LONG DAZE AT
Long Binh

24TH EVACUATION HOSPITAL
SOUTH VIETNAM, 1966-68

*The humorous adventures of two
Wisconsin draftees trained as combat
medics and sent off to set up a field
hospital in South Vietnam*

AVAILABLE NOW IN
PAPERBACK & EBOOK
at Amazon.com

STEPHEN DONOVAN
and
FREDERICK BORCHARDT

Published by DCI Communications
Madison, Wisconsin
www.longbinhdaze.com

Copyright © 2017 DCI Communications
All rights reserved
Printed in the United States of America
First Edition

ISBN   978-0-9986159-0-5 (paperback)

Library of Congress Cataloging-in-Publication Data

Donovan, Stephen H., 1945—
Long Daze at Long Binh: The humorous adventures of
two Wisconsin draftees trained as combat medics and
sent off to set up a field hospital in South Vietnam/
Steve Donovan and Fred Borchardt

1. History / Military / Vietnam War
2. History / Military / Veterans
3. Humor / General
I. Title. II. Title: The humorous adventures of two
Wisconsin draftees trained as combat medics and
sent off to set up a field hospital in South Vietnam

Library of Congress Control Number:
2017900785

DCI Communications, Publishers
Box 44625, Madison, Wisconsin 53744-4625
www.longbinhdaze.com

This book is dedicated to all those who've ever found themselves in the throes of compulsory military service— past, present or future. (Yes folks, it's bound to happen again.)

Happy Reading —
Steve Donovan

EMAIL YOUR BOOK
REVIEW TO STEVE AT:
stdonova@sprynet.com

The authors wish to thank the many individuals who so graciously helped them to recollect or reconstruct details regarding the people and events described in this book.

CONTENTS

From the Authors

War is a serious and deadly business. No one knows that better than the young men and women who are called upon to serve their country in times of armed conflict. But in South Vietnam, as in previous wars, roughly five out of every six military personnel sent to the War Zone went not as combat troops but as support personnel. Cooks, clerks, mechanics, electricians, engineers, policemen, surveyors, translators, pilots, pharmacists, truck drivers, doctors, nurses and medics, just to name a few.

This is a story of war as seen through the eyes of two of those individuals. It's a tale that was sometimes hilarious, sometimes heart-rending, sometimes horrific– but always an adventure for those who never knew what might be lurking around the next bend in the circuitous road of life. After all, none of us had experienced anything like this be-fore– nor would we ever again. Next time it would be some-one else's turn, just as it once was for us.

Nearly everything in this book reflects our best recol-lections of things that happened 50 years ago. Naturally there were names of many individuals and details of many events that we had to try to reconstruct– or else, in some cases, just fill in the blanks to make the story whole. Most names have been altered to protect individual privacy.

And of course, to keep the book editors happy, we some-times had to tweak the narrative a bit to prevent our read-ers from falling asleep. We hope you will appreciate our efforts in that regard.

Steve Donovan and Fred Borchardt
24th Evac Hospital, U.S. Army
Long Binh, South Vietnam 1966-67

CHAPTER 1

A FORTUITOUS MEETING IN THE BEER CITY

Let's see... five years in an orange jumpsuit or two years in green jungle fatigues? Hmmm....

STEVE DONOVAN: My first exposure to the concept of armed combat occurred when I was around seven years old. The Korean War had been going on for a few years and my two older brothers, aged 14 and 16, were facing the prospect of being drafted and sent off to fight the communists. They didn't discuss it much— but they did bring home "war comics" and hide them under the mattress.

FRED BORCHARDT: And you snuck them out from under the mattress to take a peek when your brothers weren't around, right? But why did they have to hide them?

STEVE: The only comics allowed in our house had characters like Bugs Bunny on the cover, but I found war comics fascinating. On just about every page, somebody would be yelling AAAIEEEEE!!! Usually it was a crazed, ferocious looking Chinese or North Korean commie who was leaping into some GI's foxhole, about to meet the wrong end of a bayonet. But what really intrigued me were the drawings themselves, since I was planning to be a cartoonist.

FRED: At that age I knew virtually nothing about the Korean War. I had my first thoughts about combat when I started learning to hunt at around the age of 13. Walking quietly through the woods and stalking live prey, it occurred to me that if my quarry had the ability to shoot back, it would have been not unlike jungle warfare.

STEVE: I had similar thoughts when I played army with my playground buddies at age ten. By the age of eleven I had participated in more combat assaults than I would ever see once Uncle Sam furnished me with an actual rifle and bayonet. But during that period I knew that way in the back of my mind, I was preparing myself for the day when I'd be staring down genuine commies— just like in the comics.

FRED: I don't recall playing army specifically, but we kids all had BB rifles for hunting rats and squirrels at the town dump. Occasionally the situation would get out of hand and we'd start shooting at each other. It's amazing that none of us got blinded in the process, but those are things you seldom think about when you're a typical dumb kid.

STEVE: Then 1965 rolls around... The Vietnam War was heating up and I was a 20-year-old college dropout. I asked myself: Was I willing to give up two years of my life (or perhaps life itself) just because my country said it needed me in uniform? Yup, I was. I certainly wasn't looking forward to it, nor was I about to go down to the recruiter and volunteer. But I'd known since the age of six that there was a military draft and that once I turned 18, it was my duty as a citizen to answer the call if it should come. By then, my two older brothers had already been in the Army and Navy, so once that draft notice showed up in my mailbox I just thought "Okay Uncle Sam, it's my turn now. Ya got me for 24 months."

FRED: My circumstances were similar, except that I was still 19 when I got mine. To my knowledge, no one in my family had ever been in the armed forces, so I had never given much thought to the military or the draft. Or to a war in some faraway place called Vietnam, wherever that was. You could say it was a bit of a shock when out of the blue, I received this notice to report for a pre-induction physical. I felt somewhat bewildered, but the letter from the government said "you are hereby required," so I went.

STEVE: The anti-draft, anti-war movement was just beginning to heat up where I lived in Madison, Wisconsin. But I knew I was not a pacifist or a coward or a communist sympathizer or a spoiled rich kid or a homosexual or a draft dodger. So any thoughts of faking a physical or mental defect, going on the lam, running off to Canada— or chopping off a few toes that I didn't need— were totally out of the question for me, despite the urgings of some of my peers.

FRED: And up in Oshkosh where I grew up, hardly anybody was talking about the Vietnam war or the draft, so nobody was bending my ear about either entering or avoiding the service. It wasn't until I got to the Army Induction Center that I heard a sergeant explain to us the "Domino Theory"— Eisenhower's ominous warning that if Vietnam fell to the communists, all of southeast Asia would soon follow. It sounded plausible to me, so I didn't really question it. After all, my government wouldn't lie to me, would it? Ike? No way!

STEVE: Supposedly one of the major (but lesser known) fears was that once the commies had taken southeast Asia, they'd gobble up Australia and New Zealand as well. There are some who claim the real reason we fought in Vietnam was to save the Aussies, not the Vietnamese.

FRED: I had not heard that one before, but I suppose it makes sense if you subscribe to the Domino Theory. That might explain why in Nam we sometimes saw infantry troops from countries like Australia, New Zealand, South Korea, the Philippines... I always assumed they were there to show their gratitude for our having saved their butts from the Japanese in WW II. It never occurred to me that they would be fighting the commies in Vietnam because they were afraid their own countries might be next.

STEVE: The South Koreans were really vicious, hard-core fighters too. "Charlie" (a common term we used for the Viet Cong, or VC— "Victor Charlie" in the Military Phonetic Alphabet) never wanted to engage the ROK (Republic of Korea) forces because the ROKs took no prisoners and had a reputation for being extremely ruthless. In Nam, the American forces had a declared kill ratio of 5 to 1, meaning five enemy soldiers killed for every one of ours killed. The ROKs had a declared kill ratio of a little over 10 to 1, meaning they were twice as "efficient" at killing as we were. Supposedly many of them carried souvenir strings of enemy ears as a demonstration of their prowess.

FRED: So anyway, when you got your draft notice did you have any fears or misgivings about having to face mortal combat?

STEVE: My biggest fear was not that I might get maimed or killed. I didn't have any dependents counting on me to provide them with food or shelter, so it wouldn't be any big loss if I didn't come back. Nor was I worried about being yelled at by a tag-team of sadistic drill instructors— I'd heard plenty of that stuff throughout my childhood.

LONG DAZE AT LONG BINH

What I dreaded most was the possibility of being surrounded for two years by a bunch of high school dropouts who might lack the ability to recognize a good joke if it bit them in the butt.

FRED: Personally, the maimed or killed business probably would have been my first choice. But when you're 19, you tend to think of yourself as being invincible. So the idea of dying scarcely entered my mind. I was more than a bit miffed that the government would be allowed to totally run my life for the next two years, but other than that I just looked at military service as a major inconvenience and an adventure to mark the beginning of the next phase of my life.

STEVE: I knew several draftees who were absolutely convinced they would never make it home alive. But as it turns out, the casualty rates were often blown out of proportion with statements like "the average life expectancy of a helicopter pilot is three weeks," or "for a door gunner, it's four weeks," or "for a combat medic, it's six weeks."

FRED: What none of us could have known then was that out of the nearly three million Americans who were sent to Vietnam from 1962 to 1972, roughly 97% came home alive. And something like 94% came home without being permanently maimed or injured. Of course it was also true that certain occupations— like radio telephone operator (RTO) or combat medic— were far more hazardous than others.

STEVE: And the job of carrying a radio in the jungle was extremely hazardous because...?

FRED: Charlie knew that any time he could knock out our radio transmissions, the Americans wouldn't be able to call for artillery support, air strikes or reinforcements. Plus the RTO had a whip antenna sprouting up directly above his head to a height of 10 feet. That would make him real easy to spot. And wherever the RTO went, the platoon leader was usually close by— the two of 'em together made a very tempting target. Of course the RTO also tended to be better protected, since his platoon wouldn't want to lose its ability to call for help or call for a helicopter ambulance to evacuate the wounded.

STEVE: As for combat medics, supposedly they were considered prime targets because Charlie believed that if an infantry platoon lost its medic and the soldiers no longer had someone to provide medical aid if they were wounded, they would no longer have the will to fight.

That probably explains why American medics in Nam didn't have big red crosses on their helmets like they did in World War II. They wore no distinguishing insignia, although they did carry a fairly large medical aid bag that the enemy undoubtedly learned to recognize.

FRED: Another measure of safety for medics was the fact that a platoon sergeant or platoon leader (usually a lieutenant) would often tell the platoon medic not to take foolish risks on the battlefield because the troops didn't want to lose their "doc." Sometimes they would assign a rifleman to the sole responsibility of protecting their medic.

STEVE: The official stats say 58,000 Americans died in Vietnam, but 10,000 of those were non-combat fatalities due to accidents, homicides, suicides, natural causes or diseases like malaria and rabies. So 48,000 combat fatalities out of 3 million would be a fatality rate (due to hostile action) of around 2% of all American military personnel sent to the War Zone. By comparison, the annual death rate in the US general population today is .0082, or a little less than one percent.

FRED: If you were in the infantry, you might be looking at a fatality rate as high as 10 percent. Which explains why most draftees hoped they'd be made a clerk or cook or mechanic rather than an infantry "ground pounder." But none of that information was available to us in 1965, so if someone said there was a 50% chance that we wouldn't make it back, for all we knew that could have been an accurate statement. In fact, the survival rate turned out to be 97 percent for draftees unless they wound up in the infantry— then it was closer to 90 percent. For chopper pilots it turned out to be 94 percent.

STEVE: And so, despite assumptions that things were probably going to be much worse than these statistics would eventually show, Fred and I met for the first time on a chilly gray morning in September 1965. Along with 18 other young "invincibles," the two of us descended upon the US Army Induction Center in Milwaukee— me from 80 miles to the west, Fred from 90 miles to the north. The process that would determine our fate was about to begin.

FRED: We were there to be sworn in and then hustled off to some place where we'd have an opportunity to learn the ancient art of soldiering. Though we barely knew it, we were about to become part of a massive troop buildup for the rapidly escalating war in Vietnam— and we were getting in on the ground floor.

STEVE: At the Induction Center we were put in a room with several rows of numbered circles painted on the floor. Each of us was assigned a number to stand on. After some preliminaries, it came time to raise our right hands in unison and recite the oath. We were told to first do a right face and take one step forward, thereby vacating our circles and signifying that we were accepting induction into the Army.

FRED: Apparently there were a couple reasons for doing this. One was so the sergeant could look down each row of circles and see at a glance whether anyone had failed to take that critical step. Another was so that no recruit could later say "I never swore to that oath!" Because the only thing that really mattered was— did he take that step forward or didn't he?

STEVE: I figured they probably snapped a photo of each row of vacant circles to establish proof that every single recruit had indeed taken that symbolic step.

FRED: One guy, kind of a long-haired hippie type named Melnick, didn't step forward. The sergeant went over to him and said "Come with me son," whereupon they went into the next room and closed the door. We thought we might hear shouting, screaming or sounds of general mayhem, but we didn't. After about five minutes they came out. The recruit went back to his circle and took one step forward with the rest of us. We all repeated the oath and they said we were now members of the United States Army.

STEVE: Of course we were dying to find out what the sergeant told Melnick, so at the first opportunity we asked him what had been said behind closed doors. Answer: "The dude asked me if I'd rather spend five years in prison for refusing induction or two years serving my country in the armed forces. I thought about it for a couple minutes and then said OK, I'll take the two. Tough choice, ya know?"

FRED: The proceedings resumed and at one point they asked us to introduce ourselves to the group by stating our name, nickname, home town and previous occupation— plus one "secret" about ourselves. It sounded pretty corny at the time but was actually a good "ice breaker" to help us begin conversing with one another.

STEVE: I said I was from Madison, had been a student at UW and my secret was that I couldn't swim. Then, since I was desperate to find someone intelligent whom I could talk to, I listened intently as the others spoke. Fortunately I didn't have to wait long, as the two fellows right behind me in line said exactly what I wanted to hear.

FRED: Right behind Steve was a large, distinguished looking black fellow who said his name was Leroy "Woody" Woodson. He had just graduated from UW-Madison with a degree in photojournalism and his secret was that he grew up in France.

STEVE: I immediately thought "Wow, I gotta talk to this guy! He's from my home town, he's a college graduate, we went to the same university— and I've had 4 years of French! I'm dying to know why he grew up in France! Sounds like a typical American to me."

FRED: Next it was my turn. (Steve's eight-digit serial number ended in 463, Woody's ended in 464. Mine ended in 465. Forty years later, the two of us would be signing our emails to each other as "463" and "465." We had to remind Woody that he was 464.) I said I was from Oshkosh, had been a student at UW-Oshkosh, and probably said my secret was that I'm color blind.

STEVE: And I immediately thought "I gotta talk to this Fred from Oshkosh too! He sounds intelligent, he went to UW-Oshkosh— and I had some friends in my dorm who were from Oshkosh. He might know some of 'em." Plus it didn't hurt that a short time later they named him as "Acting Sergeant" for our trip from Milwaukee to Fort Leonard Wood, Missouri. At which point I thought "Now I've definitely gotta make friends with this guy. He's already been singled out as the leader of our group!"

FRED: I had no idea why they picked me. I was never in ROTC, nor did I have any other qualifications that I could think of. Maybe they went in alphabetical order and I was at the top of the list, being a "B."

STEVE: I said later they might have perceived you as having outstanding leadership qualities— or maybe you were a natural brown noser! That wouldn't be the last time you'd be singled out for special recognition— however obscure the reasons might have seemed.

FRED: True, the next time would be in Medic School where once again I was made Squad Leader as an Acting Sergeant. Maybe it was already on my record by then that I had experience at that position.

STEVE: And once we got to Nam, you were picked for the Rapid Response Team— the only guy in our hooch who was given a fully automatic weapon instead of a puny semi-automatic like the rest of us had. Dang, you must have had the magic touch!

FRED: I guess the moral would be that sooner or later, greatness always triumphs. But back to the Induction Center. Ten spots behind me in line— weighing in at serial number 475— was a rather diminutive young man named Ken Stumpf from Menasha. His nickname was Kenny— but it wouldn't be long before his infantry platoon mates would be calling him "Stumpy." (It was generally considered a badge of honor to be given such a nickname by your fellow grunts.)

STEVE: A year later, Woody would be working in Germany as an aircraft mechanic while Fred and I would be toiling as medics at a field hospital in Long Binh, Vietnam. And Stumpy would be "humping the boonies" in the Central Highlands, where he was destined to earn the Medal of Honor for extreme bravery. All he did was save the lives of a number of his comrades in the face of hostile enemy fire— during which most of his platoon was wiped out.

FRED: Later he'd end up serving three tours in Nam and eventually retiring as a Sergeant Major, the highest enlisted rank attainable. And Woody, who became Stumpy's Squad Leader in Basic Training, would discover that despite being sent to opposite sides of the globe, he and Stumpy had not yet seen the last of each other.

STEVE: At the conclusion of our induction, the NCO in charge had some parting words: "Gentlemen, you will soon find out that in the Army, there are three ways of doing things— the right way, the wrong way and the Army way! The sooner you learn to do things the Army way, the better off you'll be. Remember, you cannot beat the fuggin' system no matter how hard you try. Many have tried it before you. None have succeeded, and neither will you! I will repeat: YA CAN'T BEAT THE FUGGIN' SYSTEM, SO DON'T BOTHER TRYING!"

FRED: Words we'd hear repeated numerous times over the next six months, usually by some training sergeant, sometimes by a fellow GI. Apparently the sergeant at the Induction Center truly believed his admonition, even if some of us recruits were a bit more skeptical.

STEVE: And I immediately took it as a personal challenge. To relieve the boredom, I'd keep my eyes open for every possible opportunity to beat the system... provided that I could do it without getting my ass in a sling. Can't beat the fuggin' system, eh? We'll see about that!

FRED: Eventually we'd find out that others had figured out ways to beat the system long before we ever donned the uniform. But in the meantime, we had several hours to kill before our train left the Milwaukee station for Chicago. And it fell upon me to keep those 19 other guys in line— because I was now the Acting Jack! Some of 'em would probably be heading for the nearest saloon, while I wasn't even old enough to drink hard liquor. (Now beer, that's another story!)

STEVE: I talked to Woody and found out he was indeed a gentleman with a degree in photojournalism. He'd grown up in France because his dad was in the Foreign Service. I pretended to know what that meant— but I didn't find out 'til later that it meant he worked in various US Embassies in Europe. Fred and I hit it off immediately. He was friendly, intelligent, easygoing, unusually polite and quick to see the humor in things— an essential quality as far as I was concerned. We started to hang together without realizing we'd have the chance to continue doing so for most of the next 24 months.

FRED: And without realizing that we'd be writing a book together some 50 years later about our experiences! We left the Induction Center and headed for the nearby USO Club where we ate sandwiches and shot some pool. Then it was a few more blocks to the Milwaukee train station.

STEVE: It was probably 7 or 8 pm by the time our train arrived in Chicago, where we joined several other groups of recruits waiting for the train to St. Louis. Before we could board, we each had to empty our pockets and open up our single piece of luggage for inspection. As the suitcases and gym bags lay open on the concrete platform, a couple sergeants rifled through them and confiscated any booze, drugs, snacks, weapons, girlie magazines, books, etc.

FRED: Up 'til then the Army had been real nice to us. But at that point we were suddenly awakened to the fact that somebody else was now running our lives— and we had absolutely no say in the matter. Welcome to military life, boys!

STEVE: Not only that, but in the process I lost my switchblade, brass knuckles and nunchucks! How in the hell was I gonna defend myself against the commies without 'em?

FRED: No problem. Fortunately your Uncle Sam was fixin' to give you a 16-pound, semi-automatic weapon... plus an ample supply of 20-round magazines to replace all those magazines you had to leave on the platform at Union Station!

&&&&&&&&&&&&&&&&&&&&

FACT OR FICTION? *The story goes that during his first interview at the Reception Center for new recruits, one private gave his name as L. B. Henley. "What do the initials stand for?" asked the clerk. The recruit's answer: "Nothin' man, muh name's just L. B. Henley." So the clerk typed: First name— L ONLY, Middle name— B ONLY, Last name— HENLEY. Two days later, the young soldier received dog tags bearing his official new name: LONLY BONLY HENLEY. (Supposedly the first version of this tale originated sometime during World War II. But it could just as well have happened a number of times since then, too.)*

**SEE MORE THAN 30 PHOTOS
INCLUDING FRED, STEVE, WOODY
AND STUMPY AT:
www.longbinhdaze.com**

CHAPTER 2

HOLIDAY IN THE OZARKS

Welcome to Fort Lost in the Woods... what, you
don't believe this area is a tourist destination?

FRED: Our train ride from Chicago took us to Rolla, Missouri, some 80 miles southwest of St. Louis. From Rolla it was a 20-mile bus ride to Waynesville, followed by a 10-mile ride to Fort Leonard Wood. By then we were really out in the sticks— no city within 50 miles had a population of more than 12,000.

STEVE: Fort Lost in the Woods, as some liked to call it, was located off Route 66 on the northern fringes of the Ozark Mountain Range. A Training Center for the Army Corps of Engineers, it had also been an internment camp for German POW's during World War II.

FRED: We thought maybe they decided to make Engineers out of us, but— no such luck! In fact, before long they'd be making us feel more like POW's than Engineers. Shoot, I could easily have gotten accustomed to driving around in a big dozer with a fat cigar clenched between my teeth. Sounded better than humping the boonies in Nam carrying a rifle— or a medical aid bag!

STEVE: Or both, as turned out to be the case for infantry medics. Climbing off the bus at the Reception Station, we were marched up a sloping gravel driveway between two rows of wooden barracks. As we trudged up the hill carrying our gym bags, we couldn't help but notice a solid row of young, bald-headed recruits on either side of the road wearing what were obviously brand new green Army fatigues bearing no rank or insignia of any kind.

FRED: We assumed they had to be new recruits just like us, but as we began passing them they opened up on us with whistles, taunts and jeers as if they were the veterans mocking the newbies. Rather rude and crude, we thought.

STEVE: Yeah, weren't we all supposed to be in the same army, fer cryin' out loud? What a bunch of assholes! Who the hell did these guys think they were, anyway?

FRED: And then of course it was only about 24 hours later that we were the bald-headed ones standing in that same company street, wearing our brand new fatigues, and watching as each busload of "new meat" would arrive. Naturally we'd be whistling and jeering at them as they trudged past. I'd prefer to think we didn't participate in the taunting ourselves, but I really can't say for sure.

STEVE: I'm sure I laughed at the ironic turnabout, but I doubt that I actually did any taunting since in my view that amounted to kicking a fella when he was down.

FRED: The reason for all the standing around in new fatigues was because we'd been put in a holding company while we waited to be assigned to a Training Company that had not yet started its new cycle. Then I was sent to another holding company while Woody, Stumpy and Steve remained at the first. Woody and Steve developed an instant bond since they'd both gone to UW-Madison. When they started to converse, they developed an immediate respect and appreciation for one another.

STEVE: We spent a week or more as buddies, eating chow together and going on various work details together. I point this out only because while the Army was fully integrated when the men were on duty, the troops tended to "self-segregate" during their off-duty time. Whites tended to congregate with the whites, blacks with the blacks and Hispanics with the Hispanics.

FRED: Then you got assigned to Charlie Company while Woody and Stumpy were assigned to Bravo and I went to Alpha a week later. Woody was made a Squad Leader while Stumpy was assigned to his squad, which is how they became good friends.

STEVE: A week later I was marching to class with C Company when A Company passed us going in the opposite direction. I spotted you and yelled "Hey, Fred!" whereupon we waved to one another. But you were carrying a big duffel bag on your shoulder containing your new uniforms and equipment, so I knew you must have been a week behind us in the training schedule. I remember thinking "Well, at least I know Fred's still alive!"

FRED: At that point we probably both assumed it was the last time we'd see each other, since I'd be going to the Medics after Basic while you were destined for Military Intelligence... theoretically.

STEVE: Right. So the Army set about teaching us young recruits how to march, salute, shoot... and kill. Kill with bullets, kill with bayonets, kill with grenades, kill with our bare hands. Lots of killing, as well as being whipped into top physical condition... theoretically.

FRED: You forgot killing with kindness. Come to think of it, the Army forgot that one, too.

STEVE: But when you got right down to it, there were three burning questions that dogged us throughout Basic. First, would we pass the Physical Combat Proficiency Test (PCPT) given during the final week, or would we flunk it and have to repeat Basic all over again?

FRED: Second, what Military Occupational Specialty (MOS) would we be assigned to at the end of Basic? Would I be a medic as I had requested, or would the Army make me something else, like a truck driver, clerk typist or infantry "ground pounder?" For draftees there were few assurances that you'd get what you supposedly had been recommended for.

STEVE: The third and final burning question was "Will I be sent to Vietnam, or will I luck out and go someplace like Germany or Japan?" Later on I talked to a fellow who said their Drill Sergeant in Basic, who'd never been to Nam, told them to "Listen to me carefully. Six months from now you will all be in Nam, and half of you will not be coming back! Your ability to pay attention to what we're teaching you now will determine which half you wind up in!"

FRED: Certainly a strong motivator. But in hindsight we know now that if he'd really known what he was talking about and was totally honest, he would have said "Six months from now, most of you will be in Vietnam, and four percent of you will not be coming back!"

STEVE: Speaking of learning when, where and how to salute, I believe it was the second weekend of Basic when we were allowed to leave the company area for the first time. But we had to be wearing our dress green uniforms and we were authorized to go only to the PX about five blocks away so we could buy toothpaste, cigarettes and razor blades. I'm walking along the sidewalk in my fancy new duds when this nerdy little private approaches me wearing brand new fatigues. He had this rather concerned look on his face and then as we're just about to pass each other, he salutes me!

FRED: And of course you stopped and said "No private, I'm not an officer— I'm a private just like you. If I were an officer I'd have gold or silver bars on my shoulders, plus gold insignia on my lapels and a gold band above the brim of my hat."

STEVE: Naah... I just returned his salute and said "Good afternoon, private!" Here I had only been in the Army for less than two weeks and I already knew what it felt like to be an officer, if only for 30 seconds! Does that qualify as beatin' the fuggin' system?

FRED: I would think not. But once we got to Nam I tried to always salute the nurses left-handed to see if any of 'em would notice. None did— they just returned my salute. Maybe that nerdy kid was just testing you, too. Later he probably told his buddies "Hey, I got some dumb private to return my salute today!"

STEVE: I never thought of that— good point! Anyway, the PCPT Test in Basic consisted of five events, each worth up to 100 points, so that a perfect score would be 500 with a minimum acceptable score of something like 320.

FRED: The five events were: 1) The Monkey Bars, an overhead ladder on which you had to swing from rung to rung and complete as many rungs as possible in 30 seconds; 2) the Low Crawl, under strands of barbed wire for 30 yards in as few seconds as possible; 3) the One Mile Run in 8 minutes or less; 4) the Grenade Toss, where you threw three dummy grenades at a horseshoe pit; and 5) the Run, Dodge & Jump, where you had to run around an obstacle, leap over a trench, run around another obstacle, leap back over the trench and then repeat the whole process, all in something like 30 seconds or less.

STEVE: Some guys have insisted they had to run four miles every morning before breakfast in Basic, but that sounds like hogwash to me. We had to run four laps around a circular path through the woods in the pre-dawn darkness, with each lap being a quarter mile. Some guys— me included — would run the first lap and a half and then hide behind a tree for a lap or two before rejoining the group for the finish.

FRED: In that case you had to be careful not to come in first, which would raise all sorts of suspicions, or that you didn't come in last— because then they'd make you run it again while your buddies were standing in the chow line waiting for pancakes! Being a bit on the pudgy side myself, I was warned by a sergeant that I was in danger of not being able to pass the PCPT if I didn't pick up the pace. He took me aside and said something like "Son, I may be old and fat, but I can sure as hell outrun YOU!" So I really started working on it and got my time down to 6:15 wearing combat boots. That would have been a decent time even in tennis shoes and shorts!

STEVE: In my case I barely made it under the eight-minute limit, which included a bit of walking as well as running. We also had to run sprints every afternoon. A sergeant stopped me and said "Donovan, you mean to tell me a big long-legged sumbitch like you can't run any faster than that?" I said "Sarge, I may be skinny but I'm weak!"

FRED: But your physical conditioning was interrupted twice. Once by a severe flu-like illness that hospitalized you for a week, and once for a severely sprained ankle that put you on crutches for a week. So whatever gains you'd made in terms of conditioning during Basic had been pretty much wiped out by those two periods of inactivity.

STEVE: Yeah, on the Obstacle Course we had to jump off a 12-foot high platform into a sand pit. When I landed I rolled my ankle and heard a loud crunch. I assumed it was broken, but x-rays showed it was just a severe sprain, so I spent most of that week on crutches pulling KP in the Mess Hall. My ankle was so swollen I couldn't lace my boot. Meanwhile the other troops were out doing stuff like beating each other with "Pugil Sticks" and crawling through the mud as live machine gun rounds whizzed over their heads.

FRED: You missed all the fun stuff! Did you learn anything useful by spending all that time in the Mess Hall?

STEVE: I learned that in the modern Army, GI's didn't sit around peeling potatoes with paring knives all day long. We were blessed with a potato peeling machine! You'd open the lid of this large drum, dump in a big sack of potatoes, flip the switch to turn the machine on and then step outside the back door for a smoke.

FRED: The machine with the rotating drum that would sand the skins off the potatoes, thus saving you many man-hours of drudgery?

STEVE: That's the one! Except one day I went outside and there was another guy there already. We started jabbering to pass the time and I probably smoked two or three cancer sticks. When I went back in and shut off the machine, I looked inside and the potatoes, which had been roughly the size of softballs, were now the size of golf balls. I had to mix 'em in with a batch of full-sized ones so the Mess Sergeant wouldn't blow a gasket.

FRED: Did he notice any of the pint-sized spuds?

STEVE: He found a few, held 'em up and said "What the hell is this?" I said "Yeah, some of those suckers were pretty damned small!"

FRED: So you'd already beaten the system by not having to do the Pugil Sticks and the Infiltration Course, and now you were beatin' the rap for the shrunken potatoes. A double whammy!

STEVE: True. I had managed to barely pass the first PCPT at the beginning of Basic by getting a near perfect score (95) on the Grenade Toss. So in light of my ankle being the size of a cantaloupe, I wasn't required to take it again during the final week. I'm guessing I would have flunked the second one, with or without a sprained ankle.

FRED: But following your illness, you had to be recycled into a different company to make up the week of training you'd missed— which put you right there in Alpha Company with me!

STEVE: And that's where I learned that some training companies seemed to be a lot easier than others. Alpha was a breeze compared to "Double-Time Charlie," where we ran everywhere we went and the Drill Sergeants were cruel hard-asses who drove us mercilessly— all while constantly yelling and threatening us with bodily harm.

FRED: Now I did read an account by a former Drill Instructor that might have offered an explanation for this apparent discrepancy. He said that during the first four weeks of Basic they were supposed to ride our asses and strike the fear of God into us at every opportunity, the purpose being to dehumanize us and turn us into robots. Then after tearing us down, they were supposed to build us up again during the final four weeks by giving us as much encouragement and praise as they could muster. The goal was to turn out soldiers brimming with self-confidence, pride and vigor who "loved the Army" and would walk through walls if ordered to do so.

STEVE: A plausible theory. Maybe the whole thing was really just a con job? Speaking of tossing grenades, one interesting event during Basic was our visit to the grenade range where we got a chance to throw some live ones. I'm sure this was done as a confidence builder, since I was damned scared when they handed me that first one. But after I had chucked a few, it was no big deal.

FRED: The range consisted of about eight bunkers with concrete blast walls some 4 feet high and no roofs. One recruit would stand in each bunker along with a sergeant. Arming the grenade was a two-step process. You had to pull the safety pin and then release the spring-loaded "spoon" handle which would normally fly off as soon as you threw the device. Once the spoon came off, the grenade would explode after a five second delay. The sergeant was there to make sure you did everything correctly and didn't blow up either him or you.

STEVE: The interesting part was the safety procedures. The Range Officer in the tower made it very clear to us through his loudspeaker that each one of the those sergeants had a wife and kids he would be going home to that evening, that he knew exactly what he was doing, and that no sergeant had ever been killed on that range. The officer further stressed that if a recruit should accidentally drop his grenade after pulling the pin, he should freeze rather than trying to pick it up. The sergeant, who was standing face to face with the recruit, would then have two options: pick up the grenade and toss it over the wall, or tell the recruit to dive over the wall with him and let the grenade explode inside the empty bunker.

FRED: If you foolishly attempted to pick it up yourself, the two of you might collide and nobody would pick it up! In my case I had already pulled the pin on a grenade, as instructed by the tower, when the Range Officer suddenly called a halt. The sergeant immediately wrapped both his hands around my throwing hand which held the grenade. There was no way that spoon was coming off before it was supposed to! We stood motionless in that position for a few minutes until the tower gave the command to resume the exercise. The sergeant then let go, I let 'er fly and neither one of us got blown up.

STEVE: Excellent. So did you feel a newfound closeness with the sergeant after that? I remember a target downrange that we were supposed to aim at when we let 'er go. I had intended to try to hit it, but once I released that sucker I just wanted to get down behind the wall as fast as I could, so I never did get to see where any of 'em landed. I think the sergeant complimented me on my accuracy. What's funny is that six months later we were walking around in Nam on guard duty with live grenades hanging from the lapels of our flak vests. We tossed them around like they were navel oranges.

FRED: Then there was the gas mask orientation. Didn't you once tell me you figured out how to "beat the fuggin' system" when you went through that event?

STEVE: Yeah, the purpose of the exercise was twofold: To practice donning and clearing the gas mask in a pressure situation, and to give us some exposure to what tear gas actually felt like. We went into this building that was like a miniature barn. A sergeant stood in the center while a couple dozen of us formed a ring around him. My mask was in its case attached to my hip.

FRED: The sergeant would then set off a couple tear gas grenades and yell "GAS! GAS! GAS!" whereupon the troops were supposed to open the case, pull out the mask, put it on and clear the inside by clapping both hands over the intake filters and blowing hard through the exhaust valve. This was all supposed to be accomplished in something like seven seconds.

STEVE: Soon the gas clouded up the entire room. The sergeant would point to one soldier at a time, whereupon the recruit was supposed to rip off his mask and state his name, rank and serial number. This would ensure that he'd get just enough of a dose to overcome his fear of the gas. Once the sergeant waved him off, he'd hot-foot it for the door so he could get outside and breathe some fresh air.

FRED: But you thought you had a better idea?

STEVE: Yeah, I reasoned that if I took a great big inhale just before removing the mask, I could rattle off my name, rank and serial number while exhaling. Then he'd give me the thumb and I'd be gone without ever having to inhale any of that nasty stuff. I started mentally rehearsing as I waited for my turn: "Great big gulp of air, rip off that mask, spit out my line and get waved out! Great big gulp of air, rip off that mask, spit out my line..."

FRED: You had it all figured out, you crafty bastard.

STEVE: Sure as shootin', I did! No way in hell they were gonna make ME inhale that crap, no sir! I kept repeating the strategy in my head: "Great big gulp of air, rip off that mask..." Then suddenly the sergeant pointed to me! I immediately swung into action by ripping off my mask, taking a great big gulp of air...

FRED: Oops!

STEVE: Oops is right! In my haste I had screwed up the sequence. Instead of not inhaling any of that gas, I inhaled a huge dose which immediately attacked my nose, throat and lungs to the point that I could barely talk at all, let alone say my name. After hacking and coughing for what seemed like an eternity, I managed to mutter the required words and bolt for the door.

FRED: So that one would have had to be scored as "fuggin' system one, Donovan zero!"

STEVE: Indeed. When I got outside it probably took me a half hour to recover. What's strange is that once we got to Nam, we always had to report for guard duty wearing the gas mask on the hip— despite the fact that no one had heard of any instance where the VC or NVA had used gas on American troops.

FRED: But later we learned the greatest danger actually lay in the fact that the Americans would sometimes use tear gas on the enemy, usually dropping it from aircraft or putting it in artillery shells. Depending on which way the wind was blowing, they could wind up gassing our own troops. So in other words— those gas masks were there mainly to protect us from ourselves!

STEVE: As for the question of what MOS we'd get assigned to after Basic, I always suspected that anyone who qualified as "Expert" on the rifle range had a much better chance of being put in the infantry than someone who merely fired "Sharpshooter" or "Marksman" (the lowest possible rating one could get and still qualify.)

FRED: That would stand to reason, although if that were true they must have kept it a closely guarded secret so as not to have guys deliberately getting bad scores on the range. I'm sure some guys intentionally messed up anyway, using that logic. What's ironic is that in the dense jungles of Nam, the ability to hit a target at 300 meters— or even 100— was quite often irrelevant. But the Army wouldn't realize that for another year or two, when they began adding the "Quick Kill" method to their training agenda in 1967.

STEVE: Quick Kill was based on the principle that in jungle warfare, if you took the time to raise your weapon to your shoulder and look through the sights, Charlie would already have gotten off a burst and gunned you down. So GI's had to be taught the instinctive "point and shoot" method for targets in the range of 50 meters or less.

FRED: A friend of mine who went through the Quick Kill training said they used a Daisy BB rifle instead of an M-16. Since the copper BB's were reflective in the sunlight, the shooter could see exactly where his rounds were going. Some guys claimed that with a little practice, they could shoot ping pong balls out of the air. But we never got that training. If we had been sent out into the boonies, we'd have been at a distinct disadvantage— since Charlie was using some version of "Quick Kill" while we would still have been trying to look through our gunsights and hold our breath. Thanks a lot, Uncle Sam!

STEVE: I had never fired a rifle other than in an amusement park shooting gallery, so shooting on a range was a completely new experience for me. The first thing we had to do was zero the weapon— a totally foreign concept to a non-hunter like myself.

FRED: When your weapon was zeroed for 100 meters, that meant your sights had been adjusted so that when you put them directly on a target that was 100 meters out, you'd hit it. For anything closer, you'd have to aim low. For anything farther away, you'd have to aim high. The trick was learning how low or how high to adjust your aim, depending on the distance to the target.

STEVE: The range had a series of electrically operated pop-up targets ranging in distance from 25 to either 300 or 500 meters. (It seems to me the farthest one was 500 meters out, but that would be nearly a third of a mile, so I could be wrong.) Anyway, in practice firing I remember taking aim on that 500-meter baby and thinking

"No way in hell I'm ever gonna hit that sonofabitch!" But I followed the instructions on how to control my breathing and slowly squeeze the trigger... and down she went on the first try!

FRED: Of course it's possible that the guy in the next lane was the one who actually hit it! But most of the time we weren't allowed to shoot at the 500 meter target because they knew it would just be a waste of ammo. Then when we "Fired for Record" (to earn our final qualifying score) it was the last one on the list of designated targets, and it was obviously there to separate "the men from the boys."

STEVE: There I was heavily conflicted. I thought I was shooting a decent score and the last target would be the icing on the cake. On the one hand, if I fired "Expert" it would earn me a badge of honor I could wear proudly on my chest— and be a sign that I had passed the ultimate test of my masculinity with flying colors! But I also knew that could quite possibly be my ticket to the infantry.

FRED: So how did you resolve this quandary?

STEVE: When it came time to go for the 500-meter grand prize, I sincerely tried to hit it but all along I was hoping I'd miss! (Does that make any sense?) I did miss, and as it turned out I graded out as a lowly Marksman— the bottom of the barrel.

FRED: Nevertheless, when you went home with that Marksman badge on your chest, everyone would congratulate you and say "Oh, you made Marksman! An outstanding achievement!" (What did they know?) I fired Sharpsooter and was somewhat disappointed, but like you said— it might have kept me from being an infantry grunt.

STEVE: Then with about two days to go, we got our orders for AIT— Advanced Individual Training. The results were posted on the bulletin board, which of course everyone clamored to see. Most of the guys were thinking "Please, anything but infantry!"

FRED: I got Medics as I was expecting, so I couldn't complain. It meant I'd be out in the bush with the infantry, but I'd be carrying a Medical Aid Bag instead of a machine gun or grenade launcher.

STEVE: I had already been told the Army had to cut new orders for me because of my extra week in Basic. So Military Intelligence was probably out the window. The list said: Donovan, S.— Combat Medic. Whaddaya know, the two of us would be going to AIT together! I rationalized that if I had to go humping through the jungles and rice paddies, I'd rather be trying to save lives than trying to take them.

FRED: Soon we reported to our new duty station— Medic School at Fort Sam Houston in San Antonio. It would be another ten weeks before we'd find out whether we were going to Nam— but if you're a trained combat medic, where the hell else are ya gonna go?

STEVE: The Army had already spent eight weeks teaching us how to kill. Now they were gonna spend another ten teaching us how to save lives... and be a certified "pecker checker," as some would say.

&&&&&&&&&&&&&&&&&&&

FACT OR FICTION? The story goes that after PFC Nowitzke got to Long Binh, he found out his cousin was stationed at Tan Son Nhut Airbase in Saigon. The cousin had a big Honda 650 motorcycle that could outrun the MP's and the Saigon cops, so the two of them would go out for high-speed joyrides on Highway 1. One day the zipper broke on Nowitzke's leather jacket, so he put it on backwards to keep the wind out. They were flying down the road when an old truck pulled out in front of them and they had to dump the bike. When the MP's arrived at the scene to check on the victims, a pair of young medics who had stopped to help said "The motorcycle driver escaped with only minor injuries. Unfortunately his passenger appeared to be in pretty good shape until we tried to turn his head back around."

SEE MORE THAN 30 PHOTOS AT:
www.longbinhdaze.com

CHAPTER 3

YOU TOO CAN BECOME
A "DOC" IN 10 SHORT WEEKS
Forget all that stuff about how to kill... Now
you're gonna learn how to keep 'em alive

STEVE: Our medic training at Fort Sam Houston consisted of three modes. The first was Classroom Instruction where we learned things like basic anatomy; diagnosis of common symptoms; disease prevention; and the uses for common medical drugs. It also included "desensitization" training where we were shown a number of gory films featuring close-ups of surgeries and badly wounded casualties.

FRED: Any trainees who became nauseated or freaked out by such sights would have to either quickly learn to adapt to the situation or else get washed out of the medics.

STEVE: Yeah, the Army definitely didn't want corpsmen who'd be throwing up all over the patients or going berserk when the going got rough! Those sights didn't bother me for more than 10 seconds or so, but several guys fainted or nearly passed out.

FRED: The second training mode was Field Exercises, where we learned things like emergency medical treatment; the application of pressure bandages, splints and tourniquets; treatment of snake and insect bites; treatment for shock; administering morphine; initiating the Field Medical Card for each patient; transporting the sick and wounded on litters; loading and unloading patients from helicopters; and field sanitation procedures (disposal of human waste.)

STEVE: Included was a litter obstacle course where we divided into five-man teams. The lightest guy (me, at 140 pounds) would be the patient and get strapped to the litter. The other four would each grab a corner and carry the litter through the course. The grand finale was a river crossing in a collapsible canvas boat— guided by a rope that was stretched across to the other side. I kept reminding my teammates to "Don't drop me in that damned river, fellas— I can't swim!"

FRED: As I recall, that "river" was only about three feet deep. You did have the ability to stand up, did you not?

STEVE: Not as long as I was lashed to that damned litter, I didn't!

FRED: I suppose not. The third mode was Ward Training, where we learned hospital procedures and basic nursing techniques in a mock-up of a typical hospital ward. On each side of the room was a row of patient beds occupied by "anatomically correct" dummies. Two-man teams would man each bed, taking turns performing the required tasks while the other trainee observed and coached.

STEVE: On day one of Ward Training, the NCO in charge warned us that our "patients" would be checked at the end of each day to make sure all their parts were still there. Before we left each day, he'd pull back the sheets on each bed to check for missing dicks.

FRED: We figured it was probably the WAC (Women's Army Corps) trainees who were stealing the rubber peckers. Still, I have to admit that a rubber pecker would have made a nice conversation piece!

STEVE: For sure. The procedures we learned on the ward included things like drawing blood, administering shots, taking blood pressure readings, recording vital signs, catheterizing a patient, giving sponge baths and developing a proper "bedside manner" by reassuring the wounded patients. The trainees used each other as guinea pigs for drawing blood, giving injections and so on.

FRED: When drawing blood or administering an IV, you didn't want a chubby guy for a partner because it would be damn near impossible to hit a vein. Steve was ideal because he was nice and skinny— those veins would pop out in a matter of seconds!

STEVE: Yeah, but when it came time to give shots they told us to remove the plastic cap from the syringe and be careful not to touch the needle because it was sterile. If you contaminated it, this could cause an infection in the patient. I thought "what kind of an idiot would touch the needle?" Then they gave the order to remove the caps and immediately I absent-mindedly touched the side of it with the tip of my index finger! I was so embarrassed that I just plunged that sucker into my partner's arm. But I did watch him carefully for the next few weeks and he didn't seem to have suffered any ill effects, so I guess I got away clean. At least I would know better next time!

FRED: That's Donovan for ya, always looking for the silver lining in every cloud! Meanwhile I was drawing blood from another trainee when the power went out and the lights went off. I've got the needle right in the guy's vein when the room goes black. I was concerned, but not as much as he was. He stands up rather abruptly and yells "Get that needle out of my arm, buster!" I thought he was about to start a fistfight when the instructor came over, calmed him down and removed the needle. Only time I ever drew blood as a medic.

STEVE: That was about the time I began to realize that if they're teaching us all this hospital stuff on top of the combat medic stuff, that must mean we might not be going into combat after all! And I remember thinking that wherever we went, it was quite unlikely that we'd have to use all of that knowledge they were feeding us.

FRED: So rather than trying to memorize everything they said, you figured you'd just wait to see where you'd be deployed, and then you could concentrate on learning what you really needed to know?

STEVE: Exactly. But in the meantime, once we got to Medic School you were singled out once again for your superior leadership skills, right? They made you a Grapehead?

FRED: They did. Each platoon in our company had four squads of roughly 18-20 trainees and each squad had a Squad Leader or LPC (which stood for Leadership Prep Course or Leadership Prep Candidate, I believe.) I was named the LPC for Third Squad.

STEVE: You were being prepped for leadership! And how did getting this LPC designation affect your life?

FRED: The LPC's got to wear shiny maroon helmet liners, as befitting our station in life, instead of olive drab ones like the other troops. That's where the nickname "Grapeheads" came from. We were being trained as future leaders, which meant we got our own private two-man rooms— with a tv set, no less— instead of having to sleep in the troop bays with everyone else. Unlike the peons, we didn't have to pull any details like KP or latrine cleaning or firewatch— instead we got to evaluate the performance of those who did the work. And we'd get weekend passes just about any time we wanted, whereas the others didn't get any until about the fifth or sixth week of training.

STEVE: And what duties did you have to perform in order to earn these various perquisites?

FRED: We were considered to be Acting Sergeants. My job was to keep guys in line and help them out if they were having difficulties. If a certain guy wasn't pulling his weight so to speak, I was supposed to make sure that he did. If I observed that one of my men was screwing up or violating any rules or regulations, I was to report him to my superiors if I couldn't get him squared away on my own.

STEVE: And you were also expected to rat guys out if you caught them doing anything out of line, right?

FRED: Yeah, we had to walk a fine line between trying not to alienate the NCO's to whom we reported and trying not to alienate the troops whom we were supposed to be leading. The easiest way to not alienate the troops was to look the other way if we saw them doing something wrong. But if the NCO's found out an LPC had deliberately ignored a violation, they'd come down hard on him— and there goes his maroon helmet, along with his privileges as an LPC.

STEVE: So it was a constant balancing act. You didn't want to lose your leadership position or the benefits that came with it, but you didn't want the men in your squad to despise you either.

FRED: True, and some did seem to have contempt for anyone in a position of authority, triggered I suppose by our mere existence. They often saw us as little more than power-drunk squealers, whereas those who might need our help were genuinely appreciative of our efforts.

STEVE: You said you were supposed to help guys out if they were having difficulties or couldn't hack it. What sort of difficulties?

FRED: You name it. A few were just general screw-ups who couldn't seem to do anything right. Others had personal problems for which I was supposed to lend a sympathetic ear or else help them find a resource to deal with it. Then there was Private Hinshaw, who had a problem that could get him out of the Army very quickly.

STEVE: I'm sure lots of other guys would have liked to know about it so they could get themselves out of the Army too— assuming that it was something they could try to fake.

FRED: That's the thing, he could have been faking. It started when another troop came into my room for a private conversation (my door was always open, as they say.) He said Hinshaw was directly above him in the upper bunk. It seems that on several occasions, he awakened to find a liquid dripping on him from the upper bunk and he assumed Hinshaw must have been wetting his bed.

STEVE: If the guy was a bedwetter, how in hell did he ever make it through Basic and get as far as Medic School?

FRED: My thoughts exactly. I called Hinshaw into my room for a private talk and told him there were some indications that he might be wetting his bed. He said yes, he had sometimes had problems with that in the past. I asked how he made it through Basic and he said "First, by being extra careful... and second, by having a lower bunk. Nobody noticed." It did seem kind of fishy, like maybe he decided he wanted out of the Army so he began pretending he had a condition that would get him out. But of course the determination of whether or not he was faking was not my call.

STEVE: So what were you supposed to do with a bedwetter?

FRED: I said the Army would send him to a counselor and if it was determined that he was truly an involuntary bedwetter, he'd receive a medical discharge. Then I made a report to the platoon sergeant and within a day or so, Hinshaw disappeared. I presume he got his discharge but I'm not sure. Usually once those things were out of your hands, you never got a chance to find out how they turned out.

STEVE: Or maybe he wound up in Leavenworth for trying to fake a medical condition. Did anyone in your squad ever claim to be gay?

FRED: Yeah, one guy told me he was, although I don't think the word "gay" had the same connotation at the time. It seems to me the term didn't achieve mainstream usage as meaning homosexual until the late 60's or early 70's, depending on where you lived. Anyway, he said he was attracted to men and didn't really become aware of it until he started showering with other soldiers.

STEVE: At the time, gays weren't permitted in the military. They'd automatically be discharged if their story could be authenticated.

FRED: Right, I think they got undesirable discharges (as opposed to medical.) But he could have been faking it. Same thing happened to him as with the bedwetter— he was sent to counseling and after that, we never saw the guy again.

STEVE: I must say I don't remember anyone having any conflicts with our squad leader, although I suppose it would depend a lot on just who was in the squad. Did you have any troublemakers in yours?

FRED: A few. There were these two goof-off pals, Privates Enders and Pularski, who didn't exactly cotton to military life and were always coming up with schemes to subvert the rules in one way or another. They liked to pull stunts like sloughing off on firewatch or going AWOL without being caught.

STEVE: Firewatch was a critical assignment because the Army kept telling us those wooden barracks would burn to the ground in a matter of minutes if someone wasn't awake and ready to sound the alarm in an instant. Forty men (two squads) slept in bunk beds on the first floor and 40 more slept on the second. So each night from 10 pm to 6 am, guys would take one-hour firewatch shifts, one on each floor.

FRED: This meant that of the 80 men sleeping in the two squad bays, 16 of 'em would have firewatch duty each night. The schedule might say you were on from 2 am to 3 am, so at 0200 hours the guy on the shift before yours would wake you up and he'd hit the sack. Then you'd walk the floor quietly 'til 0300, when you'd wake the next guy on the roster and then you could go back to sleep.

STEVE: But a guy on one shift might fall asleep in the latrine and then fail to wake his replacement to take the next shift. In which case everyone could die in minutes if a fire should break out. To prevent this, the sergeant on CQ duty each night would make his rounds from HQ to each barracks about once an hour to make sure the people on firewatch duty were awake.

FRED: Enders and Pularski decided they didn't like having to get up at 2 am, so they devised a little scheme for gaming the system. If Enders was on firewatch, he'd be awakened at 0200 and then wait for the guy from the previous shift to sack out. Then he'd immediately wake up the next guy, say Private Crouch, and allow him to think the 0200 shift was his. At 0300 Crouch would wake the next guy, and so on. Eventually someone would either get stuck having to pull a two hour shift by himself or else leave nobody on firewatch from 0500 to 0600. But Enders was sound asleep, so it wasn't his problem.

STEVE: So how did you find out this was going on?

FRED: Well normally a man would pull firewatch about once every sixth night. I would get complaints once or twice a week that the schedule was screwed up somehow. Looking at the rosters, I noticed that either Enders or Pularski always seemed to be on firewatch on the nights in question. After interviewing several of the other guys I managed to put two and two together.

STEVE: What did you do then?

FRED: I was supposed to handle the discipline problems myself if possible, so I called them both into my private room and told 'em I was on to their little scheme. I said if it happened again I would make sure the other troops knew who it was that was bucking the system. Then I would let nature take its course, meaning the other men would likely assume the responsibility for meting out the necessary punishment. There were no more firewatch problems after that.

STEVE: But as it turned out, that was not gonna be the last of your problems with Enders and Pularski.

FRED: Nope. I'd sometimes get a weekend pass and be gone from Friday evening til Sunday evening. Those two jokers figured out a way to beat the nightly bedcheck after lights out at 10 pm. Every night at around 10:30, the NCO on CQ duty would walk quietly through each barracks with his flashlight, checking to make sure every bed was occupied. But some squads might only have 17 or 18 guys, so there would only be 17 or 18 bunks in the row for that squad.

STEVE: So on Friday and Saturday nights when you weren't there, the "dynamic duo" figured out how to make two more bunks disappear so they could continue drinking and carousing into the wee hours?

FRED: Right. The bunk beds were the collapsible metal type that folded flat for storage. They swapped bunk assignments with someone else so that they occupied the upper and lower sections of the same bunk. In less than 10 minutes they could fold up their beds and slide them up into the rafters so they'd be resting atop the ceiling joists.

STEVE: The folded bunks in the rafters were fully visible when the lights were on, but in the dark no one would ever notice them?

FRED: Yup, the CQ kept his flashlight shining downward at the floor, flicking it briefly upward just enough to make sure each bunk was occupied. Once he saw that every bunk had someone in it, he knew everyone was accounted for. It never occurred to him to count the bunks— and even if he had, he probably wouldn't have known what the correct number was supposed to be anyway.

STEVE: So how did Enders and Pularski figure they would get away with their little prank?

FRED: On Friday evenings they'd wait 'til everyone went to chow, then they'd stash the bunks and head downtown. A few guys might see 'em doing this or see the bunks in the rafters, but everyone thought it was so hilarious and audacious that nobody wanted to be the one to squeal on 'em. Then the two AWOLs would come cruising in around 2 or 3 am, take the bunks down and sack out 'til reveille at 0600.

STEVE: So if everyone else was tolerating their behavior, how did the duo get caught?

FRED: Their downfall was all the noise they made when they came in drunk and had to retrieve their beds. They tried to be as quiet as possible, but some troops sleeping nearby were getting pissed at being awakened repeatedly in the middle of the night. Finally one of 'em decided to report it to me when I returned one Sunday evening.

STEVE: So what did you do about it?

FRED: I knew I couldn't let their escapades continue but I knew I didn't really have any solid evidence to prove their guilt. I decided to call them in for another talk. I told 'em I knew what they'd been up to but I didn't have any hard evidence and since there was no apparent harm done, I was going to let them off with a stern warning.

STEVE: What leverage did you have that you could warn them with?

FRED: I said if there were any more shenanigans I'd have to submit a full report to the platoon sergeant. I also reminded them that if they should be classified by the cadre as undesirables, they'd immediately wash out of Medic School and be sent straight to the Infantry.

STEVE: Did they clean up their act after your warning?

FRED: Yes, but in about Week Seven of our ten-week school they both had weekend passes. Along with Private Jensen, they took off in Jensen's car on Friday evening for Austin, a "swingin' town" some 70 miles north of Fort Sam. If they weren't back by 10 pm bedcheck Sunday night, they'd be AWOL. Naturally they rolled in at about 2 in the morning, making lots of noise, and I was present when they did.

STEVE: So how were you going to handle it this time?

FRED: I called them into my room and asked for an explanation. They said they had a flat on the way back from Austin and then discovered the spare had no air in it. Took 'em 'til after midnight to get squared away. Could happen to anybody, right? Except I was pretty sure they were lying and, in the process, trying to make a fool out of me.

STEVE: A little pissed, eh? What did you decide to do about it?

FRED: I handed each one a sheet of paper and said "If you're not telling the truth, you were AWOL with no legitimate excuse and I'll have to report it. So here's a little quiz. Write your name at the top of the page... Now write the answers to the following three questions, numbering them one-two-three. From this point on, no talking— and no looking at the other guy's answers or you'll be on report."

STEVE: So what, pray tell, were the three questions?

FRED: Question One was: At what time did you leave Austin on Sunday? Question Two: At what time did you arrive in San Antonio this morning? Question Three: Which tire went flat?

STEVE: Now THAT'S what I'd call leadership, Mister Grapehead!

&&&&&&&&&&&&&&&&&&&

FACT OR FICTION? The story goes that a short time after he was drafted, PFC Juan Mendoza discovered he had an identical twin brother serving in the Egyptian army named Amahl. Obsessed with trying to obtain a photo of the brother, his wife Rosie kept calling the Egyptian embassy two or three times a week. Finally the embassy clerk got so exasperated that he bellowed into the phone "Look lady, they're identical twins!! Once you've seen Juan, you've seen Amahl."

CHAPTER 4

BALLAD OF THE GREEN BRAWLERS
Surviving a brush with America's Best— while avoiding considerable pain & anguish

STEVE: For the first few weeks of Medic Training at Fort Sam, we weren't allowed to leave the company area except to go to this little PX after 6 pm where you could buy things like cigarettes, toothpaste and shaving cream. It had a cramped little snack bar— indicative of the fact that the Army wasn't fully prepared for the sudden onslaught of 160,000 new cooks, machine gunners, tank drivers, radiomen, military policemen, medics... all preparing to go to war!

FRED: But to us, that tiny snack bar was an oasis where you could get mediocre hot dogs, potato chips, decent ice cream cones— and 3.2 beer. For the uninitiated, this was a beverage that looked and tasted (somewhat) like regular beer, except that it only had about one fourth the alcohol content. Which meant you'd have to drink at least a dozen cans of the stuff to achieve the same "buzz" you'd get from three or four cans of the real McCoy. They looked like regular cans of Pabst, Bud or Hamm's— except that the small print on the label revealed the truth. It was fake beer!

STEVE: And just to make sure nobody got a good buzz on, they made you stand in line for 15 minutes just to buy two cans of that golden liquid— the maximum number allowed in a single purchase. But... the joint had a jukebox! Thanks to the 3.2 beer, the jukebox and the fact that it was the only place we were allowed to go when we were off duty, that snack bar was packed every evening.

FRED: It had about eight little tables, the kind you might see in an ice cream parlor— and it was always standing room only, as dozens of our fellow medic trainees waited for someone to vacate a table so they could sit down to relax with their "near beers." Each little table had four chairs. Now here was an interesting dilemma. If four troops wanted to drink and shoot the breeze together, they'd have to stand in line together— otherwise there'd be a 15 minute wait while some of 'em stood in line and others sat at the table.

STEVE: And your beer would get warm while you waited for your buddies! But if you all stood up to get in line at the same time, you'd have to surrender your table to the next group of four. So it was a continuing cycle of stand in line, get your two beers, wait for a table, sit down and make wisecracks while you drink your two beers. Then stand up, vacate your table and do the whole procedure all over again.

FRED: A good way to kill time, for sure! But it was the only game in town, and there was nothing else to do on post but watch TV in the Dayroom or read your mail for the umpteenth time. Of course when the first episodes of Batman appeared on the TV scene— starting on Jan. 12, 1966 and featuring the "Riddler" as the villain— just about everyone packed into the Company Dayroom to watch.

STEVE: That was quite a phenomenon. The Batman show had been hyped like crazy, even making the cover of Time magazine. This was accompanied by a story explaining that nothing like it had ever been seen on TV before. Which was certainly true— plus there were only three commercial networks then, not the the 60 or so that we see today on cable. So half the TV sets in the nation were tuned in when the show premiered on a Wednesday night and garnered a 52 percent audience share.

FRED: It was basically a cartoon acted out by real people. I still remember how odd it felt to be in a room packed with young men in combat fatigues. We were preparing to go fight the commies to the death, and yet here we were, transfixed by these two slapstick crimefighters named Batman & Robin. We were mesmerized as we watched them jump into their Batmobile and roar out of the Batcave to go defend Gotham City. Did this mean we were still juveniles at heart... or trained killers... or both? Or none of the above?

STEVE: Nobody in the room would dare speak, out of fear that they might miss one of those wacky lines like "Holy catfish, Batman!!!" or "To the Batpoles, Robin!" One of the things that made it unique was that it was loaded with generous doses of satire so it would appeal to adults as well as children. I guess you could say it succeeded, since it ended the year as one of the top five shows of 1966.

FRED: Anyway, back to the little PX with the cramped snack bar...

STEVE: I had quickly made friends with several guys from my platoon, including Private Bill Nortunen from Ohio. Bill and I, along with a couple pals, waited for a vacant table and then sat down to drink our two "near beers" apiece.

FRED: And your table happened to be about five feet away from the jukebox, which kept playing "Ballad of the Green Berets" by Barry Sadler— over and over and over. Sadler had himself been a Special Forces medic who was trained at Fort Sam, then sent to Vietnam. He was severely wounded by a "punji stick" booby trap in May '65— four months prior to our induction.

STEVE: He wrote the song while recuperating at Walter Reed Hospital and debuted it on the Ed Sullivan Show in January '66. It became an instant smash hit and shot up to Number 1 on the Billboard Hot 100 chart for March. Eventually it tied with "California Dreamin" (by the Mamas and Papas) for the Number 1 record of 1966. Across the country, the pro-war faction loved it while the anti-war faction ridiculed it.

FRED: Two years later it was sung by a chorus in the 1968 John Wayne film "The Green Berets." While copyright law precludes us from printing the lyrics here, we can describe what it said about the Special Forces: They wore airborne wings on their chest. They were fearless soldiers who were "America's Best." They were fighting men who meant exactly what they said. They jumped out of the sky and had no fear of ending up dead. You get the idea.

STEVE: Over the next several years, the song would be parodied by numerous artists— some in a pro-war version, some in an anti-war version. But in February of '66, someone at Fort Sam had already coined parody lyrics that were similar to this:
"Airborne wings... adorn their chest...
These brave men... are America's Best!
Men who jump... from Army planes...
Cuz they ain't got... no fuggin' brains!"

FRED: Now we had nothing but the greatest respect for the Green Berets— we considered them to be the ultimate in exemplary soldiers and were proud to have them representing us as they walked through airports and train stations wearing their snappy berets, shoulder braids and combat boots. But completely separate from that was the fact that most everyone found the parody lyrics pretty hilarious, regardless of their personal feelings toward the Special Forces or the military. Any time we would hear the song on the radio, somebody would chime in with the "no fuggin' brains" line and everyone would chuckle.

STEVE: I would have found it hilarious even if I had been a Green Beret myself! But anyway, we were always looking for ways to share a good laugh, especially after guzzling several cans of lukewarm 3.2 beer. Plus this damned hokey song that kept playing over and over again was getting downright annoying. Obviously somebody really liked it, because they kept plugging the jukebox to repeat it.

FRED: Did you try playing some different songs on the jukebox?

STEVE: Well if you recall, our salary as buck privates was 83 bucks a month— less than 21 dollars a week. I would invite anyone to try living on $21 a week and see how many quarters they want to stuff into a jukebox! But we wanted to hear some rock 'n roll as we sipped our near beers, dammit! So after a few more replays, we started singing the blasphemous lyrics along with the record, laughing as we did so.

FRED: What were your intentions at that point— assuming you had any— as far as why you were singing those lyrics?

STEVE: Like you said, we meant no disrespect to the Green Berets. But after all, we were in South Texas and they were 1200 miles away in Fort Bragg, North Carolina! So what possible harm could it do to sing a few bars right there at Fort Sam? If anything, we were trying to send a message to the jerk who kept playing that record over and over. We weren't trying to make fun of the Special Forces— we were just making fun of that damned song. And each time we did so, we got louder and louder— until we were really belting out the parody version.

FRED: And you did all this without realizing that the four dudes at the next table were all junior Green Berets, sent to Fort Sam to be trained as Special Forces medics?

STEVE: Indeed they were, and indeed we had not noticed! Later we would see that they appeared to be no more than a year out of high school, where they'd probably been star athletes. But they weren't wearing berets— you probably didn't get a beret until you completed your training— and we didn't notice their shoulder patches that said "Special Forces" in quarter-inch high letters.

FRED: You were digging your own graves without knowing it.

STEVE: For sure! They must have had a prearranged signal, because all of a sudden we heard the simultaneous screeching of four chairs pushing back from their table as they all jumped up together and lunged for us. Now our foursome consisted of two skinny weaklings, one certifiably overweight guy and one little nerdy dude— certainly no match for the likes of those four!

FRED: And nobody else was about to come to your aid, either.

STEVE: No such luck. Everybody in the whole place was a medic trainee like us— but so were the four Greenies! Their ringleader hollered "That's about enough of that crap, boys! We're Green Berets and we don't like being ridiculed!" They were just about to yank us out of our seats— presumably their honor code said you don't slug a fellow GI when he's sitting down— when I blurted "Hey, it's just a harmless joke, man! We didn't mean anything by it and we certainly didn't notice your shoulder patches. We meant no disrespect and we apologize! Cease fire, dude!" Fortunately I was able to calm them down and remind them that we were all on the same side. Otherwise we could have been pulverized. As it was, we were all feeling the effects of being severely intimidated— we even bought 'em a beer!

FRED: So what you're saying is, you nearly got your clock cleaned by four of America's Best?

STEVE: Yeah, afterward Nortunen says "Holy crap, those guys meant business! I need a smoke to calm me down." Meanwhile, the little nerdy guy says under his breath: "Fug 'em if they can't take a joke!" Up to then I had thought "America's Best" were supposed to be mature professional soldiers, average age 28, with post-graduate degrees and the ability to speak at least four or five languages. Or at the very least, they'd be way too sophisticated for such a sophomoric reaction. Guess I was wrong!

FRED: Sounds like those guys were basically ordinary shlubs like the rest of us, just a tad or two more cocky. (And a bit more athletic!) By the way, some of the parody versions of the song were not anti-military or anti-war, but anti-protester or anti-draft-dodger. One of the more famous ones, "Ballad of the Yellow Beret," was written by famed singer/songwriter Bob Seger. The lyrics described the draft dodgers as "fearless cowards" who wore Yellow Berets and bravely stayed home while watching their friends get shipped off to war.

STEVE: Yup, clearly a victory for the military industrial complex!

FRED: So in the end you saved your skin— as well as that of your buddies— with that uncanny ability of yours to talk your way out of almost any dicey situation. But having learned a valuable lesson that day, you probably steered clear of the 900 Marines on board our troop ship when we crossed the Pacific four months later.

STEVE: Well, let's just say that on board the USMSTS "General William Weigel," the only singing I did was to myself.

&&&&&&&&&&&&&&&&&&&&

FACT OR FICTION? The story goes that the final exam given to all candidates in the tenth week of Medic Training included one question designed to help the Army determine which graduates should be assigned to hospitals or clinics and which ones would be sent to the infantry as field medics. The question was: "How would you rearrange the letters NEPIS to spell the name of an essential body part through which the brain controls or governs a majority of the actions taken by combat soldiers in a war zone?" Those who gave the answer as "spine" went to hospitals or clinics. The remainder were issued medical aid bags, mosquito repellent and flak vests.

CHAPTER 5

HEY PRIVATE, NAVY INTELLIGENCE WOULD LIKE TO ASK YOU SOME QUESTIONS... DOWNTOWN!
Why? Do they wanna make me a Frogman? Sorry, I can't swim

STEVE: Toward the end of the first week of Medic School, the Army revealed to us that they had a problem— not enough helicopter pilots! One morning they announced that "Anyone who wishes to volunteer for Helicopter Pilot School should report to the Orderly Room once you're dismissed!" This meant we had ten minutes or so to think it over.

FRED: So you thought about volunteering, even though you'd have to agree to add a year to your hitch? Why would you want to do that? And what type of chopper would you want to fly?

STEVE: I figured if I had to go to Nam anyway, I'd rather learn a marketable skill— and be flying OVER the rice paddies instead of slogging through them as a medic. The workhorse of the war was rapidly becoming the Bell UH-1 "Huey." The Army had three types.

FRED: Yeah, gunships, slicks and dust-offs. The gunships were flying arsenals sporting rockets, cannons, mini-guns and grenade launchers as well as M-60 machine guns in the side doors. The slicks were so named because they had no external armament— just those twin M-60's in the doors. They were used to haul troops and resupply them with food, water and ammo.

STEVE: And "dust-off" was the nickname given to the air ambulances with no armament at all. Their job was to retrieve casualties off the battlefield. I figured if I had to fly into battle, I'd rather do it in pursuit of saving lives as opposed to trying to kill the enemy.

FRED: So you went to the Orderly Room to volunteer?

STEVE: Yes, and as far as I could tell, I was the only recruit who did. They sent me in to see the Captain and some Major who shook my hand, introduced himself and then opened my Personnel File. After about 30 seconds he says "Sorry son, but you cannot fly in the United States Army. You're color blind."

FRED: End of story. But then a few months later you found out they were so desperate for pilots that they dropped the ban on color-blind candidates? How did you feel then?

STEVE: Well, that was around the time we got assigned to the 24th Evac Hospital. So my reasoning went like this: Flying a "bird" was better than being a combat medic, but being a hospital medic was better than either one. So I figured that I lucked out after all.

FRED: Plus as it turns out, infantry platoons carried half a dozen different colors of smoke grenades to signal the chopper pilots— and Charlie could listen to their radio messages, find out what color they were going to use and then throw the same color smoke to try to lure the chopper into an ambush.

STEVE: Right. Misread the smoke and I'd be putting the lives of me, my crew and my patients at risk. But the way they foiled Charlie was to have the grunts throw smoke but not say the color over the radio. It was the pilot's job to say "OK, I've got green smoke" and the radioman on the ground would then confirm that he had the right color. If it had been me I probably would have screwed that up royally!

FRED: So you could have gotten killed if they made you a chopper pilot... or a combat medic... or an intelligence analyst out in the field. But instead they made you a hospital corpsman. You lucked out!

STEVE: That's how all of us pretty much looked at it, I would think. So then around the third week of Medic School, I stumbled out of the barracks for morning formation to find that it had snowed a bit the night before. Not unusual for January— unless you lived in South Texas!

FRED: I do remember that morning. There was an inch or so that stuck to the ground, which was highly unusual for San Antonio. (After

all, we were practically in Mexico!) Someone said it was the first mea-
surable snowfall there in something like 15 or 20 years. There were
a couple guys in my platoon from San Diego who had never seen or
touched the white stuff before. They proceeded to act like little kids,
tossing snow up in the air and giggling at each other. Neither one of
'em knew how to make a snowball— a very basic skill in the Midwest!

STEVE: For me, the arrival of the white stuff was only my first surprise of the day. The second, which would turn out to be considerably
more significant, came about 10 minutes later.

FRED: Let me guess. They called out your name, and you started
quaking in your boots!

STEVE: More or less. Valenzuela, our platoon sergeant standing at
the front of the formation, hollers "Donovan! Where's Donovan?" I
raise my hand and say "Here, sergeant!"

FRED: We should explain that later on, once we got out of training
units and into our actual duty assignments, the terminology was a bit
less formal. There, the NCO's acted more like your buddies instead of
like prison guards. So guys would answer them by yelling something
along the lines of "Hup Sarge!" or "Yo Sarge!" or in some cases, just
plain "Yo!" But we hadn't reached that point yet.

STEVE: Nope. Valenzuela says "Donovan, report to the Orderly
Room as soon as this formation is dismissed." "Yes, sergeant!"

FRED: What the hell could that be? A death in the family? You're
being sued for child support? Certainly it couldn't be good news.

STEVE: Probably not, although it did occur to me that perhaps
someone realized the Army had made a grave mistake by sending me
to Medic School instead of Military Intelligence School like I had
requested. Some 20 minutes later, this idea would be reinforced when
I arrived at the Orderly Room.

FRED: You mean they asked if you wanted to be transferred to
Military Intelligence School?

STEVE: Not exactly, but I was told to report to the Company Commander. As soon as I entered his office and saluted him, he gestured
toward this fellow sitting in an armchair— in civilian clothes— and
said "Donovan, this is Lieutenant Commander Stebbins from Navy

Intelligence." Holy catfish, Batman! Navy Intelligence! What could they possibly want with me?

FRED: I believe that in the Navy, Lieutenant Commander was a junior officer grade, equivalent in rank to a Captain in the Army. Not quite as awe-inspiring as it sounds, but impressive nonetheless. This was not gonna be some routine child support case!

STEVE: Apparently not, especially since— to the very best of my knowledge— I didn't have any offspring. The CO says "Commander Stebbins would like to ask you some questions. But first he'd like to take you downtown. I've arranged for you to be excused from this morning's training classes." And now I'm thinking "Wow, they've already decided I'm not gonna be a medic after all!"

FRED: So instead you were gonna be, what? A French-speaking undercover agent for Navy Intelligence? Wasn't the Navy just a little bit out of their jurisdiction, being on an Army post? Or maybe they thought you had committed treason or something like that.

STEVE: I considered that possibility, but Stebbins wasn't armed and didn't put any cuffs on me. I thought about asking to see some ID, but as soon as we stepped outside he led me over to a four-door Ford sedan with UNITED STATES NAVY in small letters on the doors.

FRED: It might not be hard to fake a government ID, but it would be pretty damn difficult to fake a "battleship grey" US Navy sedan!

STEVE: Agreed. I think I probably did ask to see his ID "just to make sure he wasn't an enemy agent," yuk, yuk— and we start driving. The guy apparently had no sense of humor. Maybe having one would have disqualified him from being in Navy Intelligence.

FRED: I'd think it would feel kind of cool to be driving around an Army post in a vehicle that says US NAVY on the sides. It was like a 20 minute drive to get downtown, right? What did you talk about? Did he eventually spill the beans once he got you alone in the car?

STEVE: He said practically nothing at all. I'd try to start a casual conversation and he'd give one-word answers. So I'm racking my brain trying to figure out who I know that's in the Navy. I keep coming up with just one answer— my brother Doug!

FRED: Maybe Doug was in trouble... or dead... or suspected of treason. Or... maybe he recommended you for Navy Intelligence!

STEVE: I figured it must have had something to do with Doug. So after several minutes of silence punctuated by an occasional "yup" or "nope," I turned to Stebbins and said "Does this have anything to do with my brother?" "Nope." Another long pause, then he says "Why, is your brother in the Navy?" I said "Yeah, he's on his second hitch."

FRED: That pretty much scotched the brother idea. Why do you suppose Stebbins couldn't have just said "I'm sure the suspense is probably killing you, so I'll tell you what this is about..."?

STEVE: I figured either that would have been in direct violation of whatever it said in his training manual about when, where and how to interrogate a witness, or else he was doing what military personnel are famous for— making a task expand to fill the amount of time available for its completion. Or maybe he was afraid I'd turn violent.

FRED: I can see it now... "Kidnapped Army Private assaults Navy Commander." So you get to downtown San Antonio and you go to...?

STEVE: Some big federal office building. He pulls into a space reserved for his battleship grey Ford, we go inside and up to about the fifth floor. He escorts me into one of those windowless interrogation rooms like you see in the movies, seats me at a table, asks if I'd like a beverage and says he'll be right back.

FRED: Did you consider trying to make a break for it at that point?

STEVE: Yes, but only for my own amusement. Stebbins comes back with a file folder that's about an inch thick, thwacks it on the table, sits down and says "Have you ever known an individual by the name of Thomas Hellman?" Suddenly I'm thinking to myself "Oh fer cryin' out loud, what did Tom do now?"

FRED: He was one of your roommates in college?

STEVE: Yup, they were doing a routine background check on him. I explained to Stebbins that Tom had lived in my dorm one year and then the following year we shared an apartment with three other guys. Now he was in the Navy and had applied for some sort of Top Secret clearance. It would all have been pretty routine, except that Tom had a few strange skeletons in his closet.

FRED: The two of you had attended the University of Wisconsin, which was known in Military Intelligence circles as a hotbed of communist sympathizers!

STEVE: And not only that, but he'd been friends with a few big-time student radicals who were leaders of the campus anti-war movement. He had attended some big anti-war rally in D.C. and I think he was arrested along with a bunch of non-violent protesters. He managed to escape, whereupon he was declared a fugitive by the FBI. He'd also attended college on a Navy ROTC scholarship but was AWOL from the six-week summer training cruise in which he was supposed to be participating. That I believe is what caused him to be called up for active duty, after which he presumably applied for a security clearance. Either that or Commander Stebbins was fibbing when he said that was the purpose of our interview.

FRED: So Stebbins was trying to get you to deliver the "coup de grace" that would establish Hellman as a radical pinko commie sympathizer with ties to the "traitors" in the anti-war movement.

STEVE: That seemed to be his objective. But I told him in all honesty, "Look, I lived with the guy for the better part of two years and during that time, his primary interests were foreign cars, foreign beers and American girls, in that order. I don't remember him ever uttering a political thought or expressing any radical views about communism or the war in Vietnam. He did have a few friends who were labeled as radicals, but he knew them from when he was in the Exchange Student program in high school."

FRED: Did Stebbins accept your assessment or did he keep on grilling you in the hopes of achieving a breakthrough?

STEVE: He kept trying different ways to get me to "crack" and say Tom was some sort of threat to national security. He was obviously aiming to add a notch to his belt for nailing another traitor, but he wasn't getting anywhere with me. Finally in exasperation he blurts out "Would you consider Thomas Hellman to be a loyal American?" I said I knew of no reason why Tom should not be considered a loyal American. Stebbins then looked me in the eye and said "Do you consider yourself to be a loyal American???" I said "Take a good look at me. I'm wearin' the damn uniform, aren't I?"

FRED: And Lieutenant Commander Stebbins said... ?

STEVE: "So you are."

FRED: Then he drove you back to Medic School in time for lunch?

STEVE: Yeah, he was a bit more talkative then. I guess he was satisfied that I'd been telling the truth. We started discussing my brother Doug, being as he and Stebbins were both Navy men.

FRED: So then did you ever find out whether Tom Hellman got his Top Secret clearance?

STEVE: I would assume not. About 4-5 years after Nam, I was back in Madison working for the Wisconsin State Journal when Tom came rolling through town in a windowless hippie van. It was painted flat (not glossy) brown— he always claimed he could paint any car with a mere six cans of spray paint from a hardware store.

FRED: A windowless van probably would have taken him more like eight— lots of surface area there! Did you tell him about sparring with Navy Intelligence and about your failure to crack under pressure from Lieutenant Commander Stebbins?

STEVE: Oh, yeah! I also told him that when I was on guard duty at night in Nam, I got a reputation for telling great stories to whomever was in the bunker with me. (It was the best way to keep both of us awake.) And at least half of those stories involved HIM in one way or another. By keeping us awake, his shenanigans might have saved my life— or at least saved me from a court martial!

FRED: Was he still a fugitive when he came through Madison in his hippie van??

STEVE: He was traveling in the style of an Arlo Guthrie, on his way to the west coast with a hippie pal named Klaus, plus two free-spirited hippie chicks. He claimed he was still a fugitive for resisting arrest and being AWOL from the Navy. He had been hiding out in Europe for several years and had just recently returned to the states for the first time. I knew he spoke fluent German, which he'd learned as a high school Exchange Student, plus he always did like those foreign cars— and those foreign beers.

FRED: How about the girls? Had he graduated to foreign girls too?

STEVE: I think the two hippie chicks were Americans. By the way, the four-door US Navy sedan with the lettering on the doors, driven by Commander Stebbins? It was actually dark blue. But it sounded better when you said it was battleship grey.

&&&&&&&&&&&&&&&&&&&

FACT OR FICTION? The story goes that an Army medic was sitting at a bar in Saigon when he saw a Navy corpsman walk in, order three glasses of beer and go sit at a table in the back of the room. Sipping from each glass, he eventually finished all three and came up to the bar to order three more. The medic turned to him and said "You know sailor, your beers wouldn't get so warm and flat if you ordered them and drank them one at a time like the rest of us." The swabbie replied "Yeah, but I've got a brother in the Marines and another in the Green Berets. When we left home, we agreed that we'd each drink this way, as if we were all together." A few weeks later, seeing the same corpsman come into the bar and order two beers instead of three, the medic says "My condolences on your loss. Which brother didn't make it?" The sailor replies "Oh, they're both fine— it's just that my wife informed me we've joined the Baptist Church and I'm no longer allowed to drink. Thank goodness it hasn't affected my brothers!"

CHAPTER 6

HANDS UP OR I'LL HIT YOU
WITH MY BILLY CLUB
*One day you're a lowly trainee, next day you're
fixin' to bash heads and take names*

FRED: When you're nothing more than a "slick-sleeve" private who's between assignments and living on an Army post, you're subject to being collared at any point in time and assigned to some sort of work detail... or guard duty. And so it was that during the few days between the time we graduated from Medic School and the time we were to officially report to our next duty assignment— the 24th Evac, right there at Fort Sam— Steve's name popped up on the guard duty roster. No rest for the weary!

STEVE: It said I was to report at 5 pm to a guard shack located in the southeast corner of the post, just a few blocks from the 24th Evac barracks which would soon become our new home. There were at least a dozen or so other guys there, all complete strangers to me, including the NCO's. I remember it quite clearly because there were several odd things that happened that night— plus it was the first time I ever pulled guard duty.

FRED: What sort of odd things?

STEVE: The first was when the Sergeant of the Guard asked us if we wanted to chip in a couple bucks each to rent a TV set for the evening, so of course we did. The idea being that when you weren't out at your guard post, you could relax inside the guard shack and watch TV.

FRED: That does sound odd. If they were pulling in 24 bucks a night from a bunch of young recruits, in a couple weeks they should have collected enough to buy the damned television!

STEVE: Definitely weird. It was only a 21-inch black & white, after all. Plus as soon as we said yes, the TV showed up within 5 or 10 minutes. Maybe the rental dude was driving around post with his van full of TV sets, I dunno. But I've often wondered if it wasn't just a few NCO's who had devised a little scam for making an extra 168 bucks a week off us dumb recruits. It had to be something like that.

FRED: What was the next odd thing?

STEVE: Well, no sooner had we sat down in front of our rented TV to watch the NBC Evening News at 5:30 than they started showing clips of an anti-war rally held that very day at my old school, UW-Madison. Standing at the podium in this large assembly hall was one of my former college roommates, Dave Wilner from Ohio. He was a self-styled "poet" and an avowed pacifist, and he was acting as sort of a low-key emcee, making announcements and introducing the radical guest speakers one by one. It was the first time I had seen the NBC News in five or six months, and there he was— my ex-roommate on national TV, right there with Huntley and Brinkley!

FRED: Holy mackerel, what are the odds of that???

STEVE: I'd have to say it could never happen again in a million years— especially since Chet and David are long gone!

FRED: So anyway, how long were the guard shifts that night?

STEVE: Since it was a walking post rather than a stationary one, I think the shifts were walk two hours, sleep four, walk two, sleep four. (Unlike our stationary posts in Nam, where later on we would do three on, three off, three on, three off.) The first shift started at 6 pm and I think I picked the 10 to midnight slot, followed by 4 to 6 am, since I knew I'd never be able to fall sleep before 10 but I'd be ready to crash hard by midnight.

FRED: And what was it that you were supposed to guard?

STEVE: I was assigned to guard the Fort Sam Motor Pool. At 6 pm the Sergeant of the Guard drove the first shift out in a pickup and had the rest of us tag along so he'd only have to explain things once. The Motor Pool was huge, with six or eight gigantic structures similar to aircraft hangars and open at both ends. Each one was filled with parked vehicles, mostly big trucks. There were like 40 yards of concrete pavement separating each one of the buildings— likely a safeguard in the event of a mortar attack, I suppose.

FRED: But you didn't spot any enemy activity in the area?

STEVE: Not a smidge. But here's the next odd thing that happened that night. They gave me a billy club, MP helmet, flashlight, MP armband and a whistle to wear around my neck. But nary a word of instruction on what to do with any of that stuff.

FRED: Maybe they assumed you'd done it before. Besides, everybody knows how to blow a whistle and swing a club, right?

STEVE: Right. But I'm looking at this stuff with "MP" all over it in big white letters and thinking "Hey, I'm gonna be playing cop! My purpose will be to enforce the laws and prevent crime! If necessary, I will scare the bad guys with my whistle and hit them with my billy club!" Later on I realized the Sergeant of the Guard should have given a speech in which he said: "Gentlemen, your job is to OBSERVE and REPORT. If you see any suspicious activity, you are to get on the field phone and report it! You are NOT here to PLAY COP!" But then in the Army, they never tell ya nuthin'.

FRED: Well then if they didn't tell you that, what did they say your responsibilities were?

STEVE: I was supposed to make a big circle, passing through each one of the hangars as I went, and stopping once each trip at a guard phone where I was to call and say "Post 3, all clear." I surmised that if I should witness any suspicious activity, I was supposed to check it out, blow the whistle if necessary, confront the perps and race to the guard phone to call for assistance ("bring more billy clubs, guys!") Not necessarily in that order, mind you.

FRED: In the war movies, when the sentry spots suspicious activity you usually see him raise his weapon and prepare to fire— up until he gets jumped from behind by one of the infiltrators!

STEVE: True, but I didn't have any weapons other than a billy club and a phone! Of course, depending on my location, I might be 80 yards away from that phone at any given point in time. And there was no way in hell that anyone was going to hear my whistle regardless, since the motor pool was probably half a mile from the guard shack. I believe I timed one single trip around the course at 27 minutes, which meant I'd be calling in roughly twice every hour.

FRED: Did you feel like a soldier? A sentry? A cop? A military policeman? Or none of the above?

STEVE: Well on one hand, being alone in the darkness with an MP helmet and a (wooden) weapon was the first time I actually felt like a soldier performing soldierly duties. But since it was February or March, it was damned chilly and windy— and I felt I wasn't properly dressed or armed for the task. (A billy club, fer cryin' out loud?) Besides, I reasoned that if anyone was going to be trying to commit hanky panky, he'd already know that the guard only comes by every 20 to 30 minutes— plus he'd have a lookout who'd say "here comes the guard," and then the two of 'em would hide in the darkness behind one of the trucks until I had passed by. Or else jump me and take away my billy club, if they were so inclined.

FRED: Then you'd be left with just your trusty whistle. Luckily for you, the perpetrators weren't likely to know that nobody could hear it! After all, why would a sentry bother to blow his whistle if he knew nobody would be able hear it?

STEVE: Don't forget I had a flashlight too! I probably could have shined it in their eyes and frozen them in their tracks, kind of like shining a deer. But what all this meant was that about the only intruders I would actually have any realistic chance of protecting the motor pool from would be drunks or crazy persons who had stumbled into the fenced motor pool more or less by accident when they were trying to find a shortcut home.

FRED: Sounds like that could have been a fairly daunting task. Had you ever experienced anything that might help you prepare for it?

STEVE: Well as a part-time pizza delivery driver during my college years, I'd dealt with more than my share of unruly drunks and crazy persons at all hours of the night— but I'd come to learn that it was generally a losing proposition.

FRED: Was the Army concerned that someone might try to steal the trucks, or vandalize them, or sabotage them, or what?

STEVE: All of the above, I suppose. Remember, the anti-war movement had just gotten off the ground, even though it probably hadn't reached Texas yet— maybe it never did. As for someone stealing a truck, it wasn't until we got to Nam that I found out military jeeps and trucks didn't have ignition keys— just a safety switch and a starter button. The only way they could be secured was with a heavy metal cable that was bolted to the floor and padlocked to the steering wheel so the vehicle could not be steered. Which meant that anyone with a bolt cutter or a lock picking tool could have stolen one of those trucks if he so desired. But of course the Army never tells ya nuthin', so how was I supposed to know?

FRED: Are you gonna tell me somebody tried to steal a truck while you were guarding the Fort Sam Motor Pool?

STEVE: I'm not exactly sure. I don't remember if someone tipped me off or I just thought of it myself, but I realized that if I climbed into the back of one of those parked deuce and a halfs, I could stay out of the cold wind and still have a vantage point where I could watch for trespassers without freezing my jollies. Plus I'd be able to spot the Sergeant of the Guard cruising around in his three-quarter pickup. If I picked a spot near the phone, I could still call in every half hour without expending too much unnecessary effort on my part. So after starting my second circuit around the course on the 10 pm shift, I picked out a truck and climbed into the cargo bay, at which point the biggest danger was that I might fall asleep at my post. (After all, you know what the Korean officers did to the ROK snoozers!)

FRED: Yes I do, and I also know you were in direct violation of the soldier's Second General Order. We had to learn them during the first week of Basic Training! I believe it reads: "To walk my post in a military manner, keeping always on the alert and observing everything that takes place within sight or hearing."

STEVE: Let me be the first to compliment you on your memory. But a good soldier should also be resourceful enough to adapt to circumstances and exercise independent judgement when necessary. I was merely adapting and exercising, as they say.

FRED: Actually, the military had eleven General Orders but each branch of the service "added" a 12th. For the Marines it was "To walk my post from flank to flank and take no crap from any rank." The Navy added another line to that one: "If he's a chief I'll let him pass, if he's an officer he can kiss my ass." These lines were designed to make it clear to the young enlisted man that when he was on guard duty, he was the dude in charge of his post, rank be damned.

STEVE: Yeah, but I was following the ARMY'S 12th General Order, which was "To not get caught violating any of those first eleven General Orders." We heard that one in Basic too— although not from any sergeant— and besides I never got caught, so "Ya can't beat the fuggin' system," eh? We'll see about that!

FRED: OK, so now you're sitting in the back of a deuce and a half. Did you fall asleep?

STEVE: No, I did not not. I climbed into the cargo bay at around 10:30, after making my first call to the guard house. Everything was nice and cozy and peaceful for an hour or so. I called in again around 2300 hours (11 pm) and once more just before 2330. Climbing back into my hideout, I scanned the horizon carefully and... damn! What was that? Were my eyes playing tricks on me, or did I just see a shadowy figure moving between the buildings on the far side of the Motor Pool? Why did this have to happen to me, fer cryin' out loud???

FRED: Now we're talking! This could be your first taste of (slightly) armed combat!

STEVE: By then the sense of power and invincibility that I'd felt when I first donned the MP garb was wearing off. I was rapidly turning into just another wimp with an armband and a helmet! I began to review my options. I could pretend I never saw the shadowy figure at all, and hope nothing came of it. I could dash for the phone and call for help, but then I'd feel foolish if it was a false alarm.

FRED: You could confront the perp, but what if he had a gun?

STEVE: And what if it was the Sergeant of the Guard or his CQ runner, sneaking around so they could check up on me? I continued weighing the possibilities for several more minutes until I heard what sounded like someone slamming the door of a deuce and a half. Sonofabitch, the bastard's trying to steal a 6 by 6 on my watch!

FRED: In the Army we usually called 'em deuce and a halfs, meaning two-and-a-half ton trucks. The Marines called 'em six-bys, meaning all six wheels were drive wheels.

STEVE: Another 30 seconds went by... and I heard another door slam! Now there was no question that something was goin' down. Soon, another door... 20 more seconds, and I hear another one! What the hell is going on? Is it a whole squad of truck thieves or what? I looked at my watch and realized the guard truck would be showing up in less than 20 minutes for the shift change.

FRED: If you timed it right, you should have been able to hop out of the deuce and a half, make it over to the phone and call in at just about the time the Sergeant was rolling down the street with your shift replacement, plus a few other troopers that might come in handy.

STEVE: You read my mind! I hear more doors slam as I get to the phone. I call and say "This is Donovan, Post Three. I'm hearing some noises over in Hangar 5, there must be somebody in there." The voice on the other end says "OK, hang loose and keep your eyes peeled, Donovan. The guard truck is on its way over there at this very minute."

FRED: So far, so good!

STEVE: I see the guard truck coming down the street, so I start walking over toward the gate. I approach the truck and tell 'em the situation, whereupon they dismount and follow me to the hangar. We're just about there when out comes one lone guy dressed in Army fatigues... and carrying something in his hand.

FRED: Aha, no doubt either a weapon or some contraband! Caught in the act! Your first collar, Mister MP!

STEVE: Our "perp" is now facing four "fake MP's" with billy clubs, plus a Staff Sergeant who's armed with a .45 caliber sidearm. The sergeant challenges him and says "Hold your hands out to your sides where we can see 'em!" The mysterious figure identifies himself as "SP5 Lenberg, Motor Pool. I left my transistor radio on the seat of a truck today and I knew if I didn't get it now, it wouldn't be there the next time I came lookin' for it. Couldn't remember which truck, so I had to keep lookin' til I found it." Flashlights at the ready, we check out his ID and examine his transistor radio, then turn him loose.

FRED: So much for your first collar. At least you didn't get nailed for abandoning your post— for all you knew, SP5 Lenberg could have piped up and said "Hey, I saw that dude there coppin' some Z's in the back of a deuce and a half!"

STEVE: As a matter of fact, when it was over the Sergeant of the Guard said "Good work, Donovan! You did the right thing. We're not cops here— we just observe and report. I'll put in a recommendation and see if we can't get you a PFC stripe for that sleeve of yours!"

FRED: Do you think he actually did that?

STEVE: Well, since I was due to get mine in the next week or two anyway, it would be pretty hard to say. As it turned out, that night would be the only time I ever pulled guard duty in the states. But little did I realize then that less than five months later, we'd be walking a different guard post with loaded M-14 rifles, steel pots on our heads, a couple of fragmentation grenades hanging from the lapels of our flak jackets, and some creepy little guys wearing Ho Chi Minh sandals lurking out there in the darkness. We're talkin' "Victor Charlies" who would have liked nothing better than to slit our throats— or at least I thought so at the time.

FRED: Sounds to me like you might have been reading too many of those war comics!

&&&&&&&&&&&&&&&&&&&

FACT OR FICTION? The story goes that unfortunately, Sergeant Binsdorf in the 24th Evac Motor Pool had become addicted to brake fluid. He insisted he wasn't worried about it, however, since he knew he could stop any time he wanted to.

CHAPTER 7

LET'S DO SOME OJT AT PRESIDENT JOHNSON'S FAVORITE HOSPITAL
Maybe one of us will get to take LBJ's official blood pressure reading

STEVE: After heaving a big sigh of relief at being assigned to a stateside hospital as new medics— rather than receiving orders for Nam— we were quickly jolted back to reality by some rather disturbing news. It seemed the 24th had been an inactive unit that was in the process of being staffed and activated in preparation for... a journey halfway around the world to the shores of Vietnam!

FRED: We took our duffel bags on a short truck ride across the Fort Sam post to our new home at the 24th and promptly had an orientation meeting for all new personnel. There we were informed that we'd be shipping out in a matter of a few months for the War Zone.

STEVE: Our date of departure and precise destination were "classified" military secrets— a bit of intrigue to add to the mystique of it all. But as brand new medics, we'd be getting three months of OJT (On the Job Training) on a hospital ward at Fort Sam, then it was off to Vietnam to get a chance to apply what we had learned.

FRED: So basically the bad news was "Vietnam, here we come." The good news, however, was that unlike many of our fellow trainees, we'd be hospital medics and not combat medics. That meant not having to go out and trudge through the jungles or slog through the rice paddies... no sleeping under the stars... and no dodging bullets, booby traps or deadly snakes for us!

STEVE: At least not initially. It didn't take long for us to figure out that since we'd received the same training as the combat medics, in Nam we'd be "ripe for the picking" any time new corpsmen were needed for immediate deployment to an infantry battalion.

FRED: A fact that would hang over our heads for nearly the entire 12 months of our tour overseas. But looking at the bright side, one of the first things we noticed at our new duty station was that the food was much better. In training units, where most of the cooks were fresh out of cook school, it had been mediocre at best. At the 24th, they were skilled pros who knew what they were doing and took pride in their work. The troops actually looked forward to chow each day.

STEVE: And for the first few weeks prior to the start of our OJT, we got stuck on KP a few times. The NCO's and cooks were nice to us and treated us like friends or family members.

FRED: After five months as trainees who were used to being abused and ridiculed by such types, this was a strange new experience for us. But one day you nearly got your ass in a jam on KP.

STEVE: I was working at the window where the troops turn in their dirty trays. I wore rubber gloves and had a high-powered, trigger-operated spray nozzle hanging down on a hose in front of my face. The window was about 2 feet wide and 10 inches high. It hit me just above waist level, so I couldn't see the soldier who was turning in his tray— and he couldn't see me either.

FRED: The guy on the other side could be a private... or he could be the Company Commander! The only way he'd be able to see your face would be to crouch and stick his puss right in the window.

STEVE: Right. As each tray came in, I'd grab it with my left hand and give it a blast with the sprayer in my right hand. In one continuous motion, I'd drop it on a stack to my left so the man next to me could load them into the dishwasher. This took me roughly three seconds per tray— a highly efficient operation.

FRED: Some guy had to be really proud of the system he'd devised for getting those trays cleaned and sterilized in a heartbeat!

STEVE: For sure. I'm blasting these trays like crazy when all of a sudden some wise guy named Borchardt, who just happened to know I was working at the dish window that day, sticks his face in the window and unleashes some smart-assed, derogatory comment. Now I had learned in college that when somebody did something funny at your expense, the proper response was to reciprocate by immediately doing something funny at his expense.

FRED: And having only a split second to come up with a response, you went to the only weapon in your arsenal— that trusty spray nozzle in your right hand!

STEVE: I did. But as PFC Borchardt spotted my right hand coming up with my finger on the trigger, he leaped aside so as not to get a quick dousing. In so doing, he exited my field of fire by the narrowest of margins and just missed receiving a good blast from my highly accurate nozzle. Instead, that scalding stream of high-pressure spray shot harmlessly across the room and landed on the floor.

FRED: And no sooner had that hot jet of steaming water hit the concrete than another face popped into the dish window. It was the next man in line, but this time it wasn't some private— no, it was none other than SFC Hoskins, our First Sergeant, who just happened to be the highest ranking enlisted man in the entire company!

STEVE: I had just missed hosing the First Shirt by a few inches! Naturally he had to peer into the window to see just who the jag-off was that had come so close to getting his ass handed to him.

FRED: Whereupon SFC Hoskins said.... ?

STEVE: He said "Donovan, you are one lucky bastard." I replied "Yessir, First Sergeant— sorry about that!"

FRED: So you narrowly avoided being put on KP every day for the next month or so. Which means you managed to beat the fuggin' system once again!

STEVE: Right. But then we went on OJT at Brooke Army Hospital for the next three months, so— no more KP! In addition to being a major burn treatment center for the US Army, Brooke was President Johnson's favorite hospital.

FRED: Being a native Texan, LBJ used to go there for his annual physicals as well as any major treatments he might need. They put me to work on the 7 am to 3 pm shift as an orderly on a Post-Op Ward, working with patients who were recovering from surgery.

STEVE: After spending a week or so on the day shift with several nurses and corpsmen, I was transferred to the 3 to 11 shift where it was just me and one nurse. The ward was called "Internal Medicine" but it was really a place where old war veterans in their 60's, 70's and 80's went to spend their final days.

FRED: Would you say you managed to learn a lot about how to be a hospital medic during that time?

STEVE: Maybe for the first week or so, but after that I settled into a routine of taking each patient's TPR every two hours, plus hustling a few bedpans or giving an occasional sponge bath. I did learn a few little tricks, like if a patient crapped his bed and it was just about time for the shift change, you could just close the privacy curtains around the bed and let the next shift worry about it.

FRED: Otherwise you'd never get your work done before it was time to punch out. If you had to stay late, you'd miss the bus and have to walk the two miles back to the barracks at 11:30 at night. But you did have one patient who provided you with a real learning experience.

STEVE: Yeah, old man Peterman. He was about 80 and in pretty bad shape— hooked up to various IV and drainage tubes. He also had a tracheotomy so he could breathe through a hole in his throat.

FRED: Was he able to speak?

STEVE: Not at all. With a trache, the patient is supposed to learn how to put his finger over the hole so he can talk while exhaling. But Peterman either never got the hang of it or maybe didn't care. He was extremely cantankerous and ignored everything the nurses and corpsmen tried to tell him. At times he'd start screaming at the staff, except that since he couldn't talk, he wasn't making a sound. He'd be gesturing wildly but no one had any idea what he was saying.

FRED: And since he was a sleepwalker, every night was an adventure with this patient?

STEVE: Yeah, he'd get up in the middle of the night, rip out all his tubes including the catheter, and start wandering toward the bathroom in his bare feet. Since he was unable to listen to reason or control his nightly meanderings, it was decided that drastic action was called for. So every night, to prevent him from yanking out his tubes, we had to secure his hands to the bedrails with leather wrist restraints. To prevent the sleepwalking, we had to sedate him and strap him to the bed with a contraption called a Posey Belt.

FRED: The Posey Belt was a device used to restrain combative, agitated or sleepwalking patients to prevent self injury or disruption of IV's, catheters, etc. It consisted of two heavy leather straps. One went completely around the mattress while the other went around the patient's midsection. To immobilize the patient, the two straps were attached to each other with a padlock that could only be opened with a key. For security purposes, each Posey Belt had its own unique key. Once the belt was locked, that patient was going nowhere until someone showed up with the magic key.

STEVE: The key was kept in a drawer at the nurse's station. If Peterman had to go to the latrine in the middle of the night, I'd have to get the key, undo the wrist restraints, unlock the Posey Belt, elevate his bed to a sitting position, hang his tubes and paraphernalia on a wheeled IV pole, put his slippers on his feet, help him stand up and then assist him as he shuffled slowly to the latrine while holding on to the pole. When he was done, the process would be reversed and then I'd put the key back in the drawer. The entire procedure could easily take up to a half hour, which is probably why they decided to put a catheter on him. He might have to pee once an hour, which could keep a corpsman occupied for four hours out of an 8-hour shift.

FRED: And at night you were the only corpsman on duty. Together with one nurse, you were responsible for around 30 patients— but fortunately most of 'em were asleep at that hour.

STEVE: Right. But then this one evening the nurse says "Mister Peterman has an appointment to be transported across the post at 7:30 am tomorrow to another building for a series of tests. A doctor will be here at 9 pm this evening to give him a preliminary exam. When he arrives, you'll have to unlock the belt for him. Also, Peterman's catheter is leaking, so it needs to be changed."

FRED: Now one of the procedures they spent several hours on in Medic School was how to catheterize a patient who was unable to urinate. It involved running a flexible rubber tube (a sterile urological Foley Catheter, to be precise) up through the penis until it reached the bladder. Once there, a little balloon near the tip of the tube would be inflated so as to hold the catheter in place and prevent it from sliding back out. Urine would then drain out through the tube into a collection bag attached to the bottom of the bedrail.

STEVE: To insert the catheter, everything had to be sterile to avoid introducing any stray bacteria into the patient's system. You had to wear sterile rubber gloves, apply a sterile lubricant to the tube, use a pair of sterile forceps to hold the sterile catheter, and insert it with your right hand while you held the penis with your gloved left hand.

FRED: In Medic School we would practice this procedure on anatomically correct dummies in a simulated hospital ward. We worked in pairs so your buddy could watch to make sure you were doing it correctly. Catheterizing dummies (or humans) was a little creepy— but then again, it sure beat having to go out on the battlefield and "plug the leaks" while lead or shrapnel was flying all around you. Most trainees would probably think "Well, I hope I never have to do that on a real patient!"

STEVE: Indeed they would, but now here was a lieutenant telling me I had to do it. I think she asked me if I knew how and I said "Well, we covered it in training but I've never actually done one."

FRED: So she offered to help by showing you how it was done. But rather than getting a kit containing all the sterile equipment, she just walked over to Peterman's bed and pulled back the sheet.

STEVE: Yeah, he was out cold from the sedative. I looked down at his groin, expecting to see a tube coming out of his member. Instead I saw what looked like a condom that been attached to his pecker with adhesive tape and then taped to a drainage tube at the tip. My first thought was that this was a cruel prank played by someone who was too lazy, squeamish or ignorant to do it the right way. It certainly wasn't anything they taught us in Medic School!

FRED: Did either you or the lieutenant say anything at that point?

STEVE: She never flinched, so I said "Is that what I think it is?" I expected her to say "Oh my gosh, look what someone has done!" Instead she said "Yes, that's condom drainage." Here they even had an official name for it! Then she showed me how to remove the old condom and install a new one. Turns out that Peterman needed a catheter not because he couldn't urinate. It was because he would have consumed about four to six hours per day of a medic's time with all his lengthy trips to the latrine. Condom drainage solved the problem.

FRED: So then the doc shows up at 9 pm?

STEVE: Yeah, I had to unlock the Posey Belt, wait for the physician to finish the exam, lock the belt again and then put the key back in the drawer at the nurse's station. So while I'm waiting for the exam to be completed, I put the magic key in my pocket for safekeeping.

FRED: Then when the doc was done, you were supposed to lock the Posey Belt, put the key back in the drawer, wait for the shift to end, catch the bus back to the barracks, tiptoe in so you wouldn't wake the rest of us, and you'd be in the sack before midnight.

STEVE: Right. But then around 6 am I'm rudely awakened by a loud voice. It was PFC Bonomo yelling "Hey, Donovan, your ward called! They can't find the key to the Posey Belt! Everyone's waiting to take your patient to the testing center but they can't do it because he's padlocked to the bed. What happened to the key??" Now I'm racking my brain thinking "What could I have done with that damned thing? I would swear I put it back in the drawer like I was supposed to!"

FRED: The only two people who might have had a clue would have been you or old man Peterman. Of course he wouldn't have been of any help since he couldn't talk, even if he did know the right answer. But then again... Is it possible that the always cantankerous Mister Peterman might have stolen the key from you somehow?

STEVE: Could be— I was completely baffled. So I leap out of bed, open my locker and start putting on the same "hospital whites" I had been wearing the night before. If nobody can find that key, I've got to at least go back there and help look for it by retracing my steps! As I'm about to leave, I start fumbling in my pocket for some bus fare and bingo— out comes a Posey Belt key!

FRED: Then minutes later, as I was heading out the door to catch the bus to Brooke, you grabbed me and said "Take this over to Ward 3-C right away! Just say it's the key to the Posey Belt and one of the corpsmen on duty last night accidentally left it in his pocket." Mister Peterman had been locked in that bed for eight hours already!

STEVE: Hopefully no one would bother to check and see who the dummy was that had been on duty the night before. To the best of my knowledge, nobody did because I never heard any more about it. That might have been the first time I managed to dodge a court martial for possible dereliction of duty. The second might have been the day we crossed the International Dateline in the middle of the Pacific. But that's a story for another chapter.

FRED: So while we were working OJT on the wards at Brooke, most of the 24th Evac personnel were busy packing up the hospital's equipment and loading it into trucks. These were then anchored to flatbed railroad cars for the trip to the West Coast.

STEVE: The railroad cars left San Antonio a week or so ahead of us, followed by our Advance Party of around 25 officers, NCO's and enlisted men. The trucks would travel by ship while the Advance Party would fly to Vietnam and begin setting things up for when the rest of us— roughly 200 men— would arrive by ship.

FRED: About the last thing we did before leaving the states was receive orientation on the M-16 rifle as we prepared for deployment to Nam. With their plastic stocks, the M-16's weighed half as much as an M-14 and could be fired on fully automatic at the flip of a switch.

STEVE: Fort Sam had no rifle range, so we had to be trucked some 18 miles out to Camp Bullis. Instead of pop-up targets like we had in Basic, Bullis had old fashioned "target pits" that dated back to World War II. These consisted of one long trench about eight feet deep and situated some 50 meters from the firing positions. The targets were standard black and white paper bullseyes mounted on tracks so they could be run up and down by those working in the trench.

FRED: For each firing lane, a three-man crew in the trench would wait for the shooter to fire five rounds. They'd run the target down, mark the hits with little pieces of tape so the shooter and spotter could see the results, and run the target up again. Each pit crew was equipped with a red flag on a long stick that they could wave back and forth to tell the shooter if he had missed the target entirely.

STEVE: That red flag had once been given the nickname "Maggie's Drawers," a term supposedly coined by the Wisconsin 7th Cavalry Regiment during the Civil War. According to the story, they had to borrow a pair of pantaloons belonging to one Margaret Delafield due to there being no red flags available where they had camped.

FRED: Since this was "familiarization firing" and nobody was keeping score, it didn't really matter whether guys were getting hits or not. What the shooters didn't realize was that we had a field phone in the pits connecting us to one of our guys up on top for safety. So we could call him and ask "Who's about to shoot on Lanes 5, 6 and 7?" He'd say "Carter's on 5, Lewis is on 6 and Portman's on 7."

STEVE: If there was someone we really liked, or some nerdy guy whom we knew to be a lousy shot, we'd mark five hits right smack in the bullseye. But if it was someone we wanted to have a little fun with, like PFC Lewis, we'd keep giving him the Maggie's Drawers no matter what he hit.

FRED: Lewis— a "super-macho" type— got so pissed we could hear him screaming "Goddammit, I gotta be hittin' that friggin' target! What the hell is going on down there??" Nobody said a word. Instead we'd just taunt him by sticking that flag up and waving it slowly back and forth a few more times.

STEVE: Later on, when Lewis demanded to know who was in the pit on Lane 6, the three guys who knew just played dumb.

FRED: We should have told him "Tough luck, hotshot— somebody just beat the fuggin' system at your expense!"

&&&&&&&&&&&&&&&&&&&

FACT OR FICTION? The story goes that the 9th Infantry had one soldier— Corporal Mitreske— with a very special talent: By using a highly sophisticated form of mind control, he was able to render himself invisible for periods of up to 12 hours at a time. This came in very handy for sneaking into enemy camps in the wee hours and committing sabotage. Soon his GI buddies had nicknamed him "The Invisible Grunt." The only drawback was that when he was transparent, he tended to get very nauseous. One morning Mitreske felt so awful that he went on sick call to try to find a cure for his condition. The medic on duty went into the doctor's office and said "Sir, the Invisible Grunt is here for a consultation." The captain, up to his ears in paperwork, said "Tell him I can't see him right now!" To which Mitreske replied "Well, duuuhhhh!"

CHAPTER 8

WILLIE AND THE WAVE MAKERS
Remember, your government is paying for all this—
so don't go wasting the taxpayer's dough!

FRED: From San Antonio we flew on a commercial jetliner to Oakland. For some reason it was decided that we'd carry our M-14 rifles onto the plane (without any ammo) while our duffel bags were stored in the cargo hold below. I don't know why they couldn't have just crated the weapons, but the impression left on us was that we should be ready to shoot our way ashore as soon as we arrived in the war zone. We'd all seen movies depicting that D-Day invasion of France, so we had a pretty good idea of what might lie ahead.

STEVE: And the impression it left on the airline stewardesses was that we were heading directly into combat. Since there was no place to store a couple hundred rifles onboard, we had to lay some of them in the aisle right next to our seats. This meant the stewardesses had to carefully pick their way up and down the aisle to avoid tripping over the armament. It was the first time I actually had any feelings of being "macho" in the nine months I had been in the Army!

FRED: I think we were probably wearing helmets and flak jackets too, which added to the ambience of virility. When we landed in San Francisco we were bussed to the Oakland Army Terminal, where we prepared to board what would be our "new home" for the next three weeks— the USNS General William Weigel, a transport ship with a maximum capacity of 5,200 troops and a cruising speed of 21 knots. We began referring to it as the Weigel— but soon enough, someone decided to nickname it "The Willie."

STEVE: The Willie was commissioned near the end of World War II and operated by the US Coast Guard to haul troops in both the Pacific and European Theaters. In fact one of our men, SP5 King, wrote home to tell his parents he was sailing to Vietnam on the Weigel. They wrote back and said the Willie was the sister ship to the one that had brought King's father home after he was liberated from a Japanese prison camp on the island of Corregidor in World War II.

FRED: The ship had originally been armed with a couple dozen anti-aircraft guns but I think they must have been removed by 1966. Apparently there was no longer any perceived threat from the Japanese Navy or Air Force. Looking at those "naked" gun turrets left one with the impression that "Nah, this Vietnam thing ain't a real war!"

STEVE: Ditto for the Viet Cong Navy or Air Force, since they didn't exist. The Weigel was decommissioned in '46, then called up again for the Korean War, being crewed this time by the US Navy.

FRED: As part of the Vietnam war buildup, the Willie would be brought out of mothballs once more— just a month before we were drafted— to haul troops across the Pacific as part of the Military Sea Transport System (MSTS.) This time she was crewed by civilians who looked, acted and dressed like US Navy sailors but were actually merchant seamen drawing fatter paychecks.

STEVE: It turns out they were given US Navy grades and ID cards identifying them by naval rank. In the event of capture by the enemy, this was supposed to protect them from being mistreated as spies in accordance with the international Geneva Conventions. Hollywood celebrities who visited our hospital in Nam were given similar ID cards showing "honorary" officer ranks for the same reason.

FRED: Some of the crewmen were rather colorful characters, too. One fellow we called "Mike the Magician" spent his free time on deck doing magic tricks for the troops. He was into pranks, too. He'd transmit fake news broadcasts from a hiding place with a portable FM transmitter after telling anyone who had a transistor radio to bring it up on deck and tune it to a certain frequency. Of course he knew there was no

FM radio reception out in the middle of the Pacific, but many of the unsuspecting troops did not.

FRED: So one day he might announce that LBJ had resigned the American presidency, the next day he might tell a different group of GI's that Ho Chi Minh had surrendered. Fortunately he always tried to make sure his victims got clued in to the fact that the broadcasts they had heard were bogus.

STEVE: From Oakland the Willie headed west, sailing under the Golden Gate Bridge. As we stood on deck, this prompted me to say "How many other people can ever say they crossed OVER as well as UNDER the Golden Gate on the same day?"

FRED: Yup that's Steve, always looking to find the positives even in the most dire of circumstances!

STEVE: We thought that would be our final glimpse of the Mother Land, but we soon found out we were headed south— to San Diego— to pick up some 900 US Marines who would join us on our voyage across the "Big Pond." It was something like 484 miles from the Oakland Army Terminal to the San Diego Naval Base. Cruising at 21 knots, that meant it would add at least a day and a half to the total length of our voyage. Which might cause one to wonder "Why didn't they just fly us to San Diego in the first place?"

FRED: Well, it was only the US military— what should we have expected? Besides, it would add about 36 hours to the amount of time we would never have to spend on Vietnamese turf. Okay by me!

STEVE: Sailing into San Diego Bay the next day, we stood on deck watching as the Willie pulled into its berth— and then some. Whoever was piloting her had miscalculated, thus taking out a sizeable chunk of the pier where we were supposed to dock. Not exactly a confidence builder for us passengers... maybe the captain and crew had been in mothballs for 12 years along with the ship!

FRED: I took a good look at the destruction as we walked off the pier— and hoped the collision hadn't done any similar damage to the Willie! We were given six hours of shore liberty and told we'd have to be back on board by 8 pm. Some of the guys who presumably knew what they were doing— or were easily persuaded by their peers—

immediately lit out for Tijuana, a mere 12 miles south of our crippled pier, to search out some Mexican poontang.

STEVE: As for the rest of us, we quickly found out (probably from the ship's crew) there were two topless bars within walking distance of the Navy Base. We sampled them both, only to find that one had cheap drinks but sleazy looking dancers while the other had more expensive drinks— but the dancers were well worth the extra cost. Nothing but top shelf entertainment for the likes of us!

FRED: Quite an odd juxtaposition. We had "sailed off to war" just two days before, and yet here we were sucking down booze while looking at shapely young women wearing only G-strings! We wound up drinking and getting rowdy with not only our buddies but also a number of the NCO's, including First Sergeant Hoskins.

STEVE: That in itself was quite unusual, since sergeants did not normally fraternize with the peons when they were off duty. But they probably figured it was their job to keep us out of trouble and make sure we didn't jump ship. Plus they obviously had the good taste to patronize the bar that had the better looking women!

FRED: As the time approached when we were due to be back on the Willie, First Sergeant Hoskins (who had been a medic during the Korean War and was normally a no-nonsense, spit-and-polish military type) was feeling his oats. At one point he stood up with a drink in his hand, pointed to one well-endowed dancer and addressed the entire group of us by hollering "Take a good look at those knockers, boys! You won't see anything like that again for the next twelve months!"

STEVE: Of course he didn't say "knockers." But having been in Korea, he probably knew what he was talking about. We hot-footed it back to the Willie, where our luxury accommodations awaited us— canvas bunks that were similar to stretchers, stacked about four to five layers high, depending on what part of the ship you were in.

FRED: These were about two feet above one another, with the bottom one being maybe four inches off the floor. If you had broad shoulders there wasn't enough room to turn over on your bunk, so you'd have to decide ahead of time which position you wanted to sleep in before you actually slid in there.

STEVE: That night we had a fart lighting contest in the troop bay.

Most guys who had never lived in a college dorm didn't believe farts could be lit like a blowtorch, so they were perfectly willing to lay down bets while I collected their money. Of course to pull it off you first had to find someone with that rare ability to fart on cue. Dan Berkley turned out to be the guy, and together we cleaned up— me lighting the matches and him farting through his jockeys.

FRED: That is until he eventually ran out of gas, so to speak.

STEVE: Throughout our three-week voyage across the Pacific, the most exhilarating and uplifting experience for me would always be the appearance of the dolphins. Several times a day we'd see a "pod"— maybe a couple dozen of 'em— suddenly appear alongside the ship. They'd take turns leaping out of the water, always with big smiles on their faces, as they swam along beside us.

FRED: We were doing 21 knots, so they were probably doing 25 as they gradually passed us and then disappeared. We never saw them coming out of the water until they were just about next to us, and once they passed, they'd stop leaping— which seemed to indicate that they were only doing it for our benefit.

STEVE: I'm an animal lover— with a special attachment for the intelligent ones— so I was fascinated by this apparent display of friendship and warmth. For decades afterward, I wondered why they did it. I would occasionally conjure up hypothetical explanations, as if they might have been trying to say one of these lines to us:
> *"Howdy, this is the way we greet humans!"*
> *"See how playful and adorable we are?"*
> *"Don't worry, this area is shark-free!"*
> *"Hey, look at us! We're as free as the birds!"*
> *"Throw us some fish, you cheapskate tourists!"*
> *"Betcha you guys can't do this!"*
> *"Got a sub you'd like us to find for ya?"*
> *"Please stop puking over the side! We live here!"*
> *"Let us on your ship! We wanna look around!*
> *"Come on out here in the water and play with us!"*
> *"Give us some more veal parmigiana!"*

FRED: I'm afraid that last one is a bit too cryptic. It demands some further explanation! But after many years of wondering, you finally got your answer as to why they would jump for us?

STEVE: Yup— we'll get to the famed Italian veal dish in a minute. For years, scientists debated whether those seagoing mammals were leaping to try to shed parasites... or to communicate with other dolphins or pods... or to take a breather from fighting the natural "drag" of the water... or to get a better view of their surroundings... or simply to play with each other because they had the ability to leap.

FRED: And how would the scientists know which possibility was the correct one? Did they interview a bunch of dolphins?

STEVE: Well, the clue was that we only saw them do it when they were right alongside the Willie. This means they were only doing it because we (or the Weigel itself) were there. And it so happens that, of the aforementioned possibilities posed by the scientists, only one of them fits that scenario.

FRED: Aha! Let me guess... that would be... to get a better view of their surroundings!

STEVE: Exactly. When they were under the waves and came upon our ship, the dolphins could only see what was below the water line. Boring stuff! But when they leaped, they could see the whole ship... plus all of us humans, standing there gawking at 'em! Now I don't know how many dolphins the scientists had to interview before they saw a pattern developing there, but that sure seems like the most logical conclusion anyone could come up with.

FRED: But in any event, just a few days after the Weigel had put out to sea, we weren't watching any dolphins at all— because we'd gotten stuck on KP. Fortunately events would dictate that it would be our only venture into the ship's galley for the duration of the voyage.

STEVE: Along with a dozen or so of our Army buddies, we'd each be given a pre-meal assignment and a post-meal assignment. For example, I might have been on "peeling onions and making tomato sauce" before the meal and running the "cups and bowls" machine afterward. As each man finished his assigned task, he'd be sent to help someone else so that, theoretically, we'd all be done with the post-meal cleanup at the same time.

FRED: I was the "pots & pans man" for the day. That assignment could be easy or difficult, depending on what was on the menu.

STEVE: And you picked a helluva day, pardner. The evening meal that night was veal parmigiana! Each breaded veal cutlet was placed on a large aluminum baking sheet, smothered with tomato sauce and topped with a slab of parmesan or mozzarella cheese— I think it was mozzarella, since military food tended not to get too exotic.

FRED: Then these trays, each one holding some 48 or so veal cutlets, were placed on a conveyor belt where they went through a giant oven so that every last speck of grease and flavor was baked right out of 'em— and deposited like cast iron on those baking sheets. Had I known, I would have tried to trade my pots & pans job for something else... like running the floor waxer!

STEVE: Once those baked cutlets got whisked off the trays with a large spatula, what was left on the aluminum surface of each tray was a gigantic, congealed, baked-on mess of burnt cheese, bread crumbs, tomato sauce and fried grease. Not very appetizing— and not a very welcome sight for the pots & pans man, either.

FRED: These aluminum trays were big bastards, maybe 30 by 40 inches, with a 3/4 inch lip around the edges. If you figure we served upwards of 1200 veal cutlets that night, at around 48 of 'em on each tray, that would have required a minimum of 25 baking sheets. I began scraping, scouring and steel wooling those babies as best I could— and I was getting nowhere! Figuring I must not have known the secret for swiftly accomplishing my mission, I went to ask the Chief Mess Steward who was running the galley.

STEVE: Even though there was no such thing as a sergeant among Navy (or ex-Navy) crewmen, we called him "Sarge" anyway, probably at his own suggestion. Fred goes over to him and says "Hey Sarge, I'm having a really tough time with these baking trays. Is there some secret to getting them clean?"

FRED: Sarge says "Oh, them things! Just stack 'em up over there in the corner and we'll deal with them later." I made a stack that was roughly two feet high and went on about doing the rest of my cleanup chores. Soon Steve was done with cups & bowls, so he came over to help me wash pots. Eventually we had everything done except for that stack of befouled trays. Most of the other guys had finished too, but none of us could leave our posts until a final inspection of the galley was completed by the Mess Officer.

STEVE: And that meant Sarge, the Chief Mess Steward, could not leave either. Fred goes over and again says "Hey, Sarge, we've still got that stack of trays over in the corner. What should we do with 'em?"

FRED: Sarge looks around to make sure no one is listening, then says in a hushed voice: "Tell ya what, Borchardt. Why don't you— and Donovan, here— take 'em up on the fantail and see what you do can with 'em?" Steve and I look at each other and then say... "OK Sarge!"

STEVE: Now we should mention that earlier in the day, one of the mess stewards had taken Fred up to the fantail (i.e., the stern) to show him the procedure for washing mops. They had about eight of these long, heavy-duty ropes tied to the railing at the back of the ship.

FRED: The steward showed me the proper procedure for tying the mops to the ropes so there was no way they could come loose. Then we'd throw 'em overboard and watch the Weigel tow them through the waves. It was one rough ride for those mopheads. They'd be jumping out of the water and back in, like we had just caught a whole school of marlin! And so it went until all were "washed."

STEVE: Then during the noon meal cleanup, Fred took me up top and showed me how to tie the mops to the ropes. Except I must not have been paying very close attention, because after a few minutes, three of those "marlin" had taken off with their hooks! I had to pull in three naked ropes and look around, hoping nobody was watching. The damned things had flown the coop!

FRED: I think I might have lost one or two of 'em myself. Maybe the sharks were eating them? We had no idea if that was the Navy's official method for mop washing, but what did we care? It was the most fun thing we had done all day. We just hoped they weren't counting mops down below in the galley. Actually nobody seemed to care anyway. After all, what's a few mops when the government's spending thousands for each bomb dropped in a B-52 strike?

STEVE: Indeed. But now it was past sundown and we were facing a new challenge: How to get those 25 big metal trays up the narrow stairways (in fact I think they were called ladderways) and out to the main deck so we could get to the fantail. I think we decided we'd each grab one end of a stack of about six or eight trays, since it would be virtually impossible for one man to negotiate those ladderways carrying a load like that.

FRED: Our second challenge would be deciding how to interpret Sarge's somewhat obscure directive. What did he mean by "see what you can do with 'em?" We got to the fantail with the first batch and set them down on the deck. Looking at the ropes, we assured ourselves that there was no way in hell those trays could be tied to them, so that left just one option.

STEVE: Ignoring the fact that 25 or 30 baking pans of that size would probably go for at least 300 bucks at today's prices, we started pitching them into the drink. It was dark by then, but the Weigel must have had a few spotlights shining off the stern because we could see the trays bobbing in the waves. We quickly noticed that if they hit the water perpendicular to the surface, they'd sink. But if they landed level, they would float until they were out of sight.

FRED: So naturally we started sailing 'em like Frisbees to see if we could get floaters— and we did! What had begun with a few giggles on our part was now turning into a major laugh-a-thon, as we left a trail of floating trays in our wake... literally. Then we'd giggle our way back down the ladderways to get another batch.

STEVE: Just what anyone would expect from a couple of trained killers heading off to war! Naturally we felt a few pangs of guilt about tossing taxpayer funds into the middle of the Pacific like that, but after all— we were just following orders! That's what Adolf Hitler's storm troopers said after World War II, right? Besides, if the Chief Mess Steward didn't care, who were we to voice any objection?

FRED: Well, the official Military Code of Conduct said we weren't supposed to follow an unlawful order from a superior— and this was clearly willful destruction of government property. Then again, Sarge was a civilian! And they had told us when we first came aboard the Willie that if any member of the ship's crew gave us an order, we were to follow it, no questions asked.

STEVE: There's also the possibility that the ship's captain might have been watching in horror from the bridge as the entire fiasco was playing out before him. Can you imagine what the conversation might have sounded like when the First Officer handed the binoculars to his commander? "Here sir, you'd better have a look at those people on the fantail." Captain: "Who are those men?" "They're Army privates, sir." Captain: "What the hell are they doing?" "They appear to be throwing large metal panels off the fantail, sir." Captain: "What sort of metal panels?" "That's not clear, sir— perhaps cookie sheets." Captain: "Cookie sheets??? Notify the Mess Officer that he's to report to my cabin as soon as the Galley shuts down for the night!" "Yes sir!"

FRED: Come to think of it, it was only a day or two later that the commander of the Marines volunteered to have his troops take over all work details on the ship— including KP— thus freeing us Army blokes to enjoy a leisurely ocean cruise for the remaining two weeks.

STEVE: Well then for all we know, maybe our buddies in the 24th owed us one HUGE debt of gratitude for saving them from all that drudgery! That would mean we "beat the fuggin' system" twice— first by not having to spend hours scraping those damned trays, and second by freeing ourselves from two more weeks of slaving away in the bowels of that ship.

FRED: And not only that, but we knew the guys loved to watch the dolphins swimming alongside us on the high seas. After we threw all that burnt veal and cheese into the water, I'd swear there were three times as many of 'em following us for the next four or five days!

STEVE: Maybe they were planning to turn us in for littering as soon as a Coast Guard cutter showed up. Or maybe they were hoping we'd show 'em what they were supposed to do with the mops.

&&&&&&&&&&&&&&&&&&&

FACT OR FICTION? The story goes that between 1965 and 1975, the U.S. Navy used trained dolphins to protect the harbor installations— as well as ships anchored along the coast of Vietnam— from underwater mines. If they encountered a hostile diver, they would swim up from behind and bump his air tank, thereby depositing a magnetic tracking device on the enemy frogman without being detected. The Navy maintained that humans were much more intelligent than dolphins, as evidenced by the fact that they had created things like the battleship, the submarine, the torpedo, the depth charge and the tactical nuclear missile. But the dolphins, on the other hand, believed they were far more intelligent than humans... for exactly the same reason!

CHAPTER 9

THEY STUCK YOUR HEAD
IN A BUCKET OF WHAT?

*Welcome to the Domain of the Golden Dragon, where
getting there is definitely not half the fun*

STEVE: One of the first orders we were given upon boarding the Weigel was that we were to come up on the main deck every morning after breakfast and remain there throughout the day. This maneuver was presumably intended to accomplish two things: First, to prevent us from sleeping all day or laying around in our racks below decks; and second, to make us readily available for any work details for which they might need some warm bodies. A third goal might have been to make it easy for the honchos to keep an eye on us.

FRED: The assignments for work details went something like this: One of our sergeants would come up on deck, approach a group of us and say "I need twelve men to work in the ship's laundry today. You... you... you... you..." and so on. Since we tended to cluster together with our buddies when we were on deck, we'd usually get picked together with a bunch of our close friends.

STEVE: On any given day, if you didn't get stuck on a work detail you were free to do anything you wanted as long as you remained on deck. The options were of course limited, but they included reading a book, playing cards, smoking cancer sticks, listening to some musical device, writing letters, telling jokes, exercising, shooting the bull, trying to fight off seasickness, etc.

FRED: For some, fighting seasickness was a full-time pursuit. When the seas were relatively calm, only a small number would have to get up and run to the railing so they could heave over the side. But when the seas were rough, it could be a whole lotta guys. The "regulars" would quickly learn which side of the ship to run to— the leeward side— so their vomit wouldn't get blown right back onto the ship and its passengers. It was those others you had to watch out for— the novices— because if they should run to the wrong (windward) side, there was a good chance we might all get showered with puke.

STEVE: We'd be sitting on the deck, leaning against a bulkhead or something, and someone would yell "Look out!! Reynolds is heading for the wrong side!" Whereupon we'd all duck and try to cover up as best we could. I'd try to keep one eye open, since I always found it amusing to watch the guy lean over the railing and then have his barf blown right back onto everyone else.

FRED: And then at times the winds would keep shifting back and forth, which kept everyone on their toes— novice and veteran alike. You'd think the Military Sea Transport System could have provided us with barf bags, but I don't recall ever seeing any. Maybe that would have been too un-manly. There might have been some below decks, or else guys would just have to use the butt cans (two-gallon cans with two inches of water in the bottom, to be used as ashtrays.)

STEVE: I never got seasick, although I came damned close several times when the ship was rockin' and rollin'. My strategy was mind over matter— when the Weigel started pitching from side to side, instead of fighting it I would convince myself I was merely part of the ship and this was a normal occurrence. That worked for me, but just barely.

FRED: Some guys were convinced that eating crackers held the key. I remember seeing PFC Lazaro sitting on deck all day, clutching his box of saltines, waiting for the turmoil to start. (I assume they must have sold crackers in the ship's PX.) I tried a few of his crackers but they didn't seem to have any effect on me, one way or the other. Meanwhile some of the guys just stopped eating, period.

STEVE: As for shipboard activities, I've read that some of the troop ships showed movies below decks several times a day. But I can only recall seeing a few on the Weigel and I think most were military training or propaganda films of some sort— stuff like how to avoid VD.

FRED: Some of us had a natural preference for playing cards— that being a friendly, social activity— but weather conditions on the high seas usually ranged from windy... to very windy... to gale force windy. So unless you had a foolproof method for weighing down every single card, you'd soon be down to a deck of 47 or 48, the others having been whisked away and deposited in the drink by a gust of wind. Then it would be like "OK, the Joker is now the Six of Clubs and the Two of Hearts is now the Ace of Hearts."

STEVE: It didn't take long for some of us to figure out a way to get out of the wind— and avoid those distasteful work details in the process! It seems that when the Weigel was filled to capacity with troops, it could carry around 5,000 men. But there were only 900-plus marines and 200-plus soldiers on board. We knew three-fourths of the ship must have been empty... so we started exploring.

FRED: The empty troop bays were off limits and ostensibly sealed off, but we knew if we kept searching we'd find a way to get to 'em, and we did. Once we found some empty bays, we also found some empty officers showers. And that was a big deal because officers showers were freshwater, while the EM showers were all seawater.

STEVE: When we took our first seawater shower on the Weigel, we quickly learned that an ordinary bar of soap wouldn't make any lather when mixed with saltwater. (A cruel trick indeed!) So the only way to get clean was to rub soap all over your body— whereupon we discovered that seawater wouldn't rinse it off! (Another cruel trick!) These problems were solved once we figured out how to sneak off and use one of the unoccupied freshwater showers.

FRED: So now we had empty troop bays where we could play cards in peace and quiet— but we still had one problem. If we were down below decks playing cards all day, we wouldn't be able to hear any announcements or important messages that might be disseminated on deck to the rest of our group, like chow call, mail call or whatever.

STEVE: Or "The war is over, guys! You can all go home now!" But eventually we found an empty troop bay with a ladderwell that led right up to the deck where we were supposed to be cooling our heels all day. The hatch that opened out onto that deck was locked from the inside, but we found that we could open it just a crack. This enabled us to peek through the crack to see what was happening on deck as well as hear any announcements that might be made.

FRED: We could now sit on the stairs to play cards, and every now and then one of us would peek through the crack to see what we might be missing. We had the best of both worlds! Plus we could eavesdrop on the guys who were sitting outside, just a few feet away from our sealed hatch. But because of the consant wind outside, the guys on deck couldn't hear us talking inside our stairwell.

STEVE: Then as the Weigel approached the International Dateline somewhere in the middle of the Pacific, we heard vague rumors about some sort of weird ceremony that awaited us when we crossed it.

FRED: It seemed there was an ancient seafaring tradition that when military vessels crossed the Equator or International Dateline, anyone on board who had never crossed it before would have to go through an induction ceremony to enter the "Domain of the Golden Dragon" which was supposed to be located inside "Davy Jones' Locker."

STEVE: There are similar "Line Crossing Ceremonies" on many pleasure cruise ships, except that these are much tamer and involve lots of alcohol consumption. They're basically "toga parties" where someone dresses up as King Neptune and everyone else wears a bedsheet, plays parlor games and gets roaring drunk.

FRED: On military ships like the Weigel, however, there was presumably no alcohol involved— and no parlor games either. Instead, the "shellbacks" (those who had crossed the line on a previous voyage) became drunk with power as they abused and humiliated the blindfolded "pollywogs" (unsuspecting novices like us) by subjecting them to various disgusting indignities. The inductees were sent through a hideous hazing process, sort of like an obstacle course with lots of unpleasant consequences for the participants.

STEVE: Of course we knew nothing about this until they told us that "tomorrow morning, you will stay below decks all morning and then when you're called in the afternoon, you'll all report to the main deck wearing nothing but skivvie shorts and shower shoes." Huh???

FRED: None of us knew exactly what it was all about— but whatever it was, the reason why we had to stay below decks was because the marines were going to go through it the next morning, while it would be our turn in the afternoon. And for the four of us card players, that meant we could peek out from our secret hatch the next morning and get a good look at what was in store for those marines. Which we did.

STEVE: What we saw was not unlike fraternity hazing on a college campus. The various events in the "obstacle course" included having to slide on your stomach across a greased deck in your skivvies while blindfolded. Also having your head pushed into a big tub of garbage while you were blindfolded and being told you were going to be bobbing for apples.

FRED: Another event was having to crawl blindfolded up to a big fat guy— King Neptune, who was sitting on a throne, naked from the waist up— and "kiss" his belly, whereupon he grabs your ears and rubs your face in some sort of grease or shoe polish that's covering his torso. Then you had to run a gauntlet of sorts (blindfolded, with your hand on the shoulder of the man in front of you) while you were being paddled or lashed by the ship's crewmen. Other similarly odious activities were also part of the festivities.

STEVE: According to Wikipedia, "Line Crossing ceremonies are all in good fun and are completely voluntary." Good fun my ass!

FRED: Voluntary my ass! Upon seeing this, Steve said "Bullcrap! Let's stay right here in our stairwell this afternoon— we can watch through the crack while everyone else gets abused and humiliated. If they think they're gonna play a dirty trick on us without our knowledge, we'll just play a dirty trick right back!"

STEVE: Initially, everyone seemed to agree with my plan. But over the course of the next few hours, one by one they must have had a change of heart— call it chickening out, or not wanting to abandon their fellow soldiers, or whatever you like. After noon chow, we returned to the troop bay and I said "OK, let's head for the stairwell." But there were no takers. It was a clear case of risk avoidance, kind of like when nobody wanted to sign up later on for a sex-and-booze party in Okinawa. So I said "Awright then, I'll go by myself!" And I did.

FRED: The rest of us went up top in skivvies and shower shoes— and were blindfolded the moment we set foot on deck. From that point on, we had to move about by keeping one hand on the shoulder of the man in front of us as we were put through our grotesque maneuvers. When we had to crawl, dunk our heads or kiss the fat man's belly, we'd let go and be guided by one of the shellbacks until we could once again grab on to someone's shoulder.

STEVE: Since they were blindfolded the whole time, they couldn't see who was or wasn't there— so no one noticed my absence. They also were unable to see that some of the pollywogs were in fact Army officers. But Lieutenant Bloom, who would later become our company commander after being promoted to Captain, said he also had to go through the initiation just like we did.

FRED: When it was over they told us we'd each receive a personalized certificate— suitable for framing— signifying that we had officially been inducted into the "Domain of the Golden Dragon."

STEVE: Meanwhile, I'm watching all this through the crack in the hatch, just 20 or 30 feet away from the action. Suddenly it occurs to me that I haven't formulated any plan for what to do when the "ceremony" ends! Let's see... everyone will be heading for the showers, covered in grease, shoe polish and slime... if I'm gonna blend in, I'm gonna have to get in the shower along with everyone else... but if I don't have any grease or slime on me, somebody's gonna notice right quick! I decided I'd have to get in the shower first and wait 'til I heard some other guys coming back, then turn on the water and pretend I just happened to be the first one in. With that I skedaddled down to the troop bay to get there before the others.

FRED: Steve's plan did work, although I happened to be one of the first guys into the shower and I noticed that he looked awfully clean compared to the rest of us. I said "You just watched us from the stairwell, didn't ya?" He gave me a smirk and pretended he didn't know what I was talking about. But it was obvious to me! In mock anger I said "I'm gonna make sure you don't get any certificate for this!"

STEVE: The "reward" for each pollywog who became a shellback that day was to receive the certificate— inscribed with his name and suitable for framing— plus a wallet-sized ID card that identified him as a member in good standing of the Order of the Golden Dragon. As it turned out, that card would be important to anyone who planned to make another ocean crossing by ship. Without it, he'd run the risk of having to go through that damned initiation all over again!

FRED: They passed out the individual wallet cards that evening, but the certificates inscribed with our names took several more days. When they came to hand them out, Steve wasn't there so I said I'd take his for him. I then put it away for "safekeeping."

STEVE: I wasn't really too concerned about getting my certificate, since I had the wallet card that would protect me in case they decided to send us back across the Pacific by ship once again. But about 51 weeks later we're packing up in our hooch in Vietnam, getting ready to catch our flight home the next day, when Fred says "Hey, I've got a gift for ya!" He reaches into his footlocker and pulls out... my Golden Dragon certificate! I think he might have even gotten it framed— if so, it was obviously because he felt guilty about holding onto it for a year.

FRED: Well I may have been holding it, but you still didn't deserve to have one. You never went through the official initiation!

STEVE: Maybe so, but in the long run, it turns out that the US Navy ultimately agreed with my stance on the matter. After many years of controversy, in 1997 the Navy officially banned "any Line Crossing ceremonies which are cruel, humiliating, oppressive, demeaning, abusive or harmful."

FRED: That's just great. They were only about 31 years too late!

&&&&&&&&&&&&&&&&&&&&

FACT OR FICTION? The story goes that whenever a really popular movie was going to be shown on the Weigel, a translucent movie screen would be hung in the center of the Mess Deck to accommodate the largest possible audience. This would allow the film to be viewed simultaneously from both the front and back sides of the screen. The arrangement was confirmed when the following announcement was heard over the ship's PA System: "Your attention please: Tonight's movie for those viewing on the officers and NCO's screen will be The Left Handed Gun, starring Paul Newman as Billy the Kid. For those viewing on the enlisted men's screen, the movie will be The Right Handed Gun, starring Namwen Luap as Dik Eht Yllib."

CHAPTER 10

CHICKEN BONE WIDMANN
AND THE OKINAWA FLASH

*Could a tiny skeletal fragment somehow alter the
lives of over 1,000 soldiers and marines?*

STEVE: Sailing in a West/Southwest direction from San Diego,
our next refueling stop was scheduled for Okinawa, a small island in
the East China Sea. It was some 1600 miles northeast of Da Nang,
South Vietnam, which was to be our first port of call in the war zone.
Each day we'd climb up on deck after breakfast and see the sun rising
behind the ship, maybe 15 degrees off to the port side.

FRED: But then one morning— after about two weeks at sea— we
discovered that during the night, the darned thing had suddenly
shifted to about 60 degrees off the stern— on the starboard side. The
General Weigel had made a big right turn in the middle of the Pacific!

STEVE: I said "Hey fellas, guess what? We're not goin' southwest
any more— we're heading north!" Obviously something had caused
the ship to make a drastic course change. Had we been hijacked?
Were we trying to outrun a typhoon? Had the man at the helm inadvertently steered us into the eastbound instead of the westbound
shipping lane? Maybe our rudder had been sheared off by a Russian
sub? Or maybe we'd forgotten something back in San Diego?

FRED: Or maybe up in Hanoi, Uncle Ho Chi Minh had heard that we were coming and decided to surrender before we had a chance to get a good look at his troops!

STEVE: Actually, few people realized the real architect of North Vietnam's pursuit of the war was Uncle Ho's number two man— Le Duan. He was the hard-line commie who talked Ho into supporting the Viet Cong rebels in the South— apparently he was calling the shots the whole time. Before we ever set foot in Nam, Ho's role had been reduced to one that was largely ceremonial.

FRED: So if it hadn't been for this Le Duan guy, the whole damn war might have been avoided and we could have stayed home? North Vietnam and South Vietnam could have remained in a stalemate like North Korea and South Korea are to this day?

STEVE: Possibly, except for the fact that the South Koreans didn't have to contend with communist rebels running around on their turf. Another thing few realize is that while we've always referred to the conflict as the Vietnam War, most Vietnamese have traditionally called it the American War. That kind of gives one a different perspective on the whole situation.

FRED: Anyway, back to the situation on the "Willie." The speculation was running rampant as to why the ship had suddenly changed course— until the loudspeaker finally crackled to life with an announcement heard throughout the vessel: "Your attention please! This the Captain speaking. Due to a medical emergency involving one of the troops onboard, we have altered course and are now steaming toward the nearest port with the proper medical facilities to handle the situation. The General Weigel is now en route to Tokyo, Japan."

STEVE: A big cheer went up among the hundreds of soldiers and marines on deck. Naturally we felt bad about the fellow with the medical emergency— but hey, we were all going to Tokyo!!! We'd refuel there instead of in Okinawa, and we'd probably get some shore liberty while we were there.

FRED: At the very least, we'd get a chance to see Tokyo and its harbor from just offshore. And not only that, but the more days we spent on the high seas, the fewer the days we'd have to spend on Vietnamese soil! That's because for each one of us, the DEROS (Date Eligible to Return from Overseas) was exactly 365 days after the date we left CONUS (the Continental United States.)

STEVE: Soon a chant started up among the troops— TOE-KEE-OH! TOE-KEE-OH! TOE-KEE-OH! Other than those carefree dolphins putting on their periodic shows for us, it was one of the few bright spots we'd experienced since we left Oakland some 17 days earlier.

FRED: Of course everyone wanted to know the details about the medical emergency, and soon the scuttlebutt came down through the pipeline. Since there were over 900 marines onboard, we assumed it would be one of their guys. (Probably busted a gut during their two hours of daily calisthenics, as opposed to zero hours for us.)

STEVE: But in fact the unfortunate fellow turned out to be one of our 220 Army souls. It seems that the night before we changed course, we had feasted on baked chicken in the ship's mess. And one of our radiology specialists, Sergeant Widmann, had swallowed a chicken bone which became lodged in his throat.

FRED: The ship's doctor concluded that surgery was required, but throat surgery was too delicate of an operation to be conducted on a ship that was constantly rolling from side to side on the surface of the Pacific. I suppose if I were Widmann, I wouldn't want anyone cutting on MY neck as we were crashing through the waves either— especially if that doc wasn't a "true surgeon."

STEVE: Since it was one of those rare occasions when the ship's doctor could overrule the ship's captain, he ordered that the Weigel be redirected to the nearest major port. According to my rough calculations, we were about 900 miles from Okinawa but less than 500 miles from Tokyo when we made our course correction.

FRED: So then if we hadn't changed course, it would have taken us nearly twice as long to reach a surgical hospital?

STEVE: Correct. At a top speed of 22 knots, we'd be able to make Tokyo in about 20 hours as opposed to at least 36 for Naha, Okinawa. Plus Tokyo would undoubtedly have better medical facilities.

FRED: Okinawa held a special significance for us because the ship's crew had been filling us in on what to expect there— cheap booze, cheap sex and some not-so-cheap gambling. What more could a young, single soldier or marine possibly hope for? But now we were headed for the Land of the Rising Sun— only those Neanderthals among us would prefer Okinawa to that!

STEVE: And we certainly had our share of young and not-so-young Neanderthals, although the Marines probably had considerably more, percentage-wise. But there was one individual in particular who was truly devastated by the news that we'd be refueling in Tokyo and bypassing Okinawa. And he wasn't even a soldier or marine!

FRED: If he was a civilian, he had to be a member of the ship's crew. Let me guess... was it Sarge, the Chief Mess Steward? No... Mike the Magician, who liked to do magic tricks on deck for the troops? No... I'm thinking it must have been Henry, the little bald-headed Japanese guy who ran the ship's laundry.

STEVE: That's a Roger, shipmate! Every morning Henry would welcome a new crew of young soldiers or marines who were assigned to laundry duty for that day— running the washers and dryers, operating the shirt pressing and folding machines, folding the bedsheets by hand— just like we did when we first got on board.

FRED: And each time, he'd have all day to try to recruit a pack or two of "party animals" who'd be willing to fund their own private sex-and-booze parties once we hit the docks at Okinawa!

STEVE: He was quite persuasive, using a routine he had obviously practiced many times during his frequent trips across the Pacific. First he'd watch to see who the "opinion leaders" in the group were. Once he'd selected his targets, he'd start telling them about all the fun, drinking and debauchery to be had in Okinawa. He obviously knew we were gonna get 12 hours of liberty when we arrived, and he gradually began advising us on how best to use that time.

FRED: "You know," he'd say, "instead of wasting all your time and money wandering from bar to bar, buying Saigon teas for the bar-girls and expensive drinks for yourselves, what you should do is have a private party for just you and your buddies. All the booze you can drink, all the food you can eat and all the girls you can screw!"

STEVE: And just how were we supposed to pull that off in a strange city with just 12 hours of liberty and not being able to speak the language? Well, of course— Henry knew the answer to that one too!

FRED: Yessir! All we had to do was round up a group of 12 willing guys. Each would throw in something like 40 or 50 bucks apiece— in advance— and Henry would take care of absolutely everything. The booze, the beer, the mix, the ice, the food, the "gorgeous" hostesses, the hotel suite, the music, the condoms, the towels and the barf bags. Why, 30 minutes after you got off the ship, you could be diddling some Japanese chick— with your beverage of choice in hand— while a steaming plate of lobster thermidor awaited in the next room!

STEVE: Or a fistful of boiled shrimp, at least. I suppose if you were a young Marine who thought you might never make it back from Nam, the whole idea could sound rather appealing, since this would be the last stop before the war zone. Even more so if he was still a virgin, I suspect. But the 24th Evac was a hospital unit, and we were all planning to come home again in about 49 and a half weeks— even the Neanderthals among us.

FRED: I think Henry offered the two of us a "discount" for helping to recruit and organize the group. He gave us about 12 days to think it over and let him know by a certain date if we were in, so he'd have time to make the arrangements.

STEVE: I would guess he probably had an "arrangement" with the ship's radioman to send a transmission to somebody in Okinawa on a certain date saying "This is Henry here, we've got six groups of 12, four groups of 14 and one group of 17. That's eleven parties altogether, arriving at such and such a time and date."

FRED: Hell of a smooth operation! Those eleven "parties" would have taken in at least six or seven grand, total— for just one trip. Henry's cut was probably 20 percent at a minimum, and he made maybe six to eight trips per year. Do the math, my friend!

STEVE: For all we knew, Henry might even have been running the whole shebang! When we went to noon chow that day, we nicknamed him the "Okinawa Flash"— not to his face, of course— because he was such a fast operator.

FRED: For sure! In little more than an hour or two, the Flash had gotten us talking about forking over 500 bucks or more to a total stranger— all while we were folding bedsheets! Later we discussed it with some of our buddies and about half of 'em liked the idea.

STEVE: But the Flash probably made his biggest mistake when he gave us 12 days to decide, because the longer we thought about it, the less attractive it sounded. I wasn't exactly thrilled with the idea of paying someone for sex— plus I had blown most of my cash in San Diego. And what if the girls were all ugly? I could not imagine myself being that desperate, so... count me out!

FRED: Those were pretty much my sentiments too. Nor did I like the idea of being trapped in some seedy hotel suite for 10 hours while others had gone out and found better ways to spend their time and money. Ultimately we passed on the deal, although I'd guess there were plenty of marines— plus some of our guys from the 24th— who signed up for the "deluxe package."

STEVE: I'm pretty sure there were. For young marines especially, the peer pressure alone would have been enough to goad a lot of 'em into taking part. It was like a test of their manhood, in a way.

FRED: Besides, if you were running a stable of bargirls and you were gonna send some out to hustle in the bars while the rest went to private parties that were paid for in advance, wouldn't you send the pretty ones to the bars and the homely ones to the parties?

STEVE: Sounds logical. But in any event, once the Flash heard we were going to Tokyo instead of Naha, he suddenly had much bigger problems. He'd collected the entire seven grand from his various "tour groups" and would now have to pay them back. By the next day, the troopers would be starting to ask for refunds. I hoped for his sake that he hadn't already blown his share in a card game!

FRED: It seems the crew did have a reputation for big-stakes gambling— possibly the main reason why they continued to crew a ship after they'd gotten out of the Navy.

STEVE: We hit the sack that night thinking lots of happy thoughts about waking up just as the Weigel was about to sail into Tokyo Bay. But alas, in the morning we went up top to take a peek and... damn! There was the sun, sitting off the port side of the stern once again. We were obviously heading southwest once more, no doubt about it... No "Land of the Rising Sun" for us!

FRED: So much for Tokyo— "easy come, easy go." As luck would have it, Sergeant Widmann had managed to pass the chicken bone during the night, thereby avoiding neck surgery. And in the process, making sure we avoided our Tokyo rendezvous.

STEVE: Son of a gun! After that we referred to him as "Chicken

Bone Widmann," or "C.B." for short… but not to his face. It would be more like "Hey look, here comes Chicken Bone!" or "Look, there goes ol' C.B. Widmann!"

FRED: Other than the fact that it had lengthened our voyage by a day or two— and shortened our stay in the war zone by an equal amount— the Tokyo episode was a big disappointment. But as far as Henry was concerned… the Okinawa Flash was back in business!

STEVE: And as we steered course once again for the War Zone, I began to wonder just whose fault it was that we had missed out on our only chance to visit Japan.

FRED: Let me guess…. Was it the ship's doctor? No…. Sergeant Widmann? No…. The ship's captain? No…. I think you might have me stumped this time.

STEVE: Well, let me put it this way. Maybe the Flash had more to do with the outcome than anyone suspected. I can see it now… the ship's doctor goes to sick bay to check on his patient and finds the Flash sitting by his side. "Henry," he asks, "what are you doing here in the middle of the night?" "I was worried about Sergeant Widmann, so I thought I'd come over and feed him a few bowls of extra-thick chicken broth," replies Henry, adding "I think it might have done the trick— he seems to have swallowed the bone!"

FRED: Okay, I get it— the doc checks the patient and says "By golly you're right, Henry! Get up to the bridge and tell the First Officer to turn this tub around!"

&&&&&&&&&&&&&&&&&&&

FACT OR FICTION? *The story goes that at a restaurant in Saigon, an Army Major was eating dinner when he suddenly grabbed his throat and started wheezing, thrashing around and turning blue. A young medic at a nearby table recognized the symptoms immediately, jumped up and began performing the Heimlich maneuver. After several attempts, he managed to dislodge a piece of steak stuck in the Major's throat. The officer said "Soldier, you just saved my life! How can I ever repay you? I must give you a token of my gratitude— name your price!" The medic thought for a bit and then replied, "Well sir, how about half of what you'd have offered me when that steak was still stuck in your throat?"*

CHAPTER 11

PARTY ALL DAY, PARTY ALL NIGHT! YOU CAN DO IT ALL... AT THE HOBBO-RITE!

It promised to be one final night of freedom, but what a way to go!

STEVE: Two days after not getting to see Tokyo, we were approaching the harbor at Naha, Okinawa, when we were informed that we'd be given 12 hours of shore liberty. (The Flash had hit it right on the nose!) We'd be on our own from noon to midnight, at which time the ship would be pulling out of port, headed straight for Da Nang... and our first glimpse of the war zone! For many, that meant eleven hours of drinking, puking and just about every other type of excess imaginable, depending on one's preferences.

FRED: Starting at 12 noon, over 1,000 soldiers and marines went skipping down the gangway, quickly scattering for parts (or bars, or hotels) unknown. We'd gotten stuck on a work detail that morning, so a handful of us weren't ready to disembark in our civvies until some time after 12:30. By then the dock was completely deserted and there was but one lone taxi sitting there at the curb, waiting for a fare.

STEVE: It was one of those ubiquitous yellow taxis like we saw everywhere in Okinawa and Vietnam— tiny little French Renault CV's designed to carry one (small) passenger in front and two in the back. It was possible to squeeze a third GI into the back seat, but only if he sat on the knees of the two who were already seated.

FRED: But there were seven or eight of us in total, and we wanted to stick together. So we waited in the hopes that a second cab would show up. No such luck, so Steve came up with a plan. We'd ask the driver of Taxi #1 to give us the name of a bar where he'd be taking us. Then four of us would get in Taxi #1 and take off, while the second group would wait for Taxi #2 and give the second driver the name of that same bar. Problem solved!

STEVE: Except for one catch— the driver of the first taxi could not speak a lick of English. I climbed into the front passenger seat so I could look him in the eye, the better to "communicate" with him. Through gestures and words I told him we wanted to go to a bar and drink (cupping my hand like I'm holding a beer bottle up to my mouth.) He says "Ya, bah, OK! Bah, OK! Drink! Drink! OK!"

FRED: So far so good, all we need now is the name of the bar!

STEVE: Yeah, but that turned out to be the hard part. I say "You tell name of bar." (He doesn't have a clue.) "What is name of bar? You... say... name... of... bar." Speechless, he gives me a blank stare like I'm from Mars.

FRED: Sounds like it could be an insurmountable problem. Time for some of that good old American ingenuity!

STEVE: I decide to "air draw" a big picture of the front of the bar in the vacant space next to my head. Holding the imaginary drawing in my right hand and pointing to it with my left, I say "bar." He says "Ya, bah, OK." Then I take my left hand and run it across the top half of the "bar" where the giant sign would be. I point to the imaginary sign and say "name of bar." I repeat... "name of bar." He pauses for a moment and then says "Aaaaahhhh.... Hobbo-Rite!" I repeat it: "Hobbo-Rite?" "Ya, Hobbo-Rite." I gesture to the imaginary sign once more and say slowly: "Hob... Bo... Rite?" "Ya, Hobbo-Rite!"

FRED: Steve then gets back out of the cab and tells those of us in Group #2: "OK guys, we're all goin' to the Hobbo-Rite! It must be a Japanese name, since these people are all Japanese! Remember that name, Hobbo-Rite!" We start repeating it... Hobbo-Rite, Hobbo-Rite, Hobbo-Rite. "OK, we got it! Hobbo-Rite! We'll be right behind ya!"

STEVE: With that, Group #1 gets in Taxi #1 and we take off like a bat out of hell on what would be the absolute wildest ride of my life. (Nothing else even comes close.) It was like something out of a Harold Lloyd movie from the 1920's. We're screaming past other cars, trucks and buses on blind hills and blind curves, going about 70 on a winding two-lane road where 45 would have seemed excessive. Everyone was holding on for dear life and there was no way we could tell our driver to slow down, since he didn't understand a word of English.

FRED: Suddenly your master plan wasn't looking so good after all!

STEVE: It was the closest thing to a living nightmare that I've ever experienced. In fact at that point I was thinking we'd be damn lucky if we ever made it to the shores of Vietnam. During the entire trip, every one of us was speechless. After traveling probably two to three miles which seemed like 10 or 20, we reached the downtown "strip" where it was just one bar after another after another.

FRED: It was 1 p.m. on a Tuesday afternoon and deader than a doornail— a literal ghost town. Half the bars were closed; the open ones were nearly empty, probably waiting for a ship to come in.

STEVE: Our cab comes screaming up to one of the bars, screeching to a halt in what is known in racing circles as a "four-wheel drift." I say to the driver "Hobbo-Rite?" And he says proudly "Yah, Hobbo-Rite!" We pay him, tip him and extricate ourselves from the vehicle while considering whether we should stop and kiss the ground— in fact I think PFC Denton did just that. Then we look up at the big sign across the front of the place, expecting to see something in Japanese, and begin to howl with laughter when we see the name— it was none other than the "Harbor Light."

FRED: Well, who ever would have guessed it? The Hobbo-Rite was actually the Harbor Light!

STEVE: Indeed! The Japanese are notorious for not being able to pronounce their r's, l's and v's. One authority claims it's not that they can't pronounce them, but that to many Asians the "r" and the "l" are interchangeable.

FRED: So then after much chuckling and guffawing at the "Harbor Light" sign outside, the fellas in Group #1 walk through the doors. The place is cavernous but completely deserted, except for a group of about six black Americans in civvies sitting way over in the far corner. (They were probably marines off our ship, the Weigel.)

STEVE: We stood around at the front of the bar for a few minutes, waiting for our buddies to show up. Since everyone in our group was white, I thought about going back and making a little small talk with the marines, just to acknowledge their presence and see if they had any useful information for us. But then I remembered that marines were known for liking to bust up bars and bust a few Army or Navy heads in the process, so I thought "Why push our luck?"

FRED: So instead, Group #1 turns around and leaves so they can meet up with Group #2 and find a bar with a little more action. They step outside to wait for the second cab, thinking it will be there any second. But one black marine follows them outside and hollers "Hey, did you guys leave because of us???"

STEVE: I have no idea what he might have done if we'd said yes, but Carl Denton immediately says "Naw man, we're just tryin' to find the rest of our group!" The marine seemed to buy that explanation and just then, we saw the second cab hurtling down the street. I said "Look, here they come now!" This meant the Army now outnumbered the Marines.

FRED: When the jarhead saw PFC Bronson climb out of the back seat— all six foot five and 260 pounds of him— he gave up and went back inside.

STEVE: Meanwhile, as soon as the cab had stopped, I saw that it was the same driver who'd picked us up in the first group. He'd driven like a maniac so he could go all the way back to the pier and pick up that second fare before someone else did!

FRED: And here I thought maybe he drove that way because he was trying to teach us a lesson for not signing up with the Okinawa Flash for a sex and booze party! But at least that would explain why he didn't call for a second cab to come out and pick up Group #2.

STEVE: I don't think they had any two-way radios in those little bombs they were driving. But now that we were all together, we could hunt for a bar with some action— girls, music, etc. On about the fourth try, we found one that had some 24th Evac guys in it already. The number of bargirls was equal to the number of GI's in the place. Five minutes after we showed up, about six or eight more bargirls mysteriously appeared, coming in through the back door. It looked like all these places were part of one big conglomerate!

FRED: It's funny now that I think about it— for many years afterward, we would refer to the night we spent at the Hobbo-Rite in Okinawa. But in truth we only spent 10 or 15 minutes there before we moved on and found another joint where we'd wind up spending the next ten hours!

STEVE: Yeah— the "Silver Slipper"or whatever the hell it was. Anyway, the guys who had gotten there an hour ahead of us quickly filled us in on the details. For five bucks you could have a dalliance with any one of the girls in the place. But first you had to sit and talk with her for a time while you bought her a few "Saigon Teas."

FRED: These consisted of a shot or two of Kool-Aid in a 2-ounce, long-stemmed liqueur glass. They were like two or three bucks each, I think. After a couple of those, the girl would ask if you wanted to go across the street to her "room upstairs," adding some encouraging comments like "Me love you long time!"

STEVE: Here's the interesting part. If you said yes— or you asked "how much?"— she'd explain that before she could leave, you would have to pay the bartender five bucks as compensation for the "absence of her services" during the time she was gone. Thus there was never any "money exchanged for sex," theoretically. The whole operation was basically an assembly line for carnal relations— very tidy and efficient— and yet it still allowed a young marine to be able to say afterward "No, I never paid any girl for sex!"

FRED: If you sat at the bar or one of the large tables toward the front, the bargirls would hustle you for Saigon Teas. In the back of the room, however, some of the guys had low-stakes card games going and the girls wouldn't bother them. I decided to play cards and spend my money on rum & cokes instead of playing games with the hustler girls, so to the back I went. Of course in the states I would not yet have been old enough to drink a rum & coke, but in Okinawa you were legit if you were tall enough to put your money on the bar!

STEVE: Now I went into the "Silver Slipper" having no intention of paying anybody for sex, but I knew that if the right gal showed up after I'd had several drinks, I might not be able to resist. Fortunately there weren't any "gorgeous" ones by my reckoning, so I felt safe. I was willing to buy them Saigon Teas because it was fun talking to them and learning about the nuts and bolts of their operation. But when they offered to take me across the street, I'd decline and say I was out of money. Then they'd usually get up and leave.

FRED: If you stepped back a bit and surveyed the scene, the atmosphere was a lot like a college bar as opposed to a nightclub. (In Wisconsin we had "beer only" bars where you could drink at 18.) There was a jukebox, a dance floor, waitresses and bar food. We eight guys went into the place, met a group of girls and some gradually "paired off" with them, just like in a college bar. We bought 'em drinks and eventually some of the pairs went off somewhere and had sex, just like you'd often see happening in a college bar.

STEVE: Reminded you of home, eh? About the only differences were that the girls were Japanese (dressed like westerners) and we had to pay a "ransom" to get them to leave. Plus there wasn't any risk of being rejected as long as you paid your five bucks!

FRED: At least not in most cases. But they ranged in height from 4 foot 10 to 5 foot 3. One of our guys, PFC Bronson, was a human behemoth standing 6 foot 5. He'd picked out the tiny gal he wanted, bought her a few Saigon Teas and had her sitting on his lap when he suggested they go across the street. She cups her hand over his groin and says "No, G.I.! Too big! Too big! You go with her!" as she points to another girl. (A great way to break the mood, and a story that would follow Bronson around for the next 12 months.)

STEVE: We danced with the girls, drank a lot, shot some pool, ate bar food, chatted with the honeys and watched as couples would occasionally head out the front door to go across the street. By around 9:30 that night, I was nearly down to my last 20 bucks which would have to last me a couple weeks til payday. I was determined not to spend it in that joint, and just about every guy who was going to sample the merchandise had already done so— with the exception of those who might be going for seconds or thirds.

FRED: Yet there you still sat at one of the front tables with some of the other guys and gals, which meant you should be fair game.

STEVE: Apparently so. At that point someone must have decided I was a "tough nut to crack" and it was time to dial up the emergency hotline, because suddenly the back door opened— and in walks none other than the doggone Prom Queen!

FRED: The bargirls were mostly 18-20 years old and wore slacks and smocks. The "Queen" was more like 30, dressed to the nines in a lime green, form-fitting silk dress slit on the sides up to mid-thigh. She was coiffed and made up like something out of a Hollywood movie.

She had a great figure... a beauty mark strategically placed on her cheek... and she was gorgeous. A real jaw-dropper! She'd probably just come from a private party where she was balling Marine officers.

STEVE: She stopped in the back to talk to a few of the girls and I saw them gesturing toward me. Then she turned and began to stroll toward the front. By the time she had made it halfway, I knew she was heading straight for me— and I began to wonder if there was any chance I'd be able to resist, since I was thinking "Wow, this could be the screw of a lifetime!"

FRED: I want to say she leaned over Steve's table and swept all the bottles and glasses off with her arm, producing a loud crash! It wasn't quite that bad, but she made a beeline for him and sat down in the adjacent chair, while many of us sat or stood dumbfounded. She gets nice and close— so he can get a good whiff of her perfume and a good look at her beauty mark and her cleavage— and begins talking to him in a soft, sexy voice.

STEVE: She wasn't interested in Saigon Teas, either! I'm thinking "Holy crap, how much is this gonna cost me?" After draping herself all over me for five or ten minutes, she pops the question about going across the street and I say "I don't have any money." She says "How mucha money you haff?" I knew there was still a 20 in my wallet but I also knew there was no way I was gonna blow my last 20 bucks on a hooker, so I said "Ten dollars." She says "OK, ten dollah."

FRED: And that's when you made your fatal mistake— one that would haunt you to this very day!

STEVE: You could say so, yeah. I had ordered a drink just moments before, and now the waitress shows up to collect. I had to carefully pull a few singles out of my wallet without letting Queenie see the 20. As I did so, the bitch suddenly leans over and looks straight down into my stash. Spotting the 20, she straightens up and decides to renegotiate by looking me in the eye and saying "Twenny dollah!"

FRED: Oops!

STEVE: I quickly recover by saying "No, ten dollars. You said ten dollars!" "No, twenny dollah! You say you only hap ten dollah. I see twenny dollah!" I say "Yes, but I can only spend ten dollars. I can't spend twenty dollars!" She says "You only pay ten dollah, then you go with her!" and she points to one of the bargirls— whose going rate had already been established at five bucks, just like all the rest of 'em. I say "I don't want her, I want you! Ten dollars!"

FRED: Now some of the guys are wondering what all the commotion is about and one says "Whatsa problem, Donovan?" Steve explains and one of our buddies says "Fer cryin' out loud Donovan, I'll lend ya the 20 bucks!!!"

STEVE: I think some of 'em just wanted to make sure that one of us banged the Prom Queen, since she was obviously the highlight of the evening. I, on the other hand, was sticking to my guns: "It's not the money, it's the principle of the thing! She agreed to ten bucks, then she peeked in my wallet and raised her price to twenty!" To be honest, once she reneged on our deal and began to reject me unless the terms were altered, I had pretty much lost interest in her anyway. I am a pretty sensitive guy, after all. I had thought she found me irresistible, and now I was realizing that was not the case.

FRED: You mean you were half expecting her to say "Oh what the hell, for YOU it's a freebie!"

STEVE: Sure, we each like to dwell on our own fantasies!

FRED: Maybe she was never planning to go across the street with you at all. At the very least, it sounds like she was planning to pass you off to one of the other girls all along. Or maybe she just came in there to teach you a lesson. That lesson being "Ya can't beat the fuggin' system, so don't bother trying!"

STEVE: Or maybe she was intending to show those younger girls how it's done when you've got a tough nut to crack— and she had just blown it, which must have pissed her off pretty good! At any rate, when the eight of us finally left the Hobbo-Rite around 11:15— make that the Silver Slipper— I did so with the feeling that I had achieved a moral victory by not letting myself get taken advantage of by some lady of the evening.

FRED: And of course Queenie was probably thinking exactly the same thing... a moral victory for hookers everywhere!

STEVE: Fortunately for us, someone had mysteriously arranged for a couple dozen buses to take us all back to the Weigel. (Our first clue that the whole operation was probably sanctioned by— if not actually operated by— the US military.) Needless to say, the trip took a lot longer in a 48 passenger bus than it had taken us in a four-seater Renault! When we got back to the ship, dozens of drunken troops were barfing on the pier and staggering or crawling up the gangway.

FRED: Some of the guys from the Flash's sex-and-booze parties had to be literally carried aboard by their buddies— not surprising, considering they had been drinking "unlimited free booze" since shortly after 12 noon. Once we got underway, one of our guys staggered up on deck and threatened to jump overboard— "Don't come near me or I'll jump, I swear it!!!"— until we managed to tackle him from behind. Obviously a good time was had by all in Okinawa!

STEVE: And then to top it off, for about the next 12 months— whenever a bunch of us were sitting in our hooch, tossing barbs at one another in Nam— I had to endure people like Carl saying "Hey Donovan, tell us again about how you failed to score in Okinawa!"

FRED: Except he didn't use the word "score."

&&&&&&&&&&&&&&&&&&

FACT OR FICTION? The story goes that shortly after the 24th Evac arrived in Vietnam, Major Fensler had to go to Saigon to meet with senior Vietnamese Army officers about the plans for hospital facilities in the area designated as III Corps. Arriving a day in advance, he decided to try his luck with an escort service that would provide him with a woman for the night. The young lady turned out to be very active in bed, and each time he made advances she would start screaming "Sai lo hong! Sai lo hong!" which he took to be an expression of the immense pleasure she must have been experiencing. The next day he was invited for a round of golf with the ARVN officers at the Saigon Country Club. On a fairly long par three, he hit a two iron that carried all the way to the green, bounced off the flag stick and stopped about three feet from the pin. Eager to try out his newly learned expression of joy, Fensler began yelling "Sai lo hong! Sai lo hong!" At which point one of the ARVN officers turned to him and said "I am afraid you wrong, Major. That is right hole. That is definitely right hole!"

CHAPTER 12

SHOOT TO WOUND? JUST HOW BADLY SHOULD WE WOUND THEM, SIR?

That's right, we're all non-combatants... which means no shooting to kill Charlie, boys

STEVE: Some 72 hours after leaving Okinawa, we were treated to a breathtaking sight when we climbed up on deck at dawn to get our first glimpse of the coast of Vietnam. Steaming slowly into the harbor at Da Nang, we began passing small fishing boats— sampans— and of course we couldn't help but wonder... which ones contained fishermen and which contained Viet Cong who'd like to kill us?

FRED: But those thoughts were pretty much overpowered by the magnificent scenery— the hills surrounding the city, the mountains in the distance, all of it illuminated by the newly rising sun. It was also eerily quiet and serene— no hint whatsoever that there was a war going on a few miles inland. The only sound was the faint chugging of the Willie's engines.

STEVE: It was like the scene in "King Kong" where the adventurers approach this mysterious island that's home to a 30 foot gorilla. Nice and peaceful, with nary a hint of the terror that might lie ahead.

FRED: If we'd arrived some six hours earlier, we probably would have been treated to the nightly fireworks show as American artillery and aircraft pounded the enemy while Charlie fired tracers, mortars and rockets at our planes, helicopters and ground installations. But I much preferred starting out on a positive note with that peaceful, scenic view. I wasn't in any hurry to see bombs and bullets, thank you.

STEVE: We dropped anchor in the middle of the harbor so the 900 marines onboard could disembark into landing craft. But their departure meant we Army dudes had to resume pulling all the work details, so we were immediately put to work and didn't get to watch them leave. We spent most of the day below deck— cleaning up the marines' abandoned troop bays, mainly— as the Willie sailed another 360 miles south to our ultimate destination: Cam Ranh Bay.

FRED: Cam Ranh was a natural deep water port, which meant our ship could sail right up to within 100 yards of the beach. But we still had to drop anchor offshore, and there was no obvious path for us to simply walk from the deck of the Willie to the beach.

STEVE: This was of grave concern to me, since I could envision us having to climb down some 30 feet on a rope ladder or cargo net to reach the landing craft— LCU or LST, I believe— while wearing our steel helmets, flak vests and rifles slung over our shoulders. One false step and I'd be in the drink— a non-swimmer, weighed down with all that extra crap. And in a deep water port to boot!

FRED: And from that day on, all our buddies would have spoken with great reverence about the day that PFC Donovan almost made it to Vietnam!

STEVE: Damned straight! Actually I was more concerned about the potential embarrassment than the prospect of drowning, but that's just me. So it was with considerable relief that from the deck, I could see them opening a big cargo door on the side of the ship. At least that would put us about 20 feet closer to the water line!

FRED: We still had to climb down a cargo net to get to the deck of the LST, but it was only like 6 or 8 feet, according to your recollection. I thought it was a lot more than that, but I sometimes tend to overdramatize things. We were also warned that if the LST was bobbing up and down in the water, you had to be sure to jump off the ladder as the landing craft was starting to go down. Otherwise if it was starting to come up, you could easily break a leg or an ankle.

STEVE: Fortunately there wasn't much bobbing at all. Heading into the beach, they warned us to hang on tight to something since there'd be a big jolt when we hit the sand. So we all braced ourselves and when we hit, there was a barely audible thump. No jolt at all.

FRED: So that meant we'd already dodged three bullets in less than half an hour... how long would our luck hold out? Could we make it 12 more months, perhaps?

STEVE: And we didn't realize it at the time, but exactly one week after D-Day in 1944, the 24th Evac had hit the sands of Normandy at Omaha Beach in exactly the same fashion. They proceeded to set up and then move their mobile hospital to no fewer than 19 different locations by the end of 1945.

FRED: Averaging about one move per month! Our landing zone on the beach at Cam Ranh— the first place we set foot on Vietnamese soil— was pretty much deserted. We had our weapons but no ammo, so we assumed we must be in a relatively safe location. Otherwise they'd have given us some bullets for them guns, right? Buses were waiting to take us to the Cam Ranh airfield, where a lone C-130 cargo plane awaited us.

STEVE: We still had no clue as to where we were going or what we'd find when we got there— everything was "top secret." Finally the First Shirt climbs up on the plane's open rear ramp so he could address all of us. He revealed that we were heading to a place called Bien Hoa. (He called it BIN-HOE-A, as in "you been a hoa all yer life," but later we found out it was actually pronounced BEN-WAH.)

FRED: Since our full group constituted at least three planeloads of troops, the plane took off with the first group while we waited for another aircraft to pick us up. (Or maybe it was the same plane making three trips— shades of the Hobbo-Rite!)

STEVE: It was a 180 mile flight to Bien Hoa, roughly 30 minutes in a C-130. Still no ammo. Now I was getting concerned because if our plane should get shot down or have to make a forced landing, we'd be out in the middle of nowhere. Eighty guys with eighty M-14's and not a single bullet among us. Sounded like poor planning to me.

FRED: I can just about hear Charlie now: "American prane forced to rand in jungle! Uh-oh, prane be full of American soldiers with M-14 rifles! Oh wait... they have no ammo crips? OK, shooting garrery time! Sound rike poor pranning to me!"

STEVE: We should point out that according to the International Geneva Conventions, medical personnel were allowed to carry weapons only for the defense of themselves or their patients. In other words, since we were medics we weren't allowed to shoot at anybody unless they shot at us first! A minor distinction perhaps, but we would gradually come to find out that somebody above us— the Hospital Commander, Medical Brigade Commander or whomever— was determined that the best way to make sure we didn't violate that policy was to take away our weapons or our ammo!

FRED: Sound rike poor pranning!

STEVE: At Bien Hoa Airbase we were pleasantly surprised to find a small fleet of deuce-and-a-half trucks— piloted by our own guys from the 24th Evac Advance Party— waiting to take us to Long Binh, our new home. Each truck could carry at least 20 men if some sat on the floor. Still no ammo... hmmm.

FRED: As we got ready to roll, a sergeant picked the two men sitting closest to the cab to ride "air guard" by standing up in the front of the truck bed, resting their arms on the roof of the cab and holding their weapons pointed forward toward oncoming traffic. He gave each two clips of ammo. They "locked and loaded" their weapons. That made a grand total of 80 rounds to protect 20 soldiers riding in the back. Four rounds per man. Of course the NCO never said a word to them about any rules of engagement, or whom they were authorized to shoot.

STEVE: Probably because he didn't have the faintest idea. But that wasn't the worst part. The two guys who got picked were PFC's Moffitt and Barnwell. Moffitt looked, talked and acted like a classic "Casper Milquetoast"— a timid soul who'd be unlikely to ever bring himself to squash an ant. But Barnwell was just the opposite— a Nervous Nellie who'd probably burn off his 40 allotted rounds at the first sight of a water buffalo or a civilian in black pajamas and "cone" hat.

FRED: So now we were heading out into open country guarded by Miss Nellie and Mister Milquetoast— one being a guy who'd waste all his ammo at the first opportunity, the other being someone who'd be very reluctant to pull that trigger under any circumstances whatsoever. I felt like saying "Gimme one of them damn clips!" but I held my tongue because Moffitt was, after all, a friend of mine. And Barnwell would never have given up a single bullet anyway.

STEVE: So for those two guys it was like "Hey, we just got off the ship and now they're giving us loaded weapons and telling us to shoot anything that looks suspicious!" But for the rest of us it was "Oh no, those are the last two guys in the company to whom we'd ever want to entrust our safety. C'mon Sarge, get real!"

FRED: Yeah, we shoulda taken a vote on who would get those 80 rounds. Then on the road to Long Binh we passed through the small village of Tam Hiep (population 500)— where we saw our first little kids wearing nothing below the waist— plus some small roadside businesses with big signs that said "car wash" or "truck wash."

STEVE: I figured the GI's had better things to do than constantly be washing the dust and mud off their vehicles, so that would explain why there were so many of those places. Later on we'd find out there were other things going on inside those little establishments which had nothing to do with hoses, sponges or detergent.

FRED: The lush scenery on the five mile trip to Long Binh would have been truly impressive if we hadn't found ourselves nervously watching for an ambush around every bend in the road. Nobody had said word one about the security situation in the area— either they didn't know or didn't feel it was important to tell us. So we were more or less free to assume the worst.

STEVE: I'm thinking "Well, it must be pretty damned safe here if they don't think we need ammo!" It wasn't 'til some time later that we learned somebody upstairs was deliberately trying to prevent us from having the ability to shoot at anything or anyone. After all, God forbid anyone should violate the Geneva Conventions!

FRED: In fact there was some confusion as to whether those rules even applied to us at the time, since some of the provisions supposedly weren't ratified by the USA until sometime in the 1970's. Plus there was also the argument that Charlie had no respect for any such international rules of warfare, so why should we? But at any rate, some 20 minutes later we rolled into the site of the (future) 24th Evacuation Hospital— what there was of it— which was basically a big empty field of dirt. Sure as hell didn't look like no hospital, that's for sure!

STEVE: We should explain that most people who've read or heard anything about Long Binh Junction probably picture it as an American "city" with swimming pools, movie theaters, restaurants and bowling alleys. But all of that stuff appeared long after we got there. In the summer of '66 it was mostly a big swatch of barren land that had been cleared of rubber trees and bulldozed into what looked like the world's largest parking lot. Long Binh wasn't officially classified as a "secure post" until 1969, two years after we left. By that time there were some 40,000 Americans assigned there— nearly 10 percent of all the Army personnel in country.

FRED: But we had the honor of being among the first! Our 25 man Advance Party had erected a couple dozen GP Medium (General Purpose, Medium-Sized) tents designed to house eight men (or 16 with bunk beds.) The floors were wooden shipping pallets and the only furnishings were canvas cots, as I recall.

STEVE: Initially our padlocked duffel bags served as lockers— we were literally "living out of a duffel bag," which meant you'd have to try to keep the things you were most likely to need at the top of the bag. We parked our rifles next to our bunks, but again... no ammo.

FRED: Around the hospital's perimeter, someone had constructed six or eight guard bunkers made of sandbag walls with plywood roofs. They were lightly manned in the daytime, but we had only been there a few hours when the night shift started gearing up for action. Members of the Advance Party were suiting up in their "combat gear" to go out and man those bunkers, two men to a post.

STEVE: I saw SP5 Buncis— a cook who used to fry our eggs every morning back in Texas— lock and load a 20-round clip into his weapon as he headed out to his post. That's when it hit me— "Hey man, them are live bullets! It's the real thing, sure as shootin'. Yup, there really is a war going on here!"

FRED: And that was probably the last time he ever had to pull guard duty too, since the cooks were excused once we took over. I think we ate evening chow in shifts that night as there was only one Mess Tent to feed us in. It was situated right next to the dirt road in front of our compound and its sides were rolled up due to the oppressive heat. Every time a truck went by, the wind would carry a big cloud of road dust right into the tent. As you ate you could actually watch that layer of dirt building up on top of your food. Yet another good example of poor pranning!

STEVE: That "road dust on the chow" would go on for a number of weeks— you got used to it after awhile— until the first building to be constructed by the Engineers would be a big fancy wood-framed Mess Hall capable of seating around 140 at a time.

FRED: Once we finally got to sack our weary bones that first night, we did so to the sound of artillery, bombs and small arms fire going off in the distance. I remember thinking "Man, how do they ever expect us to sleep with all that racket going on? And if we should get attacked, are we supposed to stand in line to wait for some ammo?" But as it turned out, the conscious and subconscious minds had specific ways of dealing with those questions. And you've said before that throughout your life, the only dreams you remembered were ones in which you were in some kind of predicament.

STEVE: Yeah, when my head hit the pillow my conscious brain said "Well, if we should get hit with any of that stuff, I'd rather be asleep when it happens!" And I never had any problem sleeping after that. But I had an incredible dream that first night. In it we got attacked by hordes of nasty-looking VC coming down this slope toward us. All our weapons were locked up in a CONEX... when we broke out the rifles and ammo, all the stocks on the rifles had been snapped off by some sinister saboteur... which meant we would instantly have to learn the "Quick Kill" method where ya just point and shoot!

FRED: And at that time no one had yet heard of Quick Kill. We wouldn't find out about it until a couple years later, after we'd already gotten out of the service. Heck, you should have patented the idea right then and there. How did your dream work out?

STEVE: My predicament dreams never reached a conclusion... it seemed like I always woke up before I found out how they ended. After that night, my big fear the following morning was "Holy cow, if I'm gonna be having a dream like that every night in Nam, I'm gonna go nuts before I ever get outta here!"

FRED: But in fact the result was quite the opposite.

STEVE: It was. I never once dreamt about the enemy for the next 52 weeks. I assume that was thanks to my subconscious brain saying

"OK, let's get this out of the way tonight so that from now on, you'll already know what it feels like to be attacked by the VC. It won't be any big deal from now on!"

FRED: Your subconscious was looking out for Number One!

STEVE: And just in the nick of time, too. I believe it was our second night in Long Binh that we were assigned to guard duty and given a metal box full of live ammo, plus some grenades and a handful of parachute illumination flares. Since it was the first time for all of us newbies, SFC Hanley climbed up on a deuce and a half with a bullhorn so he could address the whole company at once.

FRED: A grizzled veteran of the Korean War, Hanley looked more like Paul Bunyan than some wimpy career-type Medical NCO. He gave us some words of wisdom and then delivered a few announcements from the higher-ups. "This comes from Battalion Headquarters," he said. "Since we're a medical unit, our weapons are to be used for defensive purposes only. That means you're authorized to fire only if somebody shoots at you first."

STEVE: That sounded reasonable. We weren't there to kill anyone, only to defend ourselves and our patients. No argument there... although if it were taken literally, one could infer that if Charlie were to walk right into our camp without firing a shot, we should just wave hello to him as he walked past and headed for the Beer Tent.

FRED: But then Hanley added this: "Since we're not here to kill anyone, our orders say that if it becomes necessary to fire your weapon, you will not shoot to kill... you will only shoot to wound!"

STEVE: This was followed immediately by lots of mumbling and groaning as the men expressed their disbelief at what they had just heard. Nobody had ever taught us how to shoot to wound! They had to be kidding us, right?

FRED: Not only that, but can you imagine the letters the Army would have to write home to our families? "Dear Mrs. Suggins: We regret to inform you that your son Elwood was killed in action during an enemy assault. He courageously shot several of the attackers in the knees, but unfortunately they responded by shooting him in the chest."

STEVE: I couldn't help but wonder "Which clown or clowns came up with that strategy?" I felt like raising my hand and asking "Just how badly are we supposed to wound them, sergeant?"

FRED: But before you could do so, Hanley tossed in a comment of his own: "About 20 rounds of semi-automatic fire ought to wound 'em pretty good!" He was obviously letting us know that as far as he was concerned, we could ignore the orders from whatever fathead had conceived that directive.

STEVE: It was most likely the same bozo who decided we should travel nearly 200 miles through hostile territory with empty weapons and nary a bullet among us. Besides, who could ever have expected us to go home and say "Yeah, I saw some VC over there in Nam but I didn't get any kills... we were only allowed to wound 'em!"

FRED: What's ironic is that Charlie was supposedly trained to believe it was better to wound an American soldier than kill him— since it would take two or three other soldiers to tend to the wounded man, thus taking a total of at least three men out of action.

STEVE: Those conniving little bastards!

FRED: So anyway, the parachute flares came in aluminum tubes with a cap on one end. To shoot one up, you'd pull the cap off, aim the open end at the sky and slam the butt end down on any hard surface. The next sound you'd hear would be a loud FFFFOOOOSHHHHH!— like you'd hear on the 4th of July when fireworks were being shot into the sky. When the missile reached its apex, there'd be a faint "pop" as it blew open and released its little parachute with a burning flare hanging underneath.

STEVE: And when that sound was heard, everyone in camp knew it meant one of two things: either we had enemy contact— or a frigging false alarm. Before long we learned it could mean any one of three things, the third being that Barnwell was on guard duty. First night he was out in a bunker, a flare would go up about every 20 minutes or so. Soon everyone was asking "What the hell is going on?"

FRED: They had shown us how to operate the flares, but they never said word one about when we were, or were not, supposed to use them. It turned out that old "Nervous Nellie" Barnwell was seeing things out there that nobody else saw. Each time he did, he'd shoot up a flare— thereby putting the entire company on pins and needles— and each time the flare would burn out after several minutes, having revealed nothing whatsoever.

STEVE: By the second or third week, whenever we'd be sitting in our hooch at night and we'd hear that FFFFFOOOSHHHHH! sound, someone would holler "Barnwell must be on guard tonight!" And then everyone would go back to whatever they were doing. Ninety percent of the time they'd be right.

FRED: Oddly enough, at first we'd assume it was the real thing, grab our weapons and start putting on the combat gear. But after several weeks of false alarms, we eventually reached the point where everything got blamed on "Nervous Nellie." Whenever he was on guard, we'd bet on how long it would be before his first flare went up.

STEVE: In addition to the flares, another essential piece of equipment was a plastic bottle of insect repellent to slather on your exposed skin about once every hour. Plus you had your steel pot, canteen, M-14 rifle, flashlight, gas mask and flak vest. But once we'd settled into a comfortable routine, the toughest part of guard duty became staying awake. The shifts were three hours on, three off, three on, etc.

FRED: With two men in a bunker, it was possible to "cheat" and let one guy drift off while the other stayed awake. The danger then was that the second guy might also fall asleep, in which case both could be risking a court martial as well as putting the lives of themselves and the rest of us in peril if there should be an attack.

STEVE: It seems like the Army had no standard protocol for this. For example, some infantry units would put three guys in each bunker along with two cots. This was supposed to ensure that one or two could crash if they wanted to, but the third would remain standing so he wouldn't fall asleep.

FRED: The only problem was that if they were tired, lots of guys could fall asleep while standing up and leaning on the sandbags.

STEVE: That probably explains why the infantry made liberal use of amphetamines to keep the troops alert. One historical chronicle of the war said the US military virtually ran on Benzedrine pills during the nights in Vietnam. One GI was quoted as saying "I was dog tired from lack of sleep, but about 20 minutes after I took that little white pill, I felt like a brand new man!"

FRED: I know I had some in my possession, but I'm not sure if I got them from the Hospital Pharmacy. One of the few times I recall actually using them was when I flew on a chopper over to the 12th Evac in Cu Chi to visit a couple buddies from Medic School. I knew we'd likely be consuming mass quantities of alcohol and I also knew I had this habit of falling asleep when I was under the influence, so I popped a couple bennies and drank 'em all under the table!

STEVE: Some military records indicate that in Nam, the Army dispensed more amphetamines to its troops from 1966 to 1969 than were provided to all the British and American forces for the duration of the Second World War. Nobody ever offered any to me, or if they did I immediately thought of those "little white pills" that Dave Dudley sang about— and I declined on the spot. But staying awake was definitely a challenge.

FRED: Some nurses at various hospitals have said they used to take bennies to stay awake on the night shift. About the only other things that were useful in keeping a sentry awake on guard duty were 1) fear, which gradually wore off after we had been there awhile; 2) watching the nightly fireworks off in the distance— sometimes they were spectacular, like when "Puff the Magic Dragon" (a C-130 cargo plane armed with Gatling guns) would open up with a shower of red tracers at enemy troops on the ground; 3) smoking cigarettes, which was allowed as long as you crouched behind the sandbag wall and kept your hand covering the top of the lighter; or 4) getting involved in some good conversation.

STEVE: We'd smoke standing up and just lean over behind the wall each time we wanted to take a drag. That's when I learned that for me, smoking was no fun if I couldn't see the smoke I was exhaling. So with each puff I'd have to blow the smoke directly over the glowing tip of the cigarette so I could see it.

FRED: Yup, sounds pretty weird! Pete Ferris said when he was in Infantry Training, a sergeant said "If you're having trouble staying awake, pull the pin on a grenade and hold it in your hand so that if you drop it, it will go off. I'll guarantee that will keep you awake!

STEVE: According to the story, at least one trooper in the First Air Cavalry blew himself away in precisely that fashion. But ya never knew whether stories like that were true or not.

FRED: Meanwhile, you began getting a reputation for being a good talker on guard duty.

STEVE: I'd always try to get paired up with somebody who seemed to be a good conversationalist. Then I'd try to get him to take turns telling stories or leading philosophical discussions. I never really thought of myself as a talker but I developed a repertoire of detailed stories, most of which involved the wacky antics of me and my college buddies back in Mad-Town, Wisconsin.

FRED: So pretty soon, your fellow GI's were telling each other "Hey, next time you're on guard duty, try to get in the same bunker with Donovan. He's got some great stories!" But you got yourself into a few good arguments, too.

STEVE: Those would be arguments in the legal sense as opposed to the kind where someone threatens to punch the other guy's lights out. Having civil, reasonably intelligent disagreements with your "bunker buddy" was actually a damned good way to stay awake.

FRED: It sure beat being out there in the pitch dark with some guy who never said a word. You'd have to slap him on the shoulder every 15 minutes to see if he was still conscious.

STEVE: The argument that always comes to mind for me was one evening when we were about to stand inspection for guard mount. Next to me was a new kid, PFC Grimsley, who was wondering aloud about the principles involved in zeroing a weapon. Next to him was SP5 Riching, who outranked most of us and was therefore assumed to be an expert on just about all things military. I heard Riching say "Well ya see Grimsley, when the bullet leaves the gun, it rises due to the fact that the gun barrel is curved upward. Then it starts to fall as it approaches the target."

FRED: And you just assumed he must be having a little fun with the new guy, right?

STEVE: Yes, but before long I realized that he might be serious. I turned to Grimsley and said "Don't pay any attention to him, he's just pullin' your leg." Whereupon Riching says "I sure as hell am not! They taught us in Basic— the bullet rises and then it falls!"

FRED: Well, at least he was right on that score...

STEVE: True, but as a former physics major there was no way I could let that one pass. I said "Yeah, the bullet rises— but it's not because the barrel is curved! It's because the barrel, which is straight as an arrow, is pointed upward to begin with."

FRED: And then it became a case of "Is not!" "Is too!" "Is not!" "Is too!" So you arranged to switch posts with someone else so that you and Riching could continue the discussion in a bunker.

STEVE: As we headed out to our post, I stopped at the hooch and grabbed a notepad and pencil. In the bunker I began drawing diagrams showing how and why the bullet rises and then falls. It took a while, but I finally convinced him and he sheepishly agreed.

FRED: Then as you were gathering information for our book last year, you got hold of him by telephone and lo and behold, he remembered that discussion quite vividly. He was still a bit embarrassed about it. He even begged you not to use his real name.

STEVE: And I have now followed through on that promise. But I can't pass up this footnote: He told me on the phone that he used to work as a manager for a company that machined... gun barrels.

FRED: Now we know why he didn't want his real name used!

STEVE: Incidentally, some will find this hard to believe, but in all those hundreds of hours of bunker conversations back in 1966-67, I never heard a single guy bad-mouthing the war.

FRED: Yeah, we griped about the Army, the draft, the food, the officers, the NCO's, the lying recruiters and the Mickey-Mouse military bullshit— but I don't recall hearing anyone say he was opposed to the war. Most of that anti-war stuff came later on, after we had gotten our honorable discharges.

STEVE: And then after several weeks of mostly filling sandbags, erecting tents and building bunkers and blast walls, we were informed that our task was about to shift... to building a new hospital. Not a traditional Evac Hospital that was housed in tents so it could quickly be dismantled and moved to a new location— it would be a permanent facility made of wood-framed and pre-fabbed buildings.

FRED: To be built for the long haul, so to speak. We called the prefab aluminum buildings quonset huts, but their official name was

ADAMS huts (for Advanced Design Aluminum Military Shelters) which were invented by the Australians. They looked like giant corrugated aluminum tubes that were cut in half lengthwise and plopped face-down on concrete slabs. And surprise... we'd have to build 'em all ourselves, since there was nobody else around to do it!

STEVE: It would take us the next four months to construct what was initially a 200-bed permanent hospital that eventually would expand to 400 beds. During its first year of operation, the 24th Evac would treat over 9,000 patients. Nearly 20 percent were evacuated to the USA; some 40 percent were returned to active duty in Nam; and 38 percent were transferred to other treatment or convalescent facilities in-country. But in the meantime... all of our guys were medics! Yet back in Medic School, they had completely forgotten to teach us how to pour concrete and build quonset huts.

FRED: Sound rike poor pranning!

&&&&&&&&&&&&&&&&&&

FACT OR FICTION?   *The story goes that SP5 Rengel came into his hooch one day and said "Look what I got in Bien Hoa for ten bucks! It's a spider monkey named Chet, and it sings Christmas carols in English! Watch this." As his buddies gathered around, he lit a match and held it under the monkey's right foot, whereupon it started singing "Jingle bells, jingle bells, jingle all the way!" Then he lit another, held it under the left foot and the monkey sang "God rest ye merry gentlemen, let nothing you dismay..." At this point PFC Furman says "That's absolutely amazing! What happens if you hold the match between his two feet?" So Rengel tries it and wouldn't ya know, soon they're hearing "Chet's nuts roasting on an open fire..."*

SEE MORE THAN 30 PHOTOS AT:
www.longbinhdaze.com

CHAPTER 13

ENJOY A LOVELY EVENING
AT SUICIDE POINT

*Hey Sarge... I'd like to volunteer
for Suicide tonight*

FRED: Despite their giving us loaded weapons when we went on guard duty, someone was determined that we wouldn't have access to them at any other time. First they confiscated our rifles and locked them in a CONEX with one person being the official "gunkeeper." This prompted SP4 Kingsley to complain about it in a letter to his folks.

STEVE: His father, a WW II veteran himself, suggested that his son write his Congressman, which he did. This produced swift action. Within a week they gave us our weapons back to satisfy the politicians. The victory celebration was a brief one, however, since they made sure all the ammunition was locked up. So now if there was an alert, we'd grab our rifles and then have to send someone to the weapons CONEX to draw some ammo.

FRED: The first time this happened, there was a SNAFU and the ammo custodian said he wasn't authorized to distribute bullets. So then we were all sitting in the pitch dark in our personnel bunker wearing steel pots and flak jackets while clutching our empty rifles.

STEVE: After about ten minutes the Sergeant of the Guard comes by, sticks his head into the totally dark bunker and says "You guys got ammo?" This prompted me to take my voice down about one octave and yell "The weapons officer wouldn't give us any, so screw your dirty little war!" I was really just trying to get a laugh out of my buddies, but I had disguised my voice so no one could prove who said it— in case there were any repercussions.

FRED: The brass knew there'd be another letter to the Congressman if they didn't come up with a solution, so they locked the rifles in a makeshift gun rack inside each hooch. The ranking man would have the key to the rack and one individual would be designated as a member of the "Rapid Response Team" with a fully automatic weapon and his own supply of ammo to boot.

STEVE: Naturally Fred got picked once again. Presumably he was the guy most likely to be trusted with a loaded weapon. In all honesty, I couldn't have come up with a better choice myself!

FRED: For the first month or more that we were in Long Binh, each one of us had been pulling guard duty at least two or three nights a week. It had become a pretty routine thing— our nightly "venture into the war." We knew there might be untold dangers out to the east of our perimeter, and we could hear artillery and intermittent small arms fire at various times during the night. But there had been very little action in the immediate vicinity of our compound— and that was beginning to make us complacent.

STEVE: That is, until one day when the engineers came in and dug a big drainage ditch parallel to, and just outside of, our concertina wire. Roughly six feet wide by six feet deep, it sloped down toward the east ("Injun Country" to us) to help alleviate the mud problem.

FRED: It undoubtedly did drain off a lot of rainwater, but when we stood in a bunker on the southern perimeter at night, we realized there was no way we could see into the ditch. We were supposed to be watching intently for any signs of enemy activity, yet it was obvious that Charlie could march an entire company of, say, 120 infantrymen into that ditch and right up to within 30 feet of our perimeter without us being any the wiser.

STEVE: As we started to raise a stink about it, I was explaining the situation to every officer and NCO whom I could get to listen, and after a few days someone finally took action.

FRED: Our recommendation was to move the perimeter so that it either encompassed the ditch or butted right up against it, thereby allowing the sentries at those guard posts to see into the chasm.

STEVE: But moving the perimeter would have required us to dismantle and rebuild three guard bunkers on the southern perimeter. Each was constructed with umpteen tons of sandbags, so they weren't something you could just pick up and move on a whim.

FRED: Instead, some genius decided to build an additional bunker right on the bank of the drainage ditch and extend the concertina wire out so that it surrounded the new post. It probably seemed less disruptive to locate the bunker roughly 100 feet east and south of what was currently the southeast corner of our perimeter.

STEVE: To protect the bunker and its occupants, a narrow passageway was constructed leading out to the new post with walls of concertina on both sides. Out at the tip, the wire circled around the guard bunker so that the whole contraption was shaped like a giant soup spoon with a narrow handle and a sentry post sitting right in the middle of the bowl.

FRED: The problem was that when you stood in the new bunker, you were almost completely surrounded by "No Man's Land" and the only way to get back to friendly territory would be to dash some 40 yards through that narrow passageway with the possibility of lead flying around you on all sides. If a retreat was ever called for, Charlie would probably already be inside the wire by then— and in the dark, your own friendlies might be drawing a bead on you as you came running toward them in the ensuing chaos.

STEVE: As we were looking over the new setup, somebody muttered "Damn, anybody who takes this post is gonna be committing suicide." At which point I jokingly said "Hey, that's what we oughta name it— Suicide Point!" Needless to say, the idea caught on quickly.

FRED: That nickname must have really struck a chord with a lot of guys, because within less than 48 hours the scuttlebutt around camp was all about "Who's on Suicide tonight?" Answer: "Peterson and Blevins are on first shift, Vancil and Walters are on second." Then somebody would chime in with "Yeah, Blevins volunteered for it— that crazy bastard! And Walters tried everything he could think of to weasel out of it, but he got stuck with it anyway!"

STEVE: A few nights later, I'm standing in line for Guard Mount inspection and PFC Bronson, the big galoot, is standing next to me. As the Sergeant of the Guard strolls past, checking the shine on our boots, Bronson says "Sarge, I'd like to volunteer for Suicide tonight."

"OK, you got it, Bronson!" Which told me that the NCO's even knew what "Suicide" was! I was a bit flattered.

FRED: Our willingness to accept that assignment without batting an eye was one of the few opportunities we had to demonstrate our "bravery" to our peers, as well as our readiness to take on a task that some viewed with great dread.

STEVE: It seemed like almost every night, something would come up at Guard Mount regarding Suicide Point. One night it would be somebody saying "Aw Sarge, that's the third time in a row I got stuck on Suicide! C'mon man, gimme a break!" Another night it might be a soldier saying to his buddy, "Hey Wilkins! Let's take Suicide tonight!" Whereupon the others would heave a quiet sigh of relief.

FRED: One fellow even said he'd accept a court martial rather than agree to man that bunker. As we were standing around waiting for Guard inspection one night, we heard PFC Broyles say "I'll tell ya what, they ain't puttin' me out there, man! No way, brother! They can put my ass in the stockade for as long as they want, but I ain't goin' out to no Suicide Point!"

STEVE: I think there were a total of twelve guard posts around the perimeter so I figured on any given night, there was less than a 10 percent chance of getting picked for Suicide. I could live with those odds— and as it turned out, an occasional stint out there in "No Man's Land" was rather exhilarating anyway. A good way to get the adrenaline pumping every now and then.

FRED: This had been going on for several weeks when the Engineers decided to throw another wrinkle into the mix. They were working outside our eastern perimeter and in order to get their heavy equipment in and out of there, they opened up the wire for 100 feet or so, just to the north of the Suicide Point "pathway." When they went home at night they didn't bother to close the wire.

STEVE: So when we went on guard that night, the AOD advised us of the situation and told us we needed to be "extra alert" because the wire was open on the eastern perimeter. Suicide was Post 9, manned by PFC's Harkin and Pisarski, while Carl Denton and I were in Post 10, some 40 yards to the west. Normally our mission would be to watch and listen for any enemy activity in our sector. Except that Post 10 had the distinction of being located right next to a bunker housing two gigantic gasoline-powered generators that were so loud you could not hear a damn thing inside Bunker 10. If Carl and I wanted to communicate with each other, we had to either shout or else get right up in the other guy's ear. So listening was out and Post 10 was— de facto— solely an "OP" (Observation Post.)

FRED: Sergeant Lemke, a rather benign old lifer, was the Sergeant of the Guard that night. He'd be the first person to tell you he was a hillbilly from the backwoods of Tennessee— a "Gomer Pyle" type, you might say. Like many of the other lifers, he probably stayed in the Army because doing so enabled him to guzzle eight or ten beers every night and still have a job, a paycheck, a roof over his head and three squares a day.

STEVE: Periodically the Sergeant of the Guard was supposed to walk the perimeter line from bunker to bunker to check up on his troops and make sure they were awake. When he approached your bunker, you were supposed to challenge him with: "Halt! Who goes there?" Answer: "The Sergeant of the Guard." Then it was "Advance and be recognized!" When he got closer, you halted him a second time and asked for the password. If he knew it, you let him in. If he didn't, he was in big trouble because he might get shot!

FRED: The password changed every night but most guys didn't bother to memorize it unless they were on guard duty. Thus on any given night, less than half the personnel in our hospital could state the correct password if they were challenged. Not a problem— as long as everything remained peaceful and quiet. On the other hand, when the sirens went off and the illumination flares started going up, it could make things a little dicey.

STEVE: On a clear night with a full moon, you could easily spot anyone approaching your position from 40 yards away. On this particular night, however, it was pitch black with no moon. So in Bunker 10, not only could we not hear anything because of the damned generators, we couldn't see anything because it was dark as hell. Nor could we see into the drainage ditch. This meant that for Carl and me, our function was reduced to trying to save our own skins by protecting the area within a 30-foot radius around our own bunker.

FRED: It was approaching 2200 hours— "lights out" time in the hooches— and I was getting ready to hit the sack when the sound of small arms fire suddenly pierced the night air. We were used to hearing it in muffled tones from off in the distance, but this was up close—really close. It sounded like people were shooting from just outside our perimeter and, presumably, our sentries were probably returning fire. I knew it was either a false alarm or else we were about to have an alert, so I started getting my gear on. After all, I was the Rapid Response man with the only fully automatic weapon in our hooch!

STEVE: Out in Bunker 10, I don't think we heard any gunfire due to the noise of the generators. I had seen the silhouette of a figure about 30 yards north of our position trudging rather slowly toward the eastern perimeter. I was pretty sure it was Lemke, and he was heading straight for the opening in the wire. We knew we were supposed to challenge him if he approached our post, but he wasn't approaching us— he was going east. It occurred to me that he was probably lost and I thought about yelling at him, but I figured the generator noise would have drowned out my shouts anyway.

FRED: So it looked like he was walking right through the open wire into No Man's Land— also known as the Kill Zone to infantry types. If nothing else, Lemke would eventually reach the treeline and realize that he had wandered completely out of our compound. And since a sentry's Fifth General Order was "To quit my post only when properly relieved," you knew you weren't supposed to go out and try to retrieve him in the pitch dark night.

STEVE: Right. And whenever we had an alert, two things happened immediately— a warning siren started wailing, and they cut off the generators to create a blackout condition. Needless to say, right after Gomer wanders through the wire, both of those things happened.

FRED: So suddenly you're hearing a siren, which tells you there's an alert. And suddenly you can hear gunfire as soon as the generators are shut down. And now the boys out at Suicide Point probably have their hands full, not to mention that the Sergeant of the Guard is out there somewhere, on the wrong side of their concertina wire and dangerously close to their position.

STEVE: Roger that. And the logical thing to do would have been to pick up the guard phone, call Bunker 9 and tell Harkin and Pisarski to watch out for Sergeant Lemke, just north of their position.

FRED: Except you couldn't do that because the only call one could make on the phone in Bunker 10 was to the Guard Tent. There was no way to call Suicide Point from Bunker 10. Where did you think the small arms fire was coming from?

STEVE: That was the weird part. The shots sounded like they were being fired at very close range, yet there were no muzzle flashes, no tracers that I could see, and no movement that could be observed when a flare was fired into the sky. Of course if you're in an above ground bunker and Charlie's laying in the weeds behind a tree, those flares will only serve to give away your own position— not his. So there weren't a whole lot of flares going up. As for the tracers, I'm red and green color blind, which might explain why I didn't see any.

FRED: Some other guys said they did see tracers, but only the red ones. According to PFC Ferris, who was just about the only guy in our outfit with any infantry training, the Americans fired the red tracer rounds while the enemy used Russian or Chinese ammo that spit out green ones.

STEVE: Yeah, I once heard one of the Red Cross girls say "So who decided that we'd use the red tracers and the enemy would use the green ones?" But I don't think that's how it worked. Supposedly the Japanese used blue ones in World War II. Now THOSE I could have seen at night with no problem whatsoever!

FRED: Ferris later claimed that he flagged down a squad of MP's who were roaring past in a truck and told them it was all friendly fire— red tracers only! But to this day we don't know if Pete actually lived that story or just dreamt it.

STEVE: Meanwhile, Carl and I are hunkered down out in Bunker 10, peeking over the sandbags with our thumbs on the safeties of our M-14's and our steel pots pulled right down to our eyebrows. I'm figuring any second now, a couple of VC are gonna come hurtling out of the darkness and leap over the wall of our bunker.

FRED: And you knew exactly what to expect because you'd already read all those war comics when you were in second grade!

STEVE: No doubt about it, not only did I already know what they would look like, I already knew they'd be yelling AAAIIEEEEE!!! There was one problem, however— we had M-14 rifles and a supply of grenades, but... nobody had issued us any bayonets!

FRED: Well of course— just about everybody knows medics don't need bayonets. Bet ya wished you'd had that switchblade after all. Or at least a P-38 can opener to use in close combat!

STEVE: For sure. We knew there were rounds flying past us, yet we couldn't figure out where they were coming from or who was shooting at whom. Nobody had ever told me that when high velocity rounds are flying by, they make a loud "CRACK!" as they go past, probably because they're breaking the sound barrier. So we're hearing "CRACK!... CRACK!... CRACK! CRACK! CRACK!... CRACK!" Gradually I begin to figure out that this isn't the sound of rounds being fired from close up— it's the sound of rounds being fired from a considerable distance away that are zooming right past us.

FRED: So you and Carl are shoulder to shoulder, peering over the edge of the sandbags in anticipation of an imminent frontal assault, when one round whizzes by without making a "crack." Instead it goes by with a really loud "FZZZZZZZZZZZ!!!"

STEVE: It sounded like it might have been a tracer round, since they burn up and gradually slow down as they travel. Carl immediately says "Man, that one sounded like it went right past my ear!" I come back with "Yeah, mine too!" After a pause of several seconds, I say "Which ear?" He says "My right!" and I say "It sounded like it went past my left!" Our two ears were no more than 18 inches apart. We figured that round must have gone right between us.

FRED: But now you had a new problem when you saw a shadowy figure coming in from No Man's Land through the opening in the wire, approaching from out of the darkness... and heading straight for your bunker!

STEVE: It probably scared Carl a lot more than me, since I had an ace up my sleeve. I was pretty sure I had seen old "Gomer" Lemke walk straight through the wire and out into the darkness less than ten minutes earlier, so I figured this had to be him coming back. I calmly but firmly initiated the proper challenge procedure by leveling my weapon at him and yelling "Halt!" He didn't even let me finish my sentence before he starts screaming at the top of his lungs "DON'T SHOOT!!! IT'S ME, SERGEANT LEMKE! DON'T SHOOT! DON'T SHOOT! IT'S LEMKE! DON'T SHOOT!!!"

FRED: So much for military protocol— you didn't even get a chance to say "Advance and be recognized."

STEVE: At that point I half jokingly asked him for the password, just to make him squirm a little bit. He said something like "Hell, I don't remember the damn password! It's me, Lemke!" We let him in the bunker and the three of us crouched there for another 10 or 15 minutes. Then all was quiet.

FRED: Meanwhile, Harkin and Pisarski out at Suicide had been crapping their undies, not knowing what the hell was going on. They just knew whatever it was, it seemed to be happening all around them. They called in to the Guard Tent for instructions and were told "We don't know what's going on either!"

STEVE: Apparently they never even saw Lemke strolling through the Kill Zone in the pitch dark. As it turned out, our only casualty that night was SP5 Torborg, who took a round in the butt cheek while sleeping in his bunk— for which he was told he'd receive a Purple Heart. Some trucks had their windshields shot out while some tents had bullet holes in 'em. The holes were easy enough to patch— but in Nam, new windshields didn't exactly grow on trees!

FRED: We didn't begin to find out 'til the next day what all the shooting was about. First we heard that an American patrol had run into a VC patrol and they were exchanging gunfire for a time. Then we heard it was an American patrol that got too close to the perimeter of the Engineers up the road. The sentries started shooting and the patrol was returning fire until someone figured out that it was all friendly fire— red tracers only.

STEVE: Maybe it really was Pete Ferris who clued them in!

FRED: Of course since we were a hospital unit, we were under strict orders to never fire our weapons unless somebody shot at us first. But the Engineers nearby had no such restrictions. When our sentries got nervous, they'd shoot up a few flares. When the engineers got spooked, they'd open up with a few hundred rounds of automatic and semi-automatic fire!

STEVE: Following that night, our sentries continued to man Suicide Point for another month or two until more Engineers moved in right next to us and absorbed our southern perimeter to form one large compound. After that, we provided security for the northern half while they provided security for the southern half.

FRED: And that way there was less chance of two units shooting at each other in a "friendly fire" incident. So anyway, how well did you feel you handled the inevitable fear that must have crept in when you thought you were under imminent attack?

STEVE: I felt pretty good since I hadn't spent any time quaking in my boots or being paralyzed with fear— I was too busy wondering "What's the correct thing to be doing now?" After that I felt confident that I could perform adequately under fire and keep my wits about me, if and when the time came to do so. But the adrenaline rush was amazing— I had no idea my heart could beat that fast.

FRED: You mentioned what a Red Cross Girl said. When I heard them referred to as Donut Dollies, I assumed it was a derogatory term. But it turns out they called themselves that. It was actually a nickname given to them during WW II, and it stuck.

STEVE: Yeah, the first round-eyed female I saw in Nam— other than Martha Raye, who showed up in October when we were still building our hospital— was a young woman in a pale blue uniform. I assumed she must have been an American nurse. I thought "Well, that must be what the nurses wear in Vietnam."

FRED: But in fact they wore jungle fatigues, just like we did.

STEVE: Yup. Then I heard someone say she was a Donut Dolly, which sounded like a disparaging term. When I got close enough I could see her insignia— American Red Cross— and I realized she was a Red Cross Girl. I immediately thought of disaster relief and wondered "what would she be doing here at our hospital, which hasn't even opened yet?"

FRED: It turns out they worked in pairs and were temporarily assigned to the 24th Evac as their home base. They would visit with patients, cheer them up and help them with things like writing letters home or getting their personal affairs in order. But they'd also fly out to remote bases on helicopters to visit the troops. We assumed they took coffee and donuts to the grunts since that's what they did at disaster sites, along with handing out sandwiches. But one Donut Dolly said coffee would get cold and donuts would get stale, so they brought Kool-Aid and cookies instead.

STEVE: They also played parlor games like "Beat the Clock" with GI's in the field, many of whom thought it was wonderful to see American females when they showed up in a chopper. A helicopter that had Donut Dollies onboard would often use the radio call sign "Delta Delta" as code for the DD's. I was careful to never say "Donut Dolly" in their presence because I assumed it was an insulting term somebody had come up with. After all, some GI's did resent the fact that most of them spent their free time with the officers and seemed to have a certain disdain for enlisted men.

FRED: But as it turns out, in their training they were instructed to never fraternize with enlisted men under any circumstances. Plus the rumor was that many of them went there strictly to find a husband, preferably an officer or doctor.

STEVE: One way the Red Cross tried to prevent serious romances was to transfer the DD's every three months to different areas of Vietnam. That, plus the fact that they flew out to different bases every day, meant they actually got to see more of the country than practically anyone in the US military.

FRED: Hard to find a husband when you're constantly on the move! You said when you saw your first Donut Dolly you thought she was a nurse. Remember the first nurse you saw, other than the Chief Nurse?

STEVE: Yeah, the first two nurses we got at the 24th were males! I thought "Damn— are all the nurses going to be male over here?" One was Lieutenant Sherwood, a young handsome guy who immediately began hanging around with us enlisted men in the beer tent. (The only officer to do so.) He was a friendly, unassuming guy— somewhat effeminate, but since they told us there were no gays in the military because they weren't allowed, we just shrugged it off as a quirk.

FRED: He was constantly being mistaken for a doctor. Actually about 15% of all the nurses in Nam were male. The Army had only begun accepting male nurses a few years earlier. Since they were in desperate need of nurses for the war buildup, gender became irrelevant. I remember we had an alert the first night Sherwood was there. He stumbled entering the personnel bunker and fell flat on his face in the mud. PFC Crump promptly yelled "SAFE!!!"

STEVE: Uncle Sam had a specific use for them, too. When a new hospital was being set up in the war zone, they'd send in male nurses first because there were no shower or latrine facilities for females. This would explain why our first two male nurses didn't stick around long— they were probably shipped off to another brand new hospital as soon as we had built a latrine and shower for the females.

FRED: What's ironic is that according to an official report compiled after the war, the Army knew a lot of their new male nurses were gay, but they chose to look the other way for the purpose of expediency. Uncle Sam didn't ask... and those nurses didn't tell. Actually I did learn a new term from LT Sherwood that I had never heard before.

STEVE: What term would that be?

FRED: Well I thought he was a doctor at first, but he corrected me when he said "Nope, not a doctor... I'm a Ball Bearing Nurse!"

&&&&&&&&&&&&&&&&&&&&

FACT OR FICTION? *The story goes that a Green Beret captain (or dai-uy in Vietnamese, pronounced DYE-WEE) was inspecting the perimeter defenses at an ARVN base camp along with his trusty Kit Carson Scout, Trang. Like other Kit Carsons, Trang was a defected enemy soldier who was highly skilled and serving as the captain's guide and interpreter. They were passing the main gate when they got word that a sizable enemy force was approaching from the west. Trang immediately dropped and put his ear to the ground. After about 20 seconds, he says "Boo-coo enemy soldiers... me say two platoons, maybe 80 men... four light machine guns... two mortars... six grenade launchers... commanding officer walk with limp." "Holy Toledo!" exclaimed the captain. "Trang, you mean you can tell all that just by listening to the ground?" Trang replies "No dai-uy, me just look under gate."*

CHAPTER 14

RIDE SHOTGUN ON A GARBAGE TRUCK? WHO... ME?

Not to mention a midnight assault on Bien Hoa to rescue a prisoner... from the drunk tank

STEVE: In the 1960's, the phrase "ride shotgun on a garbage truck" had several origins or applications depending on the context in which it was used. It was a derisive term, usually said in jest, as in "Ahhhh, what does that guy know? He used to ride shotgun on a garbage truck!"

FRED: It could also be used to cast aspersions on a particular place, such as in "What's the most dangerous job in Havana? Riding shotgun on a garbage truck!"

STEVE: But in Nam, "riding shotgun" meant you were literally an armed guard riding in the front passenger seat of a vehicle. All vehicles leaving our compound had to have at least one armed guard aboard, in addition to the driver. So if you happened to be on the daytime guard shift and there was a vehicle about to leave the compound without a guard, you were immediately pressed into service.

FRED: Twice a day, one of our deuce and a halfs would leave the compound hauling a couple dozen 30-gallon aluminum garbage cans up to the US Army garbage dump. This was "out in the sticks," a few miles north of Long Binh Post and maybe a mile or so from the Long

Binh Ammo Dump— an occasional target of VC sappers who would infiltrate the perimeter and plant explosives in an attempt to blow up pads of American bombs and artillery shells.

STEVE: And on this particular day, my number was "up" when a guard was needed for the afternoon garbage run. PFC Hensen, a very polite and mild-mannered black fellow, was the driver. I grabbed my rifle, canteen and some ammo and hopped aboard. This would turn out to be my one and only trip to the Long Binh garbage dump, which I had never seen before.

FRED: Most of the cargo on Hensen's truck was "edible garbage" from the Mess Hall— food that the GI's didn't eat. In the states it would be considered "edible for livestock" but in Nam it meant "edible for hungry Vietnamese civilians." I'm sure the peasants were totally baffled as to why we'd throw away all that perfectly good food.

STEVE: We headed north on the deserted two-lane highway and before long, we came over a hill and I saw a line of trucks just like ours waiting to enter a large compound surrounded by concertina wire. As we approached, Hensen explained that the dump officially closed at 5 pm. If you timed it just right, the line would be short and the gate guards would let you in as long as you were in line by 4:30.

FRED: Only one truck was allowed through the gate at a time since each one had to go to the precise spot where they wanted you to dump your load. This was a 5-foot deep trench that was gradually filling with garbage. When you were done, the next truck would come in and dump its load either next to yours or right on top of it.

STEVE: But these weren't dump trucks, so once Hensen sidled our rig up to within a couple feet of the trench, the two of us would have to climb into the cargo bay. Together we'd start lifting these garbage cans up and over the side of the truck so we could dump the contents into the trench— while our loaded weapons were slung barrel-down over our shoulders.

FRED: And as you did so, Hensen said what...?

STEVE: He said softly, "Keep your eyes on the horizon."

FRED: What was on the horizon?

STEVE: About 30 yards beyond the trench was a ridge or man-made berm about 15 feet high— tall enough to prevent us from seeing anything that might be on the other side, even when we were standing up in the back of the truck. There could have been an NVA regiment over there or an amusement park, for all we knew. Soon I saw a few heads pop up above the ridge, then a few more, then some more. Within 10 minutes there had to be 60 or 80 Vietnamese standing motionless on that ridge, staring intently at us.

FRED: Sounds kind of spooky— like the wagon train that sees an Indian war party slowly forming on the ridges all around them.

STEVE: My thoughts exactly. Fortunately they weren't sporting any war paint. They were mostly women, children and little old men. They knew the dump officially closed at 5 pm, and then— and only then— would they be allowed to ransack the place in search of anything useful or edible. When it got down to less than five minutes to go, they were right up to the front edge of the berm. Soon it would be clear that their chief concern was to be among the first to leap into that trench so they could find the "best stuff."

FRED: How did they know when it was 5:00?

STEVE: A guard might have given them a signal, but by my calculation it was about 4:58 when they couldn't hold back any longer. Suddenly they all came streaking down that hill and leaping into the trench— lots of shrieking, chattering and cheering going on, as if they had just won the lottery or something. Some appeared to be looking for objects like empty bottles or pop cans. Some looked first for a container like a box or large can that they could put their "treasure" in. They'd start scooping up anything that looked like edible food and as soon as they filled the container, they'd hand it up to an accomplice and start filling another.

FRED: So were you done with your dumping by then?

STEVE: No, that was the weirdest part! There were women and children standing directly beneath us in the trench. Hensen and I pick up a can and we're just about to dump it when I say "Hold it! There's women and children directly below us!" He says "Don't worry about it, that's what they want." I look down and sure enough, they're looking up at us with outstretched arms as if to say "come on, let's have some more of that manna from heaven!"

FRED: How did you feel about having to dump garbage right on top of those women and children?

STEVE: Very strange, I kid you not. But for anyone who thinks it was an awful, pitiful thing to do, you have to understand that those people in the trench were as happy as a bunch of clams at high tide. It appeared that they had virtually no concept of either personal hygiene or food contamination.

FRED: If you had put a water buffalo or herd of goats in that same trench instead of civilians, those animals would have thought they'd died and gone to heaven. So you're saying these peasants felt pretty much the same way?

STEVE: Yeah, it was like we had just driven in there with a big sign on our truck that said "Free Food, Everybody!" (In Vietnamese, of course.) They were doing the same thing as what is today known as dumpster diving— except this was just "dump diving."

FRED: Well anyway, one thing is for certain— to the best of my knowledge, you're the only person I've ever known who's actually ridden shotgun on a garbage truck! Didn't you have another episode when you made Supernumerary and got stuck on day guard?

STEVE: Yeah, Supernumerary... The most important thing a new recruit learned in his first week of Basic Training was a list of General Orders. A Drill Sergeant would say in a gruff voice: "These are your eleven General Orders! Memorize every one of 'em— and you WILL be tested on this!" Of course they didn't bother to tell us what they were for, or why we needed to know them, but then that's the Army for you— they never tell ya nuthin'!

FRED: It turns out the General Orders all pertained to the way in which you were supposed to conduct yourself on guard duty. For example, report any violations of orders, pass on any instructions to your relief man, sound an alarm when necessary, etc. And the reason why you had to know them was because any time you were on guard duty, you first had to stand inspection, also known as the mounting of the guard, or "Guard Mount."

STEVE: During Guard Mount, the Sergeant of the Guard (or often the Officer of the Day) would examine your uniform, weapon and personal grooming. Then he might ask you to recite a couple General Orders.

Flunking any such tests might earn you a bit of disciplinary action such as "Go clean that weapon and report back to me!"

FRED: But there was also an incentive to pass them, since the one or two individuals who achieved the highest "scores" would be named as Supernumeraries (which basically means an "extra.") They'd be excused from having to walk (or stand) guard at a post. Instead they would get the night off but had to remain available in case someone got sick or injured— or if something should happen that required the services of an "extra" guard.

STEVE: It so happened that I was pretty good at reeling off my General Orders when asked. That's because I memorized them the same way I used to study for tests in high school: I'd create a code that was easy to remember. Then as long as I remembered the code, I could reconstruct the eleven orders in my mind. For example, my code for the first six was "Take, walk, report, repeat, quit, receive" and for the remaining five it was "Talk, give, call, salute, be."

FRED: Once again, ya just had to figure out a way to beat the fuggin' system, didn't ya?

STEVE: Natch! So when the Officer of the Day asked "What's your Fifth General Order, soldier?" I would say "Sir, my Fifth General Order is..." and while I was saying that, my brain would be reciting the list: ("Take, walk, report, repeat, quit— Number Five is QUIT!") So I would finish the sentence with "to quit my post only when properly relieved!" Then he might say "What's your Tenth General Order?" and I would reply with "Sir! My Tenth General Order is... (Ah, Number Ten is SALUTE!)... to salute all officers and all colors not cased!"

FRED: And he would say "Very good, Donovan!" So if your boots were shined and your uniform and weapon were up to snuff, he might pick you as a Supernumerary... and you'd get the night off!

STEVE: I might— and on this particular night, I did. I was sacked out in the Guard Tent and everything was going great for the first five hours. No mosquitoes... no having to smear myself with insect repellent... no having to keep my eyes peeled for Charlie... nobody waking me up every three hours. Then shortly before 11 pm, a call comes in to HQ from the MP's in Bien Hoa, about five miles west of Long Binh. PFC Firenza had been arrested for violating the nightly curfew, getting in a drunken brawl and pulling a knife on somebody.

It wasn't clear whether he'd actually stabbed or cut anyone with it, but since he already had a reputation for that type of behavior, it was indeed a serious matter.

FRED: Firenza was a mild-mannered, happy-go-lucky soul when he was sober— but when he got drunk (which was often) he could turn into a raging animal. And do a lot of damage because he was not only a large burly fellow, but he also liked to pack a blade that he didn't hesitate to reach for whenever somebody pissed him off. He had already gotten into trouble a few times for getting involved in drunken brawls, which may explain why he decided to do his drinking in Bien Hoa instead of in our hospital compound.

STEVE: For security reasons, it was unusual for anyone to leave our compound after dark or go driving on the surrounding roads at night. We were in a relatively secure area in the daytime, but at night it was anybody's guess as to who or what might be found out there. Nobody wanted to push their luck if they didn't have to.

FRED: At times the main highway was patrolled by helicopters operating under the assumption that anything moving on that road after dark was probably up to no good. In fact, one of the Red Cross girls said she hitched a ride from Saigon to Long Binh in a jeep that got stopped by a Huey using its powerful searchlight to blind the driver. So there was reason to fear not only the VC, but "friendly fire" from the Americans as well.

STEVE: In fact when we first arrived in Bien Hoa, some of us were told "Never go to Bien Hoa alone, or at night. We may own it in the daytime, but Charlie owns it after dark." Whether those warnings were just wild rumors or based on actual fact, we had no way of knowing— just like most of the other stuff we would hear.

FRED: But since Bien Hoa had a 9 pm curfew for American military personnel anyway, most of us had enough sense to make sure we were home before dark.

STEVE: Nevertheless, when the call came in from the MP's, whoever was the AOD (Administrative Officer of the Day) that night decided that rather than leave Firenza to stew in the drunk tank in Bien Hoa overnight, we should immediately send someone to retrieve him. What the heck, it was only six miles away, right?

FRED: That might have been just a foolish mistake by an inexperienced officer, or perhaps our CO didn't want to have to file a Morning Report stating that one of his men was missing because the MP's had him in the Bien Hoa jail. Or there could have been other issues at play that we knew nothing about.

STEVE: So some time after 11 pm, the Sergeant of the Guard, SGT Hamlin, was instructed to take a vehicle with an armed guard, drive to Bien Hoa and spring Firenza out of the drunk tank. For his armed guard he would take the Supernumerary— me. Yessir, my ability to faithfully recite my General Orders had earned me a free trip to Bien Hoa in a lone vehicle— on a pitch dark, moonless night. Whoopee!

FRED: So then you had like five minutes to grab your weapon and don your steel helmet, flak jacket, pistol belt, ammo pouches, insect repellent, flashlight, first aid pack, etc. What type of vehicle were you gonna take on this excursion?

STEVE: At that hour we had our pick of any vehicle in the Motor Pool. But Hamlin made a wise decision there. On a pitch dark night, any Army jeep or truck would still be recognizable by its sound as well as its silhouette against the night sky. But we had exactly one rig at our disposal that didn't fit that category. Yessir, we were about to make "Hamlin's Run" through Injun Country in our own nondescript "stealth" vehicle!

FRED: Too bad Robert Mitchum hadn't shown up at our hospital yet— we could have sent him! But anyway, Hamlin was looking for something fast, quiet, nimble— and not recognizable as a US Army vehicle in the dark. That would have to be... the Carryall!

STEVE: Precisely. This was a 6-cylinder Ford Econoline passenger van. It was painted dark green, which was as good as black on a dark night. The US Army lettering on the sides was black instead of white; it could do 75 with a tailwind; and compared to a typical truck or jeep, it was quiet as a mouse. Stealth, baby!

FRED: Hamlin was a burly black sergeant in his early 30's, kind of a no-nonsense type who rarely said much. Everyone respected him as a very level-headed guy— and Steve certainly wasn't in any position to question his judgement on this particular night.

STEVE: None whatsoever. In fact, he was in the 25-man Advance

Party that arrived three weeks ahead of the rest of us— and for some odd reason we looked up to those guys like they were experienced veterans compared to us! Anyway, we pulled out onto the highway after convincing the Long Binh gate guard it was OK to let us out. We went a half mile north on the main highway... and then turned west on Route 15 toward Bien Hoa.

FRED: Now it gets interesting— 15 was a narrow, winding two-lane road with a blind curve or blind hill about every 100 yards or so. It was completely deserted at night, but you never knew what you might find around that next bend! On the other hand, if Charlie was out there, he'd have virtually no advance warning that you were coming.

STEVE: I was sure counting on it! On that night I think the terrain favored us, rather than any VC who might be lying in wait. As soon as we turned off the main highway, Hamlin switched off the headlights so we'd be driving totally blacked out. Each time we rounded a curve or came over the crest of a hill, he would flip the headlights on for just a second or two to make sure there wasn't a water buffalo— or a platoon of VC— standing in the middle of the road. Mind you, we basically hadn't said a word to each other since we left the compound. He was making all the decisions but I was in total compliance, so no problem there. I would guess neither one of us wanted to let on that we were scared, so we both clammed up and concentrated on the task at hand.

FRED: How fast do you think you were going on that winding road?

STEVE: That was another interesting part. He had apparently decided he'd go like a bat out of hell wherever possible. This meant he'd frequently have to go clear across the center line on blind curves to maintain his velocity. Not a problem, as long as there wasn't another crazed driver coming toward us in blackout mode as well! As it turned out, during the entire 12-mile round trip we never saw a single vehicle. People, yes— vehicles, no.

FRED: Of course driving at that speed would increase the risk of leaving the road and winding up in a field or rice paddy somewhere. Had you considered that?

STEVE: Somewhat, but I still would have done everything the same way Hamlin did. If Charlie was out there somewhere, we'd be on him and gone while he was still trying to figure out whether we were friend or foe! It was roughly the same strategy the Dustoff pilots would often use to avoid detection by the enemy— come in low and fast, before Charlie could figure out what was happening. Little did I know then that as we were approaching the next blind hill, we'd soon have an opportunity to test that theory.

FRED: You ran into some VC?

STEVE: Actually we had no idea who they were. We go flying over this little hill and as soon as we level out, Hamlin hits the light switch for a second. To our great surprise, we're hurtling right between two columns of armed Vietnamese patrolling the road and coming in the opposite direction— one column on each shoulder. I think they were temporarily blinded when Hamlin suddenly hit the high beams. They sort of froze in their tracks, waiting til their night vision would return.

FRED: What happened then?

STEVE: In a matter of 4 or 5 seconds, we were past them and gone. It was obvious they had no idea who we were, just as we had no idea who they were. But we were definitely outgunned! There were maybe 30 of 'em total— a platoon size group. They were wearing khaki style uniforms with tan pith helmets— and they carried what could have been Russian or Chinese AK-47 automatic weapons. But it happened so fast I couldn't be sure about that.

FRED: Did you say anything to Hamlin at that point?

STEVE: I think I said something in a jovial tone like "Whoa, what the hell was that???" (chuckle, chuckle.) Hamlin says "I dunno man, and I don't wanna find out neither!" Thirty minutes later we've sprung Firenza from the MP station in Bien Hoa and we start heading back to Long Binh. At that point I was ostensibly holding him under armed guard, but I'm thinking "If we get in a shootout on the way back, we give Firenza a weapon— drunk or not!"

FRED: Of course you must have been hoping they'd be gone by the time you were coming back, and surely they would never have been expecting you to be on a two-way round trip at midnight anyway.

STEVE: True. We were always told Charlie did most of his moving and fighting at night so he couldn't be detected by American aircraft. I was just hoping the "mystery platoon" wouldn't be taking their midnight rice break in the middle of the road when we came roaring around the bend from the opposite direction!

FRED: My guess would have been that those guys in the khaki uniforms were most likely a local militia force— friendlies— out checking for possible saboteurs or mines planted in the road.

STEVE: That's pretty much what I thought too. But since then I've read that some NVA regiments indeed wore... tan khakis and tan pith helmets! I've even seen photos of them in such attire. I've also learned that from time to time, our hospital brass were warned that "there might be an NVA battalion operating in the Long Binh/Bien Hoa area." So I really have no idea if those guys patrolling the road that night were friendlies or maybe not-so-friendlies.

FRED: I always assumed the road from Long Binh to Bien Hoa was pretty safe, day or night.

STEVE: Me too. But I've talked to a fellow who drove a 5-ton truck for the 539th Transportation Company at roughly the same time we were there. He said their convoys would go through Bien Hoa in the middle of the night driving total blackout, bumper-to-bumper, and they were always on their toes because the roads around that area could be very dangerous at night. In fact, after reading what the Red Cross girl said about being tracked by an Army gunship, I realized SGT Hamlin and I could have been in just as much danger from our own forces as we were from Victor Charlie.

FRED: A lot of US casualties in Nam were caused by "friendly fire," since it was so difficult to tell friend from foe regardless of where you happened to be. "Friendly" indeed!

STEVE: So then once we're safely inside the gates of the 24th Evac and can heave a big sigh of relief, they tell me that since we don't have a lockup of any kind, I'm on round-the-clock armed guard of Firenza for the next 24 hours. Three hours on, three off, three on, three off.

FRED: And so once again, you were being rewarded for your uncanny ability to be named Supernumerary!

STEVE: Yeah, it was weird following a fellow G.I. around all day with a loaded weapon. Since he outweighed me by 100 pounds and there was no way I was planning to shoot him, I'm sure he could have taken it away from me any time he wanted to. But we were "casual" friends, so as long as he was sober he didn't pose any threat to me.

FRED: What finally happened to him?

STEVE: I believe he got in another drunken brawl a few weeks later, pulled a knife, got arrested by the MP's and was court martialed. After that we never saw him again, but SP5 Riching had to testify at his trial in Bien Hoa. I think Firenza got something like 90 days in the stockade plus loss of pay, then he was drummed out of the service as an undesirable. Which begs the question: Why bother to put him in the stockade at taxpayer's expense if they were planning to give him an undesirable discharge anyway?

FRED: My guess would be that the Army didn't want to be sending out the wrong signals to the rest of the troops.

STEVE: You mean signals like "Hey soldier, wanna get out of Nam quick? All ya gotta do is get drunk and stab somebody a few times, then it's back to civilian life for you..."?

FRED: Shoot! If only we had known that at the time!

&&&&&&&&&&&&&&&&&&&&

FACT OR FICTION? *The story goes that Colonel Dickerson would leave on Friday afternoons to weekend at his fancy villa in the beach resort town of Vung Tau, about 90 miles south of Long Binh. Approaching Vung Tau in the Carry-All van one Friday, he saw two peasants eating grass by the side of the road. Puzzled, the Colonel stopped and asked for an explanation. "We have no money for food," answered one, "so we have to eat grass." Dickerson says "Well then, come with me to my villa and we'll feed you." The native says "But we have our wives and three children with us." The Colonel replies "No problem, the more the merrier," whereupon everyone piles into the van. As they resume their journey, one of the peasants says "This is very kind of you, sir. We've always heard that the Americans were very generous." Dickerson says "Glad to do it. You'll love my villa— the grass is at least eight inches high!"*

CHAPTER 15

OK PRIVATE, TELL US HOW YOU MANAGED TO LET A KILLER ESCAPE

Better bring plenty of smokes... some of those guys might be accused of murder!

FRED: When you sprung Private Firenza out of the Bien Hoa drunk tank while you were on guard duty, was that the only time you ever had to hold an American prisoner under armed guard?

STEVE: Actually it was not. A couple times I got stuck on daytime guard duty during the period when we used to get prisoner details from the stockade down the road— the Long Binh Jail, or LBJ.

FRED: Its official name was the Long Binh Stockade, but everyone called it the LBJ (a play on the initials of President Lyndon Baines Johnson.) The stockade was across the road and roughly 150 yards south of our compound.

STEVE: It wasn't there the first day we arrived at Long Binh, since there was practically nothing there at all before we showed up. But it soon appeared "out of thin air," so to speak, complete with guard towers, double rows of 18-foot-high chain link fence topped with razor wire, and armed MP's manning the towers to make sure nobody escaped. A rather imposing, grim looking place.

FRED: The LBJ wasn't a POW camp. It was the main incarceration facility for all US Army personnel in Vietnam who were convicted of— or awaiting trial for— serious crimes or violations of the Uniform Code of Military Justice.

STEVE: The inmates ranged from GI's who'd gone AWOL to shack up for a few months with some bargirl or mama-san... to fellows who had deserted to avoid combat... to guys who had attempted to kill their commanding officer or senior NCO.

FRED: Since the stockade was practically across the road from us and our hospital was in the construction phase, the inmates were a convenient source of free labor that we could use for filling sandbags, digging trenches, building bunkers and so on. The only hitch was that while the LBJ was willing to send us all the prisoner work details we wanted, they weren't able to provide any security for them.

STEVE: This meant that for each work detail comprised of six or maybe eight inmates, we had to provide an armed guard to watch their every move for an entire day. So wouldn't ya know, my name pops up on the duty roster for day guard— and I get assigned to chaperone a prisoner work detail with my trusty M-14 rifle.

FRED: Like most of the other assignments we were given, nobody spent even five minutes explaining what the guards were supposed to do and how they were supposed to do it. Probably because no one in our hospital would have had the faintest idea what to tell us. Guarding prisoner work details was not something with which any of our personnel had even the slightest bit of experience.

STEVE: I tracked down a couple guys who'd already done the prisoner guard thing and asked for any tips they could give me. Their best advice was "Take a couple packs of smokes and some matches with you cuz they'll ask you for a cigarette every time there's a water break. And take several packs of chewing gum too. Don't try to be a hard-ass, just be their friend and they won't give you any trouble."

FRED: Sounds pretty simple. What could possibly go wrong?

STEVE: Good question. So the next morning I grab my rifle, canteen and ammo belt and hop on the truck to go over to the LBJ. I get assigned a detail of six or eight inmates and promptly march 'em back to the 24th Evac with my loaded weapon at the ready.

FRED: And thus for the second time in your brief military career, you found yourself playing the role of an MP— just like you did at the Fort Sam Motor Pool back in Texas!

STEVE: Except this time I had no armband, no purple helmet, no billy club and no whistle. (And as it would later turn out, we probably could have used some whistles!) But maybe it was just as well, since those inmates might have tried to take me out if they thought I was an honest-to-goodness Military Policeman.

FRED: Were these inmates wearing some sort of prison garb?

STEVE: Well they weren't wearing any prison stripes, if that's what you mean. I think they wore plain Army fatigues with no insignia or rank of any kind and a big "P" on the backs of their shirts for identification, although I wouldn't swear to it. This would become important once we went into the Mess Hall for chow.

FRED: Did you have any clue about what sorts of crimes or violations these guys were doing time for?

STEVE: Well I knew there were inmates at the LBJ who had supposedly committed murder or attempted murder, but I never dreamed the Army would let 'em outside the stockade on a work detail— let alone one guarded by some wimp medic who'd never guarded anyone or fired a weapon, other than on the rifle range.

FRED: But then at some point you found out otherwise?

STEVE: Yeah, at first I figured the guys on my detail might be guilty of disobeying an order, being a deserter, going AWOL, getting drunk and starting a fight, maybe threatening a superior... or getting high or drunk on duty. In other words, they'd be soldiers who were guilty of "victimless crimes" for the most part.

FRED: And the difference between going AWOL (Absent Without Leave) and being a deserter was that if you didn't show up for duty and nobody knew where you were, you were AWOL. But if you were AWOL for more than a specified period of time— I think it was 30 days or something like that— then you'd be declared a deserter.

STEVE: Being AWOL was a fairly minor offense where you might spend some time in the stockade before returning to your unit. But being a deserter in wartime was a major, big-time, court-martial type offense for which one could theoretically face a firing squad.

FRED: Although I'm pretty sure no one did in Nam, since ours was officially an undeclared war— a little technicality that probably saved more than a few deserters from having to stare down the barrels of a half dozen M-14's. I think the last guy to actually be executed for desertion was the highly publicized Private Slovik in World War II.

STEVE: I believe what determined whether a soldier was a deserter or just AWOL was intent. If his intent was to remain permanently absent from the military, he'd be declared a deserter. And the 30-day period was often considered sufficient evidence of his intent not to return. But oddly enough, if he retained any of his equipment or clothing— like a bayonet or entrenching tool, for example— then he'd be charged with being AWOL on the assumption that he was actually planning to return, otherwise why would he have kept the goods?

FRED: Civilians might wonder why any soldier would want to go AWOL in Vietnam. But by 1968, there were supposedly hundreds of American military deserters living "underground" in Saigon, as well as some living in Bien Hoa. Usually they were either shacking up with a bargirl, routinely engaged in alcoholic binges or else hooked on drugs.

STEVE: Anything to escape the jungles, rice paddies and rigors of combat! John Steinbeck IV, son of the famous author by the same name, was a newscaster on Armed Forces Radio & TV while we were there. He stayed in Nam for a couple of tours, lured by the Asian mystique, the ambience and perhaps the prevalence of good drugs and the "party" lifestyle in Saigon, tawdry though it was.

FRED: In his book he wrote that Americans walking around Saigon in civvies were constantly being checked by American MP's looking for AWOLs and deserters. It seemed there were quite a few GI's who found an alternative lifestyle in the "Pearl of the Orient" to be preferable to "humping the boonies" wearing an 80-pound pack. But you found out some of the prisoners on your detail were doing time for more serious offenses than just being AWOL?

STEVE: Eventually, yes. As soon as my detail got back to the 24th, we were assigned to a trench where they'd be digging up dirt and filling sandbags all day long. Even though these inmates were in my custody so to speak, I don't believe I ever saw a roster of their names. So if someone were to escape, I wouldn't even have been able to report who was missing. I told them I had smokes and gum and they could light up during the hourly water breaks. I pointed out the location of the latrine and said they'd have to ask for permission first and then go in there one at a time.

FRED: So you'd have to watch both the trench and the latrine.

STEVE: True, but I figured if someone was determined to escape, it would have been pretty damned easy to do, so I wasn't going to worry too much about it. And I sure as hell wasn't gonna shoot any of 'em if they did. But up to that point I thought these particular inmates were all doing time for minor offenses, so the idea of anyone escaping barely crossed my mind.

FRED: And no one told you when or if you were ever supposed to shoot an escaping prisoner. So when did you find out that some of their offenses weren't so minor?

STEVE: One of 'em volunteered that he was in the pokey for repeatedly being drunk on duty. I asked about the others and he said "That one over there is in for killing his company commander at his base camp. This one over here's accused of attempting to murder his platoon sergeant out in the field."

FRED: Did you believe him, or was he just blowing smoke?

STEVE: I had no way of knowing if he was telling me the truth, but he seemed completely sincere so I had no reason to doubt him.

FRED: If you'd been given any instructions on how to guard a prisoner detail, you probably would have been told not to talk to the inmates except when it was absolutely necessary. So could you believe it when you found out there were guys in your group who were crazy enough to kill, or attempt to kill, their superiors?

STEVE: Well of course I was horrified to hear it at the time, especially since I hadn't been told I was gonna be guarding any murder suspects. But later I found out some infantry units had an unwritten code that said that if an officer or platoon sergeant was so incompetent or foolhardy as to constantly be exposing his men to unnecessary risks or getting them killed, some of the troops might feel there was justification for getting rid of him by whatever means necessary.

FRED: As grotesque as that sounds, I suppose I could have seen where there might be extreme cases in which some troops, already accustomed to seeing death all around them, might see a "snuff job" as a viable option. To us it would have sounded downright barbarian, but then again we weren't used to seeing guys get gunned down or blown up as a part of everyday life... whereas they were.

STEVE: There were also unconfirmed cases of an NCO taking out one of his troopers, too. One soldier wrote that when he arrived at his new infantry unit, his platoon sergeant said "If you guys wanna smoke a little dope here in base camp, that's your business. But any man caught doing drugs when we're out in the boonies… WILL NOT be returning." How serious he was is anybody's guess, but a trooper doing dope out in the jungle was putting the lives of his fellow soldiers at risk. In combat conditions it would have been pretty easy to rub out someone like that with a little bit of "friendly fire."

FRED: And of course the preferred method usually would have been "fragging," where a fragmentation grenade would be tossed into the hooch, bunker or foxhole of the individual being targeted. That way there'd be no ballistic evidence or fingerprints at the crime scene like there would have been in the movie "Platoon" where Sergeant Barnes, played by Tom Berenger, deliberately gunned down Sergeant Elias, played by Willem Dafoe, with a single rifle shot.

STEVE: Friendly fire (or fragging) deaths were often reported to the families of the deceased as KIA's (Killed in Action) in which the fatal injuries were incurred in the line of duty. Obviously no one wanted to have to tell the surviving family members that their loved one was killed by a fellow soldier.

FRED: So anyway, it was possible that some of the prisoners on your detail might have been facing charges of murder or attempted murder. Why do you say you could have used a whistle?

STEVE: Well, everything went pretty smoothly until it came time for noon chow. I was gonna have to march my six prisoners (I'm guessing six was the number) into a crowded hospital Mess Hall where there were probably well over a hundred folks eating lunch.

FRED: And there was nobody to assist you or tell you how to maintain control of those men— you'd have to wing it! Plus once you got inside, they'd be operating on the honor system.

STEVE: For sure. I had my detail stop at the latrine to give 'em a chance to wash up a bit at the basins outside. I told them if we got separated, we'd rendezvous at the latrine in 30 minutes. We went into the Mess Hall and I staked out a table where I told them to bring their trays so they'd all be sitting together. From that point on, they were pretty much on the honor system since I couldn't very well go chasing someone through the Mess Hall with a loaded weapon.

FRED: There was no one to help you guard those guys because in a hospital setting, everyone else is normally unarmed.

STEVE: I think I got a certain amount of cooperation from a couple of the other prisoner guards so that we could keep all the guys with "P" on their backs in one area.

FRED: Did your prisoners cooperate and follow your instructions?

STEVE: It seemed to me that they were. I figured the reason they didn't try any shenanigans was because they didn't want to be excluded from future work details. After all, it was their only chance to break the monotony of sitting in a prison camp all day. But I also realized that if anyone was determined to escape— like one of the murder suspects— this would be their golden opportunity.

FRED: And did someone try to escape?

STEVE: Well, as we finished eating they'd get up, one or two at a time, and take their trays back with the understanding that we would all meet up again at 1300 hours. I went to the designated spot to wait with part of my crew. Soon there were four of them there— and as we waited for numbers five and six, one of the other guards comes by and says "One of the prisoners just beat it out the back door of the Mess Hall and got outside the wire!"

FRED: Oops! Did you suddenly start thinking you might have to surrender yourself to the Long Binh Jail so you could serve out the remaining time of your escaped prisoner?

STEVE: Something like that. My first thought was "Sonofabitch! There's an escapee, and my two murderers are missing! What could I have done wrong? What was I supposed to do that I failed to do? Whose responsibility is it to go and chase down these two fugitives now? How am I gonna explain what happened? At the very least, I'm gonna look like an incompetent stooge! Why me???"

FRED: And your buddies would forever be saying "Hey Donovan, tell us again about how you managed to let two murderers escape— after you tell us again about how you failed to score in Okinawa!" As for your prisoner, I can understand how he could walk out the back door of the Mess Hall, but what would he do then? Our compound was completely surrounded by concertina wire to keep Charlie out. I'd think it would be just as effective at keeping fugitives in.

STEVE: Apparently he had turned his fatigue shirt inside out so there was no longer a big "P" on his back. When he got outside, he grabbed a stepladder to help him negotiate the concertina. When he got to the wire he either found an opening left by the construction workers or else he found a way to go over or under it with the ladder.

FRED: Where would he go once he got outside the wire?

STEVE: Probably hitchhiked or went cross country til he reached Bien Hoa, about six miles away. That's where the MP's picked him up a few days later.

FRED: So did he turn out to be one of the prisoners you were supposed to be guarding?

STEVE: Well, as I was standing there— along with inmates number one through four— and nervously contemplating all the hot water I might be in, my two killers suddenly showed up, ready to start filling more sandbags. Hallelujah! The escapee was not from my crew! He was gonna be somebody else's problem— not mine. And I wasn't gonna need a whistle or a billy club after all!

FRED: Sounds to me like you beat the fuggin' system again. After that your buddies should have been saying "Hey Donovan... tell us once more about how damned lucky you were!" Kind of like when you just missed hosing the First Shirt back in the Mess Hall at Fort Sam.

&&&&&&&&&&&&&&&&&&&

FACT OR FICTION?   The story goes that one afternoon, Chaplain Dunleavy asked PFC Hensen for a ride over to the LBJ (the Long Binh Jail, known officially as the Long Binh Stockade) so he could visit with one of the prisoners. As they approached the LBJ, they realized there was an attempted prison break in progress. Hensen hollers "Holy cow, look at that midget climbing down the outside fence of the stockade!" After pausing briefly to collect his thoughts, the chaplain replies "Private, don't you think that's just a little con descending?"

CHAPTER 16

YA GOTTA RELEASE SOME OF THAT SEXUAL TENSION, SON!
In Nam there were about five ways to do it... not counting bestiality or necrophilia

FRED: Every man in our outfit was presumed to have the natural proclivities of a normal 20-year-old male heterosexual, even though we rarely discussed it. And despite sex being a somewhat taboo subject, the Army knew full well— as did most of those in uniform— that in wartime, some sort of provision had to be made for satisfying the sexual appetites of the troops. Once we got to Nam, we learned there were about five possible ways that could be achieved.

STEVE: Well, one of 'em surely had to involve... hookers! Going back as far as the Civil War, the US military seems to have had a long history of sanctioning or facilitating access to prostitutes for its soldiers. In fact the term "hooker" has supposedly been traced to Union General "Fighting Joe" Hooker, who was alleged to have routinely surrounded himself and his troops with ladies of the evening in a "party-type" atmosphere. In the 150 years since, many military leaders have drawn a direct connection between a soldier's access to sexual gratification and his performance in combat.

FRED: To wit: During World War II, General George Patton is famously quoted as having summed up this belief by saying "When the men don't screw, they don't fight!"

STEVE: But when it came to matters of sexual gratification, the Army had bigger problems than simply worrying about whether its troops were getting their libidos satisfied. In Vietnam, as in other wars, its chief concerns were that GI's might contract STD's from prostitutes or that some might turn to homosexuality if they were denied access to any females of the species.

FRED: So from the military's point of view, doing whatever was necessary to make hookers available seemed like the best solution to a sticky problem. Apparently there was a regulation somewhere on the books prohibiting the solicitation of prostitutes, but most of the brass were willing to ignore it by simply looking the other way. The chief objective was to try to make sure the troops had a safe, acceptable outlet for their natural sexual urges.

STEVE: Officially we weren't given any indoctrination on how to deal with sexual matters when we arrived in Nam. It was as if sex simply didn't exist. The only "off the record" advice given to us by our superiors was that if we chose to engage in such activities, we should be sure to take the necessary precautions and patronize only "approved" facilities. These were regularly checked by US medical personnel for any potential threats of VD.

FRED: I think they handed out free condoms or made 'em available at very low cost. We were also told we could get a shot of penicillin any time we might think we needed one. (A benefit that was not available to troops out in the field, but we were a hospital, after all!) As a precaution, some guys even tried to get the shot before they engaged in any sexual activity— but that was highly frowned upon.

STEVE: In cities like Bien Hoa and Saigon, there were a variety of establishments ranging from steam baths and massage parlors to brothels where soldiers could go to relieve those sexual tensions with the assistance of a young woman. Supposedly massage parlors were legal in the eyes of the South Vietnamese government while brothels were not— but again, everyone seemed to look the other way, as brothels operated openly. GI's often called them bordellos, whorehouses or "boom-boom" rooms, but most of us referred to them as cathouses, as I recall.

FRED: A bit more tasteful, no doubt! In our case, a group of four to six guys would often go to Bien Hoa on a Saturday or Sunday to shop at the PX, visit a saloon, see a movie or just relieve some of the monotony of our daily existence. Usually a couple of 'em would want to stop at a cathouse, so the rest of us would either wait in a bar or else wait at the establishment.

STEVE: I remember standing out on the second-floor veranda of this cathouse, leaning on the railing as I waited for a couple buddies who were busy inside. I was approached by a young girl who looked no more than 16, although it was hard to tell her age. She was very soft-spoken and polite as she asked if I wanted some boom-boom. She seemed downright shy, to tell you the truth, and it kind of felt like you were talking to someone's kid sister.

FRED: And you told her you didn't have any money, just like you had said in Okinawa?

STEVE: Correct. Having sex with a stranger for money never had much appeal to me, not so much for moral or religious reasons but simply because to me that was not intimacy. I never condemned anyone else for getting a little boom-boom, and I knew sooner or later I might give in to the temptation myself. But I fully expected it to be a big disappointment compared to genuine intimacy between consenting adults. Later I would find out that some of our guys had tried it once and found it so unfulfilling that they never went back.

FRED: Well, didn't you ever have any one-night stands in your late teens or early 20's? What would be the difference?

STEVE: Yes I did, but it was always a case of two people having consensual sex because they both wanted to— not because one of 'em wanted to be paid and the other was willing to pay.

FRED: Some guys had a "kid in a candy store" mentality. Once they discovered they could have sex with young women whenever they wanted— for three bucks a crack— they'd go to town at every opportunity. Often this meant spending nearly their entire monthly paycheck in the pursuit of "drinking and whoring." Some went all the time, some would go occasionally and some did it only once and never let on to anyone that they had ever tried it at all. And of course many of us simply abstained.

STEVE: But there were a few who managed to find a "girlfriend" with whom they could regularly shack up overnight, usually in exchange for paying a portion of her monthly rent. The main thing they had to worry about (besides VD) was possibly being caught in town after curfew by the MP's— or being reported as AWOL.

FRED: Those risks weren't so great at the 24th Evac. We never had bed checks and some guys always worked nights anyway, so it would have been nearly impossible to figure out which of the bunks were supposed to be occupied at any given point in time.

STEVE: Most of the "girlfriends" were bargirls who hustled drinks and turned tricks for a living, then went home to their apartments late at night to be with their temporary American "husbands." One such husband at the 24th Evac was PFC Ray Parilla, a quiet but very independent fellow who kept a low profile and was hardly ever seen during off-duty hours, but nobody really knew why.

FRED: Ray was a rugged looking dude and pretty much a loner as far as we could tell. But if he never told anyone that he had his own personal squeeze, how did you find out?

STEVE: One afternoon they needed a translator in the Emergency Room and the regular interpreter had gone home for the day. As we searched the grounds for someone who might be up to the task, Ray Parilla stepped forward and said "I can talk Dink."

FRED: Now "dink" and "gook" were slang terms used by some GI's to refer to Vietnamese civilians or enemy combatants. While both sounded highly derogatory, they were often used with little or no malice intended. It was more like "What are we supposed to call these people? Oh, dinks or gooks? OK." The point was that there had to be a short, universally understood term that could be used in an emergency— such as when someone might have to yell "Gooks in the wire!" meaning that Charlie was trying to breach the perimeter defenses.

STEVE: Personally I always called them Vietnamese or civilians or natives, especially after I became Civilian Personnel Specialist and began working with them every day. To me, dink or gook sounded too much like the N-word, which neither we nor our group of friends ever used either. As for enemy soldiers— of which some were patients in our hospital— I always referred to them as Charlie, Cong or VC, even though some were actually NVA (North Vietnamese Army.)

FRED: I imagine that if we had been in the infantry, we probably would have said dink or gook just like our fellow grunts. But in a hospital we could afford to be more respectful. So anyway, how was it possible that Ray Parilla— just a medic like the rest of us— could speak Vietnamese?

STEVE: I was dying to find out, so I asked him at the first opportunity. Ray said he "picked up the language" from talking to sandbaggers (most of whom were female) as he worked with 'em in the
trenches. That sounded damn near impossible to me, so I pressed
him some more. He said he became friends with some of 'em and
visited them in Bien Hoa, where one of the "friends" got him a Vietnamese dictionary and helped teach him to "speak Dink."

FRED: But weren't the sandbaggers pretty much just uneducated
peasants who couldn't even read or write? What possible use would
they have for a dictionary?

STEVE: My thoughts exactly. I was inclined to think his "friend"
in Bien Hoa was most likely a lady friend who had probably never
touched a sandbag in her life. Then I found out Ray was regularly
catching a ride to Long Binh on the truck that picked up the Mess Hall
workers every morning at 5:30 am in Bien Hoa, where he had obviously been spending the night.

FRED: Which meant that by hiding inside the mama-san truck, he
could smuggle himself into Long Binh Post every morning without
arousing any suspicions. So just about every afternoon or evening,
he'd walk out the front gate and catch a Lambretta to Bien Hoa.
Anybody who cared— and it was doubtful that anyone did— would
assume he was planning to be back before sundown. But instead
he'd be playing house with his make-believe "wife" for the night,
making sure he was off the streets of Bien Hoa before curfew.

STEVE: Clever indeed! And since he was strictly a loner anyway,
no one even noticed that he wasn't around at night. I suppose for
him, the lure could have been sex or romance or binge drinking or
even drugs— or perhaps some combination of those factors.

FRED: Or maybe he was into Russian Roulette, kind of like one
Corporal Nick Chevotarevich— the character played by Christopher
Walken in the movie "Deer Hunter."

STEVE: Maybe so, although Ray Parilla would probably have preferred the cockfighting! In any event, if his lady friend was not one
of our Mess Hall workers or hooch maids, she was most likely a
bargirl whom he first met by offering to pay her for a "short time."

FRED: Speaking of bargirls, I'm reminded of a story about where they allegedly came from. This Vietnamese fellow who worked as a translator for the Americans claimed that in the rural areas, young women had to have a photo ID card in order to become employed. To obtain one, the pretty ones would have to bribe the local police by providing them with sexual favors. When a girl's family found out this had happened, they'd be so ashamed that they would banish her to the city, where hustling GI's in the bars was about the only type of job she was likely to find.

STEVE: Interesting theory. Speaking of sexual favors, the two principle religions in Nam were Buddhism and Catholicism. Supposedly the Buddhist bargirls would only perform a certain type of sex act while the Catholic bargirls would do anything but. Sort of the opposite of what guys thought about Catholic girls back in high school! What's ironic about it is that many Vietnamese families practiced dual religions— they were both Catholic and Buddhist at the same time. Seemingly a contradiction to us, but not to them.

FRED: And a situation that could have prompted soldiers to say "Wait a minute, I thought you said you're Catholic!" Bargirl: "I am, but that's OK, G.I.— I am Buddhist too!" As for steam baths, some were located just outside— or just inside— certain American base camps. And in several remote areas, the US Army sanctioned the construction and operation of "brothel compounds" just outside of large bases. As an experiment, four of them were built in 1966 at Pleiku, An Khe, Lai Khe and Ban Me Thuot— each supposedly under the operational control of an American commander.

STEVE: They were given nicknames like Sin City, Disneyland and Dodge City and were officially operated by Vietnamese entrepreneurs. The Americans, however, provided armed security as well as regular medical checkups and security clearances for the female employees. All involvement by the US military was allegedly kept "off the books" so it could later be denied if necessary.

FRED: I guess these boom-boom complexes were pretty popular, with some averaging 150-200 troops visiting per day. Typically they had a number of bars or "clubs" on the premises, a bandstand for parties, and of course a large number of cubicles or rooms in which the women could ply their trade.

STEVE: Sounds like they were following the same blueprint as what we saw in Okinawa— home of the famous Hobbo-Rite!

FRED: But then the story gets more interesting. It seems that a giant monkey wrench was thrown into the works when a young GI innocently wrote a letter to his mother describing "Sin City" and what exactly went on there. She was so outraged that she wrote her congressman to complain. Before long, Senator William Fulbright was said to have publicly accused the American military— on the floor of the US Senate— of turning Vietnam into a giant brothel. According to the tale, by the end of '68 all four complexes had been shut down due to the political pressure from back home.

STEVE: Which of course meant a whole lotta GI's would be forced to seek out less safe, more risky alternatives.

FRED: Or maybe they would just choose to become celibate?

STEVE: Sure thing, why not? Meanwhile, for the GI's in Long Binh there were different "degrees" of participation. In small villages like Tam Hiep you had little roadside businesses called "car washes" or "truck washes" that you'd drive past and see two or three Army vehicles parked outside. A handful of 12-year-old kids armed with a hose would be washing one of the trucks, but no GI's were to be seen. They must have been inside, but what were they doing?

FRED: Drinking and whoring, that's what! I found out one day when PFC Harkin and I were riding in a jeep from Bien Hoa to Long Binh with SP4 Fiedler behind the wheel. As we're passing through Tam Hiep, Fiedler says "Who wants to stop for a carwash?" Nobody responded, but since he was driving we pulled into a space in the gravel parking lot under a large sign that said "car wash." Out front there was a little open-air lunch counter where you could buy beer, sodas and snacks like beef jerky. Harkin and I sat down on bar stools while Fiedler went inside through the curtains that covered the doorway. We ordered a couple ice-cold Cokes and papa-san said they'd be 75 pee (around 60 cents) each, which we paid.

STEVE: And then a couple more soldiers showed up?

FRED: They pulled in, got out of their vehicle and sat down at the other end of the bar. They ordered two Cokes and as I was talking to Harkin, I could overhear these guys haggling with papa-san over the price of the drinks. Then I remembered that when we first arrived in Nam, we were told that whenever you made a purchase, you had to negotiate over the price until you arrived at a compromise. It was the way all business was conducted by the Vietnamese. So I waited a few minutes, then turned to the two GI's and asked "How much ya pay for those Cokes?" "Fifty pee apiece." "Sonofabitch!" I replied, "I keep forgetting that ya gotta bargain for everything in this godforsaken place. We paid seventy-five!" Of course they laughed and must have assumed we were greenhorns.

STEVE: Man, that was dinky-dow (dien-cai-dau, meaning crazy.) Negotiating the price of a Coke, fer cryin' out loud!

FRED: I guess when papa-san said "75 pee" I was supposed to say "40," then he'd say "60" and I'd say "50." Then he'd say "OK, 50." Once ya got used to it, you could probably complete the whole negotiation process in less than five seconds.

STEVE: Gee, maybe that's what I should have said to Miss Queenie back at the old Silver Slipper in Okinawa! So then Fiedler came out through the curtains after 10 or 15 minutes?

FRED: Yeah, he had an embarrassed little smirk on his face. He ordered a beer, chugged it and said "Let's go, guys!" I assume he paid for oral sex but I didn't really want to know, so I never asked. He never got his jeep washed, either. He used to drive that road often, so he was probably a regular at some of those establishments.

STEVE: The American military was at times accused of "turning Vietnamese women into whores" but it should be remembered that for several hundred years, there had always been foreign armies occupying Vietnam— the Chinese, French, Japanese, the French again, and then the Americans. And all of those armies had sexual needs which many Vietnamese were willing (or forced, in some cases) to satisfy. Former CNN correspondent Peter Arnett described the situation this way: "Prostitution was a time-honored Vietnamese tradition. Certain heads of families would not think twice before routinely selling their daughters if they needed the money."

FRED: Now you said there were five ways for GI's to relieve their sexual tensions in Nam. We've talked about one— visiting those Vietnamese prostitutes or shacking up with a "girlfriend" on a regular basis for an extended period of time. What about the other four?

STEVE: Well, one was to simply do nothing at all, whereupon Nature would take its course by causing a soldier to have periodic "wet dreams." (Nocturnal emissions— an involuntary ejaculation during sleep.) In my experience, the less often one had any sort of sexual activity, the more often he would have these types of dreams.

FRED: But there were two problems with wet dreams. First, they'd mess up the sheets on your bed, as well as the skivvies you were wearing as you slept that night. And second, it seemed like if you were going to have an orgasm anyway, you might as well be fully conscious so you could get a little enjoyment out of it, however brief. That's assuming it wasn't against your religion or a violation of your personal moral standards.

STEVE: True. That leads us to Method Number Three, which was self-gratification which most of us engaged in as adolescents, despite the fact that hardly anyone ever admitted it. (Certainly not like they do today!) That would have been a perfectly acceptable solution, except for one problem: Unless you happened to have a key to some place like the Supply Room, the Arms Room, the Mail Room or the Pharmacy, there was absolutely no place in our compound where you could find any privacy whatsoever!

FRED: Right. We slept in a 10-man squad bay with no partitions of any kind. Our latrine was a 10-holer with no partitions of any kind. If you waited until after dark and went to the group shower, somebody might walk in and cause considerable embarrassment if you were caught in the act. Besides, the shower water tank was heated by the sun in the daytime, but at night it felt ice cold. No thanks!

STEVE: Well then, how about waiting until dark and sneaking off to some far corner of the compound behind a truck or bunker? Then again, if you were spotted lurking in some dark area where nobody was supposed to be, you might get shot by a sentry... or you could provoke one of 'em into shooting up a flare... or sounding the siren for a general alert!

FRED: Not good. Though we rarely discussed it, we pretty much all knew what it was like to be feeling really horny and think "Man, if I don't get my rocks off soon, I know I'm gonna have a wet dream. It's time to clean the pipes, dammit!"

STEVE: More than once I considered resorting to the piss tubes. These were long metal tubes, maybe 6 inches in diameter, that had one end buried deep in a pit full of stones and gravel with the other end sticking up a couple feet in the air.

FRED: When you had to take a leak, you'd walk some 30-40 yards out to the piss tube and step inside a solid metal privacy screen offering concealment from about your chest down to your knees. From a distance anyone could see who was out there taking a leak, but nobody could see what you were actually doing. Presumably you were peeing into the open end of that tube which was capped with window screening to keep the snakes in... and the bugs out.

STEVE: But I remember a few times when, being desperate for a little privacy, I stepped outside the hooch in the semi-darkness to light a cigarette. I stood there watching until I saw someone using the pisser. When it looked like he was about to leave and there was no one else in sight, I started walking toward it. One time I was halfway there when I saw someone else approaching from a different direction, so I had to change course and veer off toward an alternate destination.

FRED: Foiled again! You should have started looking for an empty truck like the one you found in the Motor Pool at Fort Sam.

STEVE: Yeah, but the Motor Pool in Long Binh was padlocked at night, I think. Another time, no sooner had I gotten to the tube than I spotted another GI approaching. Not wanting to get caught with my dick in my hand, I had to pretend I was finished and leave. Then a few days later, I was using the pisser for its intended purpose one morning when I spotted some residue on top of the bugscreen that told me I wasn't the first person to think of the tube as a potential source for relief. And on top of that, I found it thoroughly disgusting!

FRED: You immediately thought "What kind of a jerk would be so crass as to do something like that?" And here you had been planning to do the exact same thing yourself!

STEVE: True, but I was so creeped out after that experience that I never again considered it. I promptly crossed it off my "bucket list."

FRED: For all we knew, maybe the Army intended for us to use those tubes that way. There were no signs telling us not to! Of course if you had worked on one of the hospital wards you could have just pulled the curtains closed around one of the beds for some privacy. But no, you didn't wanna be a medic any more! You preferred punching your typewriter and driving the CO's jeep!

STEVE: That is true. The only place where I could truly find any privacy was probably the same one a lot of other guys found— under the sheets in my own bunk. While it could get up to 100 degrees in the daytime, it usually got pretty chilly at night. So we would sleep under a sheet and a blanket. And I had an advantage over most of the other guys— my good old photographic memory.

FRED: So you didn't need any visual aids!

STEVE: Nope. At around 9:45 at night, the sergeant on CQ duty would stick his head into each tent and yell "Lights out in fifteen!" That was my signal to sit down on the edge of my bunk, open my foot-locker, put away my toys, pull out the latest issue of Playboy and study those photos for 10 minutes or so. Then I'd put the magazine back, grab a few Kleenex tissues, close the footlocker, slide under the sheets and wait for the lights to go out.

FRED: And even in the dark, you could still see those photos in your mind's eye!

STEVE: For about the next 20 minutes or so, I could indeed. It was nearly the same as staring at the magazine.

FRED: OK, it's my turn to guess what Method Number Four would have been. I'll say... banging a nurse or a Donut Dolly!

STEVE: That's affirmative, Kemosabe! Generally, the opportunity to have carnal relations with a "round-eyed" woman was a privilege reserved only for officers and celebrities... but not entirely.

FRED: Army nurses, being officers, were strictly forbidden to fraternize with enlisted men. They were instructed to date or social-ize only with other officers, although married officers were not nec-essarily off limits. The same went for Donut Dollies.

STEVE: When a doctor and nurse wanted to get together for some hanky panky, they too had difficulty finding enough privacy. Most wouldn't risk getting caught in the nurse barracks, especially if one was married. One night a doctor and nurse climbed into the back of an empty ambulance so they could be alone. They were "doing the nasty" when the driver hopped in, unaware that anyone was in the back. He started 'er up, put 'er in gear and took off.

FRED: The couple had to make themselves presentable before the male officer could approach the driver and say "Hey, we fell asleep here in the back. Could you stop and let us out please?" The driver let them out on the road and they had to walk back to the front gate of the hospital. The best part of the story? The nurse had been in Nam for less than a week!

STEVE: In a similar incident, SP5 Rickman from the 24th was working in A&D over at the 93rd Evac on temporary duty. One night they saw some shadows lurking about by the helipad. Thinking it might be enemy saboteurs, they grabbed a couple flashlights from the Emergency Room and went to check it out. They opened up the side door on one of the Hueys, only to find an embarrassed doctor and nurse buck naked on the floor! Then they promptly went back to the ER and laughed their butts off.

FRED: Like their counterparts on college campuses, some nurses were extreme prudes while others were highly promiscuous. But most fell somewhere in between. A few at the 24th might qualify as knockouts in my estimation, but the majority did not. Ditto for the Donut Dollies. One officer wrote home to his wife (who happened to be great looking, from the photos I saw) that he couldn't believe how much attention all those plain looking nurses got from men of all ranks, ranging from privates all the way up to generals.

STEVE: Hey, it was all about the laws of supply and demand! The most attractive Army nurse I ever saw was the one I worked with on the night shift back at Brooke Army Hospital in Texas. She was tall, slender and blonde (like the woman I would ultimately marry some five years later.) At the time I thought "Hey, if all the nurses look like that, this Army Medic job might not be so bad after all!"

FRED: Little did you know then that the good looking ones would be so few and far between! But working on a ward with a gorgeous nurse was a bit of a distraction anyway. I could do my job better without any distractions.

STEVE: You're probably right, but if you were trying to impress the nurse, wouldn't you be more inclined to do a really good job?

FRED: I dunno. Were you trying to impress the nurse the night you locked your patient in a Posey Belt and then went home having forgotten you still had the key in your pocket?

STEVE: Good point— and it was that same attractive nurse, too. But since nobody discovered it until they tried to spring the guy to go for tests the next morning, I was hoping she'd never find out.

FRED: Wouldn't have mattered— she was a Lieutenant and you were a lousy Private.

STEVE: True, but in Nam, as it turns out, a few of the nurses at the 24th had no qualms about violating the non-fraternization rules with enlisted men. One of the knockouts, a Lieutenant Davies, was a brand new nurse just in from the states. She really stood out when you contrasted her to most of her peers.

FRED: Everyone assumed the young officers would be drooling over her, but in fact it was one of our enlisted buddies— PFC Craig Randall— who managed to get his foot in the door first, so to speak.

STEVE: Randall had "movie star" good looks despite the fact that he could have passed for 17 (he was actually 19 or 20.) He worked on a ward with Davies and they hit it off immediately, since they were both Californians, they both spoke surfer and together they looked like the King and Queen of the high school prom. They were obviously destined for each other in the same way it's inevitable that the head cheerleader and the star quarterback are going to hook up.

FRED: And hook they did. They got around the lack of privacy by having Davies smuggle Randall into the nurses barracks in the wee hours. He would bring a bottle, they'd get a good buzz on and then go at it. But of course Craig just had to tell somebody, so he'd brag to me in secret that he was banging Lieutenant Davies. Being a natural skeptic, I said "Bullshit, you are not!"

STEVE: But Craig was determined to prove it, otherwise there'd be no point in telling you if you didn't believe him. After all, she was about the best looking female in the whole compound, right?

FRED: Right. So then one night I'm snoring away when someone quietly shakes me awake at around 2 am. I open my eyes and there's Craig staring me right in the kisser. I smelled the booze on his breath, saw this silly grin on his puss and noticed he was dangling something in front of my face. Reaching for my glasses, I put 'em on and realized it was a used condom containing fresh evidence! Whereupon he says in a hushed voice "See, I told ya I was screwin' her!"

STEVE: And later on when you told me about it, I said "Oh yeah, I remember that night. I got up in the middle of the night to take a leak and saw Craig Randall standing outside our hooch. He appeared to be somewhat drunk as he unrolled a fresh condom and proceeded to hock a couple of loogies into it."

FRED: And after that I wasn't sure who to believe!

STEVE: Oh, I was just shittin' ya. I owed you one for confiscating my Golden Dragon Certificate and keeping it for a year.

FRED: Now he tells me!!! But another enlisted man, SP4 Nissler, struck up a romance with a nurse on his ward too. They couldn't find any way to be alone since they didn't want to be seen together. They finally figured out that they should both go to Tokyo on a 7-day R&R and meet up once they got there.

STEVE: But there were only so many seats on each plane— and at the last minute, Nissler was informed he would be bumped off the flight by someone with more seniority (probably an officer.) He was told he'd have to postpone his R&R!

FRED: He was so flustered that he went and spilled the beans to Maxwell, the Company Clerk, hoping he'd get some sympathy. Fortunately Max was a very accommodating fellow and good at keeping secrets. He arranged to bump somebody else off the flight instead, and Nissler got to meet his squeeze in Tokyo after all— where they got to play the roles of married tourists for a week!

STEVE: That was Max for ya, ever the romantic! So a number of young officers— plus a few celebrities and young enlisted men— were able to enjoy liaisons with young nurses from the 24th Evac. But there was another group who more or less felt entitled to the attentions of those young American nurses and Donut Dollies.

FRED: Let me guess. You must be talking about... Flag Officers!

STEVE: Yup. Groups of 24th Evac nurses would periodically be invited to attend lavish parties hosted by assorted command groups comprised of Majors, Colonels and Generals. The invitation would be posted, nurses would sign up and then on the appointed evening, several trucks (or helicopters, in some cases) would arrive to pick them up and take them to some "Magic Castle" for a night of wining, dining and dancing to live music.

FRED: And a little boom-boom, perhaps?

STEVE: Well according to some of the nurses, the drunker the big wheels got, the more they seemed to expect some sort of a payoff. It was as if they viewed the nurses as playthings who'd been brought there for the officers' own amusement.

FRED: So how did the nurses view these activities?

STEVE: Well they were very impressed with the music, the food and the wine. As for the advances of the old coots, some welcomed the attention, some tolerated the behavior while managing to ward them off, and some became highly incensed. One nurse told me later that this Colonel kept asking her to dance and then grabbing her ass on the dance floor. She kept pushing his hand away and finally slapped him a good one. She said after that she was so disgusted that she didn't sign up for any more parties.

FRED: Sometimes nurse parties were also used as bargaining chips with other units. In one case an officer at the 12th Evac (who later was transferred to the 24th) said their nurses were sent to party with the top brass at some regimental command in exchange for a large load of construction lumber.

STEVE: What, one round-eyed broad for every 100 board-feet of white pine? Were the nurses aware of the arrangement?

FRED: I don't know, but I would guess they weren't. Depends on whether the wood was for the nurses or for someone else.

STEVE: You mean as in "We'll take care of your wood if you will reciprocate by taking care of ours?"

FRED: Your guess should be about as good as mine. Now then, that should bring us to the fifth and final method for releasing some of that sexual tension in Nam... that's assuming we're not counting bestiality or necrophilia.

STEVE: You are correct sir! And while Method Number Five was barely worth mentioning as far as we were concerned, it was, after all, one of the Army's chief concerns with respect to soldiers who might be deprived of sexual contact with females.

FRED: Ah, you must be referring to the fact that there weren't any homosexuals in the US military in 1966. At induction, every recruit was asked whether he was a homosexual. If he was, he answered "yes" and would then be denied entrance into the US military.

STEVE: Or so we thought.

FRED: Gays were not allowed, and anyone who happened to slip through the cracks and was found to be gay after induction would promptly be given an undesirable discharge.

STEVE: Or so we thought.

FRED: On top of that, anyone committing a homosexual act after he was already in the armed forces would promptly be given an undesirable discharge.

STEVE: Or so we thought!

FRED: So you're saying that during induction, some gays might have said "no" when asked if they were homosexual? Why on earth would anyone do that?

STEVE: Maybe they were scared or embarrassed. Maybe they lied intentionally because they thought living in a men's barracks would be paradise. Maybe they were in denial. Maybe they were bisexual— a term which I don't believe I had ever heard back then. Or maybe they didn't know they were gay. I had a friend in college who used to say "I don't know yet if I'm gay or straight— since I've never had sex with either a woman OR a man!"

FRED: Gee, I hope you straightened him out. Are you saying that if a soldier was caught committing a homosexual act, he was not automatically discharged from the Army?

STEVE: Well it turns out that in 1966, Army regulations said "Personnel who voluntarily engage in homosexual acts will not be permitted to serve in the Army in any capacity, and their prompt separation from the service is mandatory."

FRED: Sounds pretty cut and dried to me.

STEVE: Ahhh, not so fast, Red Ryder! On the next page it listed the exceptions: "Persons involved in homosexual acts stemming solely from immaturity, curiosity, intoxication or mental illness will be immune from prosecution under this regulation."

FRED: Well holy crap! So all they'd have to do if they got caught is say they were drunk, curious or immature? I wonder how many gay guys read those regulations and said "Oh what the hell, I should be able to pull that off. Might as well go ahead and enlist!"

STEVE: The Army probably had to add those exceptions because too many old lifers were getting shit-faced and then playin' a little grab-ass with the troops! So while we assumed there weren't any gays among us, we could very well have been dead wrong.

FRED: Of course we did have a few guys who seemed to exhibit gay mannerisms or speech patterns, according to the old "gay-dar." But I assumed it was just their misfortune— or maybe they didn't realize they were gay until after they were inducted. And we also had a few episodes where somebody would get roaring drunk and then flop into bed (uninvited) with another soldier. Did that make him a homosexual or not?

STEVE: Most of us probably would have said yes, but apparently the Army would have thought otherwise. Yup, I can see it now: Two GI's get caught in the sack together and the first one says "Honest Sarge, I was drunk as a skunk!" Then the second one says "Honest Sarge, I was just curious as hell!"

FRED: So then Sarge replies "Well okay then.... but you two just make sure you're still drunk or curious the next time it happens!"

&&&&&&&&&&&&&&&&&&&

FACT OR FICTION? *The story goes that one day the hospital's Exec Officer made the following announcement at a formation of all enlisted personnel: "It's come to my attention that enlisted men have occasionally been seen inside the nurse barracks which is off limits to all non-officer personnel. From this point on, any enlisted man caught breaking this rule will be subject to a $25 fine for the first offense. A second offense will merit a $50 fine and a third will cost you an entire month's pay. Are there any questions?" Whereupon one soldier in the back of the formation replied "Yes sir, how much for a season pass?"*

CHAPTER 17

A RAYE OF NO HOPE
Three times we narrowly miss Bob Hope,
three times we settle for Martha Raye

STEVE: Ever since World War II, thousands upon thousands of American soldiers in combat zones had looked forward to a visit by Bob Hope and his Christmas USO Show featuring singers, dancers, bands, comedians, starlets and beauty queens. Of course we were no different, but unfortunately his annual schedule never quite seemed to coincide with ours.

FRED: Hope's first visit to Vietnam was in Christmas of '64 when he brought his show to Bien Hoa, just five miles west of Long Binh (but we were still civilians at the time, and Long Binh was just a big patch of dirt.) Twirling his trademark golf club, he was accompanied by actress Jill St. John, among others, who danced onstage with some of the troops. Hope's signature one-liner was "We're thrilled to be here in Sniper Valley!" He added that "I asked Defense Secretary McNamara if we could come out here and he said why not, we've tried everything else!" And of course the crowd roared their approval after every quip.

STEVE: I was never very impressed with Hope as a comedian. It seemed like throughout his career, he got laughs with corny or un-imaginative one-liners that would have gotten most comedians booed off the stage. They were more like wisecracks than jokes— and an awful lot of 'em were "groaners." To make matters worse, wrote one biographer, in the latter stages of his career, Hope seemed disengaged and was basically "just reading the cue cards and walking through his performances."

FRED: Still, everyone was glad to see him because he was an icon. Besides, it wasn't really the content of the quips that captivated his audiences— it was his style of delivery. Almost as if he was saying "OK, I'm gonna talk for 10 seconds and then you guys are all going to laugh like hell. Then we'll repeat the process over and over until you've laughed so much that your sides hurt." And laugh they did.

STEVE: Security was extremely tight for his first trip. The locations of his performances remained secret and no announcements were made concerning his itinerary. Soldiers who attended the shows weren't told whom they were going to see until the last minute. Then, just before the troupe returned from Bien Hoa to their Saigon hotel— the Caravelle— a truck bomb went off in front of the Brinks Hotel directly across the street. The Brinks, which was used as a Bachelor Officers Quarters (BOQ) for American officers at the time, was severely damaged and there were many casualties.

FRED: It was later claimed that the attack was an assassination attempt on Bob Hope. He had arrived late at the hotel, according to the story, because he traveled with more than a ton of giant cardboard cue cards for his show and his cue-card man was having difficulty getting the cards off the aircraft at Tan Son Nhut. Had Hope arrived on time, he might have been right in front of the hotel at the moment the blast occurred. This prompted the comedian to later say he was "saved by the idiot cards again!"

STEVE: The true target of the attack was more likely to have been the BOQ, but it was a close enough call that on most of his subsequent visits to Nam, Hope stayed in hotels in Thailand and just flew in for the actual performances. He would return by air to Bangkok or to an American aircraft carrier cruising in the South China Sea. From then on, his entourage traveled with a 10-man security team provided by the US military. They were told to stay away from doors and windows— and drop to the floor if they heard an explosion.

FRED: For anyone who wondered why the VC might try to take out Bob Hope, the theory was that doing so would be a major blow to the morale of the American forces. One captured VC agent supposedly indicated that this was in fact the objective of the hotel bombing. Personally I'd think killing Hope would have angered the American people, making them more hostile toward the Vietnamese communists. So I would say if Hope was the target, they're lucky they missed.

STEVE: Several years later, when James Brown (the "Godfather of Soul") toured Vietnam for a few weeks, the Army wanted Brown and his band members to be armed. At first James said "Hey man, we're entertainers, not killers!" But after they played a gig out in the sticks and saw a firefight break out just outside the camp, the Godfather agreed to carry a pistol. In his autobiography he said "I felt a hell of a lot safer once I had that big .357 on my hip!"

FRED: Then at Christmastime in '65, we had just finished Basic Training in Missouri and were on our way to Medic School in Texas when Hope brought his troupe to Tan Son Nhut airbase in Saigon, just 14 miles south of Long Binh. In less than two weeks he had performed 22 shows while managing to visit five hospitals in the process. His touring performers included crooner Eddie Fisher along with dancer and female sex bomb Joey Heatherton, while his repertoire of one-liners included "I don't know what you guys did to wind up here, but let that be a lesson to ya!"

STEVE: For Christmas of '66, we were right there in Long Binh waiting to see old "Ski-Nose" bring us his holiday show. It included actress Chris Noel, the knockout Heatherton again, plus an appearance by none other than Miss World. But instead of coming to Long Binh they went to Cu Chi, 20 miles west of us! Hope's signature one-liner at that show, referring to the war protesters at home, was: "I want to assure you the entire country is behind you 50 percent!"

FRED: In December '67 he finally came to Long Binh with Barbara McNair and none other than Raquel Welch herself, the reigning pin-up queen for the GI's. She danced around in a tight mini-dress and got the troops all riled up (of course.) But by then we had already returned home and been discharged. We had to watch it on TV! One of his jokes referred to the new craze of draft card burning on college campuses: "To foil the student protesters back home, the government has now come up with an asbestos draft card!"

STEVE: The following year, when he traveled with Dean Martin's "Golddigger Dancers" in '68, a dancer named Nancy Sinclair said that when they visited the hospitals, Hope would always go into the wards with the most serious casualties. But to protect the girls from seeing the horror of it, he wouldn't let them go in.

FRED: By 1970, as Hope tried to remain "hip" and relevant to the young soldiers in his audience, he was working drug jokes into his Christmas show. He was reported to have told this one in front of the 101st Airborne troops: "I hear you guys are interested in gardening here. Our security officer said a lot of you are growing your own grass!" NBC was wisely editing out all the drug jokes— probably the war protester jokes too— before airing the program on national TV.

STEVE: Everyone appreciated all the sacrifices Bob Hope made to be able to entertain the troops overseas, but there was another side to his story that wasn't so well known. (While we had no firsthand knowledge of the behind-the-scenes stuff, a number of books and articles have been written about such things over the years— including a book called "The Secret Life of Bob Hope.")

FRED: For one thing, NBC was reported to have paid him $150,000 for the broadcast rights to his Christmas show, over and above the travel costs and production costs for his trip. (By the time of the Gulf War two dozen years later, the figure had risen to $250,000.)

STEVE: So that alone should have been incentive enough for him to continue making his annual treks. (The Bob Hope Christmas in Vietnam Show, broadcast in January each year, was annually one of NBC's top-rated shows and biggest money-makers.)

FRED: Another little-known aspect of his trips was the fact that he had a reputation for being a notorious skirt-chaser with "an enormous appetite, even by Hollywood standards." Of course this was part of the comedic image he crafted for himself, so it would be difficult to verify how much of it was actually true.

STEVE: Hey, nothin' wrong with chasing 'em— it's only when ya catch 'em that you get in trouble! Supposedly his wife Dorothy did travel with him on some of the trips to Nam— although he probably would have left her at the hotel in Bangkok! Anyway, we never did get to see any Bob Hope shows except on TV. But as a consolation of sorts, we did get to see comedienne Martha Raye several times at the 24th Evac. It turns out she and Hope had been friends for nearly 30 years, ever since she appeared in three of his comedy films in the late 30's when she was in her early 20's.

STEVE: Her first appearance at the 24th was rather strange. It was probably late August or early September and we weren't even a hospital yet— just a construction site where we'd be wallowing in the mud all day as we filled sandbags, poured concrete, built bunkers, erected tents and so on. One day she suddenly just appeared out of nowhere, wearing a raincoat and strolling into our work area wearing civilian clothes. A couple guys dropped their tools and walked over to greet her. Then several more... and soon she had drawn a crowd. She was the first entertainer— or American female, for that matter— whom we had seen since leaving San Diego.

FRED: We had all grown up in the 50's when Martha Raye was a fixture on TV variety shows and even had her own weekly show for awhile. She was that wacky comedy lady with the huge mouth and gigantic toothy smile, and back then we were all young kids and very impressionable. So to us she was like an old friend we hadn't seen in years, though few of us realized that she had been a movie star since before we were born.

STEVE: We didn't know it at the time, but like her friend Hope, she had a long history of visiting and entertaining the troops going all the way back to World War II. In fact, though she's now deceased and buried in the Special Forces cemetery at Fort Bragg at her own request, she's still revered today by career military types and aging veterans who like to refer to her as "Colonel Maggie."

FRED: One doctor at a base in Soc Trang, about 100 miles south of Saigon in the Mekong Delta, said he was starting to work on a flood of casualties that had just arrived when he heard a woman's voice say "Need some help, Doc?" He turned around and saw Martha Raye, who said "I'm a trained nurse— got my experience in the Civil War!" He asked if she had any Operating Room knowledge and she replied

"Sure, plenty!" So he took her inside the OR and she began assisting him with the surgeries.

STEVE: Later when she was visiting the patients in recovery, she'd take every opportunity to crack jokes with them. The doctor said he always knew where she was because he could hear the bursts of laughter coming from off in the distance. When he visited a nearby base at Bac Lieu, he discovered there was a small hooch there with Colonel Maggie's name over the door. Out of curiosity, he knocked— and she answered! As it turned out, that was one of the places where she often stayed during her extensive travels in country.

FRED: On her first visit to the 24th, she climbed up on a little platform and— with the aid of a bullhorn, I think— began telling jokes, chatting with the crowd and singing a few tunes "a capella." It was clearly an impromptu one-woman show, totally unlike any of the USO shows— large or small— that would be coming to our compound over the course of the next eight months.

STEVE: Meanwhile I'm standing at the back of the crowd scratching my head. It was really nice that she had come to see us, but what was she doing there? How did she get there? Why did she come to our hospital when it was still just a big muddy field? Who sent her there? Where was her military escort? Who was she traveling with? Why didn't she have any musicians or assistants accompanying her?

FRED: These questions would not truly be answered (for us, at least) until after a couple of authors wrote biographies of "Colonel Maggie" some 30 years later. She was undoubtedly a big star when she visited the troops in Korea in her mid-30's. But by age 50, when she came to Long Binh, she was kind of a has-been as far as sought-after celebrities go. Later she would claim she'd been blacklisted by Hollywood because of her strong support for the (rather unpopular) Vietnam War. That story was debunked by her biographers, who pointed out that lots of other big stars weren't shunned just because they supported the war— and that Maggie actually made dozens of TV appearances during and after the conflict. They surmised that her difficulties may have been due to the fact that film and TV roles for actresses "in their mid-50's and beyond" were relatively scarce.

STEVE: Anyway, after chatting with us for 30 or 40 minutes, she signed some autographs and then disappeared as quietly as she had arrived. We didn't see her again for several months. The next time she was accompanied by a couple of musicians, a handler, a sound system and a somewhat scripted act. It was more like one of the traditional "small" USO shows that showed up unannounced about once a week. This time she wore tailored military fatigues, a Special Forces green beret, a camo scarf and a Light Colonel's insignia on her shirt collar (which raised a few eyebrows— impersonating an officer perhaps?)

FRED: Not a crime if you were a civilian— only if you were an enlisted man. Maggie made eight trips to Vietnam, traveling mostly on her own dime and staying in country for up to six months at a clip. It was reported that she had five parachute jumps under her belt and spent so much time in Vietnam that a blinded soldier on one of the hospital wards recognized her solely by the scent of her perfume.

STEVE: Her favorite activity was heading out into the boonies to the Special Forces camps where she could drink, gamble, trade jokes and carouse with the Green Berets, most of whom treated her like a favorite aunt. Being both a woman and a celebrity who was very popular among the military, she had no problem hitching rides on helicopters or planes to whatever destination she had in mind.

FRED: If she planned her own itinerary, that could explain why she visited our hospital when it was still a big empty field— nobody bothered explaining to her that we weren't operational yet.

STEVE: Anyway, once she returned to CONUS after many months, she would call or write the soldiers' wives and families and give interviews to reporters in which she said the troops were very discouraged by the lack of support they were receiving at home. In one case she described the war protesters as "a minority of idiots."

FRED: Now THAT might very well have gotten her blackballed by Hollywood! She was given the honorary rank of Lieutenant Colonel by the Special Forces (which explains her insignia and beret) as well as the honorary rank of Bird Colonel by the Marines. She was so enthralled with the Special Forces that she even went so far as to build a guest house for the Green Berets on the grounds of her Los Angeles residence. In 1993, one year before her death, she was awarded the Presidential Medal of Freedom by President Bill Clinton for her service to her country in three wars.

STEVE: At around the same time she visited us, an Associated Press article in October '66 said "Comedienne Martha Raye... a former nurse... donned fatigues and worked for two days in an Army field dispensary, cleansing wounds, changing bandages and comforting GIs wounded in a Mekong Delta battle." Apparently she didn't have any problem with letting folks believe she was (or had been) a registered nurse as well as a Colonel in the Army Reserve.

FRED: According to her biographers, however, neither story was true. Her rank was purely honorary, and her only medical training consisted of working as a candy striper in the 1930's and helping to provide care for wounded soldiers while entertaining troops in Africa and England during World War II. The myth-debunking website Snopes.com reports that once she received the honorary rank of Colonel, "Raye took to wearing a Special Forces uniform and beret everywhere she went on subsequent tours of Vietnam."

STEVE: That would explain why she was in civvies the first time we saw her. After that it was green or camo fatigues and a beret, which would suggest that part of her motivation could have been that she was a Special Forces "wannabe." None of which diminishes all the great things she did for the troops in at least three different wars. You could say she loved and supported the GI's with all her heart—but at the same time, she had a few quirks in her private life.

FRED: She was married seven times, had many battles with booze and pills, and was described as having a "roller coaster life." The movie website Imdb.com pointed out a possible reason for Maggie's difficulties in finding film and TV roles: She had a lifelong fear of flying, but her profession and her overseas journeys required her to make regular air trips. So to muster the courage, she would first have to "drink herself into a near alcoholic stupor." And in at least one instance she became so obnoxious and belligerent on an airliner that she had to be forcibly removed from the plane.

STEVE: This of course made news headlines, further sullying her reputation and causing some airlines to refuse to let her purchase a ticket. She would have had to do a lot of flying to travel around in Nam— I wonder if she had to get tipsy first before she could board a plane or chopper?

FRED: Well, with all the drinking the troops did on a daily basis over there, she should have fit right in. Maybe that's why she liked to stay in country for six months at a time!

&&&&&&&&&&&&&&&&&&&

FACT OR FICTION? The story goes that to deflate the morale of the American troops, two VC commandos were given orders to kidnap Funnyman Bob Hope, whom they would easily be able to recognize because he'd be wearing a baseball cap and twirling a golf club. They did exactly what they were told, except they didn't realize the guy they captured was not Funnyman Bob Hope. Since they hadn't eaten for several days, they decided to cook and eat their prisoner. From their position on a hilltop, they could see the American base camp off in the distance. As they began eating, the first VC said "Boy, wouldn't those yankee dogs be surprised if they knew we were sitting over here eating Funnyman Bob Hope?" To which the second VC replied: "I'm not so sure. Does this taste funny to you?"

CHAPTER 18

FREDDIE AND THE MORTAR FORKERS

We come up with a concrete proposal
for turning ourselves into celebrities

FRED: In April 1965— just five months before Steve and I were destined to meet at the Army Induction Center in Milwaukee— the hit single "I'm Telling You Now," by the British rock group Freddie and the Dreamers, made it to Number 1 on the Billboard Hot 100 List. They followed that up in June with their second hit, "Do the Freddie," which made it to Number 18. At the time, some critics considered the group to be just about the least talented of any rock band in history that had managed to produce five record albums, one film soundtrack and two Top 20 singles, all in one year.

STEVE: But little did we know then that 14 months later, our own "Freddie" would be the front man for yet another group with its own unique style— possibly the least talented group of concrete finishers to ever arm themselves with trowels, screeds, groovers and edgers!

FRED: Obviously you must be referring to the "Long Binh Mortar Forkers." We might have been the least talented when we started, but once we had a few pads under our belts we were ready to take on all comers! Now the pros say that a good concrete finisher is produced only through years of training, experience and practice. Mastery is achieved not only by learning how to use all the tools, but also by learning how to expertly time the various steps in the process, based on temperature, humidity and atmospheric conditions. And here we had what— two days to metamorphose from beginners into experts?

STEVE: I'd say a day and a half, certainly no more than two. It all started after we'd spent weeks filling sandbags, erecting gigantic tents and constructing guard bunkers, blast walls and personnel bunkers. One morning they called us all together to tell us we were about to learn how to pour concrete pads and build quonset huts. The method of instruction was quite unique, to say the least.

FRED: By golly, we were gonna get a chance to learn yet another marketable skill! They told us "Tomorrow the engineers are going to come in here and pour a couple of concrete pads. And YOU MEN are going to watch everything they do VERY CAREFULLY— because in two days they'll be gone, after which you'll be doing the exact same things you watched them do!"

STEVE: The good news was that we were going to get to loll around for two days watching these other dudes work. The bad news was that if we didn't pay close attention to what they were doing, we'd have an excellent opportunity to screw things up royally.

FRED: You mean like when you tried to tie the mops to the fantail on the General Weigel?

STEVE: That would be a good example, yeah. So the next morning we're out there fixin' to do some learnin' when the engineers show up. As I start to watch 'em work, I'm keeping my eyes peeled for a job that would require some skill, dexterity and artistry as opposed to brute strength or endurance, neither of which were my strong suits.

FRED: We watched them put together the steel forms for the perimeter of the pad. Then a cement truck came in and about 30 GI's with big heavy-duty wheelbarrows set up a daisy chain where they would continually lug barrowloads of fresh concrete from the truck to the pad, dumping their loads inside the forms as they went.

STEVE: And now I'm getting nervous because humping those big heavy wheelbarrows did not look like the sort of job that a skinny weakling like myself was cut out for. Or at least it wasn't anything I was looking forward to. As they dumped their loads, several other guys with long wooden rake-type tools would try to even out the distribution of the concrete. Then when the form was just about full, they'd bring out these long boards called screeds to slide back and forth, leveling off the top surface and forcing the large chunks of aggregate down toward the bottom of the pad.

FRED: Then they'd have to wait an hour or two for the concrete to set up properly before the cement finishing crew would take over. These fellows would lay boards over the fresh concrete, walk out on them and kneel down so they could work the surface using these tools called a darby, a float and a trowel (although nobody bothered to tell us the names of any of those devices— we just had to watch 'em and see what they did with the things.) These were used to flatten the surface, push down any lumps, fill any voids and finally compact and even out the surface so that it had a smooth, level finish.

STEVE: And lo and behold, this was a job that required not brute strength or great endurance— it called for skill, dexterity, artistry and finesse. Just exactly what we were looking for! I told Fred to watch these guys VERY, VERY carefully because we were gonna pass ourselves off as expert cement finishers. So while most of our buddies had gotten bored with watching by the time the finishers got to work, we studied their every move, hanging right over them much of the time.

FRED: We also noted that one crew could pour and finish two pads per day. The wheelbarrow men would start pouring at 8 am, finishing their first pour by 11. Then they'd eat chow and start their second pour at noon. The cement finishers would start working the first pad around 12 noon and finish by 3 pm. They'd eat chow, start their second pad at 4 o'clock and finish by 7 pm.

STEVE: This meant that if we were on the finishing crew, then we couldn't possibly get stuck on the wheelbarrow crew because both were working at the same time. Just what we were looking for! So we decided to go see Sergeant Pickering, who was in charge of the work details, and sign up for the finishing crew.

FRED: We walked into his tent and I said "Sarge, we're both experienced cement finishers and we'd like to sign up for that detail starting tomorrow." He looked at me and said "Have you worked construction before?" I said "Yeah, the last two summers I worked construction and did some work with concrete. Donovan did too. And we've been watching the engineers do it for the past two days. Piece of cake!" Actually it was true that I had worked construction, but my job had practically nothing to do with concrete. And Steve had never been near a construction site in his life, other than a few times when he deliberately ignored a "No Trespassing" sign.

STEVE: But Pickering knew even less about cement than we did! He says "Okay, great! Put your names on this list here. Be ready to do your first pad at around 12 noon tomorrow." This meant we could sleep 'til 10:30 am while most of the guys were out busting their butts with those wheelbarrows. Then once they had showered up by 4 pm, they would basically have nothing to do but grab a few beers, pull up some folding chairs and sit around watching us "artists" at work. So when we'd do our second shift later in the day, we'd have an audience of "fans" cheering us on as they watched "their" concrete pad finally taking shape. It was at that point that someone gave our little crew of cement finishers its nickname: the Long Binh Mortar Forkers!

FRED: For the first couple days we had to act like we knew exactly what we were doing when in fact we were really just "feeling our way along." The important thing was to look and act like pros so nobody would question how on earth we had gotten that job. But since we didn't know any of the terminology, we'd have to say things like "Hey, hand me that square thing there!" Fortunately we had a couple guys on our crew who apparently had some experience with finishing cement, so that helped us a lot.

STEVE: After a few days we were getting pretty good at it. We soon figured out that on a hot, sunny, dry day, the hardening process was accelerated, so we had to work really fast to complete all the steps in time. But when it was cool, cloudy and humid, everything slowed down. And as soon as we'd finish, the pad had to be covered up immediately with tarps to keep it moist for a few days. Otherwise the surface would dry out while the bottom remained wet, which would produce cracks in the concrete. Fortunately the engineers had left behind a "Project Manager" who knew about these things and could bail us out when we needed advice. But if it started raining, all bets were off.

FRED: Since it was toward the end of monsoon season, every few days it would start raining while we were working, or while we were waiting for the concrete to set up. Then it was like a thunderstorm at a major league baseball park— crews would have to race out with big tarps to cover the pads before the rain ruined the cement. Meanwhile we'd go relax and endure the suspense to see if we could get back out there before it had hardened too much. I don't think we ever "lost" a pad, but we did have some pretty hairy moments along the way.

STEVE: If there was a "rain delay" of more than an hour or two, it meant we'd have to be working after dark— because that concrete wasn't going to wait until the next day to harden. To get enough light to enable us to see what we were doing, we'd have to park about six or eight jeeps and trucks around the edges of the pad with their headlights shining on the surface. Then we'd get out there on our boards and start "floating and troweling" like crazy— with a huge audience of drunks cheering us on!

FRED: Here in a matter of a few days we'd gone from "pretenders"— rank amateurs, really— to celebrities performing in the spotlight before an adoring crowd. The Long Binh Mortar Forkers were "heroes" in a symbolic sense— and we were getting way more recognition than we actually deserved. It was great!!

STEVE: I think there were a couple nights when it didn't stop raining 'til 10 or 11 pm and they had to wake us up so we could get out there and start troweling in the headlights at midnight. We felt like the "Pros from Dover"— Hawkeye Pierce and Trapper John in the movie M*A*S*H. (Of course the book didn't come out 'til '68; the hit movie followed two years afterward.)

FRED: Some three decades later, Steve would post a statement on the 24th Evac website to the effect that "If you were a doctor, nurse or corpsman who worked on one of the wards, we probably finished the concrete that you walked on every day— and painted the walls that surrounded you— despite the fact that we were all medics."

STEVE: Or at least that's what they told us we were supposed to be. As it turned out, I would spend an entire year in Nam without ever getting a chance to utilize my medical training. Not that I'm complaining, mind you. But that's the Army for ya!

FRED: I read a statement not too long ago that said "The strong alkalinity of cement can cause chemical burns that will damage the skin. Therefore, it is essential to wear rubber gloves and goggles when working with wet concrete." We do have a photo of you wearing gloves to protect your "tender hands," but in the same photo the rest of us are working barehanded. And I'm damned sure none of us ever saw any goggles.

STEVE: So you could say that for those of us on the Mortar Forkers team, it was actually a case of "If the Agent Orange don't get ya, you can bet the wet concrete will!"

FRED: You could say that, yes. Speaking of Agent Orange, when and how did we first find out about that evil stuff? I don't recall the Army ever mentioning it to us in any way, shape or form. Of course we peons didn't have a "need to know," not to mention the fact that the Army never told ya nuthin' anyway!

STEVE: I think the first I heard of it was when I read about it one day in Time magazine while I was sitting in our hooch in Long Binh. Its existence wasn't a secret to those who actually handled the stuff or flew the missions that sprayed it over several million acres of Vietnam countryside. But as a general rule, the troops on the ground knew nothing about it until they inadvertently got sprayed with it— or they witnessed its after-effects on just about any type of vegetation.

FRED: Agent Orange (AO) was a defoliant used by the US military to kill vegetation in areas where they wanted to: a) deny the enemy its favorite sources of cover, b) destroy crops that enemy soldiers might be using for food, or c) protect roadsides, waterways, airfields and other US installations from ambush by eliminating any hiding places where the enemy might want to lie in wait.

STEVE: It got its name not from being orange in color but from the orange stripes around the 55 gallon drums used to transport it. Agents Blue, White, Pink and Green were other herbicides similarly named for their colored stripes, but Agent Orange turned out to be the preferred defoliant used to "denude" some two million acres of Vietnam's jungles and forests over a ten-year period from 1962 to 1971.

FRED: And it killed the vegetation in a most unorthodox way— by causing certain species of plants to experience such rapid growth that their cells would literally "explode" and die in a very short period of time. Its first use was for clearing roadsides along major highways and strategic routes, after which the Army produced color-coded maps

showing which roads were relatively safe in the daytime and which remained highly dangerous. Then they began using it along the banks of waterways as well as the perimeters of military bases.

STEVE: I don't think I ever saw a roadmap the entire time I was in Nam— color-coded or otherwise— despite the fact that I would eventually become the Company Commander's jeep driver. But I'm color blind, so color codes would have been of limited use to me!

FRED: Later on they started using AO to destroy crops and eliminate strategic hiding places for enemy troops. From 1965 to 1970, an estimated 12 million gallons of the herbicide were sprayed by aircraft, patrol boats and vehicles as well as by men on the ground wearing spray tanks on their backs.

STEVE: Supposedly soldiers or marines who did the hand spraying would sometimes spray each other when they were horsing around, being unaware of the potential dangers involved. In our case, we assumed that AO was only being used way out in "the boonies"— uninhabited areas that didn't affect us. But a few years later we began hearing claims that it had been heavily used in Long Binh to defoliate areas where structures were to be placed, as well as the perimeter areas where enemy snipers or attackers might want to hide.

FRED: Of course Agent Orange was not without controversy. The first potential "scandal" regarding the herbicide involved its use in destroying crops to deny sources of food to the enemy. Before we even arrived in Nam, this was being hotly debated behind closed doors in the US Senate because destroying crops could possibly be viewed as a violation of international law or a war crime. Supposedly the way our government got around this was to "give" the defoliants to the South Vietnamese government. Their taking ownership assured that if any crimes were to be committed, the USA would not be the guilty party.

STEVE: The later scandal, which exists to this day, involved the potential toxicity of AO to both American military personnel as well as Vietnamese soldiers and civilians. Of course at the time it was known to be very effective at killing plant life, but nobody knew how dangerous it could be to humans. An official Air Force document said AO was a standard defoliant "widely used throughout the world" that had "no harmful effects of any kind on human or animal life." Apparently the Air Force failed to consider the fact that AO was being used in much higher concentrations in Vietnam— or that the harmful effects might not appear for some period of years after exposure.

FRED: Several years later, researchers began to confirm that one of AO's key ingredients, dioxin, could cause cancer, birth defects, tumors, infertility and other permanent injuries to humans. One research study supposedly claimed that a mere 80 grams of dioxin, if poured into the water supply system of New York City, would be capable of gradually annihilating the entire population of Manhattan. (We have no way of knowing whether this was actually true.)

STEVE: A third scandal involved accusations that the manufacturers of AO— Dow Chemical and Monsanto, in particular— already knew it was toxic to humans when they began supplying it to the US government. A related accusation was that the US military knew about its dangers but sprayed it over the countryside anyway.

FRED: Meanwhile, since the Army tried to never let anything go to waste, the empty AO barrels were often used to store water, fuel or other substances to be used by the troops for various purposes such as washing or showering. This meant that even GI's who had no direct exposure to the spraying might still come in contact with AO residue through other means.

STEVE: Every hooch or building in our compound had "fire barrels" sitting right outside the entrances. These were 55-gallon drums filled with water for use as fire extinguishers. Outside the hooches we also had a number of charcoal grills made by cutting the steel drums in half lengthwise and placing them on wooden stands.

FRED: If those drums had any colored stripes on them, I doubt that we would even have noticed. And if they contained any residue, it's quite likely that they were never thoroughly cleaned out.

STEVE: It also turns out that when AO was sprayed by aircraft, the mist could travel up to six miles through the air before settling to the ground, which meant that many soldiers were undoubtedly contaminated by airborne herbicide without ever knowing it. For years we wondered if we might have been directly exposed to AO ourselves.

FRED: The 1991 Agent Orange Act mandated that certain diseases and conditions associated with defoliants be treated as a result of wartime service, and a vet suffering from any of them would be eligible for disability compensation. It was further established that anyone who set foot on Vietnamese soil was considered as having been exposed to AO, regardless of where he was stationed or what he did.

STEVE: In fact one unofficial report stated that "If you were in Long Binh, your risk of exposure was exceptionally high"— a direct contradiction of what we had thought when we first came back to the USA.

FRED: In 2002 we held a reunion with about a half dozen guys who had lived in our 10-man hooch. In trying to locate as many of our buddies as we could, we managed to track down nearly two dozen and found that several had already died of brain tumors. At the reunion, two others had existing brain tumors and both are now deceased as a result. Thus far, neither of us are aware of any conditions we have that might be attributable to Agent Orange.

STEVE: In other words, you could say that when it comes to experiencing the effects of Agent Orange, we still don't know whether we "beat the fuggin' system" or not!

&&&&&&&&&&&&&&&&&&&

FACT OR FICTION? *The story goes that Colonel Dickerson, who fancied himself a gourmet cook, wanted to hunt some wild mushrooms outside the perimeter. With SP4 Soder driving the jeep and PFC Krump riding shotgun, he kept telling them to move further away from Long Binh and out into the sticks. Soon they were captured by a VC patrol near an abandoned village and lined up against a wall for execution by a firing squad. The VC leader says "ready... aim..." and Soder shouts "earthquake!!!" As everyone dives for cover, Soder leaps over the wall and escapes. They try it again and when the leader says "ready... aim..." Krump yells "typhoon!!!" Everyone hits the deck— and Krump escapes over the wall. Now the Colonel's thinking "OK, I just need to yell out some type of natural disaster and then I'll get a chance to escape like the others." So when the platoon leader says "ready... aim..." Dickerson yells "fire!!!"*

CHAPTER 19

SORRY SIR, DIDN'T RECOGNIZE YOU IN YOUR BIRTHDAY SUIT
Barbarians at the gate? No, just jet jockeys looking for some entertainment

FRED: At night, gate guard at the 24th Evac was considered pretty boring duty because rarely did any vehicles enter or leave after dark. The main thing you had to worry about was the Sergeant of the Guard suddenly showing up to make sure you were awake and alert. Usually they'd approach by walking down the middle of the company street where they could easily be seen. But a few were wise guys who liked to sneak up on the bunker from a random direction to try to catch you "off guard"— no pun intended.

STEVE: One night I was out there with SP4 Dawkins and suddenly realized I was about to throw up. It was all I could do to say "I'll be right back!" and step outside behind the bunker, where I promptly tossed my cookies on the ground next to the sandbag wall. I assumed it was food poisoning so I took a few swigs from my canteen, stuck a stick of Wrigley's Doublemint in my craw and said "I think I'm okay. Musta been somethin' I ate!"

FRED: But while the two of you were preoccupied with the puking crisis, Benitez, the Sergeant of the Guard, was quietly sneaking up on you in the shadows— from the rear.

STEVE: He was one of those gung-ho types who liked to pull that kind of crap. Dawkins suddenly spots him from 20 feet away, wheels around and levels his weapon while simultaneously yelling "Halt!"

FRED: Was Dawkins about to start shooting?

STEVE: Nah, we could see it was obviously Benitez. He continues moving forward as he says "Everything all right here? You're not supposed to let anyone get this close without challenging them!" By now he's walked right up to the outside of the back wall of the bunker and we're eyeing him over the tops of the sandbags. We give him some feeble answer and then get a mild ass-chewing. Then he goes on his merry way, determined to sneak up on his next victims.

FRED: And when did it occur to you that he might have been standing right in that puddle of puke with his spit-shined boots on?

STEVE: Well I thought about it after a minute or two, grabbed my flashlight and went outside behind the bunker. I said "Hey Dawkins, ya gotta see this!" There were the footprints of "Benny" Benitez right where he had been standing in that pool of fresh vomit! We had a good laugh— it served him right for being such a gung-ho hard-ass.

FRED: I wish I could have seen him when he got back to the Guard Tent and checked the mirror shine on his boots— "Hmmm, what the hell is this? It looks like... that chicken fricasee we had for dinner!"

STEVE: It did indeed... except we didn't have chicken fricasee that night! It never would have happened if he had just walked down the company street like a normal person. Come to think of it, I later heard about some guys in other units setting up trip wires to alert them when the Sergeant of the Guard was trying to sneak up on 'em.

FRED: Hope they remembered to tell the guys on the next shift, otherwise there could be some sparks flying! Like you said, not much happened on gate guard after dark. Although I did have an interesting experience there one night, shortly after I started my 3 am shift.

STEVE: Was that the night you heard those blood-curdling screams coming from the nurse barracks about 30 yards away? I always wondered why they put the nurse hooches so close to the front gate, but it makes perfect sense to me now— armed guards always nearby.

FRED: I did hear screams, but the sentry's Fifth General Order says you're not supposed to leave your post until properly relieved! On the other hand, the first order is "To take charge of my post and all government property within view." The nurse barracks was definitely within my view, so I was supposed to take charge of it, right?

STEVE: Beats me! As usual, confusion and contradictions ruled the day (or night, in this case.) But as a certified combat medic you were perceived as having the ability to exercise independent judgement on the battlefield — or wherever else it might be required, right?

FRED: Indeed. Some screaming nurse sounds like she's in a life or death situation. But which General Order am I supposed to follow? I compromised. I told PFC Furman to remain in the bunker, get on the field phone and call the Guard Shack for assistance. Then I grabbed my flashlight and trusty M-14 and headed for the nurses hooch.

STEVE: What did you think you were gonna find?

FRED: I had no idea— maybe some enemy infiltrators? As I got close to where I thought the screams were coming from, I heard someone shouting "Man in the barracks! Man in the barracks!" I entered and found several nurses standing around in pajamas holding makeshift weapons like baseball bats or whatever. They were staring down a caucasian male— a total stranger to me— who appeared to be in his 20's and, in addition to looking very disoriented, was stark naked.

STEVE: Now a little background information is required here. It involves a female Head Nurse on one of the wards, Major Cooksey, whom we later named "Hot Lips" after the book "M*A*S*H" came out and was made into a hit movie. One of the fictitious characters in the book was a female Chief Nurse the men had nicknamed "Hot Lips" Houlihan. The moniker seemed to fit, so we borrowed it.

FRED: On the one hand, Hot Lips Cooksey was very straight-laced and rather prudish— probably in her early forties, and definitely not as good looking as Houlihan! I guess she was quick to lecture the other nurses on how they should conduct their personal lives so as to maintain the high standards of the Army Nurse Corps. She did, however, like to enjoy a vodka gimlet or two in her off-duty hours.

STEVE: We witnessed this at times when we tended bar during the evenings (for a modest wage, plus all we could drink) in the little make-shift officers club which was attached to the end of one of the three nurse barracks. After two or three gimlets, she was capable of becoming quite amorous toward any one of the young male officers who happened to be in attendance that evening.

FRED: Most of the male officers in our outfit were either doctors or Medical Service Corps "career types" who didn't feel it was prudent to be messing around with our own nurses— at least not in public. Still, there was no shortage of male officers in our little club. Most were pilots from the Long Binh helicopter units or jet jockeys from the Bien Hoa Airbase. They were drawn to our club because it featured an attraction that few other clubs in the area could match— the combination of cheap booze plus American nurses with their own private or semi-private bedrooms close by!

STEVE: The club had a tiny dance floor next to the jukebox and by her third or fourth cocktail, Hot Lips would at times begin to virtually molest her dance partner. As nurse Carline Brown said later, Major Cooksey would "dance with some of the young bucks fresh from the field and wrap herself around them like a second skin." Eventually the major would either scare the fellow off or else succeed in inviting him to her room inside the nurse barracks.

FRED: Sometime between 3 and 4 am on the night in question, the Head Nurse on Ward ICU-3, Captain Brown, was walking to the mess hall to get a cup of coffee with Janet Jenson, another Head Nurse from the adjacent ward. Hearing a big commotion— screaming and shouting— they headed for the nurse barracks. She said they went in and found the gate guard holding his weapon on Major Cooksey as well as a young male officer, both of whom were wearing women's bathrobes, while several nurses looked on.

STEVE: Supposedly no males were allowed in the nurse barracks. In fact, one nurse had to get special permission from the Chief Nurse to let her husband, a captain, sleep with her in the barracks.

FRED: Another nurse living in that same hooch later wrote a book in which she complained that she not only had to endure the inconvenience of having a male in their private quarters, but she also had to listen to the sounds of the married couple's lovemaking every night. This was supposedly due to the fact that the rooms had no ceilings— the roof of the building forming one common ceiling for all.

STEVE: Some 10 years after THAT, the married nurse also wrote a book. She said a lot of the nurses appreciated having a man around who could fix things and provide some security. She also said if any lovemaking sounds were heard, they had to be made by someone else, not by her and her husband. So anyway, who was this naked guy in the nurses barracks?

FRED: Well I figured he was most likely an American officer of some type, so I decided to apply the US Marine sentry's "12th General

Order" which said I should "walk my post from flank to flank and take no crap from any rank." I proceeded to level my weapon, order him to sit on the floor and ask someone to get him a robe or blanket.

STEVE: Did you take any crap from him?

FRED: No, he was fairly incoherent and didn't offer any resistance. Furman had called the Guard Tent so the reinforcements arrived in a matter of a few minutes, first the Sergeant of the Guard and then the Officer of the Day. At that point I was released to return to my post at the front gate while the OD interrogated the guy.

STEVE: So who was he, and how did he get in there butt naked?

FRED: It seems he was an Air Force pilot who had gotten drunk in the lounge with Hot Lips. She invited him to her room and then in the middle of the night he had to get up to pee. In a drunken stupor, he stumbled down the hall— naked as a jaybird— looking for the head, but what he found instead was the nurses shower. He went in and was taking a leak on the shower floor when another nurse came in to use the latrine. Seeing a naked man in there, she decided to "scream first and ask questions later."

STEVE: At which point it was SP4 Borchardt to the rescue!

FRED: Yeah, but of course if she had just talked to the naked man instead of starting to scream, there probably wouldn't have been any need for a "rescue." Here I had gone in there with visions of VC commandos infiltrating the nurse barracks, fer cryin' out loud!

STEVE: Okay, make that "Rambo" Borchardt to the rescue... the only guy in our hooch authorized to have a fully automatic weapon!

FRED: So when it was all over, did they ever decide how to discipline Hot Lips or prevent her from engaging in that type of conduct?

STEVE: Well according to Brown, they put Hot Lips Cooksey on permanent nights so she couldn't spend hours soaking up gimlets and striking up acquaintances with young pilots in the officers lounge. Apparently that did the trick. In a somewhat similar episode, another senior nurse— a Major— was supposedly having an affair with an enlisted man. According to several of the nurses, when the Hospital Administration found out about it, she was transferred out of the 24th Evac in the blink of an eye, never to be seen again.

FRED: Reminds me of the incident where a jet jockey from Bien Hoa Airbase was trying to impress one of our nurses. He was coming up empty, so he made a last ditch effort just as we were closing up the place. On his way out the door he called to her and said "Say, I'm flying tomorrow so I'll give you a buzz on my way back to base!" Nobody knew exactly what he meant by that and we quickly forgot about it.

STEVE: The next day we were having our usual Saturday afternoon (water buffalo) steak cookout in the area between our hooch and the next one. I'm stretched out on a reclining lawn chair with a beer in one hand and a cigarette in the other, staring up at the little patch of blue sky I can see between the two tents. All of a sudden we hear this tremendous roar. Then for a split second my field of vision is completely blocked by the underbelly of an F-4 Phantom jet screaming directly overhead, no more than 50 feet off the ground, if that.

FRED: For a moment we had no idea what was happening— were we about to witness a crash landing? Had the pilot already ejected? His plane was but a speck in the western sky by the time we realized it was just our flyboy friend trying to impress the target of his affections as he made his approach to the Bien Hoa airfield, six miles away.

STEVE: Then again, he could have been merely trying to taunt or punish her for her failure to come across!

FRED: At night we had some 24 guys per shift manning all the perimeter bunkers. During daylight hours, however, we just had two at the front gate and one in each bunker at the northeast and southeast corners of our perimeter. That's because Charlie hunkered down in the daytime to avoid detection by American aircraft, coming out mostly at night to engage in troop movements, ambushes or attacks.

STEVE: And one day you were on gate guard when you witnessed a lumber truck dropping its load right in front of our compound. Lumber was a hot commodity, since new American units were coming into the country and building permanent quarters just like we were.

FRED: Getting lumber to build shelving, tables and cabinets was a real trick. You couldn't just pick up the phone and order a big load of it. Instead you'd have to resort to one of the "scrounging" techniques commonly used by the military in a war zone.

STEVE: Let me guess! You must be referring to the four B's.... Begging, Bribing, Bartering or Borrowing— the last one being known euphemistically in the military as "requisitioning," or just plain stealing. To beg effectively, you needed a good sob story— but just about everybody could come up with one in Nam. To bribe effectively, you needed to find someone willing to accept a personal gift (or gifts) in exchange for access to whatever it was you needed. For example, one captain in desperate need of lumber for his signal battalion noticed that when he ordered truck parts, they'd come in big crates that could be dismantled for the lumber. He managed to find a supply sergeant who was willing to send him truck parts each week in exchange for an expensive bottle of scotch. The parts would then be sent back, minus the crates, so the sergeant still had his full complement of truck parts— uncrated— while the captain had the lumber he needed.

FRED: And of course the sergeant had his new bottle of Chivas Regal every week! Bartering, on the other hand, was considered a legitimate and time-honored way of obtaining necessary supplies in the military. For example, a transportation company with access to plenty of lumber might need a supply of surgical masks for its truck drivers to wear on those horribly dusty roads during the dry season. The supply sergeant then finds a hospital that's got a surplus of masks but has a need for his lumber— and it's a done deal, completely off the books!

STEVE: And then there was the fourth and final entry in the scrounging category— "requisitioning." The dictionary defines it as "seizing property that belongs to someone else." On the one hand, theft was treated very harshly in the military. For example, if a soldier was caught stealing from his fellow trainees in Basic Training, the troops were encouraged to hold a "Blanket Party" in which a blanket was thrown over the offending G.I. and a couple of soldiers would sit on the ends. Then everyone beat on the guy with blunt objects such as a large bar of soap wrapped in a towel or sock. The thief would usually learn his lesson from that point on.

FRED: But in a combat zone, theft by one unit from another unit (to obtain needed equipment or supplies) was considered a fairly normal and acceptable activity, as long as it was for the common good and not the personal enrichment of a few individuals. It was justified by the rationale that if Company A stole needed materiel from Company B, the transfer of goods was actually Company B's fault for not providing better security for their own equipment.

STEVE: And when it occurred, there would be a tendency for Company A's officers to "look the other way" unless (and until) the perpetrators were caught red-handed.

FRED: So on this particular day, the 24th Evac was in desperate need of lumber with which to build cabinets and shelving for our new hospital. I'm on guard at the front gate when I see a deuce and a half truck go roaring past in a cloud of dust with a big load of (precariously balanced) lumber hanging out of the back end. Some 40 yards past our gate, it hits a nasty bump and the entire load gets dumped right there on the dirt road. I thought the truck would immediately stop, but it just kept on going. The driver apparently didn't know— or didn't care— about what had just happened.

STEVE: So did you immediately think about trying to requisition that lumber before someone else did?

FRED: No, I was thinking about the Golden Rule we learned in grade school: "Do unto others as you would have them do unto you." At that time nobody had explained the rules to me about when it was, or was not, okay to "seize property belonging to someone else." So I got on the field phone and called the Sergeant of the Guard to report the matter, thinking someone would immediately try to locate the unit that owned that truck and tell them to come back for their lumber.

STEVE: Did anyone do that?

FRED: Someone did take swift action, but it wasn't exactly what I expected. Within minutes, our own deuce and a half goes roaring out of the front gate and screeches to a stop at the lumber pile, whereupon Sergeant Parlor and a couple other guys from the 24th jump out and start frantically throwing that wood into the back of their truck. They appeared to be laughing as they did so— kind of like when we were tossing the baking sheets off the stern of the Weigel. Before long PFC Tidwell and I— both watching from the guard bunker— were laughing too as we watched those guys trying to play "beat the clock" before that empty lumber truck came back!

STEVE: So much for the Golden Rule. Willie Parlor, a Wardmaster by trade, was temporarily in charge of the cabinet building crew and must have been tickled pink to see all that good wood.

FRED: For sure! I tried to imagine what would happen when that other deuce and a half rolled into its own compound, triumphantly delivering its big load of wooden treasure, only to have the NCOIC say to the driver "What in the hell are you tryin' to pull, soldier? Your rig is empty! Where's your load?" "Gee Sarge, I know it was there when I made the turn off Highway One. I watched it to make sure the load didn't shift!" "Well it sure as hell musta shifted before ya got HERE, butthead! Get out there and find it— and don't come back til you do!"

STEVE: Did that other truck ever come back for its lumber?

FRED: Well, Tidwell and I quickly realized that each time a truck went by heading in the opposite direction from where that one had gone, we'd have to play it stonefaced and nonchalant, like we didn't even notice that a truck was passing by. After 10 or 15 minutes we saw one go barreling past at a high rate of speed, so we figured that was probably the one that was out searching for its wayward load. We never batted an eye, and it never even slowed down.

STEVE: That cargo probably went down in history as "The Phantom Lumber Load of Long Binh!" But anyway, the most memorable event on daytime gate guard for me was the day Robert Mitchum showed up, riding alone in a jeep with some colonel behind the wheel. It was around the end of February '67.

FRED: Sounds like a good subject for the next chapter of our book!

&&&&&&&&&&&&&&&&&

FACT OR FICTION? *The story goes that PFC Elmendorf was walking past the nurses shower one evening when he heard a woman's voice loudly moaning "Thirteen.... thirteen.... thirteen.... thirteen...." Noticing a 2-inch knothole in the wall a foot or two above his head, plus an empty ammo crate sitting on the ground, he climbed up on the crate to look in and see if someone might be in trouble. At first he saw nothing— until the end of a mop handle was suddenly thrust through the hole, poking him in the eye and knocking him off his crate. Laying on the ground, he heard the mysterious moaning again: "Fourteen.... fourteen.... fourteen.... fourteen...."*

CHAPTER 20

ROBERT MITCHUM NEEDS
TO LEARN HOW TO SALUTE

*Hey, Mister Mitchum.... why not take
your shirt off and stay awhile?*

FRED: One morning near the end of February, Steve was on daytime guard at the front gate. He saw a jeep pull in and spotted the little flags flapping in the breeze on the fenders indicating a field grade officer was on board. Time to straighten up and fly right!

STEVE: Right— it was a colonel. Military protocol said the highest ranking man in the vehicle was supposed to sit in the front passenger seat unless he was driving himself, which must have been the case because the guy in the passenger seat was wearing civvies— a cream-colored "safari suit" like the Big Game Hunters used to wear.

FRED: But you knew there must have been a colonel in the vehicle, and you knew you were supposed to salute him, right?

STEVE: Yeah, ya don't wanna be messin' with no colonel. I just wanted to salute and wave him through as quickly as I could. So I gave a rifle salute to the vehicle and caught a brief glimpse of the driver's right arm going up, which told me that he returned it— even though I couldn't see squat due to the glare off the windshield.

FRED: Mission accomplished! So you dropped your weapon down to "port arms" and waved them on in.

STEVE: As the jeep started up, I noticed that the guy in the safari suit was slouched way down in the seat with a goofy grin on his face, like he was sloshed. He tried to return my salute in a half-assed, almost mocking way and gave me another clownish grin as he passed within a few feet of me. He was obviously plastered... and on top of that, he looked a lot like Robert Mitchum.

FRED: But you didn't think it was him.

STEVE: Not at first. Celebrities usually traveled with a small entourage of at least two or three people, and he had none if you didn't count the driver. I said to the other sentry "Did you see that guy in the passenger seat? He looked like Robert Mitchum... Hey, wait a minute! I heard the other day that Mitchum was probably gonna be here some time this week. That was him! He saluted me.... and he was bombed!"

FRED: Something for you to pass on to your grandchildren!

STEVE: Yup, there I was being saluted by Robert Mitchum— while he was in his cups, no less— in 1967! What I didn't realize until later was that Mitchum would spend a total of three days and three nights at the 24th Evac in various states of inebriation.

FRED: Usually when celebrities showed up they'd be wearing green jungle fatigues so they could blend in. Why do you suppose Mitchum wore a cream-colored safari suit instead? Do you think he was trying to look cool, or maybe impress the ladies?

STEVE: Well it could have been that, or perhaps he figured that if he was going out in the boonies, he'd prefer not to be mistaken by the enemy for an American officer with a 5000-dong bounty on his head (roughly 50 bucks, give or take.) Although some people might surmise that he'd be safer if he blended in with the rest of the troops.

FRED: If it had been me, I probably would have gone with the olive drab. After all, if your chopper should get shot down, ya don't wanna be runnin' around the jungle in a cream-colored suit, I would think. If Charlie don't get ya, the tigers might. Especially if they should recognize that Big Game Hunter getup— they just might not be in any mood to form a welcoming committee!

STEVE: It's been said that Mitchum loved being worshipped by the troops out in the field, as well as visiting with the hospital patients— and especially socializing with the nurses and Donut Dollies. Whenever he wasn't talking with wounded soldiers at the 24th Evac, he would spend the majority of his time having cocktails in the officers club or the nurses lounge.

FRED: One patient, Dennis Schelinski from Illinois, said "he was nice to everyone on the ward and very generous with his time. He talked to me about sports, women and so on. The nurses eventually tried to move him along, but he wouldn't leave until he was ready to go." Dennis also said Mitchum spoke about "which one of the nurses might be going to visit him later," as if he more or less "had his pick."

STEVE: Now before we go any further, we should state that everything we know about Robert Mitchum is stuff we've either read or been told by others who interacted with him. In the legal sense, this would all qualify as "hearsay" since we didn't witness any of it ourselves— other than his performance at the front gate. But we did learn some interesting hearsay about Mister Mitchum— much of which he freely acknowledged to biographers and interviewers.

FRED: For one thing, over the years he often admitted that he liked to tell "tall tales" whenever the opportunity arose. One of his famous quotes was "I learned early in life that by telling stories far more colorful than the truth... one's real truth is left alone." Probably a reference to the fact that he had a very rough upbringing which he preferred not to discuss. Or perhaps a reference to his mundane life prior to becoming a movie star in the 1940's.

STEVE: In his biography he acknowledged that he loved booze, tobacco and entertaining the ladies. One famous quote was "The pretty women come to me with their troubles and I, uhhh... cheer them up a little." During his three days at the 24th Evac, some people thought he acted like an absolute gentleman while others saw him more as a drunken lout. But over 72 hours, it's quite possible that both of those impressions could have been correct at various points in time.

FRED: A nurse on one ward, Maureen Robinson, said she was working with a patient when Mitchum came on the ward and started shaking hands and making small talk with each one of the troops. Her patient was taking it all in and got so excited that when Mitchum reached out for a handshake, he said "It's a great pleasure to meet you, Mister Wayne!" Some of the others laughed and the soldier was obviously embarrassed, but Mitchum didn't flinch— he just said "That's OK, I get that a lot. People often mistake me for the Duke!"

STEVE: One of our Head Nurses, Captain Carolyn Tanaka, took the letters she had written home to her family and had them published in the National Archive in Washington. In one she says "I felt good enough to attend a party last night at the 24th Evac. Robert Mitchum was next door in one of the nurse's quarters, but he was so drunk and obnoxious that we didn't invite him to the party." We have no way of knowing how many others might have shared that view.

FRED: Another nurse at the 24th, Lieutenant Jeanne Markle, was quoted in an interview for the Veterans History Project of the Library of Congress. She said Mitchum had been traveling around the country entertaining the troops. When he got to the 24th Evac he decided to "take a little R&R" and hunker down for three or four days. She said "We entertained him in the living room of our nurses hooch, and he stayed there for three nights. He wouldn't let us take his picture, but he autographed a bunch of military currency for us as souvenirs."

STEVE: Now why do you suppose someone presumably as vain as your typical movie star wouldn't want his picture taken? Maybe he was concerned about being out of shape and sporting a good hangover. He looked pretty wasted when he gave me that half-assed salute at the front gate. (Of course he was trying to get a laugh from me— I think— and he succeeded before I realized who he was!)

FRED: Then again, maybe he didn't want pictures floating around of him being surrounded by a bevy of female nurses in their own bar- racks. He was married to the same woman, after all, for over half a century. And rumors of him being a skirt chaser followed him around for years— but for all we know, he may have been deliberately perpetu- ating those "tall tales" to enhhance his macho image.

STEVE: Far be it from us to try to surmise what was or wasn't true. Besides, Mitchum undoubtedly had a temporary ID card bestowing on him the honorary rank of Major or Light Colonel. And I think the sign at the entrance to the nurse barracks simply said OFFICERS ONLY BEYOND THIS POINT. So therefore he would have been within his rights to hang out there, wouldn't he?

FRED: By golly, he just might! One thing we did hear from several sources— including patients, nurses and at least one medical officer— was that Mitchum liked to brag about "having fun in the dark" with a few of the nurses and/or Red Cross girls (the Donut Dollies.) Then again, since he was famous for telling tall tales throughout his life, he could have been making it all up.

STEVE: If he was, he would have had to be fighting off the women, since he was one handsome, sexy dude— even at age 50!

FRED: But another nurse, Captain Cherie Boudwin, said "I had a long conversation with Mitchum during cocktail hour in the nurse's lounge. He was a perfect gentleman and while he may have had a lot to drink, he didn't show any obvious signs that it was affecting him."

STEVE: She said he was very polite and engaging. He talked a lot about Marilyn Monroe and how down-to-earth and reserved she was. He claimed that he probably could have prevented her suicide if he hadn't been filming on the East Coast when it happened.

FRED: Cherie Boudwin also said "If Mitchum was having one night stands while he was at the 24th Evac, I clearly was NOT one of them. Maybe I was the only one who didn't realize what he was up to. He certainly was one hunk of a man though.... I guess I missed out on that one!" She said she was under the impression he had been spending his free time with one of the Red Cross girls.

FRED: Cherie, who went by the nickname of Posie, said the first time she ever saw Mitchum was late at night when she was coming out of the latrine. She saw a suspicious man squatting on the ground near the latrine and assumed he was probably a pervert. She was about to read him the riot act when a Red Cross girl came out of the women's latrine, pointed to the squatter and said "Hi Posie, I'd like you to meet Robert Mitchum!" Mitchum stood up and smiled, shook her hand and then Posie watched as the two of them strolled off into the darkness. She added that "We then proceeded to have a four-day party— in his honor— in the living room of one of the nurse hooches."

STEVE: The fact that he liked to "drink good booze and entertain the ladies" might explain why Mitchum seemed to be traveling alone with a rather loose itinerary.

FRED: He particularly liked getting out in the field with the troops where he could drink and gamble with the boys, fire off some "practice rounds" on an M-60 machine gun and trade war stories with the GI's. In one instance described in his biography, Mitchum flew to a remote firebase in a Huey helicopter accompanied by a lieutenant as his guide. His routine was to pose for photos, sign autographs, shake hands, meet some of the brass, chat with the troops and collect messages and phone numbers from the soldiers so he could phone their families when he got back to the states. The young lieutenant, wanting to make sure they got home before dark, was trying to hurry things along when Mitchum said "Relax man, what's your hurry? Where can we get a drink around here?"

STEVE: They were directed to a makeshift clubhouse where he asked how much it would cost him to "buy the bar." He produced a fat roll of bills and laid down a couple hundred bucks— enough so that those troops wound up drinking on Mitchum's tab for the next month or so, according to the story. (Booze was incredibly cheap in Nam, since there was no tax and no middleman.) Then he drank and played craps with the soldiers 'til he lost most of his roll. Hopping back into the chopper, he and his escort took off as twilight was approaching.

FRED: In another episode, Mitchum said he was flying in a chopper when his pilot got lost and had to touch down at an American outpost that was bracing for an imminent attack. The commanding officer was stunned, saying "Robert Mitchum! What in the hell are you doing here?" Mitchum's answer was "Anything to get out of the house!" As soon as the pilot got his bearings, they took off again— and according to Mitchum, "Eleven minutes later, that camp got hit. When the smoke cleared, there were only six survivors."

STEVE: Now that sounds like it could be the same type of "tall tale" that got Brian Williams booted off the air by NBC News. But Mitchum could get away with it because he was, after all, just an actor!

FRED: Indeed he was. Mitchum had gotten his start in films in the 1940's by appearing in seven "Hopalong Cassidy" western movies starring William Boyd as "Hoppy." He said he carefully studied the star dressed all in black and later tried to model his acting style after Boyd's calm, quiet and understated method.

STEVE: Occasionally Hoppy would brandish his twin pearl-handled sixguns to mete out justice for average folks who couldn't fend for themselves— although he always tried to capture the bad guys rather than shoot them. And when gunplay was inevitable, he would always let the villain draw first (I wonder how many guys got killed trying to follow that advice? Kind of like "no shooting Charlie unless he fires first!")

FRED: If we had only known about the Hopalong connection back then, we could have set up a meeting with Mitchum and William Boyd right there at the 24th Evac!

STEVE: You're referring to one of our medics named Bill Boyd. I used to call him "Hopalong" until one day I was passing him on the sidewalk and said "Hey Hopalong, how's it goin'?" He stops, glares at me and says "Hey man, muh name's Boyd. WILLIAM BOYD."

FRED: He was a short fellow but built like a fireplug, so you got the feeling you didn't want to mess with him.

STEVE: Certainly not. But I had meant no disrespect; it was generally considered a badge of honor to be given a nickname like that by your fellow soldiers. I suppose he might have thought it sounded like he was being ridiculed if somebody called him Hopalong.

FRED: Yeah, some of the guys used to call you "Mellow Yellow" or "Sunshine Superman" because those were two hit songs by the rock star Donovan. It was supposed to be a sign of respect and friendship for them to give you special recognition like that.

STEVE: Personally I didn't mind being called Mellow Yellow, but I didn't especially like it when they would shorten the other name to just "Sunshine." I guess I never really got used to guys saying "Hey Sunshine, how's it goin'?"

FRED: Another one of Mitchum's stories that sounded like it might be an exaggeration involved his having to lie about his horsemanship skills in order to get the first Hoppy movie. He said the horse they gave him kept throwing him— until he finally punched it in the mouth, after which he had no problems.

STEVE: This was reminiscent of the scenario portrayed later in "Blazing Saddles" (1974) when Mongo, played by NFL star Alex Karras, appeared to slug a horse in the jaw and knock it to the ground. If you watch Mongo's performance on YouTube, you can see that just as he punches, the rider yanks hard on the right rein, which causes the horse's head to swing around and the horse to fall down, just as he was trained to do. We all got fooled by a stunt horse!

FRED: Mitchum's personal assistant said when he returned from Nam, he brought hundreds of scraps of paper bearing names and phone numbers given to him by the GI's. He'd spend days calling them and saying "Hi, this is Robert Mitchum. I just wanted to say I saw your son while I was in Vietnam and he asked me to give you a call. He looks fine, he feels good and he's doing a great job over there."

STEVE: The personal assistant said she'd overhear him telling interviewers that he had participated in dozens of unspecified "missions sanctioned by the government," some involving the CIA, but the reporters never bothered to verify the stories. She would wonder "where's this stuff coming from?" But she knew how he liked to embellish. Afterward they'd both laugh about it.

FRED: Brian Williams, eat your heart out! Mitchum probably did get debriefed by the CIA when he came back, just like many others who spent time traveling around the war zone. But if indeed he had been involved in top secret government missions, there probably wouldn't have been any way to verify those stories anyway.

STEVE: As for his supposed exploits with the ladies, he was alleged to have had a three-year relationship in the early 60's with the actress Shirley MacLaine— 17 years his junior. (She described it in her autobiography.) That was right about the time I had the hots for her myself (big time!) while I was in high school. If only I had known that when he saluted me back in '67.

FRED: Why? What would you have done if you knew?

STEVE: Well at the very least I would have wanted to shake the hand... that shook the whatever... of the woman of my dreams!

&&&&&&&&&&&&&&&&&&&

FACT OR FICTION? *The story goes that one of the Donut Dollies (AKA Red Cross girls) went on sick call for an examination to determine why she was experiencing itching and pain in her genital area. After some tests, the doctor told her "You have acute vaginitis." Whereupon she replied "Why thank you, doctor. And you have a dashing mustache!"*

CHAPTER 21

HE WHO CASTS THE FIRST STONER

What? You spent a whole year in Nam and never saw a single drug-crazed, baby-killing rapist?

FRED: When I was a teenager, if somebody got "stoned" it meant he was drunk out of his mind on an alcoholic beverage. But starting in the mid-60's, a person could also be stoned if he got really high on marijuana or some other type of mind-altering drug.

STEVE: If the term was used by some pot-smoking hippie, you knew he meant stoned on drugs. But if it was some beer-swilling frat boy or football jock, he probably meant stoned on alcohol. Gradually the druggies co-opted the term until it became the property of the "stoners"— those who got high on weed or some illicit drug.

FRED: If one adhered to the dual meanings, it was safe to say there were plenty of stoners in the 24th Evac in 1966. But most were stoned on beer or booze, not on illegal substances. And the majority confined their "altered states" to off-duty hours only.

STEVE: As construction workers engaged in building a hospital from scratch, we all knocked off around 4 or 5 pm and many proceeded to guzzle large quantities of the golden fluid until "lights out" at 2200 hours (10 pm.) Later when we were staffing a hospital 24 hours a day, the drinking was far more subdued.

FRED: A lot has been written about soldiers in Vietnam being a wild bunch of "pot smoking, drug-crazed baby killers." It's also been reported that anywhere from 40 to 70 percent used marijuana or hard drugs like heroin during their tours. We saw no evidence to support those conclusions during the year we spent there. Whatever truth there might have been to those statements, most of the heavy drug use and abysmal behavior didn't begin until about '68 or '69— a year or more after we'd returned to civilian life.

STEVE: By then, many (if not most) of the new draftees were at least mildly opposed to the war, if not downright antagonistic toward it. It's also been reported that most of the military personnel who used drugs in Nam were already drug users in civilian life before they were inducted. This I would tend to believe, since public tolerance of marijuana use was much greater in the states by '69 than it had been when we were inducted in '65. I think it was during my sophomore year in college that some of my classmates on the Madison campus started experimenting with grass, though I had no interest in it myself.

FRED: At that time I don't think the drug culture had made it to Oshkosh yet. But in Nam, there were a relatively small number of pot smokers in our camp who quickly found out that dirt-cheap weed was readily available in Bien Hoa. We had several friends from California and Texas who brought their pot-smoking habits with them from civilian life and continued such pursuits in the war zone. As for me, Budweiser and Pabst Blue Ribbon were about the only mind-altering substances I ever needed, so I had little interest in experimenting with drugs despite frequent offers from some of our friends to sample the wares.

STEVE: And at times there were no American beers available, so we'd have to drink Tiger Ale from Singapore or Ba Muoi Ba ("33") Beer made in Saigon. Except I couldn't drink more than two cans of either one before they'd give me a splitting headache.

FRED: Just about every Vietnam vet will tell you that 33 Beer was rumored to be brewed with formaldehyde as a preservative. This was commonly employed as an embalming fluid, so it gave the beer some extra kick as well as making it somewhat lethal. That might explain your headaches— though some historians maintain that there never was any truth to the formaldehyde rumors in the first place.

STEVE: To some degree there was a bit of a racial component to the determination of whether you were a "juicer" or a "stoner." You were more likely to favor grass if you were black; tequila if you were Hispanic; and beer or whiskey if you were white. In the evenings there were several hooches you'd walk past where you could always count on getting a good whiff of marijuana smoke wafting out of the open tent flaps. You probably could have gotten high just by going in the tent and standing around for ten minutes. Some guys who were "non-tokers" were moved to a different hooch at their own request.

FRED: If there were any prohibitions against smoking the stuff, we were unaware of them. We knew it was illegal in the states, so we assumed it would be in the military too. But historians say pot was largely ignored by the US Army prior to '68. Officially we received no warnings or threats of any kind. It was as if the higher-ups had no idea what was going on— nor any idea as to what that very distinctive odor might have been.

STEVE: It was pretty obvious that the Army treated pot differently from other drugs. This could have been due in part to the fact that prior to '68, the military had no crime lab in country that could test drug samples. They had to be sent to a lab in Japan, which took six weeks or more— too much time to waste on a relatively minor offense.

FRED: American commanders often considered alcohol to be a bigger problem than weed or hashish, which was derived from marijuana resin. One officer summed it up by saying "A soldier is much more likely to be fresh and alert in the morning if he smoked grass the night before than if he got juiced up on alcohol." Apparently the Army didn't begin cracking down on pot possession until '68, after we had left. At that time they started prosecuting users and even had South Vietnamese troops going out into rural areas to destroy large fields of marijuana that was being grown as a cash crop.

STEVE: It wasn't until '71 that the Army started subjecting returning soldiers to drug testing before they could leave Nam. Any GI who flunked a drug test was sent to detox for a week or so until he could "get clean." The Army also guaranteed that returning troops could receive treatment for addiction when they arrived in the states.

FRED: Back in 1966, about twice a year a Drug Education Officer would come around to the 24th Evac from the CID (Criminal Investigation Division) to give us a lecture about the dangers of drugs. I paid little attention since I had no interest in drugs anyway, but I don't remember any mention of penalties for smoking marijuana.

STEVE: I do remember him warning us that the pot for sale in Bien Hoa was often soaked in an opium solution and then dried out before being sold. This was allegedly done to try to get us hooked on hard drugs, but it sounded more like a story made up by the CID to try to scare us into staying away from Vietnamese weed.

FRED: It was also fairly common for infantry grunts out in the field to discover quantities of opium or pot in the knapsacks of dead VC or NVA soldiers, almost as if it was routine for their troops to use the stuff regularly. Some GI's claimed that enemy soldiers would toke up before a battle to reduce their fear and give themselves extra measures of courage and endurance.

STEVE: Some VC also carried a supply of betel nut, a mild narcotic that was commonly chewed in a mixture with lime, tobacco and betel leaves. Betel was supposed to give one a feeling of calmness and well-being as well as boosting the chewer's energy and stamina. It also numbed the gums and caused many older Vietnamese, especially the elder mama-sans, to have reddish-black teeth and gums.

FRED: Yeah, the first time a GI saw an old mama-san give him one of those big black-toothed grins, it was a shock he would not soon forget! They always seemed to be real happy, too. The betel chewers used to spit dark-colored juice frequently, similar to the way men spit when they chew tobacco.

STEVE: That probably explains why I got sick when I tried some chewing tobacco one day in college. I forgot to spit!

FRED: Some of our guys probably bought weed directly from the mama-sans who cleaned their hooches. But I'm not exactly sure, since nobody in our tent used the stuff.

STEVE: One of my college dorm buddies— everyone called him "Scooter"— was stationed at Bien Hoa Airbase. He said every guy in his outfit was either a juicer— like him— or a stoner. Their hooch maid explained that she sold pot to the troops because she was saving her money to put her daughters through college.

FRED: And then one evening she gave Scooter a mild shock while he was on guard duty, right?

STEVE: He was standing in the guard tower next to the airstrip when he spotted a Vietnamese doing something suspicious at the far end of the runway. Suspecting a saboteur, he took a look through his field glasses and saw someone cutting marijuana that was growing wild just inside the perimeter of the base. After adjusting the focus on the binoculars, he realized it was none other than his own hooch maid— harvesting the next day's profits!

FRED: Mama-san was working overtime to bolster the educational fund! And with no need for a supplier— or a middleman. That would have to qualify as being super-industrious, I would think.

STEVE: I had no interest whatsoever in being a pot smoker myself, but I recognized that the situation in Nam presented a golden opportunity to try it and find out what it was like— purely for future reference— without fear of consequences. Our California buddies would regularly offer us weed and one, SP4 Dan Berkley, even offered to share little pieces of his "letters from home."

FRED: It seems that his brother would mail him letters on pastel-colored stationery. The last three or four pages would be completely blank— but Dan knew that meant they were painted with a solution of LSD which had dried before the letters were mailed. He'd be relaxing in a chair in our hooch, tearing off little bits of paper from one of the blank pages and sucking on them. Then after several "hits" he'd sit for a while in a hallucinatory stupor without saying or doing much of anything. The slight grin on his face meant he was getting a lot of enjoyment from it. Afterward he'd try to describe his hallucinations, but they seemed to have little appeal for us.

STEVE: He offered to let us try sucking on some paper ourselves, but being from Madison I already knew LSD was an unpredictable drug that could severely mess with your head, so I declined. Berkley's brother also used to send him "primo California weed" packed into those little round aluminum film canisters commonly used to send camera film off to be developed.

FRED: So then you eventually decided to smoke some reefer?

STEVE: Yeah, basically I just wanted to know how a marijuana high compared to an alcohol high. Dan offered me a pre-rolled joint that came out of a Marlboro box he bought in Bien Hoa for something like 5 bucks. It seems that the Vietnamese would take filtered Marlboros and carefully roll them between thumb and finger until all the tobacco fell out. Then they'd pack them with weed, twist the ends closed and stick 'em back in the box.

FRED: That explains where they got their tobacco to mix with the betel nut! I've heard that they even wrapped the boxes in cellophane, but I never saw one like that so I don't know if it was true. Supposedly when you opened the box you could tell if they were cigarettes or "ready-rolls" only by the fact that the marijuana sticks were a little bit shorter due to the twisted ends.

STEVE: Meanwhile I set up a controlled experiment where I was basically sitting alone with no outside influences to alter the experience— it was just me and the weed. I smoked an entire joint and then waited for something to happen.

FRED: And what happened?

STEVE: Not a damned thing. It was a complete bust. I tried it again a few days later and it was the same story. I began to think it was either bad weed or maybe the whole thing was a myth. Finally a week later I decided maybe I wasn't doing it right, so I'd give it one more shot. I inhaled as deeply as I could, held it in my lungs as long as possible and then slowly exhaled— just like I'd seen in the movies.

FRED: Was there any difference?

STEVE: Sure enough. Not only did I proceed to get higher than a kite, but I was sitting in a wicker chair smoking this joint when my keen senses detected a powerful smell of acrid smoke. I knew something must be on fire, so I leaped out of my chair, stepped into the center aisle of our tent and hollered loud enough for all the guys to hear: "Hey, what the hell is burning?"

FRED: Did someone answer?

STEVE: Yeah, SP4 Bonomo pointed at me from 20 feet away and said "YOU ARE!!" I looked down and saw that a flaming cinder had set my green Amy T-shirt on fire. It created a perfectly round hole on my chest that was getting bigger and bigger by the second. After I put out the flames, I sat down and finished the doobie. At that point I realized I was totally wasted and ready to either fall asleep or pass out, I'm not sure which. I "floated" the length of our hooch— feeling like I was a foot or so off the ground— to get to my bunk and flopped on top of it. Within seconds I was out like a light.

FRED: So after that, did you form any conclusions about comparing the effects of marijuana and booze?

STEVE: Yes, a couple of 'em. I noticed that being high on weed was similar to being drunk on alcohol but without the negative side effects like slurred speech, loss of balance or impaired vision. But I also concluded weed was highly unpredictable, given the fact that it caused me to pass out in short order. I concluded right then that I wanted to have nothing more to do with the stuff— I'd stick to alcohol, thank you very much, since at least I would know what to expect.

FRED: I did try Dan's weed once or twice but on one occasion I threw up afterward, so that was the last time for me. Did it ever occur to you that perhaps you had just smoked an opium-laced joint?

STEVE: At the time, no. But later we learned that out in the bush, the VC would sometimes use opium-soaked joints to knock out the GI's just before staging a night attack.

FRED: Well wait a minute now, just how was Charlie going to get G.I. Joe to smoke a joint that was of dubious origin?

STEVE: It was pretty simple, actually. At firebases, base camps and nightly bivouacs out in the boonies, young Vietnamese girls would walk up to the perimeter defenses and sell ready-rolls to the GI's at twilight. Once they had earned the trust of the Americans, they could easily switch to spiked joints any time Charlie directed them to.

FRED: So then when they did, half the troops would be out cold by 10 pm— and the Cong could overrun the camp with relative ease?

STEVE: Exactly. Now whether this actually occurred is anyone's guess. It could have been just another of those CID "scare stories" designed to prevent GI's from wanting to try Vietnamese weed. The brass undoubtedly knew the "rumor mill" was a very effective means for disseminating fabrications as well as actual facts. But at least it could explain why I barely made it to my bunk before I passed out— someone had slipped a "mickey" into my "reefer!"

FRED: Reminds me of another story. A patient at the 24th Evac was a "cannon cocker" (artilleryman) who received a bullet wound in the leg at a firebase. When he saw this Colonel coming on the ward to present Purple Hearts to all the wounded, he turned over and pretended to be asleep. Afterward the fellow in the adjacent bed asked him why he was so reluctant to participate.

STEVE: And the artilleryman said it was because he'd been shot not by the Cong, but by his Vietnamese drug dealer?

FRED: Right. He had an arrangement with a civilian from a nearby village. Every afternoon the guy would stick a bag of weed in a hiding place outside the perimeter. The GI would go out, pick up the pot and leave a bundle of cash in its place. Then he'd sell it in small quantities to the other guys in his outfit and make a handsome profit.

STEVE: But then something must have gone wrong if he got shot. What went wrong?

FRED: The artillery unit got orders to abandon the camp in two days and move to a new site. On their last day, the soldier went out to pick up his weed and decided not to bother leaving any money. But then the unit's departure was delayed by half a day. The next morning he got shot by a sniper while he was loading supplies on a truck. This brought helicopter gunships and the whole nine yards searching for Charlie, but not a single enemy soldier was found.

STEVE: Did anyone think it was odd that he was the only guy who got shot... and that no enemy troops were found?

FRED: Sure, especially since their firebase had never been attacked by small arms before. But he and some of his buddies were the only ones who knew why he was shot and who did it— naturally they didn't dare tell anybody it was his pot dealer. He finally felt guilty enough to confess to the man in the next bed at the 24th Evac!

STEVE: Well anyway, one thing I learned from my adventure in trying a little grass was that if the Army was gonna be sending us into a combat zone, then by golly they should at least have provided us with flame retardant T-shirts!

FRED: Okay, so like the vast majority of guys in our outfit, we were juicers and not stoners. As long as I got my three or four cans of Schlitz or PBR every night, I was reasonably happy.

STEVE: Usually by that point you would have lost count anyway, right? I, on the other hand, was partial to hard liquor mixed with something like fruit juice or 7-Up. But often the mix was harder to find than the booze, so I wound up drinking a lot of beer too.

FRED: For about the first six months of our tour, we could buy as many cases of (warm) beer as we wanted for like 2 bucks a case. Of course you could buy ice cold cans in the beer tent for 10 cents apiece, but only two at a time— and they had to be opened.

STEVE: To buy hard liquor at the PX, I think you had to be an E-5 or higher (meaning at least a sergeant or an SP5.) Since our buddies were E-3's and E-4's like us, I would have to find an E-5 willing to accept a small bribe in exchange for buying me a bottle. Top shelf brands were usually less than $1.50 for a fifth.

FRED: About halfway through our tour, the Army went to ration cards that allowed you to buy something like two bottles of liquor and three cases of beer per month. They'd punch your card at the PX when you made a purchase. If you wanted more than the allotted amount, you'd have to find a buddy who either didn't drink or was willing to let you rent or borrow his ration card.

STEVE: But still, if you wanted to drink anything other than beer, both the liquor and the mix could at times be damned hard to get. That is, until one day when the heavens seemed to open up... and offer an answer to our prayers!

FRED: You must be referring to the episode where an epidemic of venereal disease was magically transformed into the World's Longest Wapatuli Party! (That's pronounced WOPPA-TOOLEY.)

STEVE: The problem for us was that thanks to SP4 Talbot, we had plenty of "Woppa" but not much "Tooley." Wapatuli was invented on college campuses some time in the 1950's. It's had other names like Trash Can Punch, Panty Dropper Punch, Killer Kool-Aid or Purple Jesus, but in Nam it was often called "Jungle Juice."

FRED: The basic concept for a Wapatuli Party in high school or college was that every guest would bring a bottle of booze and/or a bottle of mixer like fruit juice, ginger ale or 7-Up. Some of the more common types of liquor would be rum, vodka, gin or cheap champagne. They'd all be mixed together in a trash can or wastebasket. Then you'd throw in a little fresh fruit, sugar and ice... get a ladle... and start filling everyone's glass!

STEVE: If you were lucky you'd get a fairly pleasant tasting (but highly potent) punch that was capable of knocking everyone on their keester. When it was all gone, those who could still stand up would proceed to eat the liquor-soaked fruit left at the bottom of the barrel. But what really put the "WOPPA" in the mixture was pure grain alcohol, often known commercially as Everclear (which today is illegal in about 15 states because it can be lethal— especially to amateur drinkers who don't know when to quit.)

FRED: With an alcohol content of 95 percent, Everclear was 190 proof— the highest possible proof for an alcoholic beverage. Any higher and it would start to evaporate before you could even get it up to your lips. In comparison, beer was usually 5-6 percent alcohol, meaning that a glass of Everclear was 17 times more potent than an equal sized glass of beer. It tended to take on the flavor of whatever you mixed it with, so it didn't interfere with the other ingredients in the mixture and was virtually undetectable to the novice drinker. (But if you were foolish enough to try to drink it straight, it would produce a severe burning sensation in the throat.)

STEVE: Once you had all the ingredients in your Wapatuli vat, you'd dump in a quart or two of Everclear. This yielded a concoction which, while pleasant tasting enough, was so potent that it would sneak up on folks and get them totally smashed before they even realized what was happening. At times they could be babbling like chimps as they were attempting to get up off the floor.

FRED: But to make Jungle Juice in a combat zone, you didn't have access to whatever ingredients your heart desired. Instead you had to make do with whatever was available. Just about everything you needed was scarce— and nothing more so than the Everclear! The Hospital Pharmacy had a supply of grain alcohol but it was needed as an antiseptic, a topical anesthetic and a solvent for cleaning and sterilizing equipment. Plus every drop had to be accounted for so that nobody would be pilfering it for personal consumption.

STEVE: One of the most important functions of a good Supply Sergeant in a combat zone was the ability to scrounge and barter for needed materials and equipment. For example, infantry grunts seldom wore flak vests in the bush because they were too hot and cumbersome— and because once a GI learned his flak vest weighed just as much as six canteens of water, he'd usually say "Screw it, I'd rather carry the water!" Units like ours, on the other hand, had a use for flak vests since our sentries wore them on guard duty at night.

FRED: So if an infantry Supply Sergeant needed some truck tires in a hurry, he couldn't just pick up the phone and call Sears Roebuck. He'd have to find another unit that had some to spare— and then he'd have to offer something to trade, like several cases of flak jackets. This was the type of situation SP4 Talbot found himself in one day.

STEVE: The phone rings in the 24th Evac Pharmacy where Talbot was working. He answers and it's a Supply Sergeant from one of the infantry divisions we supported. It seems that their grunts had encountered a sizable "nest" of prostitutes somewhere out in the bush. As a result, a terrible outbreak of gonorrhea (a sexually transmitted disease also known as "the clap") had infected the troops— so much so that the platoon medics had completely exhausted their supply of the miracle drugs needed to deal with the problem.

FRED: Naturally the sergeant's first thought was to start calling hospital pharmacies to find some penicillin or tetracycline. Talbot says "Yeah, we've got a pretty good supply. Whatcha got to trade for it?" He rejects the first few offers before the sergeant says "How about four 5-gallon cans of pure grain alcohol?" Suddenly Talbot's eyes light up— 20 gallons of Everclear that would be completely off the books! Nobody would even know he had it, let alone make him account for every single drop! "Okay, ya got a deal," he answers.

STEVE: Hmmm... that would be 80 quarts of 190 proof booze— the alcohol equivalent of nearly 200 quarts of 80 proof vodka!

FRED: The infantry troops used alcohol as a solvent for cleaning weapons and other equipment. Naturally the sergeant didn't want word to get out that their troops all had VD, while SP4 Talbot didn't want word to get out that he had somehow acquired a large supply of grain alcohol. It was "hush-hush" on both sides of the equation.

STEVE: So Talbot packs up several hundred doses of "clap killer" and soon a chopper's landing at our helipad, ready to swap 20 gallons of "Jungle Juice starter" for a batch of miracle drugs. Talbot then stashes the Everclear in the Pharmacy and begins to quietly spread the word to a couple dozen of his "closest friends."

FRED: Imagine what that chopper pilot was thinking: "Here I am, flying a top secret mission in a combat zone where I could get shot out of the sky at any moment. And I'm doing it all to enable the guys at one end to get totally wasted on Everclear for some unspecified period of days, while the guys at the other end will all be saved in the nick of time from having their peckers shrivel up and drop off!"

STEVE: A noble undertaking, to be sure! Ain't war a bitch???

FRED: You can say that again. Since Everclear was undrinkable by itself, we had to find suitable liquids to cut it with. At the PX we bought what little fruit juice they had, plus some Ginger Ale, 7-Up and Mountain Dew. I remember mixing the stuff with tomato juice I got from the Mess Hall.

STEVE: By the way, they say grape juice was supposed to be an essential ingredient for making a "Screaming Purple Jesus."

FRED: Duly noted. If you brought Talbot some mix, he'd reward you by doling out small quantities of Everclear (it didn't take much, that's for sure!) Meanwhile he was stockpiling ingredients in the Pharmacy refrigerators as he prepared for a wild Wapatuli Party featuring genuine Vietnam Jungle Juice!

STEVE: A date was set for the "secret bash"— an evening when my name just happened to show up on the guard duty roster. This meant that a) I would not be participating, and b) I'd have to remain sober that night. Which didn't bother me a whole lot, since I didn't particularly enjoy getting "rip-roaring, falling-down drunk" anyway.

FRED: But you drank alcohol every night, just like the rest of us.

STEVE: True, but I always tried to pace myself so I could maintain control. In college I once got so wasted on Brandy Manhattans that after a certain point I had absolutely no recollection the next day of what had transpired.

FRED: And that bothered you a lot?

STEVE: Sure did, for two reasons. First, people said "Man, you were a riot last night!" But I had missed nearly the entire event insofar as my ability to remember any of it. And second, since I had no recollection of what transpired, that meant I could have insulted, raped or killed someone and yet not had any knowledge of it whatsoever. And that scared the hell out of me!

FRED: Or gotten someone pregnant, perhaps! As for me, my only defense against getting roaring drunk was that after consuming a certain amount of alcohol, I tended to either fall asleep or pass out, such that my friends had a hell of a time waking me up. I figured at least that would prevent me from ever drinking myself to death.

STEVE: So then I'm on guard duty when our buddies start hittin' the Jungle Juice. As I'm heading out for my shift, I notice some guys staggering or stumbling around outside and slurring their speech. And I'm thinking "Man, I hope this isn't the night we get attacked!"

FRED: As for me, I had several cups of Jungle Juice from out of the "community trough," got pretty trashed and then— true to form— I went and passed out on my bunk. End of Wapatuli for Fred.

STEVE: I had to wait 'til the next day to do any Jungle Juicin.' Talbot was still handing out cupfuls of Everclear on the sly— as he continued to do for the next week or so, since he had 80 quarts of the stuff— but we were on our own as far as what to mix it with. Every last drop of available fruit juice or mixer in our compound had been scarfed up already by the Jungle Juicers. The only thing I could find to mix with my Everclear was a packet of Kool-Aid that came out of a C-Rations box I had under my bunk. The concoction was virtually undrinkable, but I still drank it out of a sense of duty. Needless to say, the stuff gave me a splitting headache.

FRED: Although theoretically nobody had a hangover the next day. Since Everclear was 95 percent alcohol, there was almost no room for the impurities found in traditional liquors that are only 40 percent alcohol. And those impurities, plus dehydration, are supposed to be what causes hangovers.

STEVE: All in all, it was the principle of the thing that counted. We had figured out how to take a couple hundred cases of the clap and turn them into the world's longest Wapatuli Party. And not only that, but it hadn't cost us a cent. We had beaten that fuggin' system one more time, pardner! Take that, Mister Drill Sergeant!

FRED: Should we go back to Milwaukee and look him up?

&&&&&&&&&&&&&&&&&&&&

FACT OR FICTION? *The story goes that Chief Nurse Taylor told the Chief Surgeon that she'd read a book about Vietnamese culture and customs. "It said the women normally walk 10 paces behind their husbands out of respect," she told him. "Now I see the men are walking 20 paces behind their wives. What do you suppose it was that enabled the women to achieve such a momentous reversal of roles?" she asked. "Land mines," replied the surgeon.*

CHAPTER 22

HEY! NOBODY VOLUNTEERS
FOR ANYTHING, GOT IT?

*Why would our platoon sergeant care whether
we're working with shovels or paintbrushes?*

STEVE: When we were inducted in '65, I wondered whether or not I should make a big deal out of the fact that I had 4 years of French in high school and college. Most educated Vietnamese spoke French— due to the fact that the country was once French Indochina— while relatively few spoke English. So the Army might jump at the chance to utilize my talents as a translator by putting me in a position where I'd have frequent contact with French-speaking Vietnamese.

FRED: Thereby assuring, in the process, that you'd have little or no contact with those nasty Viet Cong, most of whom couldn't read or write any language at all— let alone English or French!

STEVE: Then again, if some Army lackey was gonna be looking at my records while trying to decide whether I should be sent to, say, Vietnam or Germany— he'd probably see "four years of French" and think "Whoa, jackpot! This boy's goin' straight to Nam, baby!"

FRED: So when we had our personal interviews at Fort Leonard Wood prior to Basic, you decided not to mention anything about your proficiency in French. But the sergeant saw it in your file.

STEVE: He said "I see you have a foreign language." Never mentioned that it was French, or that lots of Vietnamese spoke French— in fact if I had to guess, I'd say he wasn't even aware of it.

FRED: Well after all, the Army only told its personnel what they needed to know. In my case, the sergeant kept asking me what field I was interested in, then trying to change my mind when I answered him. I'd had a relative who'd been in the ASA (Army Security Agency) and that sounded intriguing, but the sergeant said I'd have to serve a three-year hitch because the training was so extensive. I ruled that out immediately!

STEVE: So then since you'd had summer jobs working construction, you thought you might like to be an Army electrician since it seemed like a pretty easy, low-stress occupation?

FRED: Yes, but he said "that wouldn't work because electricians have to be able to read color-coded wires and you showed some deficiencies on the color blindness test. Besides, you have pretty good test scores so you ought to be able to do better than that." It seemed like no matter what I proposed, he'd find a reason to reject it.

STEVE: I always thought the interviews were a bunch of hogwash anyway. The army knew it needed x number of electricians, x number of artillerymen, etc., in any given week— and there's no way he was going to recommend you for a job that wasn't on his quota sheet. I asked my interviewer to read off the choices and one was Military Intelligence. It sounded kinda cool, so I said "How about that?" He said "Well, your test scores are good and you have a foreign language, so I'll recommend you for it."

FRED: I finally told my interviewer I knew someone who'd been in the Medics and that sounded pretty good. I guess that must have been the magic word because he said "Okay, that'll work. Medics it is!" So ultimately I did get what I asked for, although in reality it was probably my fourth or fifth choice.

STEVE: I'll never know whether I actually would have gotten assigned to Military Intelligence. Halfway through Basic, I came down with a brutal "URI" (upper respiratory infection) and had to spend a week in the Fort Leonard Wood Hospital. Though I could barely stand up, I don't remember ever seeing a doctor while I was there.

FRED: Your first exposure to the Army's system for medical treatment ! If you didn't see a doctor, how did they diagnose your illness?

STEVE: I suppose they sent my samples to the lab. The nurses kept giving me pills four times a day. When I was released, I had missed a week of Basic so I had to be "recycled" into Alpha Company which was a week behind my previous one— "Double Time Charlie!"

FRED: And four weeks later, your original orders for Military Intelligence (or whatever they might have said) had to be rescinded because you weren't done with Basic yet.

STEVE: That's what I was told. I figured that when we graduated from Basic, they had a quota of Medical Corpsmen to be filled that week, so they put both of us in the Medics. My mysterious URI might have saved me from winding up in the Infantry, or it might have precluded my chance to be in Intelligence— I never did find out. Either way, I probably would have wound up in Nam regardless.

FRED: And now you were at the 24th Evac, working on a construction crew made up entirely of US Army medics. Still no opportunities to test your French— but that situation would soon change!

STEVE: Eventually, yes. Every day we'd all fall out for morning formation, after which everyone who was already assigned to a work detail would go and report for duty. Anyone still left standing there would be assigned to some sort of manual labor like filling sandbags or building bunkers. Then one morning the First Sergeant says "Does anybody here know how to paint signs?"

FRED: A simple question— either you do or you don't, right?

STEVE: It was a bit more complicated. I had only a couple seconds to make a decision, but I thought "Heck, I made posters in high school and I used to fill in color keys on advertising layouts for my old man— that should qualify me to paint a damned sign or two!" Nobody else had volunteered, so my hand shot up. The First Shirt said "OK Donovan, report to the Orderly Room after this formation." No questions asked— I didn't even have to interview for the job!

FRED: And presto, you were instantly transformed from a sandbag filler into a sign painter!

STEVE: At which point our platoon NCO, SFC Price, immediately twists his body around so he can glare at me without having to move his feet from the "at rest" position. He was obviously pissed when he bellowed in a loud voice "NOBODY in my outfit volunteers for anything!" I thought "What's his problem? Why on earth should he care whether I'm filling sandbags or painting signs?"

FRED: But the damage was already done— the First Shirt had ordered you to report to the Orderly Room, and you were now the official sign dude! I think Price was looking at the big picture. He had his full complement of men for his Admissions & Dispositions platoon, where I would ultimately be working, and he was busy making plans for how his group would function when the hospital opened for business. He knew qualified replacements didn't exactly grow on trees— especially since the Army had just recently lowered the intelligence requirements for draftees!

STEVE: I didn't find out 'til later that manpower was considered a very precious commodity in a war zone— and I had just cost Price one of his valued men! Now he'd have to beat the bushes to try to find someone with the required skills to fill that position. And of course he blamed me for his predicament. I don't think the guy ever spoke to me again after that.

FRED: And here all you were trying to do was help out your poor First Sergeant who needed a sign painter! There's a standing joke in the military about "Never volunteer for anything because you'll invariably wind up being sorry you did." But in this case, you eventually wound up being damned glad you did, correct?

STEVE: I was a little doubtful at first. Maybe Price assumed that "sign painter" would be a permanent assignment (eventually it did lead to one, in a round-about way.) I figured the job would last only a few weeks. They'd probably give me some space over in the Motor Pool, some big plywood boards, some paint and a list of what the signs were supposed to say. Then I'd stretch the work out for as long as I could before having to return to the mindless drudgery of those daily work details. As for the actual painting of the signs, I planned to learn how to do it through OJST— On the Job Self-Training!

FRED: So did they send you over to the Motor Pool and give you a couple buckets of paint?

STEVE: Hardly. When I reported to HQ, they sat me down to wait for a private meeting with Colonel Dickerson. "Holy cow!" I thought. "This sign job is so important that the Colonel himself is taking command of it! What is it, top secret?" It turned out that old Dickerson had a little pet project of his own, reminiscent of what you'd see in one of those military comedies where the CO sits at his desk all day and plays with an assortment of toy soldiers.

FRED: Some guys thought he was a super-military "career officer" jerk who was just trying to finish out his 30 years so he could collect a fat pension. One junior officer wrote a letter to a friend in which he described the Colonel as an overpaid buffoon. But apparently some folks really liked and admired the guy, so I guess it takes all kinds. What did you think of him personally?

STEVE: Up 'til then I had no opinion of him at all, since I'd hardly ever seen the guy or been within earshot of him. He was a very distinguished looking man in his late 40's, I would guess, but I've heard him described as having no personality whatsoever.

FRED: And what sort of items did he have on his desk in place of the toy soldiers?

STEVE: Well, the 24th had up to that point been a semimobile hospital in previous wars. The MASH unit was fully mobile, meaning it could be packed up and moved to an entirely new location in a single trip— within 24 hours. Then there was the "semimobile" (SMBL) hospital that was capable of moving to an entirely new location in "multiple trips" within something like 72 hours.

FRED: Both types were housed in large tents that could quickly be erected, then struck and folded up for transport. The purpose of moving them at a moment's notice was to try to keep them as close to the front lines as possible to expedite the rapid treatment of battle casualties. But in Vietnam, there weren't any front lines.

STEVE: And with the advent of medical evacuation helicopters that began operating there just a few years before we arrived, it became far more efficient to fly casualties directly from the battlefield to a hospital within 30 minutes instead of trying to have the medical facilities pick up and chase all over the countryside after the troops.

FRED: This meant units like the 24th Evac would be permanent installations instead of "pack up & go" hospitals housed in tents. Once we arrived in Nam, we set about building a permanent installation. Our Military Table of Organization and Equipment authorized us to have a certain number of desks, chairs, typewriters, filing cabinets, etc.

STEVE: But among the many items not included in the standard equipment for a mobile medical facility in 1966 were little nameplates to go on all the administrative officers' desks and above the doorways of their respective offices. Obviously that would never do in a permanent installation! The Colonel apparently felt this need so strongly that he took it upon himself to personally oversee their creation. It was to be his contribution to the transition from a semimobile to a stationary (non-mobile) facility.

FRED: Colonel Lynn Dickerson, Commanding Officer of Nameplates! (Not to be confused with famed Packers QB and Heisman Trophy nominee Lynn Dickey, who at the time was being recruited by Kansas State.) So what did the Colonel have on his desk?

STEVE: A stack of about three dozen balsa wood slats, each one being 12 inches long and 3 inches wide. My mission— should I choose to accept it— was to paint 'em battleship grey and then apply dark blue lettering to spell out each officer's name, rank and title. Dickerson had already obtained the slats, the paint and several paint brushes of varying sizes. All he needed was some wizard who could wield those brushes and turn those slats into masterpieces!

FRED: Would you say you were you able to detect whether or not he had a personality at that point?

STEVE: Can't say as I did. He was all business, never smiled or gave the slightest hint that he possessed a sense of humor. Quite impersonal and gruff, almost as if it irked him to have to talk to a lowly PFC. I got the feeling that he had never been that close to one before, just like I had never been that close to a colonel.

FRED: Did he seem like a gung-ho military hard-ass type?

STEVE: From my brief contact with him, yes— probably the first one I'd encountered since Basic. Virtually all the officers in our hospital were either doctors, nurses or Medical Service Corps (MSC) officers who were looking for careers in hospital administration, not looking for opportunities to chew out some private for failing to shine his belt buckle. Dickerson, on the other hand, was MSC but he seemed to be the old-school, spit-and-polish, no-nonsense, salute-me-or-be-court-martialed type of disciplinarian.

FRED: We never stopped to realize how easy we had it, being in a medical unit with a bunch of doctors and nurses! We hardly ever saw any gung-ho military types who were out to hassle us over petty nickel-and-dime bullshit. Most of the doctors were draftees like us— and a majority of the nurses were under 25 and had been sent to Nam against their will.

STEVE: That comes as a big surprise to a lot of people. The Army didn't draft female nurses (males, yes— females, no) since women weren't eligible for the draft. But instead what they did was offer to pay for their nursing education in exchange for three or four years of service as a lieutenant in the Army Nurse Corps.

FRED: Countless nurses have said they accepted that deal only after being assured by a recruiter that assignments to Vietnam were strictly voluntary. Then six months after they'd completed nursing school and accepted their commission, they'd get orders for Vietnam. When they'd protest and say "Wait a minute, I was told that Vietnam duty was strictly voluntary!" they would get an answer along the lines of "Welcome to the US Army, Lieutenant." One nurse was quoted as saying "There were nearly 30 new nurses onboard this plane bound for Vietnam, and not one of us wanted to be going there."

STEVE: Just like most of those guys we knew who had avoided the draft by enlisting in the Army so they could have the duty station of their choice. Somehow they managed to wind up in Nam regardless.

FRED: Welcome to the US Army, son!

&&&&&&&&&&&&&&&&&&&&&&&

FACT OR FICTION?   The story goes that Colonel Dickerson had started a melon patch growing at his private villa in the beach resort town of Vung Tau. When he went down there on weekends, he discovered that the natives were stealing his best melons while he was gone. To foil them, he had a sign put up that said in Vietnamese: "WARNING: One of these melons contains poison that will kill you and your family!" When he came back the following weekend, he was pleased to see that no melons had been stolen. Then he noticed that his sign had been replaced by another that said: "WARNING: Two of these melons now contain poison that will kill you and your family!"

CHAPTER 23

COULD YOU REPEAT
THAT IN FRENCH PLEASE?
There's more than one way to skin a cat—
as long as it can say "bonjour"

FRED: So after Steve was suddenly anointed as the Company Sign Painter, he was shocked to be sent in to see Colonel Lynn Dickerson himself. Steve, what was your first clue that he was a cold, spit-and-polish, "STRAC" military type who did everything by the book?

STEVE: I went into his office, saluted and he directed me to sit in a chair. He started showing me the slats and the paint and as he was explaining what he wanted, at one point I said softly "Okay..." to indicate that I understood what he was saying. Perfectly normal conversation between two individuals who had just met for the first time, right? Except he stops in mid-sentence, rears back, glares at me and says "O-KAY????" For a moment I was stunned. I had no clue as to what his problem was. Then I realized he was being a hard-core, two-bit, Mickey-Mouse, military-bullshit asshole.

FRED: You had forgotten what they were like because you'd become so used to dealing with reasonably normal human beings!

STEVE: Exactly. I said "I mean... Yes Sir!" He replied with something like "That's more like it!" and from that point on, I barely heard anything he said because I was so steamed. He probably thought he was doing me a favor by teaching me some military discipline so I might someday be worthy of sitting on his side of the desk.

FRED: Maybe he just enjoyed insulting and humiliating people who didn't have the option of responding in anything like a normal fashion. He probably got a secret thrill every time someone saluted him or snapped to attention when he walked into a room— combat zone or no combat zone. (In Nam, soldiers in any branch of the combat arms were usually forbidden to salute because it might tip off the enemy as to who the officers were.) As for me, I tended to agree with the idea that Dickerson was an overpaid buffoon. But if that was the case, why do you suppose SP4 Ronley said the colonel was such a swell guy who was "like a father to him?"

STEVE: I wondered about that. I suspect Dickerson just detested college-boy wise guys like me. He knew we had little use for the Army and he probably figured we made fun of him behind his back because he had a girl's first name. Ronley, on the other hand, was more like Dickerson's type of soldier, I would guess.

FRED: Maybe Dickerson was overcompensating for having been teased about his name throughout his childhood! Or perhaps he just didn't like guys with mustaches because they were too "un-military." So then did you get banished to a dark corner of the Motor Pool to work your sign magic?

STEVE: No. To my surprise, there was an empty desk right there in Headquarters. So they sat me down there with my slats, paint and brushes. Maybe the colonel wanted to be able to keep a close eye on his pet project so he could stop me if he saw that I was ruining his precious slats. I figured if there were 30 of 'em and I completed four per day, I'd finish in less than 10 days— and then I'd be back to filling sandbags or painting walls inside the new quonset huts.

FRED: But before long you realized you preferred working in an office environment to doing manual labor?

STEVE: Yeah, it probably took me a good 10 minutes to reach that conclusion. I liked working on my own too, since nobody bothered me (except kibitzers) and Dickerson rarely spoke to me at all. It also occurred to me that if there was an empty desk in that office, that probably meant they were short a man in HQ. Which meant that if I played my cards right, I might be able to wrangle a permanent position there. I just needed to prove to them that I could type— and most importantly, spell!

FRED: And how did you plan to accomplish that when all you were doing was painting slats?

STEVE: Since I was working in a very limited amount of space, I'd have to paint a half dozen slats grey on one side and then set 'em out to dry for an hour before I could turn them over and paint the other side. After I painted the second side, they'd have to dry for another hour before I could start the lettering. As each one was lettered, it would have to dry for another hour before space would be available for more slats. As a result, there were lots of periods when I didn't have anything to do until the paint dried. I didn't want to look like I was goofing off, so I would ask one of the three clerks in HQ if there was anything I could do to help them.

FRED: And of course they welcomed the opportunity to have someone share their workload!

STEVE: They certainly did. Soon I was typing various forms, correspondence and reports. And before long the Company Commander, Captain Bloom, was bringing things to me to type. The other three fellows— the Company Clerk, Morning Report Clerk and Personnel Specialist— had all been trained to type by the Army, and of course they used all ten fingers. I was a two-fingered typist, which meant I was the slowest— but I had one distinct advantage over the others.

FRED: Hunt 'n peck! Reminds me of the joke about the female WAC who worked as a typist in HQ and kept getting in trouble because everyone knew she was a-huntin' pecker. But how could two fingers possibly be better than ten? Sounds rather implausible to me.

STEVE: For official Army documents that had to be filled out in triplicate, accuracy was far more important than speed. The best example was the daily Morning Report that every unit had to submit to its higher command. This was a detailed accounting of the on-duty status of every single man assigned to the unit. It included a listing of who was missing, sick, killed, wounded, AWOL, incarcerated, on leave or otherwise unavailable for duty on that particular day.

FRED: Why were spelling and accuracy so important?

STEVE: Because it was an official document that had to be typed with about six carbons (there were no copy machines back then) and it had to be absolutely letter-perfect. There couldn't be any strike-overs (corrections) on it because they might be an indication that someone altered the report after it had been signed by the commanding officer. Theoretically there weren't supposed to be any misspelled words either, but if neither the typist nor the CO were very good spellers, obviously some errors were bound to sneak through. Usually they'd get kicked back down to us if it was a glaring error.

FRED: And then PFC Bonomo, the Morning Report Clerk, would have to do the whole damned thing all over again.

STEVE: And not only that, but since Captain Bloom had to sign it, he had to hang around the office until it was done. That meant no jaunts to Saigon or Bien Hoa for him!

FRED: That probably ticked him off more than just a little bit. But why would two fingers be more accurate than ten?

STEVE: Because I had to find each key before I hit it. If I made sure to go slow enough to look at each key before I'd strike it, my method was guaranteed to produce an error-free document. That report would come out letter-perfect as long as I maintained my concentration. The other guys were faster, but when accuracy was essential, I would beat 'em hands down since I only had to do it once. And once I got rolling, I was almost as fast as they were. My only disadvantage was that since I had to look at the keys, I couldn't be simultaneously looking at a sheet of notes like the other fellows could.

FRED: Which is where a photographic memory can come in handy. But you were not the Morning Report Clerk, so you weren't assigned to that job anyway.

STEVE: No, but each morning Bonomo would start typing the Morning Report after he'd collected the data. He'd get his official form (DA Form #1) with the six carbons all lined up in the typewriter, start banging away— and then sooner or later he'd hit a wrong key. At which point he'd curse out loud and have to start all over again. After the third or fourth try, he'd yell "SONOFABITCH!!!" as he screwed up yet another one and ripped it out of the typewriter with a loud flourish. Hearing this, Captain Bloom would come out of his office, go over to Bonomo and say "Let's give this one to Donovan." Then I'd do it— a little slower to be sure, but it would be right the first time.

FRED: And once Bloom had approved and signed it, he was free to go off and do other things like work on his suntan... write some personal letters... or have a beer while playing cards with a few cronies in one of the officer hooches.

STEVE: That soon brought him to the realization that I was a pretty valuable man to have in Headquarters... because I was having a direct effect on the amount of free time available to him each day!

FRED: So you were an excellent speller too?

STEVE: Yeah, I won some spelling bees as a kid because I've got a photographic memory. Soon the other clerks discovered they didn't need dictionaries any more. It became a matter of "Just ask Donovan, he's a walkin' fuggin' dictionary!" So all day long it would be "Hey Donovan... pneumonia!" "Hey Donovan... penicillin!" And the Captain would overhear this as well, from inside his office. I think he figured out that if I could spell those words and the other guys couldn't, he needed to keep me in HQ.

FRED: But your sign painting job was only going to last for a few weeks, then it would be back to the A&D platoon for you.

STEVE: Right. So just as I was finishing up with the sign business, Captain Bloom calls me into his office to tell me he's created a new position for me. He says "There are around 80 Vietnamese civilians working in our compound and we need someone to maintain their employment and pay records, see that they all have proper security clearances and health exams, see that they get paid— and take care of any problems, disputes or grievances that should pop up. So I've decided to make you our new Civilian Personnel Specialist. Any questions?" "Yes," I said, "how will I get around the language barrier?"

FRED: There was your opportunity to tell him you spoke French! Or were you afraid of making promises you'd be unable to keep?

STEVE: Precisely that— I didn't mention my background in French. I figured he'd probably already seen it in my Personnel File anyway, but I knew my language skills were pretty rusty. His reply was "No problem, we're gonna get you an interpreter just as soon as we can."

FRED: And what was your reaction to this new assignment?

STEVE: My thoughts— which I kept to myself— were "Hot damn! I get a desk... a title... and an office job that sounds like it could be quite an adventure. Plus I'll more or less be my own boss, since I'll be reporting directly to the captain... and it's pretty obvious that he doesn't want to be bothered with any of this crap himself!"

FRED: Who had the job before it was given to you?

STEVE: I never really figured that out, exactly. But I found out later on that before Captain Bloom came to the 24th Evac as Company Commander, he had been a First Lieutenant at another hospital. There, one of his "miscellaneous" duties was to be in charge of the civilian personnel, along with other assignments like being Motor Pool Officer and Morale Officer. My guess is that at the 24th, one of our lieutenants had the Civilian Personnel job and got transferred out. Since Bloom already knew what the job entailed and didn't have another officer he could give it to, he figured I could handle it so he gave it to me. And that way he'd still be able to keep me around in HQ, since I had already demonstrated my value there.

FRED: Meaning you'd still be available to type his Morning Reports. He was killing two or three birds with one stone! So suddenly you're now the honcho for all the civilians. What was the first thing you did?

STEVE: They brought me this big box of records— each one of those workers had a personnel file, albeit a brief one. I figured I'd start by browsing through their files to see what I could learn about them individually and about the civilian population in general.

FRED: And what did you learn?

STEVE: Not a damned thing. Every word in those files was in Vietnamese... it might as well have been in Sanskrit!

FRED: So you're the official custodian of a big box of records of which you cannot read a single word.

STEVE: Right. But if I couldn't read any of the documents, I thought I'd better at least try to figure out how to communicate with the civilians if and when the need should arise. If there were 80 of 'em on post, surely there must have been someone who spoke either English or French. I started walking around the compound asking every civilian I saw "Do you speak English?" "No speak." Then I'd say "Francais? Parlez-vous Francais?" "No speak."

FRED: They were all mess hall workers, hooch maids or sandbag fillers. Meaning they were poorly educated peasant types who'd never been taught any French or English. Your new job wasn't looking like the piece of cake you thought it was gonna be, right?

STEVE: No, and it was becoming clear that qualified interpreters didn't exactly grow on trees, either. Naturally they were in extremely high demand among American units in the field. It looked like we might have to wait a month or two before we got one. My new job was about to go up in smoke before it even got started!

FRED: But then there was one last hope— a single Vietnamese civilian who worked in our compound and, unlike the others, was not a member of the peasant class.

STEVE: Indeed there was. A few weeks earlier, the powers that be had installed a small PX (Post Exchange) right on the grounds of our hospital. It was the equivalent of what today would be called a convenience store, selling items like shaving needs, cigarettes, candy bars, magazines and liquor. And a few days after it opened for business, I was walking through the compound when, from a distance, I saw two people come out of the new PX, walking briskly together. One was a middle-aged Caucasian man dressed in civvies, but the other was what really caught my eye: a young slender Vietnamese woman, probably 20 to 25 years old.

FRED: And unlike all the mama-sans in their flip-flops, tunics and black pajama bottoms, she wore a brightly colored, tight fitting, floor-length ao-dai dress, slit up to the waist on the sides with the traditional silk floor-length slacks underneath. What a sight for sore eyes! Probably the first female we had seen in roughly five or six months who actually looked sexy, even though she was covered in silk from her neck to her toes!

STEVE: In fact the sexiest part was her black high-heeled sandals with ankle straps— something we definitely hadn't seen since we left CONUS. She was taller than most Vietnamese women, maybe five foot five instead of five feet even. And not bad looking at all, except that she had a somewhat severe overbite, commonly known back then as buck teeth. As I gazed upon her I immediately found myself thinking about things I hadn't thought of in many months. (Though when I try to picture her now, my brain keeps coming up with an image of the Japanese character with buck teeth that Jerry Lewis used to play in his comedy skits. Wish I could get that one out of my mind!)

FRED: And then the next time you went into the PX to buy some smokes, there she was. But at the time you had no hint that you were about to become the Civilian Personnel Specialist and would soon be needing a translator.

STEVE: Right. She was working behind the cashier's counter. I figured that since she appeared to be educated and cultured, she probably spoke English or French. Once I got my new job, I went and asked her. She said no on the English, but when I said "Parlez-vous Francais?" she perked up and said "Mais oui!" ("but yes") in a rather excited and enthusiastic tone. She told me her name was Linh and she lived in Bien Hoa. She was the only civilian in our compound who didn't fall under my "jurisdiction"— she was employed by the Army and Air Force Exchange System (AAFES), a somewhat nebulous organization that was completely separate from the 24th Evac.

FRED: So now you'd found just about the only Vietnamese person in the whole compound who spoke either English or French— and on top of that, she was the only woman in the vicinity who "oozed sex appeal" in your eyes! Of course for all you knew, Linh might have sounded excited simply because she had finally found an American GI with whom she could communicate.

STEVE: True. But regardless, I knew I needed to try to charm her since I wasn't going to be able to perform my new job without her assistance. I began by "hanging around" in the PX and conversing with Linh frequently after explaining that my French vocabulary was extremely limited.

FRED: What did you talk about?

STEVE: Well honestly, we enjoyed our chats but we spent most of our time just trying to figure out what the other person was trying to say. I always took a notepad with me so I could draw visual aids when necessary. For example, she wanted to know where I was from so I drew a crude map of the USA pinpointing New York, Chicago and Los Angeles (Hollywood to her.) Then I showed her where Wisconsin was and explained that I originally lived in the Big Apple but moved to Wisconsin to go to college.

FRED: And since Wisconsin was virtually touching Canada on your little diagram, she decided you must be Canadian because you spoke such good French?

STEVE: Apparently so. Since I hadn't spoken a word of French for nearly two years, my vocabulary was pretty weak. But my pronunciation and enunciation were— if I do say so myself— quite precise. That's only because my high school French teacher grew up in Belgium and spoke French all her life. She demanded that every student pronounce the words correctly. If you didn't, she'd humiliate you in front of the entire class and make you keep repeating the word over and over until you got it right.

FRED: So as a result of your domineering teacher, Linh would say "I've never heard an American speak French as well as you do, therefore you must be from Canada!"

STEVE: That's right. I would insist I was from Wisconsin but she refused to believe it. She was probably just teasing me, but it's kinda hard to tell when there's a fairly severe language barrier.

FRED: And this teasing was often of a flirtatious nature?

STEVE: You could say so. We'd laugh, smile and giggle a lot. I'd always be writing or drawing visual aids on the notepad and she'd be "innocently" touching my hand as I did so. Definitely the highlight of my day! Within a few days I was bringing my civilians into the PX to have Linh translate for me, and if she needed to communicate with an American she'd bring him over to HQ so I could translate for her.

FRED: And that's how the Johnny Carson thing got started?

STEVE: Actually I think it might have been Jack Paar— Carson's predecessor on the Tonight Show. When I was in high school, Paar would have like four celebrity guests sitting on his couch who were fluent in various languages. He'd put all but one in a soundproof room and tell Guest Number One a joke in English. Then Number Two would come out and Number One would translate the joke from

English to German. Number Three would come out and Two would translate the joke from German to Spanish. Four would come out and Three would translate the joke from Spanish to Arabic. Then Number Four would translate the joke from Arabic back into English. Invariably it would get all fouled up by the time it had been translated four or five times, whereupon everyone would howl with laughter. On rare occasions when the joke would emerge intact, the comedy bit would be a failure and they'd try it again.

FRED: And you would soon find yourself in similar situations with Linh on a regular basis?

STEVE: I did, minus the jokes. Typically it would be some minor beef or misunderstanding between an American officer or NCO and a Vietnamese woman, usually a hooch maid. The American would ask me a question in English and I'd translate it into fractured French for Linh. She'd translate it from French to Vietnamese for the civilian. Mama-san would then answer in Vietnamese, whereupon Linh would translate the answer into French, which I would translate back into English for the American officer.

FRED: So the questions and answers would go through four or five separate translations before they'd get back to the person with the original query. What sort of subjects did these sessions cover?

STEVE: Mostly it was mundane stuff like "Tell her I don't want any more starch in my fatigues!" But occasionally it would be something major, like an accusation of theft. The Vietnamese struck me as very honest on the whole, but naturally there'd be a few bad apples who couldn't resist temptation— especially when they were left alone in our hooches all day long. In some areas of Vietnam— where all the civilians were considered as being potentially hostile— the workers would be strip-searched every day before leaving the compound. But in Long Binh, the gate guards just did cursory searches of their dirty laundry bags before they got on the trucks to go back to Bien Hoa.

FRED: So did these multiple translations by you and Linh produce lots of confusion and comical situations like Jack Paar did?

STEVE: For sure. And not only that, but when we were all done I'd invariably realize there was no way for me to tell whether mama-san actually understood the questions— or for that matter, whether I actually understood Linh's answers when she translated them from Vietnamese back to French. But as long as all parties appeared to be satisfied, I figured my job was done, even if none of 'em had understood what was actually being said!

FRED: At any rate, you and Linh probably got some good chuckles out of it. Shared experiences like that would give a great boost to your flirtations as well.

STEVE: True, we'd automatically smile and giggle each time we'd see one another. I'd occasionally fantasize about getting together with her outside of the compound sometime, but there was no way I ever intended to do anything about it— too many complications.

FRED: Famous last words!

&&&&&&&&&&&&&&&&&&&&

FACT OR FICTION? *The story goes that PFC Timmins in HQ was supposed to bring Colonel Dickerson a cup of hot coffee every morning at precisely 8:30. In rushing to try to get it there from the mess hall before it got cold, Timmins would invariably spill about a third of it by the time he got to the Colonel's office. This pissed off Dickerson to the point where he finally threatened to have Timmins transferred to the infantry if it continued. The next morning the colonel's cup was full to the brim, as it was every morning after that. When someone asked Timmins how he managed to solve the problem, he replied "It was easy. Just before I leave the mess hall, I take a big swig from the cup and hold it in my mouth. Then when I get to Dickerson's office, I spit it back into the cup just before I knock on his door."*

SEE MORE THAN 30 PHOTOS AT:
www.longbinhdaze.com

CHAPTER 24

CHUCK CONNORS, YOU
OWE ME A TOOTH

We tangle with none other than Bret
Maverick and Lucas McCain

FRED: Once the 24th Evac became fully operational in January, we began to see a steady stream of celebrities popping in to visit with the patients. Often they would come in unannounced, accompanied only by a couple of PIO's— Public Information Officers (the Army's version of PR flacks.) Every week or two we might see a crooner, a comedian or a sports star. But the majority tended to be movie stars like Robert Mitchum or TV stars like James Garner.

STEVE: As I grew up during the late 50's, it seemed like three out of every four prime time TV shows were shoot-em-up westerns. My Dad and I watched 'em all— our favorites were Gunsmoke, starring Jim Arness as Matt Dillon, and Maverick, played by James Garner.

FRED: Same here. In fact, if you had asked me back then, I would have said my secret ambition in life was to be Bret Maverick. He had those great wisecracks and he never took himself seriously. He was always coming up with ingenious ways to get out of any scrape, no matter how perilous the situation. If it was a showdown gunfight with some bad cat out in the street, he would inevitably figure out a way to outwit his opponent. Plus he was a big hit with the ladies too!

STEVE: Plus the show usually had a funny ending too, often at Bret's expense. But running a distant third (or maybe sixth?) behind those two shows was the Rifleman, in which Chuck Connors played Lucas McCain. His specialty was rapid firing his lever-action Winchester 44-40 rifle by pumping the lever up and down in a continuous motion... Kaboom! Kaboom! Kaboom! Kaboom!

FRED: And little did either of us know then that just a decade or so later, we'd be meeting face to face with both Bret Maverick and Lucas McCain in a faraway hamlet called Long Binh.

STEVE: Nor did I know at the age of ten that Chuck Connors was about to have an impact on me personally— one that would affect me every day for the rest of my life.

FRED: Man, that is one bold and extremely cryptic statement! What on earth could you be talking about?

STEVE: OK, so I'm ten years old and one day my friend Johnny Chopak shows up with a Daisy air rifle— the kind that shoots BB's. He didn't have any BB's, but the thing still made a loud "pop" each time he cocked and fired it. So he was busily moving about the playground, popping away and scaring the other kids with it.

FRED: And he shot you with it? No wait, he didn't have any ammo.

STEVE: Right. But since Johnny and I were good friends, he was perfectly willing to let me try my hand at the popping and scaring business. Now this was one of those air rifles where you had to hold the barrel in your left hand, put the stock against your left hip, and then pull on the lever with all your might to cock the weapon.

FRED: Because you were only ten years old— and because you were manually building up the air pressure that was supposed to fire the BB when you pulled that trigger.

STEVE: Yup, and it would also make the loud popping noise when that pressure was released out the muzzle. I fired off a good dozen or so blasts until I felt like a grizzled veteran. Soon I felt myself starting to get bored until... I thought of Chuck Connors!!

FRED: You were going to rapid fire that BB gun and impress all the other kids with your dead-on impression of the Rifleman!

STEVE: Exactly. But not having the benefit of adult supervision, there was one important detail that hadn't occurred to me. Namely, if I held that rifle in Chuck's legendary waist-high firing position and pushed that lever down as hard as I could with my right hand, I had better have a damn good grip on that barrel with my left.

FRED: Oops!!!

STEVE: That barrel came flying up so fast that I literally didn't know what had hit me. I stood stunned for a moment. Had a meteorite just come hurtling out of the sky? Had the Russians finally started World War III like everyone thought they would? I looked down at the Daisy Sure-Shot laying harmlessly on the ground. Then my tongue reported to my brain that there seemed to be a vacancy at the front of my mouth where a tooth had been, just moments before.

FRED: Oops!!!

STEVE: My first thought was to frantically try to recall how many front teeth I had yet to grow in that spot. Let's see... I had a baby tooth, lost that one... then I grew a second tooth, lost that one too... shoot! That's it! I don't get any more! I'm doomed to spend the rest of my life with only one front tooth, like Blackbeard the Pirate or...

FRED: Tom Cruise has only one front tooth.

STEVE: Yeah, but he's got another one on either side of it! He doesn't have any gaps! I suddenly had a big gap like Blackbeard!!! I began to stagger toward the house, hoping my Mom would have some magical cure for my sudden affliction. And as I went, I began to think about just whose fault it was that this had happened. Certainly it couldn't have been mine!

FRED: Let me guess. Johnny Chopak? No... the Daisy Company? No... the adult who failed to supervise you? No... it had to be...

STEVE: You got it. Lucas McCain! That damned Rifleman! I began to think about the hundreds or thousands of little kids across America who were probably trying to rapid-fire a Daisy Sure-Shot at that very moment. It occurred to me that if I had been eight months younger, the damn thing would have hit me in the eye instead of the mouth. Then I'd be wearing an eye patch for the rest of my life!

FRED: Well at least an eye patch would have kept you out of Nam for sure! But you should have felt fortunate then, that it was your tooth and not your eye.

STEVE: Actually I did. When something bad happens, I try to rationalize that it could have been worse. But I did make a mental note that if I ever got the chance, I'd have a stern talk with Chuck Connors about all the kids he must have maimed over the years.

FRED: So how do you figure that this unfortunate incident has affected you every day since?

STEVE: Well, the temporary crown that the dentist put on began to get yellower and yellower as the years went by. (He said I couldn't get a permanent one until I had stopped growing.) By the time I was in high school, my close friends were calling me "Fang" because of my yellow tooth. Every morning I would look in the mirror and see that darned thing. It was embarrassing. Damn you, Chuck Connors!

FRED: Couldn't you have gotten a different one?

STEVE: I suppose so, but I was never one of those kids who felt entitled to things. My parents never mentioned it, so I didn't either. Perhaps they were trying to teach me not to play with guns.

FRED: So you let an Army dentist fix you up for free.

STEVE: I did. One of the features of the pre-Vietnam deployment physical was a thorough check of each soldier's dental needs— since it was unlikely that he'd see a dentist again for the next 12 months. The "doc" took one look and said "We've gotta get you a permanent crown on there, son. How'd ya knock it out, anyway?" (He called me son despite being no more than three years older.) So I had to repeat the Rifleman story and then he gave me a new tooth.

FRED: So if the Army dentist took care of your problem back then, how is it still affecting you today?

STEVE: Well the new white "permanent" false tooth was great for a while. But as we age, our real teeth tend to discolor— especially when we consume massive quantities of coffee and nicotine— while the false teeth remain bright white. So I look in the mirror every day and see one bright white tooth in a sea of gray ones. It's ol' Fang all over again! And it's all Lucas McCain's fault!

FRED: Then lo and behold, who shows up at the 24th Evac but...

STEVE: It was late morning— Tuesday, the 11th of April, to be exact. I'm coming out of the Mess Hall and I see this big hulk of a guy loping down the sidewalk with two PIO's trying to keep up with him. From a distance he looked a lot like a gorilla in jungle fatigues. Big long arms, knuckles nearly draggin' on the wooden walkway, cigarette dangling from his lips.

FRED: Sergeant McMillan says the Rifleman chain smoked the entire time he was on post. Then again, lots of us did back then.

STEVE: As they approached, the big hulk starts looking familiar. Suddenly I thought "Holy crap, that's Chuck Connors himself!" I knew I had only a few seconds to decide what I was going to do, if anything. So just as we were about to pass each other, like ships in the night, I took one step to the left.

FRED: And you blocked his path?

STEVE: Natch! Up close he looked pretty well-worn. Turns out he was 46, but he looked more like 56. Still had that big square jaw though. I said "Hello Mister Connors, ya got a minute? I have a story that involves you directly." The conversation went like this:
  CONNORS: Why sure, son! Donovan is it? Good Irish name, just like mine! Where ya from, Donovan?
  ME: Well I grew up just outside of New York City, but I was living in Wisconsin when I got drafted.
  CONNORS: New York, eh? I grew up in Brooklyn! Did you know I played first base for the Brooklyn Dodgers in '49? Only lasted a few weeks though— they shipped me off to the Cubs! Then once it became obvious that I'd never be able to hit a major league curveball, I decided to try the acting gig. What was it you wanted to tell me about?

FRED: Oh boy, here it comes!

STEVE: He quickly field-stripped his cigarette and lit another. Obviously his 48 hours of advanced military training was paying off! The two PIO's were now looking at their watches and getting nervous, but I was determined to tell Chuck my Daisy Sure-Shot story. When I finished I said "So I've always wondered if you got letters from the parents of other little kids who managed to injure themselves trying to perfect their techniques at rapid firing from the hip?" He leaned in close— the guy must have been at least 6 foot 5— and lowered his voice to a gravelly hush:

CONNORS: Well just between you and me Donovan, yes we did get quite a few letters of complaint, for various reasons. The Daisy company got their share too, but then again they also sold a whole mess o' them air rifles. So overall they were pretty satisfied with the situation, if ya know what I mean. Besides, lots of kids tried jumping off the roof wearing a bath towel as a makeshift cape, but nobody tried to cancel the Superman show as a result. Oh, and one more thing: Do me a favor— keep it under your hat that the Rifleman grew up in Brooklyn. Wouldn't exactly fit the image, ya know? Naturally I'm sorry to hear about your misfortune, but at least your tooth looks good as new now!

STEVE: As he reached out to shake my hand, I said "Okay Chuck, thanks for listening to my story." And then he was gone.

FRED: You had your chance to ream him and you blew it!

STEVE: Maybe so, but I was satisfied that I had finally gotten my revenge. After 10 years, I had shamed Chuck Connors into admitting his guilt... and giving me a personal apology!

FRED: Well, look at it this way: If you hadn't lost your tooth, you wouldn't have had an excuse for talking to the Rifleman, a veritable TV legend, in the flesh!

STEVE: When he visited the 91st Evac a few days later, one of the surgical nurses there was a died in the wool Connors fanatic who was dying to meet him. Unfortunately she had already scrubbed for surgery when he arrived, so the ward NCO outfitted him in a surgical gown, mask and cap— and marched him right into the Operating Room! Of course the nurse was quite surprised and thrilled to meet him. She later said "I gave Chuck a big hug, whereupon he turned me around and wrote his autograph across the back of my scrub suit with a magic marker! I was in seventh heaven!"

FRED: That scrub suit would have been government property, so I'm sure she turned it in with all the others (yuk, yuk.) When Connors visited the hospital wards he'd present Purple Heart medals to some of those wounded who were due to receive one. He also carried a portable tape recorder wherever he went and would invite soldiers to record a message for him to deliver to their families back home.

STEVE: Once he got back to the states, he'd call the GI's wife or mom and say "Hello Mrs. Jones, this is Chuck Connors calling from Hollywood. Do you believe that? I've just come back from Vietnam where your son Ralph is stationed. I had quite a chat with him and several other members of his unit. Ralph's a pretty smart cookie and he's doing well. Would you like to hear his voice on tape, along with some of the other fellows?" Then he'd play the tape over the phone and of course the family would be thrilled to hear it.

FRED: Incidentally, Connors not only played pro baseball— he also played pro basketball for the Celtics! Anyway, two weeks before the Rifleman made his appearance at the 24th, word had come down through the old grapevine that James Garner would be stopping in on a Thursday afternoon. I promptly swapped duty shifts with SP4 Tompkins so as to be sure that nothing would deter me from meeting Bret Maverick— my boyhood hero!

STEVE: So you loaded your Nikon A-35 with a fresh roll of film and then began lurking in the shadows, right?

FRED: About every half hour or so I would stick my head in the door over at headquarters and ask "Is he here yet? When is he due?" Eventually he shows up and I see him walking with the two PIO's, plus two Donut Dollies, plus Captain Fulton and the XO. (He definitely merited a bigger entourage than Connors did!) They were moving at a very brisk pace and I realized it was going to be tough to try to get anything more than a handshake with Garner.

STEVE: Those groups didn't waste any time— they were probably hitting at least two or three hospitals a day if they were traveling by chopper. Plus a few other stops, most likely.

FRED: Garner was a big dude like Connors— maybe 6 foot 3. I saw them turn and head into Ward 7, so I knew they'd be coming back out within 15 or 20 minutes. I waited outside the door, focused my camera and test-fired the shutter. I figured getting a picture was the most important thing, getting to talk to him would just be a bonus.

STEVE: You were like a sniper waiting for his unsuspecting target to show. You might have been the first paparazzi in Army history!

FRED: Kind of, yeah. The door swung open, he took a step or two and I fired, as it were. Then I quickly blurted "Hello Mr. Garner! When I was in fifth grade, my main goal in life was to be Bret Maverick!"

GARNER: No kidding! Well I certainly hope you've come to your senses by now, haven't ya?"

ME: Yes sir... now my main goal in life is to be a civilian!

GARNER: That's a good one, Borchert. Is it Borchert or Borkert?

ME: Actually it's pronounced Bor-Kart. But I'm used to people only getting it right about 20 percent of the time anyway.

GARNER: What do you do here at the 24th, Bor-Kart?

ME: I work in the Emergency Room and the Admissions Office, receiving patients that come in by helicopter or ambulance.

GARNER: I'll bet you see some pretty scary stuff. Just remember those fellows on the litters are even more scared than you are. I was wounded twice in Korea, so I know that routine fairly well. But you folks are doing a fine job here, and we want you to know we're very proud of you back home. Where's home for you, Borchardt?"

ME: Oshkosh Wisconsin, sir.

GARNER: Call me Jim. "Sir" is reserved for people way above MY pay grade, if ya know what I mean. And don't forget to write a letter to the folks back home. Tell 'em Bret Maverick says hello!

FRED: With that he patted me on the shoulder, chuckled, flashed his "million dollar grin" and was gone. It took all of 60 seconds and poof! My brush with greatness was over. But I do have that photo for all of posterity— plus he gave me permission to call him Jim.

STEVE: You should have said "Hello, Mister Bumgarner!" That would have gotten his attention. It happens to be the name he was born with— James Bumgarner.

FRED: In his autobiography, Garner said he had only been in Korea for a few days when he was hit by mortar fire and suffered superficial wounds to the hand and face. Several weeks later, he got caught in some "friendly fire" when he was inadvertently strafed by a couple of Navy jets. Those wounds got him airlifted to Japan, and it sounds like he never had to return to the war zone after that.

STEVE: That was one short tour for sure! Another quote in his book was "I smoked grass for 50 years. It made me more tolerant and forgiving, whereas alcohol made me more belligerent."

FRED: One of the Donut Dollies said she spent a day flying around the countryside on a chopper with Garner, visiting one unit after another. The excited soldiers would crowd around him at each stop and he'd charm them as he signed autographs, shook hands and posed for pictures. He made a special point of spending his time talking to the enlisted men as opposed to the officers and bigshots. On top of that, she said he never ate lunch that day! She was starved, so she went to eat with the GI's in their mess while Garner talked to more troops.

STEVE: She said the Army wanted to assign Garner a simulated rank of Colonel for his 10-day "Handshake Tour." He declined on the grounds that it would have involved special protocols that would slow him down and interfere with his ability to meet as many troops as he could. Eventually he accepted a temporary rank of Lieutenant Colonel with an ID card so he could be admitted to the officers clubs.

FRED: When I got my photo of Garner developed a week later, I gazed at it and realized that as he was coming out the door of Ward 7, you could clearly see he had just stepped off the edge of the concrete pad that formed the floor of the quonset hut.

STEVE: One of the pads showcasing the cement finishing artistry of none other than the Long Binh Mortar Forkers!

FRED: Bingo. Incidentally, long before his Bret Maverick days, James Bumgarner was nicknamed "Little Bum" by his two older brothers. Many years later, Giants pitcher Madison Bumgarner became MVP of the 2014 World Series as he pitched while Hall of Famer George Brett watched from the stands. He was nicknamed "Mad Bum" by the San Francisco fans.

STEVE: So if I understand you correctly, what you're saying is that way before millions stared at their TV's watching one Bum playing in front of Brett, millions more had stared at their TV's watching another Bum playing just Bret, period?

FRED: You got it! The genealogy freaks say it appears that Little Bum and Mad Bum had a common ancestor: John Bumgarner, born in 1754 in North Carolina. And just three years after we saw Connors and Bumgarner in Long Binh, the two of 'em would co-star in the comedy Western movie "Support Your Local Gunfighter."

STEVE: As these celebrities traveled around the country visiting the troops, their itineraries were kept secret since the Army feared the VC would attempt to assassinate someone like Martha Raye, Bob Hope or James Garner to demoralize the American troops. (In fact they apparently did try to assassinate Hope in '64 when they set off a bomb in front of his Saigon hotel.) Supposedly that's why we seldom knew in advance that they were going to pay us a visit.

FRED: I suspect they also had another reason for not wanting to tell the troops in advance. They knew it could disrupt their mission for an entire day or longer— everyone would basically take the day off in anticipation of a visit from the big movie star.

STEVE: Probably so. Yet despite the Army's attempts at secrecy, I managed to get an apology from the Rifleman and you managed to get a photo of Maverick stepping off our concrete pad. It sounds like we "beat the fuggin' system" again, didn't we?

FRED: I'd say that should probably qualify! What's more, I've got a photo that will prove for all of eternity that Bret Maverick walked on the very cement that we finished with our own four hands.

STEVE: And for that matter, who knows? He might still have had some of our DNA on the soles of his jungle boots.

&&&&&&&&&&&&&&&&&&&

FACT OR FICTION? *The story goes that PFC Flanagan went to the Company Commander and said "Sir, I would like to report the theft of my wallet!" The CO says "Where did this happen, Private?" Flanagan answers "I was driving through Bien Hoa and saw two attractive young ladies hitchhiking. They asked if I could give them a ride to Tam Hiep. Since I was going that way anyway, I said sure, hop in. Along the way, they both started undressing. When they were practically naked, one started climbing all over me while the other one stole my wallet!" The captain says "I see. Exactly when did this happen, Flanagan?" "Sir, it's happened twice this week and three times last week!"*

SEE MORE THAN 30 PHOTOS AT:
www.longbinhdaze.com

CHAPTER 25

PRAYING FOR RAIN...
AND RAQUEL WELCH

Weather permitting, she just might
do an encore performance for us

FRED: One of the few "fringe benefits" of living in Long Binh was getting to see a free Hollywood movie every night of the week at our makeshift outdoor theater. The elevated screen was roughly 12 feet high and made of plywood boards covered with white bedsheets. Seating consisted of some wooden benches backed by a large open space where guys could arrange their personal wicker armchairs which just about everyone bought in Bien Hoa for 5 bucks apiece.

STEVE: We used to get double features, too. The first flick— usually a real dog— started as soon as it was barely dark enough to see the image on the screen. It would be plenty dark, however, by the time the "feature presentation" came on— typically a recent Hollywood flick that was popular in the states.

FRED: This was our one and only form of nightly entertainment other than reading, playing cards, listening to music or getting mildly drunk (or high, for a relatively small number of guys back in '66.) There was no TV at night and no one was permitted to leave the compound after sundown. If you wanted to go to Bien Hoa for any reason, it had to be during daylight hours.

STEVE: The movie projector was housed in a corrugated steel cargo container (a "CONEX") that was roughly 6 by 10 by 8 feet tall. Woe be to any projectionist who allowed the film to break, the reels to get shown in the wrong order or the bulb to burn out in the middle of the movie when there was no spare.

FRED: PFC Scott McGregor had somehow managed to wangle that assignment, probably by raising his hand when they asked "who knows how to run a movie projector?" Scott valued his job so much that he spent all his waking hours checking and double checking the films and projectors. It was a convenient way for him to always manage to look busy— and to remind everyone how valuable he was as the projectionist. To the rest of us, he was a veritable god.

STEVE: One night I'm sipping a brewski as I sit in my wicker chair facing south toward the movie screen. We're watching sex bomb Ann-Margret do her thing in "The Swinger." All eyes are glued to the screen as she starts to do a sexy dance number— just about the best thing we'd seen since San Diego! But then suddenly the entire screen— and everything else around it— lights up as if the sun had suddenly and miraculously arisen on the northern horizon.

FRED: As guys jumped up and ran for cover, you knew something was very wrong, yet you didn't turn to look at the source of the brilliant light. McGregor immediately shut off the projector, prompting some guys to yell "Hey, turn it back on! C'mon, man!" They knew if they didn't see Ann-Margret finish her act right then, they'd probably never get another chance!

STEVE: The spookiest part was the total silence once the projector stopped. That told me whatever it was had to be a long way off, since light travels much faster than sound. And the intense brilliance told me it must be something huge, like an atomic bomb exploding. As I grabbed my chair and began running toward the hooch to get my gear, I heard the sound I'd been expecting— BOOOOMMMMM!!! The ground was vibrating like crazy. It had to be the biggest explosion I've ever heard in my life.

FRED: That was followed immediately by what sounded like the high-pitched whistle of incoming artillery rounds. Except that we couldn't hear any detonations when they hit. When the whistling ceased, we looked out and saw a giant fireball on the horizon at the Long Binh ammo dump, three-quarters of a mile north of us.

STEVE: We figured VC sappers must have sabotaged the dump by planting charges under some of the big pads of bombs and artillery shells. The whistling sounds were unarmed shells being blown sky-high and hurled up to a mile away from the blast.

FRED: One landed in the center of our compound, 20 feet from a building that was under construction and 50 feet from the movie crowd. Which meant that if you had jumped up and run north instead of west, you could have been crushed by the damned thing.

STEVE: True. It was unarmed but still a live shell, which meant the EOD team (Explosive Ordnance Disposal, also nicknamed Elimination Of Duds) would have to come and disarm it in the morning. They'd have their work cut out for them, since shells just like it were now scattered all over Long Binh.

FRED: The ammo dump was huge— its perimeter was anywhere from 7 to 13 miles long, depending on whom you believed. The pallets of bombs and artillery shells were placed far enough apart so that if one were set off, it wouldn't necessarily detonate the others. MP's patrolled inside the wire in jeeps with mounted machine guns. They were constantly looking for saboteurs who might have cut their way through (or tunneled under) the barbed concertina wire. By the way, did you ever figure out why you didn't look at the fireball?

STEVE: Well I did wonder about that— until I realized it was my Army training kicking in! In Basic they said if we ever saw a bright light at night— regardless of whether it was from a flare, a fire, a floodlight or an explosion— we should immediately close our eyes or look away. If we didn't, our night vision could be knocked out for the next ten minutes or whatever. At the very least, we should be sure to keep one eye shut at all times. That's why I kept looking south, even though the explosion was to the north of our position.

FRED: Ah, the old survival instinct takes over! I had been in our hooch at the time of the blast, so I didn't see anything at all until after I heard the big boom and the artillery rounds flying by. Then I looked out and saw that huge yellow fireball. It was pretty damned scary, up until we eventually came to the conclusion that we were not about to come under attack ourselves.

STEVE: I was curious about how much attention the event got in the news media back home. Soon it was time for my monthly letter to the folks, so I told them what happened and said "I'm not trying to alarm you, but I'm curious as to whether this got any news coverage in the states." My mother sent me back the front page of the New York Herald Tribune with a photo and banner headline saying something like "Viet Cong sappers blow up largest American ammo dump." Naturally they got a few of the critical details wrong, but I've long forgotten what those were.

FRED: And on top of that, you never did get to see Ann-Margret finish her dance!

STEVE: No, but we got to see Raquel Welch do hers several weeks later. Given a choice between the two, I'd have to go with Raquel. She was on the cover of Esquire (along with a sexy but tasteful photo spread) just a few days before our induction in Milwaukee. Like most people, I'd never heard of her before. But I thought "I've gotta take this magazine with me to Basic Training, otherwise I'll never see it again!" And then the Army goes and confiscates it on the concrete platform at Union Station in Chicago.

FRED: Bummer— you coulda been the most popular guy in your barracks! So then about a year later, Raquel's new movie was about to show up on the Long Binh circuit during our monsoon season, correct? That was the period when, every afternoon between 2 and 3 pm, it would rain like hell for about 20 minutes or so. Absolutely blinding rain. In broad daylight you couldn't see more than 20-30 feet. It would stop just as suddenly as it started. Then there'd often be some light rain again in the evening around 8 pm.

STEVE: Right. So if it looked like rain around dusk, guys would show up for the evening movie wearing their rain ponchos so they could continue watching the flick while sitting in their wicker chairs, even if it was raining. If it really started to pour, McGregor would shut down the projector— but if it was a light or moderate rain, then... the show must go on!

FRED: And that's when you found out some of those guys were praying for rain?

STEVE: I did. One night PFC Adkinson shows up for the movie and sits down next to me wearing his poncho. We're about to view one of those "Beach Blanket" flicks starring Annette Funicello and a cast of bikini-clad go-go dancers. I say "Hey Benny, it's a warm night with not a cloud in the sky, so why are you wearin' a poncho?" He says "Well, you never know when it might start raining. After all, it is monsoon season." Then he leans closer and says "Besides, as long as I'm wearin' this poncho, nobody can see what I'm doin' with muh hands, ya know what I'm sayin'?" I chuckled and said "Yeah, OK. I get it."

FRED: So that started those wheels turning in your head. We've already talked about the fact that for most guys, there was absolutely no place in the entire camp where one could find total privacy, other than under the sheets in his own bunk.

STEVE: If I didn't know any better I'd say it was almost as if the Army was trying to force us to go to Bien Hoa and get some nooky from time to time. I did contemplate the "Adkinson Method" for a bit but it sounded highly impractical, since one would have no idea when that "crucial scene" was about to suddenly appear on the screen. One would have to sort of prepare himself in advance, so to speak.

FRED: And then as you contemplated this, a minor miracle suddenly unfolded before your very eyes?

STEVE: Indeed. One day I walked out of our hooch and discovered that a company of Army Engineers had moved in right next to us. In the process they absorbed our southern perimeter so that it was all one big compound now— ours plus theirs. Not only that, but there sat their outdoor movie screen facing us, no more than 30 yards south of what used to be our southern perimeter.

FRED: And what else did you notice besides the location of their outdoor theater?

STEVE: I noticed that the movie they showed each evening was the same one we had shown the night before at our theater! Which meant that any time you wanted to see a repeat of last night's movie, all ya had to do was grab your wicker chair... plus a couple beers... walk less than 50 yards over to the Engineers' movie screen... plop your chair down... and take a seat.

FRED: And if you waited 'til dark and wore your poncho, no one over there would even know (or care) who you were or what you were doing! So you began making plans to test the "Adkinson Method?"

STEVE: Yeah, I figured if I saw a scene one night in our compound that was a real turn-on, I could go over to the Engineers the next night and see it again— plus I'd know exactly where the scene was going to appear, so I could be ready for it. And I'd be surrounded by complete strangers in the audience, so I wouldn't have to worry about being discovered or ridiculed by my buddies.

FRED: Each day McGregor would post the name of that night's feature on the bulletin board. Then along comes a Raquel Welch flick where she dances around in bikinis and skimpy costumes. Which meant all you had to do was pray for a little rain that evening!

STEVE: Actually it would be the following night that I'd be hoping for a little mist or drizzle. In fact since it was Raquel, all I would need would be a cloud or two in the sky! I don't remember the name of the movie, but there were indeed several scenes where she was dancing or running around wearing very little. The one that really got me was where she's on this bandstand wearing a little red micro-mini skirt and a tight fitting striped tank top. She starts doing a sexy dance to the music, then reaches for her left hip where she magically releases this break-away skirt to reveal a pair of red panties. She's doing the "frug" in a tank top and panties on a 12-foot high screen. Dynamite!

FRED: So did it happen to rain the next night?

STEVE: It was misting a bit. I took my chair over to the Engineers shortly after dark, sat down in my poncho and waited for the first flick to end. I skipped the two beers so as to keep my hands free if needed. I noticed that half the guys were wearing ponchos due to the threat of rain. The Raquel movie starts and I'm waiting patiently for the bandstand scene. Eventually, there it is. She starts dancing in her little red mini-skirt. I'm thinking "OK, here we go, wait til she reaches for that skirt!" And then all of a sudden... heh heh...

FRED: Yes? All of a sudden what? What happened at that point?

STEVE: All of a sudden a guy on the far side of the audience yells "Hey, Clinkner's beatin' off under his poncho!" Others start laughing and one of 'em shouts "Hey Clinkner, yank one out for me!" Then I see some guy in a poncho get up and start making fast tracks for his hooch as another one yells "Hey Clinkner, just keep doin' it til ya need glasses!" Now some are yelling "Shut the hell up!" and there's so much commotion that the projectionist turns off the movie. Whereupon guys start yelling "Hey, turn it back on, dammit!"

FRED: What happened next?

STEVE: As soon as everything quieted down they started up the movie again, at which point two or three other guys in ponchos also got up and left under cover of darkness. My guess is they had been attempting to give the Adkinson Method a try also. I never completed my mission that night, since all the noise and commotion broke my concentration. I did, however, manage to convince myself that PFC Adkinson's procedure could surely work in the future.

FRED: So eventually you managed to beat the fuggin' system... in more ways than one!

STEVE: Well, let's just say that monsoon season became one of my favorite times of the year.

FRED: Ironically, Bob Hope brought Raquel to Long Binh for his Christmas Show in December of '67, but we had already left by then. What's strange is that after she returned home, she was quoted in the press as saying "Honestly, they should just send whores over there to Vietnam. That's all those men wanted!"

STEVE: I guess she was unaware that Vietnam already had plenty of whores. Plus she goes to all this trouble to establish herself as the number one sex goddess in the land, then gets upset when a bunch of young, single men and boys (who happen to be suffering from severe deprivation) start leering and making suggestive comments in her presence. Make up yer mind, fer cryin' out loud!

FRED: You mentioned that Raquel was on the cover of Esquire. Wasn't there some episode with Playboy magazine that resurfaced some 30 years later?

STEVE: Yeah, I thought about making it a separate chapter in this book and calling it "Hugh Hefner pulls a fast one." But instead I'll try to keep it short, if that's possible.

FRED: First we need to explain that Playboy was very popular in Nam (no surprise there) and there were at least three different sources from which GI's could obtain a copy. They could buy it at the PX, buy a subscription and receive it in the mail, or have a friend or relative back home mail them a copy. We assumed that all copies of the magazine would naturally be identical, regardless of the source.

STEVE: Guess again, my compadre! The ones that were mailed always arrived ahead of the PX copies. And of course PFC Ronley, the mail clerk, would be the first to read each new issue because as soon as the first copy showed up in his mailbag, he'd open it and read it— regardless of whom it was addressed to.

FRED: One day PFC Harkin is reading his new issue, mailed from home, when he suddenly blurts "Holy cow! Listen to this!" And he proceeds to read aloud a "letter to Playboy" purporting to be from a young woman who was on a diet. She said she enjoyed performing oral sex on her boyfriend and was concerned about just how many calories she was ingesting in the process. Could the Playboy Advisor provide her with an answer?

STEVE: The magazine did print a reply, but nobody cared what the answer was— it was the question itself that had every guy in our hooch howling or screaming with laughter, shock or disgust! (Of course this was 1967 and oral sex was hardly ever discussed in polite company, even in an Army barracks. And it certainly was not to be found in any nationally circulated magazine.)

FRED: The guys were still buzzing about it when Ronley walked in and someone said "Hey Ron, did you see the letter in the new Playboy from the woman who wanted to know how many calories there are in oral sex?" He replied "Bullcrap! I just read that issue from cover to cover and there was no such letter!"

STEVE: We showed him the magazine page and he said "That was not in the issue I saw!" He went and got the other copy— a subscriber version— and we laid them side by side. Sure enough, the two issues were identical except that in his copy, the "calories" letter had been replaced by a different letter of identical length. We weren't terribly surprised, given the amount of "shock value" inherent in that first letter, and we wondered who decided that it was too sensitive a subject for the troops overseas.

FRED: Then you quickly forgot all about it until some 34 years later, when a controversy emerged about yet another surprising "letter" that appeared in the pages of Playboy.

STEVE: Right. A year or two after we came home from Nam, a letter appeared inquiring as to which universities were rated as the nation's "top party schools." (This was before Playboy or any other publication published those annual rankings.) The editors listed a half dozen or so schools, followed by an asterisk indicating a foot-note. At the bottom of the page was another asterisk with a footnote that read: "Of course we could not include Wisconsin in this list be-cause it would be unfair to rank professionals with amateurs." Natu-rally this caused a huge "buzz" on the UW campus where I happened to be a student in the process of completing my degree.

FRED: And I read the same letter in Playboy at UW-Oshkosh. I was impressed, although I couldn't help but wonder "Who would put that in there, and for what possible purpose?"

STEVE: Exactly my thoughts. I speculated about that for a while and then forgot all about it— although it continued to be a topic of conversation on the UW campus for at least the next five years or so. Some students even said "My parents threatened to yank me out of school" or "My parents forced me to change my plans to attend UW and made me enroll somewhere else."

FRED: Now fast forward to the year 2001. A newspaper columnist in Madison published a column referring to the Playboy party school story as an "urban myth" that never really happened at all.

STEVE: Several hundred readers, including me and the Mayor of Madison, called or emailed the columnist— I'll call him Elmer Fudge, but he knows who he is— to tell him he was mistaken because we remembered reading that Playboy letter 33 years earlier.

FRED: But instead of printing a retraction and thanking his many readers for helping to set the record straight, he elected to stick to his guns— even contacting the editors at Playboy, who promptly denied any knowledge of the letter in question. (It's important to note that they never denied it actually happened. They just denied having any knowledge of it. They did say they went through some back issues from the 1960's and did not find any evidence of such a letter.)

STEVE: And that might have seemed to put an end to the matter, except for one problem. I, together with hundreds of other alumni, knew we had all read that letter in the magazine and knew Playboy was either lying or else woefully uninformed. Could Hefner be lying to his loyal readers? To make matters worse, Elmer Fudge had also ridi-culed those "balding, delusional old geezers" who contacted him to insist they had seen the item in the magazine.

FRED: Foul! That would have to be a clear case of adding insult to injury. So you set about trying to prove you and the other geezers were right and Elmer Fudge was wrong?

STEVE: Yes, I assumed I'd solve the puzzle within a matter of a few weeks by finding the "smoking gun." (How hard could it be, after all?) But after several years of contacting hundreds of UW alumni and searching through stacks and stacks of old Playboys, I still had not found the letter in question. I had, however, accumulated a number of interesting clues relative to the mystery.

FRED: And there was absolutely no doubt in your mind that the "phantom issue" was out there somewhere, yet to be found? Did you recall the "calories" letter we saw in our hooch back in Long Binh?

STEVE: I did indeed, and that's when I realized Playboy had a history of "switching letters" for whatever purpose. I learned that in '68, Playboy was publishing eight regional editions of the magazine— printed in eight different printing plants around the USA— with different ad content for each region.

FRED: Which meant they could easily have been switching the letters for different regional editions. Then you discovered the same thing had happened at other universities?

STEVE: Yup, when the Elmer Fudge column hit the wires and found a national audience, several columnists at other newspapers read it and then proceeded to write about similar experiences they remembered from their own college days. One in particular was a graduate of the University of Missouri and another attended the University of Georgia. They remembered seeing that "professional party school" quote in Playboy— but the footnote didn't say Wisconsin, it said Missouri in the one case and Georgia in the other. And they too soon found themselves embroiled in a controversy over whether the whole thing was just an "urban myth."

FRED: And yet nobody could produce a copy of any magazine containing one of these quotes?

STEVE: Nope. I was determined to either a) find a copy of the magazine, b) locate someone who possessed a copy of it, or c) force Playboy to admit they had indeed published those statements. But after five years of searching and amassing a mountain of clues, I had still come up empty.

FRED: Until you thought of a way to flush out someone who could end the controversy by producing the smoking gun!

STEVE: Through a long process I had managed to figure out what issue it was in and what page it was on, but I still couldn't find a copy of the page from the regional edition that had been distributed in Wisconsin. So I decided to see if I could create one myself.

FRED: Starting from scratch?

STEVE: Well I had a copy of the correct page but without the "party school" comment. Plus it so happened that on my computer I had a font that was an exact match for what Playboy was using in 1968. And I knew almost verbatim what the original text had said (thanks to my trusty old photographic memory.) So it was pretty easy to "fake" the letter and footnote, place them on the actual page and then make a photocopy of the whole thing.

FRED: And you sent a copy to Elmer?

STEVE: Since we had been sparring for several years over the matter, I figured he'd be suspicious if it came from me. So I had someone else send it to him anonymously. I watched the daily paper expecting to see either a declaration by Fudge that he'd been hoaxed or an admission that he'd been wrong all along. But... no reaction whatsoever. Several more years went by until the subject came up again, which gave me an excuse to send another anonymous copy.

FRED: So did you think your "fake page" was good enough to deceive most folks, or would Elmer recognize it as a hoax?

STEVE: It was good enough to fool the average bloke, although I was sure it would never pass muster from a professional document examiner. But this time Elmer Fudge took the bait— and sent a copy of my page to Playboy. Lo and behold, they didn't bother to have it examined— a good sign that they already knew they'd been exposed. A Playboy editor wrote back to Mister Fudge and confessed that "In the 60's, our editors had the ability to slip slightly altered content into the magazine's zoned editions for both our own amusement and the amusement of our readers... it's highly likely that they were the ones who swapped out that Playboy Advisor question."

FRED: What they failed to mention was that the whole thing was an ad gimmick designed to draw the attention of UW students to that particular page. Adjacent to the footnote about UW was a list of store locations in Wisconsin where one could purchase the men's apparel featured in a full page ad on the facing page. The University of Missouri version listed store locations in Missouri. The University of Georgia version listed store locations in Georgia. And there's evidence that a number of other schools around the country were named in different regional versions.

STEVE: Then in Madison some 47 years later, the story got a front page write-up (along with a photo of the "mystery page") in the local paper. And old Elmer Fudge, instead of being ridiculed for his obstinance in refusing to accept the word of hundreds of his readers, was applauded as a hero for his having finally solved the mystery. So... everybody wins! Except for Playboy, that is. They fessed up after insisting for 12 years that it could never have happened.

FRED: Which must have left them wondering just whose fault it was that their little prank— and their lying about it for umpteen years— had finally been revealed to the world. Let's see.... Elmer Fudge? No.... Steve Donovan? No.... The PR Department at Playboy? No.... It had to be....

STEVE: You've nailed it, Sherlock! We never would have solved that "UW party school" mystery if it hadn't been for PFC Ronley, the mail clerk at the 24th Evac, who always made it a point to be the first guy in our company to read each new issue of Playboy!

FRED: My guess is he probably looked at the photos, too.

&&&&&&&&&&&&&&&&&&&&

FACT OR FICTION? The story goes that a dead mule was found by two sentries just outside the hospital's front gate. They were arguing about whether it was a horse or a donkey when the Sergeant of the Guard came along and decided to settle the matter. "That's an ass," he said, "bury it now!" As they were digging, Colonel Dickerson passed by in his jeep, then stopped and said "What are you men digging out here, a foxhole?" Whereupon PFC Adkinson— one of the sentries— replies "No sir! Ass hole!"

CHAPTER 26

CAN YOU TEACH US SUMMA INGRISH?
We go over to ARVN Headquarters to
teach Ingrish to the ARVN's

STEVE: The choices available for how you spent your free time in Nam were quite limited, so any time someone came up with a suggestion for an inexpensive, novel way to kill some time and feel good doing it, we would listen intently to see if it sounded worthwhile.

FRED: One day some ARVN (Army of the Republic of Vietnam) officers made a request for some Americans to come over to their compound in Long Binh in the evenings for the purpose of teaching them English. We assumed they must have wanted to learn English so they could interact more efficiently with the Americans, do their jobs better and improve their chances for career advancement.

STEVE: It seemed a bit odd that the ARVN forces wouldn't have their own means for teaching English to their officers. But it sounded like an interesting, noble and challenging endeavor— and a welcome diversion from playing cards, telling stories and guzzling an indeterminate number of beers every night. Or watching an outdoor movie each evening, weather permitting.

FRED: Plus it would give us a chance to interact with Vietnamese other than the hooch maids, mess hall workers and sandbag fillers— and perhaps develop a new perspective on what the educated natives were actually like. So we were quick to volunteer, and somewhat surprised that there were only about half a dozen takers.

STEVE: I had an added advantage— I'd taken four years of French in school. Since parts of Vietnam had once been French Indochina, many educated Vietnamese spoke French rather than English. While my French was more than a little bit rusty, I figured it might be useful in helping us communicate with the ARVN officers.

FRED: We were scheduled to go over to the ARVN officers compound the following Tuesday evening. Steve talked to each one of us about developing an action plan for how we were going to handle the task, but for the most part we all said we'd just play it by ear and see what develops after we get there.

STEVE: I was concerned that if we didn't at least do some advance preparation— like making crude flash cards or whatever— we'd accomplish very little and probably make fools of ourselves in the process. But I finally gave in to the "play it by ear" philosophy. Fortunately I managed to scrounge up a pocket-sized French/English dictionary that I thought might come in handy.

FRED: Tuesday evening we piled into a pickup truck, headed over to the ARVN compound and were waved in by the guards. Entering the Headquarters lobby we were greeted by a handful of ARVN officers. There was a lot of smiling, gesturing and hand shaking going on, but little speaking— since we knew only the half-dozen standard Vietnamese phrases that every GI knew, and the ARVN's didn't seem to know any English.

STEVE: Or French either, for that matter. I was inclined to think the whole thing was going to be a disaster. I couldn't imagine anything we were going to be able to accomplish other than staring at each other and smiling a lot. I asked once more if anyone spoke French— "est ce qu'on parle francais?" One young officer smiled and rather sheepishly raised his hand, saying "oui" in a very soft voice. I said "Parlez-vous francais?" He responded quietly in what sounded like fluent French, so I had to quickly put the brakes on by saying "Je parle francais, mais seulement un peu! J'ai un dictionnaire francais/anglais." ("I speak French, but only a little bit. I've brought a French/English dictionary.")

FRED: Despite the language barrier, the ARVN's seemed completely comfortable and acted like they knew exactly what they were doing, so we forged ahead. They ushered us very politely into a large room that appeared to be a mess hall. We expected it to be full of ARVN officers, but it was empty. Then after a few minutes, a door opened at the opposite end of the room and in walked a dozen or so children ranging in age from about 6 to 12. They were followed quickly by another group, then another, and finally one more until there were some 30 to 40 kids in the room with us.

STEVE: And not a single adult! As they quickly swarmed around us they were all smiling, laughing and chatting— and very obviously happy that we were there. But ever since our first or second day in country, we had been conditioned to be wary of swarming kids.

FRED: In towns like Bien Hoa, as soon as you stopped at the open-air shops and exited your vehicle, the peasant kids would swarm around you. The ones in front would smile and try to distract you by making loud conversation about who knows what. The ones at your side would keep asking you for candy, food, money or anything else you might be willing to part with.

STEVE: While all this was going on, the ones behind you would be trying to pick your pockets. Many a GI found this out the hard way. If he hadn't been warned in advance, he could easily lose his wallet, watch or whatever. Supposedly some of the kids even carried razor blades so they could slit your back pocket open.

FRED: We soon figured out that these kids at ARVN HQ were children of the officers who lived in the compound, so we didn't think they would dare try to pick our pockets. We also began to realize that we had been brought there to teach English not to the officers, but to their offspring! Forty laughing, smiling, shrieking kids who were quite eager to engage us in conversation.

STEVE: Except it was becoming clear they really had no interest in learning English from us— all they wanted to do was teach us some Vietnamese! We divided them roughly into age groups and each one of us took a group to a different area of the room.

FRED: There we stood while they chattered away and attempted to teach us fragments of their language. One kid would tug on his shirt and say "ao so mi." Another would point to a cup on the table and say "chen." A third would point to the sandals on his feet and say "dep."

STEVE: Now the Vietnamese language can be difficult to learn because a simple three or four-letter word can easily have four or five different meanings, depending on how it's pronounced. And most are actually combinations of two or three short words like "ao so mi" for shirt or "dien cai dau" for crazy. So when they'd say a word or a phrase, we'd repeat it in Vietnamese, then say the English translation such as "shirt" and they'd repeat it in English. This way there was at least some semblance of us teaching them while they taught us.

FRED: This went on for close to an hour before we managed to make a gracious exit, with the officers thanking us profusely. It was an interesting and enjoyable diversion for us, and the kids seemed to enjoy themselves immensely. But I don't think we could say that we learned a single thing from them, nor they from us.

STEVE: I'm just glad we didn't have to stick around while those officers asked the kids what English words and phrases they'd learned from us! Hopefully the kids concluded we were a great bunch of GI's. But we sincerely hoped we would not be invited back, and as far as I know we never were. Not only that, but once we went in that room, I never got to speak a single word of French!

FRED: Bummer. Wasn't that episode right around the time we tried our hand at doing a little dowsing? (Defined by the dictionary as using "divining rods" or forked sticks to locate sources of underground water.)

STEVE: Yeah, one day in the Spring of '67 the waste water drain in our mess hall backed up due to a clogged grease trap. It was buried roughly two feet under the soil, some 40-50 yards out in the middle of an open field at the intersection of two underground drainpipes. After several futile attempts at digging holes to find the crucial spot, the mess hall crew contacted some American (civilian) engineers working nearby. In a matter of minutes they came over with a couple of stiff copper wire "divining rods" and located the two underground pipes as well as the spot where they intersected.

FRED: One engineer said "dig here." Warrant Officer Gomez, the Mess Officer, said "if you find it on the first try, I'll eat my green boxer shorts." Of course the diggers did hit that grease trap on the first try, and Gomez had to at least eat crow, if not his shorts.

STEVE: A bit later I went into the Mess Hall to check on one of my civilian workers. Gomez stopped me and said with a chuckle, "Donovan, you're not gonna believe what just happened!" He told me the story, including the part about the boxer shorts. I said I'd have to see it for myself before I'd be inclined to believe it, so I went to find the American engineers and ask about the divining rods.

FRED: What did you think they would do?

STEVE: Well I was hoping for a demonstration, but one of them said "You can do it yourself. Take these two L-shaped copper wires (brass actually works better, but we don't have any brass) and hold them out in front of you, about 10-12 inches apart. Let them slope downward just slightly. Then walk slowly across the field and when you get right above the pipe, the wires will cross."

FRED: Fully intending to debunk this thing right quick, Steve grabbed me, PFC Harkin and SP4 Marotta to serve as witnesses. All the while he was expecting that the whole thing was total malarkey and he was going to prove it.

STEVE: When "Yogi" Marotta (from the Bronx) heard what we were about to do, he wasted little time in exclaiming "No way, man! It's a buncha crap— a myth that's been around for centuries. And I got five bucks that says it ain't gonna happen here today!"

FRED: Bill Harkin, from Detroit, took the opposite approach: "If Gomez says he saw it, then I believe it. I'll see your five spot, Yogi."

STEVE: Now five bucks was not an insignificant sum of money to a lowly GI in Vietnam— it could buy you two cases of beer, or four cartons of smokes, plus a dozen packs of gum.

FRED: And regardless of whether they were gamblers or not, most guys wouldn't want to get a reputation for welching on a bet, since we had to live with each other 24 hours a day. For a GI to be willing to risk five smackers, he had to be pretty drunk or pretty well convinced that he was right. Since I'd always believed "water witching" was nothing more than a hoax or myth, I had no problem siding with Yogi Marotta. I tossed in my five bucks too.

STEVE: And I was still fairly skeptical about what those engineers had told me— I figured if I went back and told them it didn't work, they might laugh like hell and say "You musta done it wrong, pal!" But to balance the odds, I threw in my five with Harkin. That way, two of us would be winners and the other two would be losers— plus that would prevent Harkin from taking five off each one of us!

FRED: Soon Steve was walking across the field, holding those copper rods out in front of him. When he got directly above the pipe, the wires crossed. He tried it a half dozen times from different directions, including walking backwards. Each time, the result was the same. We were all astonished as Yogi blurted "Sonofabitch! That's gotta be rigged! Awright, how'd ya do that Donovan?"

STEVE: I said I was just as surprised as he was, but he didn't believe me. Fred then tried it himself, as did Bill and Yogi, and it worked just the same for all three of 'em. But being a natural skeptic, I then devised a test in which they blindfolded me so I couldn't possibly know when I was walking directly above the pipe.

FRED: The rest of us watched as he crossed over that drainpipe. Each time, the wires swung toward each other, even with the blindfold on. The damn thing worked! And not only that, but Yogi Marotta and I were now out five bucks apiece!

STEVE: As for why it worked, I learned in high school physics that when a liquid runs through a pipe, the molecules rub against the inside walls of the pipe and generate a static electric charge around the outside of the pipe. My guess would be that this charge probably caused the copper wires to be attracted toward each other in much the same way that a balloon will stick to your chest after you've rubbed it on your sweater to create a static charge.

FRED: That could also explain why the wires remained crossed when the dowser continued walking forward. There was no longer any electric charge to exert a force on the copper rods and cause them to move, so they remained stationary in the crossed position. Sounds like a good theory, anyway.

STEVE: I took the rods back to where I had gotten 'em. The last thing that engineer told me was "You can do it with a green forked stick just as easily, but we don't have any green forked sticks." At the time I thought he was just pulling my leg. But my wife, having grown up on a farm in Wisconsin, says her Dad used to find water by dowsing with a forked stick.

FRED: Did her Dad actually find that water, or was it just a coincidence that there happened to be water directly under the spot where the dowsing device told him to look? Guess we'll never know. So after that experience, did you pursue the matter any further after you came back to the states?

STEVE: I more or less forgot about dowsing after Nam— that is until some 30 years later when I saw the famed author and magician James Randi ("The Amazing Randi") on TV. He had been a regular guest on Johnny Carson's show for years and his specialty was debunking mind readers, spoon benders and most especially— dowsers! He would routinely describe them as looneys, crackpots and swindlers. I thought he might be mistaken, so solely in the interests of furthering our collective scientific knowledge on the subject, I thought he'd appreciate hearing my dowsing story. I sent him a very polite and gracious email detailing our experience at the 24th Evac in 1967. Even told him he had been a hero of mine for years.

FRED: Did he appreciate hearing your dowsing story?

STEVE: Well if he did, it was only because it gave him an opportunity to send me an incredibly rude and nasty reply in which he called me an idiot and a moron, among other things. I promptly crossed him off my list of heroes.

FRED: Yet "water witching" is still a hotly debated topic to this day. Those in the scientific community tend to dismiss it as hokum, but on the internet many examples can be found like this one: "I used to work at a water utility company. One of the old-timers on the crew used metal rods to locate burst water pipes. If the evidence produced by his rods did not agree with the official city plan, the crew always dug first at the spot he indicated. And his call would always turn out to be the right one."

STEVE: In reviewing findings like ours, scientists will often give themselves an out by saying "Well, you didn't find ground water, you found underground water pipes! We've never said a dowser cannot legitimately find underground pipes!" Amazing Randi, on the other hand, insists they cannot. At the time of this writing, he was still in the debunking business at age 88.

FRED: A 2004 article in Popular Mechanics said "There's no scientific reason why dowsing should work, yet it apparently works well enough and reliably enough to keep the practice alive." The article added that "a massive set of data now suggests there may be some validity to dowsers' claims... this is contained in a study financed by the German government and appearing in the Journal of Scientific Exploration published at Stanford University." And nowadays there are YouTube videos on the internet showing how it's done. I wonder if Amazing Randi ever saw them, or if he thought they're all hoaxes? I suppose it would be pretty easy to fake.

STEVE: Some of those on YouTube do look like they were faked. But that's why I had to do it blindfolded, so it would be impossible to fake it. At least we know the truth, even if Randi didn't!

FRED: Maybe Randi wasn't quite as amazing as he thought?

&&&&&&&&&&&&&&&&&&&

FACT OR FICTION? The story goes that a $60,000 cash payroll mysteriously disappeared and Tran, a Vietnamese civilian working on post, was observed taking a courier pouch from the XO's office. LTC Dickerson sends for the interpreter so he can interrogate Tran. The Colonel says "Ask him where the money is." The interpreter asks Tran, then tells Dickerson "Him say he know nothing about this." With that, the Colonel pulls out his .45, cocks it and holds it to Tran's temple, saying "Tell him I'll kill him if he doesn't tell me where the money is!" The interpreter tells Tran, whereupon the suspect starts trembling and blurts in Vietnamese: "OK, don't shoot me! It's underneath the third stall in the officer's latrine, right behind the shit can!" Dickerson then asks "What did he say?" and the interpreter replies, "Him say you no have the guts to pull trigger!"

SEE MORE THAN 30 PHOTOS AT:
www.longbinhdaze.com

CHAPTER 27

WE'VE BEEN ADOPTED BY THE DATE CAPITAL OF THE WORLD? REALLY?

Yet another reminder that in the long run, it's the thought that counts

FRED: One of the highlights of our rather humdrum existence was the arrival of a care package from home, usually chocked full of yummy stuff like cookies, brownies, chips, candy bars and so on. The unwritten rule was that any guy who received one would open it up and set it out on the table in our 10-man hooch, whereupon the goodies would disappear in two blinks of an eye.

STEVE: Another common ingredient in these shipments would be several cartons of cigarettes. Most of us smoked like chimneys, since there was little else to do, but we usually had to choose from what few brands they happened to have at the PX.

FRED: It might be Philip Morris or Old Golds or whatever— but they were only 11 cents a pack, since there was no middleman and no tax. At that price we couldn't afford NOT to smoke! But you smoked those damned Larks. How did you manage to find 'em in Nam when we couldn't even get popular brands like Winstons or Marlboros?

STEVE: They hardly ever had them at the PX, so I had to wait until Liggett & Myers Tobacco was giving away free cartons of Larks in the Mess Hall, which probably happened about once a month. Then I'd have to beg guys to pick up a free carton for me. I offered to pay 'em, but most just gave them to me. It was definitely a case of feast or famine with my supply of Larks!

FRED: But then every once in a while someone would get a care package with some sort of surprise inside. For example, PFC Shipley opened up a box from home and at the bottom he found a strange package which turned out to contain an inflatable love doll— a gag gift from his brother, I think.

STEVE: Most of us had never seen one before, even though the first "sex dolls" were actually manufactured in Europe some 30 years before we arrived in Nam.

FRED: There's also been a persistent rumor for many years that Hitler had a top secret project in the early 40's designed to equip his soldiers with inflatable dolls they could carry in their packs. This was allegedly supposed to prevent VD among the Nazi troops. But when they were field tested, according to the story, the troops were too embarrassed to carry them. Today the tale of the "Hitler love dolls" is still being told— you can find it on the internet— but some sources insist it was most likely a hoax to begin with.

STEVE: PFC Shipley, from Tennessee, was a little guy but very solidly built. Though he always had a big toothy grin on his face, he hardly ever said anything due to his extreme shyness. It was as if he used his broad smile as a substitute for conversation.

FRED: His boyish good looks, plus the fact that his voice sounded kind of like that of an eight-year-old, may have contributed to his reticence. But whoever sent him that doll probably did so knowing it would embarrass him to no end, which it did. I asked Shipley if he was planning to try it out and he said "What do I look like, a perv?" I said "No, I don't think so... but if someone were to get intimate with what is essentially a large plastic balloon, would that qualify him as a pervert? I'm afraid I have no idea."

STEVE: He really just wanted to get rid of the thing, but a few guys offered to "test out" Shipley's new playmate overnight. That is until a rumor started about gonorrhea being transmitted via love dolls, whereupon the volunteers all backed off. Soon the guys in Shipley's hooch had named the doll "Hannah" (after Hanoi Hannah, the Vietnamese radio version of Tokyo Rose from World War II.)

FRED: Supposedly Hannah could be heard on Radio Hanoi in

Saigon and Bien Hoa, but I don't remember ever hearing her in Long Binh. On the other hand, I guess she came on at 11 pm when we were already in the sack, so maybe we slept through her broadcasts.

STEVE: The guys mounted Hannah on the wall as a decoration after first outfitting her in a lovely floor-length purple "ao-dai" dress they got in Bien Hoa for like 10 bucks. They even got a pair of high-heeled sandals to attach to her rather dainty little feet.

FRED: She definitely classed up the joint! But while some of the hooch maids found her quite amusing, others perceived her as somewhat of an embarrassment or an insult to them. Or perhaps a veiled threat that they could wind up mounted on the wall, too.

STEVE: Several weeks later there was a firefight outside the perimeter with hot tracers flying through our compound. One of our medics, SP5 Torborg, was hit in the butt cheek as he lay sleeping in his bunk. Hannah took a slug through her upper left arm, shredding and melting the vinyl so badly that an emergency amputation was required. Fortunately we had plenty of medics on hand!

FRED: They said Torborg would receive a Purple Heart, although I don't think he ever got it due to some technicality— maybe because it was "friendly fire" or because we were officially non-combatants.

STEVE: In any event, from that point on the doll in the purple ao-dai was known as "Hannah, the One-Armed Wench." And some of the mama-sans seemed rather pleased that she had gotten hers.

FRED: Another care package "surprise" was received by SP4 Pete Ferris, who had been an infantry ground pounder until he slipped a couple discs in his back and got assigned to light duty at the 24th Evac. His platoon had been out on a three week "search and destroy" mission, trudging through the jungle every day and setting up an NDP (Night Defensive Position) in a different location every night.

STEVE: One day he got a message from base camp that there was a care package waiting for him and he could either have it brought out on the re-supply chopper or wait two weeks 'til he got back to camp.

FRED: He assumed it was full of treats, so he asked to have it sent out on the next Log (Logistical Supply) Flight. When the slick showed up, it off-loaded its cargo as rapidly as possible and then skedaddled within minutes so as not to draw the enemy's attention any more than necessary. (Depending on the situation, the Log flights would sometimes land or hover in two or three different spots to confuse Charlie about the platoon's true location.)

STEVE: With the ship safely out of sight, Ferris got his care package. He could see that it was a corrugated box roughly two feet square and not heavy enough to be full of cookies and brownies. So naturally he opened it with some wonderment.

FRED: Being from Georgia, Ferris was a huge Bulldogs fan. Inside the box was a big stuffed toy "Uga," the white bulldog mascot of the Georgia football team. It was decked out in a bright red turtleneck sweater with a big white "G" on the front. It would have made a great decoration for his hooch, except for one problem— he was out in the jungle, some 16 miles away from base camp! And the next Log flight wasn't due to return for another 3-4 days.

STEVE: Even if he could have sent "Uga" back to camp, he had no way to tell somebody to put it in his footlocker, since he had the only key. He thought about trying to strap the mascot to his pack and haul it around on patrol. That is, until his platoon sergeant said "No way, Ferris! Charlie will spot that thing from half a mile away, making YOU, as well as the rest of us, a prime target!" He figured his only option was to bury it right there— until the platoon's machine gunner came up with a bright idea.

FRED: The gunner said "Let's execute the danged thing!" Now normally they would never fire a weapon unnecessarily out in the boonies, not wanting to alert the enemy to their presence. But there was one exception to this rule.

STEVE: Like a lot of infantry platoons, they had a morning ritual called the "Mad Minute" when they were in a Free Fire Zone. (Any Vietnamese found in such uninhabited areas were considered hostile and could be engaged by our troops without first getting authorization.) Shortly before breaking camp, they'd spread out around the perimeter with all of their weapons pointed out toward the jungle. At the appropriate moment, the platoon leader would give the signal and all guns would start blazing away for up to 60 seconds.

FRED: This served several purposes. It gave them an opportunity to check their weapons to make sure they were working while offering a way to appease those grunts who might be feeling some itchiness in their trigger fingers. But it also gave them a chance to scare off or blow away any VC who might be lurking in the immediate vicinity.

STEVE: I've also heard the Mad Minute allegedly gave them a way to get rid of "old ammunition." Didn't know there was such a thing. But anyway, the reason why the VC might be lurking was...?

FRED: When Charlie planned to attack in the morning, he would often wait until after the GI's had filled in their foxholes— that way there'd be no holes for the Americans to dive into for cover.

STEVE: Dirty sneaky. But in this case, the Mad Minute also made an ideal firing squad for Uga! Ferris proceeded to lash his Georgia Bulldog to a tree some 30 yards out from the perimeter. When the signal was given, everybody on that side opened up on the defenseless pooch, ripping it to shreds.

FRED: Normally when they broke camp they were required to bury all evidence that they'd been there, right down to the cigarette butts. This was intended to prevent the VC from finding it or using it in some fashion. But the platoon sergeant took one look at what was left of that stuffed Georgia mascot, still tied to the tree, and said "Nah, leave him there. Let's see Charlie try to figger this one out!"

STEVE: But for the rest of us, the biggest surprise involving care packages began when we received a proclamation in the mail informing us that the 24th Evac had been adopted by the City of Indio, California— the self-proclaimed "International Date Capital of the World." (The slogan referred to the kind of dates one eats, not the kind one takes to a dance.)

FRED: We weren't sure exactly what that meant until a month or so later when we started receiving care packages from the residents of Indio. The packages kept coming... and coming... and coming. And they were filled with every type of date concoction you could imagine— from date bars, date cookies, date cakes and date pudding to things like date butter and date candy.

STEVE: You forgot date bread— one of my favorites! Unfortunately there seemed to be one nasty little problem that all these packages had in common. Since they came by ship and took a minimum of six weeks to cross the Pacific, the contents were all covered with mold by the time we got our hands on 'em. So we basically had to throw away nearly all of those scrumptious goodies.

FRED: Captain Bloom, our Company Commander, said that with some of the items we might be able to take a scalpel and surgically remove all the moldy parts so that some edible material remained. But most of the guys lost their appetites after seeing what the stuff looked like when the boxes were opened.

STEVE: Eventually the deluge of care packages subsided, somewhat mercifully. You might say that receiving all those cartons of inedible goodies was worse than receiving none at all. It was sort of like coming within a few inches of making love to the woman of your dreams— so near, and yet so far!

FRED: But having to throw away all those treats, sad as it may have been, was not the end of the story.

STEVE: No, it was not. Since I usually typed (and often wrote) Captain Bloom's correspondence for him, one day I said "Sir, I think we need to send a nice thank you to the people of Indio for all of their efforts and kindness." He said "Good idea Donovan, go ahead and do it. And sign your own name to it too."

FRED: But of course you couldn't bring yourself to tell the good people of Indio that the stuff had to be thrown away because it was all moldy. Especially since the cash value of all those packages could easily have been a couple thousand bucks. Not to mention all the time and energy those folks invested in baking, packaging and shipping that mountain of tasty delicacies!

STEVE: Indeed. So instead, I wrote this flowery piece about how much we enjoyed the date products. And especially how much it meant to us to know that the people back home thought so much of us and supported our efforts so admirably. I downplayed the "tasty treats" aspect and pumped up the "touching symbolism" of their largesse— that way I wouldn't have to fib much.

FRED: And once your letter to the Mayor of Indio was mailed, you thought the matter had been laid to rest, once and for all. It was one more thing you could check off your daily "to do" list.

STEVE: Precisely. But unbeknownst to me, the Mayor proceeded to send copies to all the schools— and at least one school principal read it aloud to the entire student body over the PA system. A month or so later, another round of (moldy) care packages started arriving— and we went through the whole process all over again!

FRED: Get out them scalpels, boys!!!

STEVE: Right. Only this time we also started receiving dozens of letters from fourth graders in Indio, all addressed to SP4 Donovan at the 24th Evac. They were from 10-year-old boys and girls, and a number of the girls even enclosed snapshots of themselves.

FRED: We passed the photos around and some guys remarked as to which of the girls they would like to go back to Indio and visit about eight years hence.

STEVE: Since the letters were addressed to me, I felt a personal sense of responsibility to try to answer them all. But as I thought about it, discretion gradually took the better part of valor. I decided I'd learned my lesson about writing letters, so I'd have to just break their little hearts and not respond in any way, shape or form.

FRED: It was either that or tell 'em the whole truth— which could have broken their hearts even more. Maybe Captain Bloom knew what he was doing when he told YOU to sign that letter!

STEVE: And maybe those poor kids in Indio surmised that if SP4 Donovan didn't write back, it must have been because he probably perished in "WW Nam."

FRED: With a half-eaten date bar still clutched in his fist!

&&&&&&&&&&&&&&&&&&&

FACT OR FICTION? The story goes that a soldier once received an inflatable love doll in a care package, blew it up and discovered it was equipped as a male doll instead of a female. He was about to wrap it up and send it back when his platoon sergeant took a close look at it and exclaimed "You dummy! You blew it up inside out!"

CHAPTER 28

IF HIS DAUGHTER MARRIED LBJ, SHE'D BE JANE FONDA JOHNSON

Henry Fonda didn't sing, dance or tell jokes...
what the hell was he gonna do in Nam?

FRED: It's funny how a brief trip to the war zone could change some people's opinions of the war, yet for others it only reinforced the beliefs they had before they arrived there. When we were drafted in '65, a majority of "average citizens" supported the war effort— over 60 percent, according to polls.

STEVE: But by the middle of '67, when we were approaching the end of our tour in Nam, the anti-war movement had begun to pick up steam in many parts of the USA— and public support had dropped to 48 percent. By mid-'68 it would be 36 percent, and by the time the war was winding down in '72, a mere 27 percent of Americans thought we should still have troops there.

FRED: According to Robert Mitchum's biographer, Lee Server, Mitchum had never shown much interest in the war, one way or the other. When the government offered to send him on a "Handshake Tour" to visit with the troops in '67, he thought he should probably go take a look for himself. But once he viewed the mangled bodies of soldiers on the hospital wards, he found he could no longer remain neutral. His attitude became "look at what those damned commies are doing to our boys, who are only here to try to help the Vietnamese people. They are enemies of humanity and they need to be stopped!"

STEVE: By the time he returned to the states he was making speeches in strong support of the war effort.

FRED: Legendary movie star Henry Fonda freely admitted he was opposed to the war when the government asked him to take a Hand-shake Tour. He agreed to go, but found it extremely difficult to view the badly wounded patients in the hospital wards. Unlike Mitchum, his reaction was to become more convinced that the war was a complete waste. He did say afterward that his trip had been very rewarding, but his conclusions were quite the opposite of Mitchum's.

STEVE: In his autobiography, Fonda said when the US Government tried to recruit him for a three-week "Handshake Tour," he initially said "You've got the wrong guy, I don't approve of that action in Viet-nam." He was told "your approval has nothing to do with it— it's all about boosting troop morale by letting them see a familiar face. Just go over there and talk to them. Sit with them while they eat in their mess halls; listen to them talk in their barracks."

FRED: Henry was persuaded to go, but he thought "What the hell am I going to do once I get there? I'm not an entertainer, I'm no Bob Hope! I'm not even good at mixing with people I don't know." Then he thought of a gimmick: "I would buy a Polaroid camera, have somebody take pictures of me with the soldiers, and give them the autographed prints to keep or send home. Well, that's what I did. I bought a bag full of film, a camera and off I went to Saigon."

STEVE: With a Major assigned to him as a guide, he flew around Vietnam by helicopter and stopped at three or four bases every day. They'd visit mess halls, officers clubs, enlisted men's clubs, hospitals and aid stations. He quickly used up all his film, but luckily he was able to buy more at just about any PX in country.

FRED: On April 18th, 1967, Fonda visited the 24th Evac as well as the 93rd Evac, located a mile or so up the road from us. It was a few days after 10,000 anti-war protesters had marched in San Francisco— and several years before Henry's daughter would earn the nickname "Hanoi Jane" for her two-week visit to North Vietnam.

STEVE: On one of the hospital wards there was a patient who'd been shot through the jaw, with the bullet entering one cheek and exiting through the opposite cheek. Since his jaw was wired up and his head was heavily bandaged, he was unable to speak when he saw Fonda coming toward him. Henry, trying to sound cheerful as he approached, said "Well, what happened to you, soldier?"

FRED: Since he couldn't answer verbally, the patient made the classic symbol of a gun with his thumb and forefinger. He held the "barrel" up to his cheek and clicked the "hammer" to signify that he'd been shot through the cheek. Henry, appearing to be shocked at this, recoiled in horror and quickly moved away. The soldier was rather puzzled until he thought for a moment and realized Fonda thought he was telling him he had intentionally held a gun to his own cheek and pulled the trigger! He wanted to try to correct the record, but Henry was gone in a flash.

STEVE: It wouldn't have been the first time we had a patient with a self-inflicted wound, but usually they'd go for the leg or foot— not the jaw. In this case, however, it was just a case of misinterpretation by a movie star.

FRED: Fonda later wrote that he had considerable difficulty viewing the wounded patients. "I had a terrible time controlling my emotions when I looked at those hundreds of casualties. .. that was the roughest part of the whole trip."

STEVE: Nurse Cherie Boudwin said that when Fonda came on her ward, ICU-3, he looked extremely apprehensive, like he really didn't want to be there. She said he talked briefly to one of her patients and had a look on his face that said "please get me out of here." He seemed to her to be cold and insensitive toward the whole episode, and didn't spend much time on her ward.

FRED: Then again, Henry Fonda often looked like that in his films anyway. If, as he said, seeing those wounded soldiers was a highly traumatic experience for him, it's understandable why he might have looked so uncomfortable and out of place. I didn't hear anyone mention that he took Polaroids, though.

STEVE: Maybe he didn't think he should be photographing patients who might be seriously wounded. I wonder if he realized Polaroids didn't last very long in all that heat and humidity, even when they were coated with the preservative solution that came with the film?

FRED: Some of our buddies learned that the hard way. They'd send

Polaroids home and by the time they arrived, the images were nearly unrecognizable. Regarding "Hanoi Jane," Fonda wrote that his daughter was falsely labeled a communist when in fact she merely had a few friends who were "true believers." He added that "I've always been for the underdog, but I personally believe that communism is full of lies. I am definitely anti-communist."

STEVE: Jane herself apologized many years later and said her trip was a mistake because it sent the wrong message to the troops as well as to the American public— one she had never intended to convey.

FRED: After he returned home, Henry wrote: "I carried dozens of enlisted men's telephone numbers with me and when I got back, I made damn sure to call every one of their families. It was a trip this 62-year-old man didn't want to take, but I felt I had to... not for me, but for the guys sweating it out and dying in the rice paddies and jungles."

STEVE: At that time his daughter Jane was best known for movie roles as a hooker in "Walk on the Wild Side" and a gunslinger in "Cat Ballou." On the day Henry's appearance had everyone in our camp buzzing about both of them, Craig Randall walked into our hooch that afternoon and said "Say, did you hear that Jane Fonda had been planning to marry President LBJ until she realized that for the rest of her life she'd be known as Jane Fonda Johnson?"

FRED: A bit of tasteless college-boy humor there! But instead she went to Hanoi and became known for the rest of her life, at least by many vets, as "Hanoi Jane." If she'd known that was gonna happen, she probably would have preferred marrying Lyndon.

STEVE: A month after Fonda's visit, famed advice columnist Ann Landers visited the 24th Evac on May 22nd, exhibiting a no-nonsense, take-charge attitude. Nurse Boudwin said she was very well groomed, very assertive and very focused on visiting with every single one of the patients on ICU-3. She seemed genuinely interested in each one, although she hardly spoke to the hospital staff at all.

FRED: In a biography of Landers, her daughter wrote that "unlike some celebrities who popped into a ward or two for a photo op, Ann wanted to see as many of the injured as she could.... which she did, from early morning 'til late at night." Ann carried a spiral notebook with her and invited the patients to give her names and phone numbers of their families back home. Her daughter wrote that when Ann returned to the states, she spent four days calling every one of those numbers so she could relay greetings from "the boys in the beds."

STEVE: Then there was Reverend Billy Graham, the famed evangelist known as the "pastor to the presidents" ever since Harry Truman was in office. He was very outspoken against communism as well as a staunch supporter of the war. He made an appearance at Long Binh just before Christmas in December of '66. I remember that week for one reason: I received two Christmas gifts sent from the states— one from my parents in New York, one from a girl I had been dating in Wisconsin— and the two were identical. Black Ronson Varaflame Comet butane lighters, guaranteed to light in any type of weather— wind, rain, monsoon or tropical heat.

FRED: Wow, what are the odds of that? Ronson must have had one hell of an ad campaign going for those butane lighters— the perfect Christmas gift for that GI sweating it out in a combat zone! Then again... where would you get more butane to refill them with?

STEVE: Well fortunately when I got two lighters, I also received two cylinders of butane that came with 'em!

FRED: Meanwhile, thousands of troops and hospital patients gathered to hear Graham speak in the makeshift amphitheater just north of the 24th Evac compound. I wasn't a huge fan of evangelistic soul saving, but I was raised as a Christian and considered myself a believer, so I was looking forward to hearing his sermon and pep talk. Toward the end he asked all of us to lower our heads, keep them down, and raise our hands if we were willing to devote the rest of our lives to Christ. As hands started going up, he said "Good, there's a few hands. Great! There are some more... some more... and now some more." This went on for several minutes.

STEVE: So, did you put your hand up at some point?

FRED: I didn't raise my hand, partly because I wasn't exactly sure what he meant by "devote my life to Christ" and partly because of my aversion to the whole "saved by an evangelist" process. But I found that I desperately wanted to lift my head, look around and see for myself how many hands were raised. Was it a few? Hundreds? Nobody knew! I tried to peek out of the corner of my eye but couldn't quite see anything without raising my head. And out of deference, I suppose, to Reverend Billy Graham, I never did look around— but I still wish to this day that I had.

STEVE: He was not without controversy, both during and after the Vietnam war, due to his extremely hawkish views. He was a close confidant of President Johnson, who apparently considered making the Reverend a member of his presidential cabinet. Supposedly LBJ also considered grooming him to be his successor as president, but Graham insisted he had no political ambitions.

FRED: In the late 80's it was revealed in the National Archives that Graham had sent a secret letter to President Nixon in 1969. In it he recommended that if the Paris Peace Talks failed to reach a negotiated settlement of the war, Nixon should bomb all the dikes across North Vietnam to bring a quick and decisive end to the conflict by flooding the cities and industrial areas.

STEVE: Graham explained that his dike plan would destroy the economy of North Vietnam overnight and preclude the enemy from continuing the war effort. The Defense Department estimated it also would have killed a million North Vietnamese civilians.

FRED: That would be what... killing commies for Jesus?

STEVE: I suppose so. The next celebrity to make use of the amphiteater was probably Nancy Sinatra (daughter of crooner Frank) who headlined a USO Show at Long Binh in February. Wearing a horizontally striped micro-mini dress along with her patented knee-high boots, she had only one problem— she was an emotional wreck.

FRED: As I recall, she didn't come out on stage for like a half hour after the warm-up act had come and gone. The band kept playing, stopping and then playing some more. Everyone knew Nancy had been there for more than an hour already, because they had all seen her arrive. Yet every five minutes or so, the Master of Ceremonies would come up to the mike and say "Nancy will be out in a few minutes, boys. Is everyone excited to see her?" And of course the troops would all cheer and scream like hell— which, as it turns out, was apparently the source of the problem.

STEVE: We didn't know it at the time, but she later told an interviewer that when she first scheduled her tour, she was so frightened and anxiety-ridden about it that she canceled the trip, went home and "cried her eyes out." Then, thanks to a lot of yoga and some consultation with her dad— Ol' Blue Eyes himself— she decided she had to go to Nam after all, so she scheduled another excursion.

FRED: Do you suppose her fears stemmed from the fact that it was a dangerous war zone or from the fact that she would have to face all those adoring fans? My guess is the latter. When she finally made her appearance, she looked rather messed up. My first thought was a drug overdose.

STEVE: But eventually it was explained to us that she had been overwhelmed by all the cheering and adoration being shown to her by these thousands of 19 and 20-year-old soldiers. She had been sitting in her dressing room crying her eyes out, consumed by a peculiar type of stage fright. She was a wreck because the troops obviously worshipped her... and she didn't feel worthy.

FRED: I think she sang a couple tunes, then broke down and had to go backstage. After 10 minutes or so, she reappeared and finished an abbreviated version of her act. The whole scene was kind of weird and uncomfortable. It appeared that she was overwhelmed by the ear-splitting exuberance of the crowd.

STEVE: As for the knee-high boots, most people assumed that she always wore them because her big hit song at the time was "These Boots are Made for Walkin'." It was named Billboard's Number 2 song of the year for 1966. But I discovered the real reason for the boots— which I had long suspected.

FRED: And how, pray tell, would you have discovered that?

STEVE: Well, first I should explain that I've always been a leg man. It's the first thing I attempt to ascertain about a woman if I'm trying to evaluate her "visual" sex appeal. But in Miss Sinatra's case, she was always wearing those damned boots! The harder I tried, the more I began to realize she was deliberately concealing her legs from the public because... they must have been bad news.

FRED: And then she came to Long Binh. But she was still wearing those boots when we saw her, so what were you able to find out?

STEVE: Well, I was working that day as CQ runner in HQ. The CO asked me to deliver a message to Major Fensler, who was doing duty as part of the "welcoming committee" for Nancy Sinatra. I had to go over to the backstage area at the amphitheater which I believe was located underneath the big stage. The MP's wouldn't let me in until I convinced them I had a message from the Colonel which I had to deliver personally to the Major.

FRED: And then they let you into Nancy Sinatra's backstage digs?

STEVE: Yeah, I was supposed to deliver my message and then wait for a reply from the Major. While I'm standing there, I see Nancy through a partially open doorway as she was about to put on her legendary boots— and I could see her legs quite clearly.

FRED: Finally, a chance to satisfy your curiosity! What did you see?

STEVE: Unfortunately they were about as breathtaking as a couple of tongue depressors. I thought "Sonofabitch! I knew it! They're terrible!" From the knees down, they looked more like flippers than female celebrity gams. Big disappointment.

FRED: But as long as she continued to wear those boots, nobody was any the wiser... except you!

STEVE: So from that point on, whenever I heard her singing her trademark song, the lyrics may have said "These Boots are Made for Walkin'".... but I always sang a slightly different, more accurate version. Which would often prompt someone to ask "Whaddaya mean by that?" And then I would have to explain.

FRED: So how did your version go?

STEVE: "These Boots are Made for Hidin'!"

&&&&&&&&&&&&&&&&&&&

FACT OR FICTION? *The story goes that PFC Gilman knew he'd eventually need a blood transfusion. Nevertheless, when they were about to airlift him to Taiwan, he started yelling "No! No! I'm not getting on that plane! No way!" The flight nurse came over and asked "What's the problem, soldier?" Gilman replied that the medic back in Long Binh had told him "Whatever happens, don't let them give you Taipei blood!"*

CHAPTER 29

IT'S A DEATH CARD... LETS CHARLIE KNOW WHO DID THIS
Why on earth is everyone carrying decks with only 51 cards in them?

FRED: Once the 24th Evac went operational, I was assigned to Admissions and Dispositions (A&D) which was involved primarily in processing admissions, maintaining and updating patient medical records and processing patients out once they were discharged or transferred to another facility. But being the only one in A&D who was actually a trained medical corpsman, I was frequently pressed into service next door in the Emergency Room (ER) when they were short-handed— or when things got hectic.

STEVE: Like a number of the other guys, I started thinking about possibly becoming a doctor or EMT when I was in Medic School. But by the time we got to Nam, a medical career was no longer on my radar. I wanted an occupation where folks were looser, less serious and more likely to be cracking jokes at any given point in time.

FRED: Like being a bartender!

STEVE: Well, maybe not THAT loose... although we'd soon get an opportunity to tend bar in the evenings (for modest pay) at the 24th Evac Officers Club. But since we were enlisted men and the club patrons were all officers, most of 'em kept a certain distance from us. We were just the hired help— not much looseness there!

FRED: Since most people at the 24th Evac didn't even realize you were a medic, it meant you didn't have to worry about suddenly being transferred to the infantry where you could be sent out to slog through the jungles and rice paddies. I guess some of our medics did get transferred to the ground pounders, but I don't know if it was at their own request or not.

STEVE: That was one of our main fears as hospital medics— that we could suddenly find ourselves out in the boonies hauling a medical aid bag through the swamps and forests. But perceptions did vary on that subject. One corpsman, Jim Rothblatt with the nearby 199th Light Infantry Brigade, had spent time as both a field medic and ambulance driver. When he drove over to the 24th Evac to visit one of our patients, he was horrified to see all the mangled bodies on the ward and later told me "I thanked my lucky stars that I didn't have to work in that place every day!" Much to our surprise, he preferred being a field medic to having to work on a hospital ward.

FRED: Jim was like a lot of infantrymen who would admit that when they were out in the bush, they only encountered the enemy about once a week on average. The rest of the time they were extremely bored and weary from the heat, rain, bugs, snakes, marching and so forth. It all depended on where you were and what sort of activities your unit was engaged in.

STEVE: And in 1967, as infantry tactics gradually shifted from "search and destroy" to "helicopter assaults," contact with Charlie became more frequent, since the troops would often be airlifted directly to areas of known or suspected enemy activity.

FRED: But at least once their mission was completed, they could usually count on being flown back to their base camp for showers, hot food and a reasonably comfortable bed. Prior to the period when combat troops were being moved by chopper, some infantry companies might at times spend four to six weeks out in the bush with virtually no respite from the harsh conditions.

STEVE: Like you said, I'm not sure if anyone got transferred out of our hospital and into the infantry against their will. In some cases, corpsmen like Rothblatt who got assigned to the infantry upon their arrival in Nam might spend six months in the field, then three months at an infantry aid station and three months at some rear-echelon job like ambulance driver or hospital medic. The theory was that in the eyes of some infantry brass, a platoon medic's job in the field was too demanding, draining and risky to warrant a 12-month assignment.

FRED: A lot of guys who spent their entire 12 months as field medics are going to be surprised to hear that one! But they'd probably tell you that not all of the wounds incurred on the battlefield were necessarily inflicted by the enemy. Which is why another one of my duties in A&D was to fill out these long forms they had for injury investigations.

STEVE: Whenever a patient came in with a self-inflicted injury— and there were quite a few— the Army's Criminal Investigation Division (CID) would have to investigate to determine if it was accidental or intentional. If it was ruled intentional, the soldier could be subject to severe disciplinary action, up to and including a court martial.

FRED: Depending on the severity of the offense, the result could be forfeiture of all pay and allowances; a dishonorable discharge; or imprisonment for a period of up to 5 years or more, if the offense occurred in a hostile fire zone.

STEVE: In reality, the Army's chief concern was to prevent other soldiers from thinking they could get away with avoiding combat duty by shooting themselves in the leg or foot. Thus the prevailing strategies were to either return the soldier to active duty as quickly as possible or else prosecute him to the fullest extent. Nevertheless, if the soldier's ultimate goal was to avoid combat action no matter what it cost him, he often succeeded.

FRED: Another option the Army could employ in a combat zone was the concept of "bad time." If a soldier spent two months in the stockade or hospital as a result of an intentional act that was not in the line of duty, he might automatically get his tour in Vietnam extended by two months of "bad time" to make up for the amount of active duty time that he missed. This too was intended to discourage anyone else from thinking they could get out of combat duty as a result of a self-inflicted illness or injury.

STEVE: The most common example of a "self-inflicted illness" was when soldiers deliberately avoided taking their daily and weekly malaria pills. Some would do this in the hopes of contracting the disease and spending a month or two in a nice convalescent hospital, such as the one at Cam Ranh Bay, instead of having to sweat it out in the jungle. But if it could be proven by their immediate superiors that they'd deliberately skipped their pills, they might have earned themselves some bad time.

FRED: Lots of our buddies in the 24th Evac quit taking the pills too, but not in the hopes of contracting malaria. It was mainly because the pills gave 'em constant diarrhea.

STEVE: I was one who stopped taking 'em for that reason. Fortunately we were in an area where the malaria-bearing mosquitoes were pretty rare. Some other parts of the country were totally infested with 'em. I don't recall a single one of our guys ever having malaria— if they had, I'm sure we all would have been taking those damned pills. Malaria was often fatal if it wasn't treated immediately and properly. There were at least two different strains, and if you tried to treat the patient before determining which type he had, you could make the problem a whole lot worse if you gave him the wrong meds.

FRED: With self-inflicted wounds, there were rarely any witnesses to the act. This meant it was extremely difficult to prove the action causing the injury was deliberate. My job was to initiate the investigation process by filling out a form including any facts that were known at the time, plus a physician's statement regarding the nature of the injuries and their probable cause, plus the names of any potential witnesses— as well as a brief statement from the patient.

STEVE: So would you say you found the stories of most of those patients to be credible?

FRED: Well, some would admit they had done it on purpose or only because they were drunk or stoned at the time. Others maintained their innocence but seemed like they were probably lying. And then there were those who were either telling the truth or else they were damned good actors. But it wasn't my function to try to assess the truth of their statements— in fact I had to be careful not to let personal opinions influence what I reported on the form.

STEVE: I suppose if someone in your position were prejudiced for or against a certain patient, it would be easy to let that affect what you put on the form. But at least you weren't in the French Army during World War I. Back then, many French soldiers were supposedly executed for self-inflicted wounds. The British had a similar rule on the books at the time, but apparently the 4,000 or so troops presumed to be guilty of the offense were rarely if ever executed. Instead they'd be given a choice of facing a firing squad or leading the next charge into battle.

FRED: A great way to drum up volunteers for the next combat assault! But anyway, in addition to my working in A&D plus the ER,

I spent some time helping out next door in a structure given the rather un-military-sounding name of the "Baggage Room." There we were responsible for storing and securing patients' personal items, clothing and valuables. Since they usually got their clothing cut off when they came into the ER, we had to keep a supply of new uniforms to issue to them if they were going back out into the field.

STEVE: And that meant you had access to... jungle fatigues! When we arrived in Nam, we were wearing the old-fashioned fatigue shirts and pants just like most other non-combat units. The lightweight, loose-fitting jungle fatigues with the big pockets were in short supply and thus were being issued only to combat units out in the field. We were authorized to wear them if we wanted to, but the only way to obtain a set was to literally buy them— or else you had to know somebody who knew somebody. In this case, that second somebody was anyone who worked in the Baggage Room!

FRED: Jungle fatigues were lighter, cooler and more comfortable— plus they looked more impressive and were considered a "status symbol" among the non-combatants. So guys like Carl Denton and I, who spent time working in the Baggage Room, "issued ourselves" some new jungle fatigues and got a few sets for our friends as well.

STEVE: I turned down the offer, figuring anyone who saw me suddenly appear in jungle fatigues would assume that a) I probably got them through some sort of devious means, and b) I was only wearing them out of vanity, i.e., I wanted to look like a combat veteran. So instead I chose to continue wearing the old dorky-looking fatigues that Uncle Sam issued us— the ones that made us look like gas station attendants. (Yes, gas stations had such people back in 1966.)

FRED: When we logged a patient's personal possessions for secure storage, we'd sometimes run across interesting stuff they had in their pockets. Of course there were the essentials like toilet paper, matches, gum, insect repellent, can openers, etc. But we also found things we didn't expect— like comic books, sewing kits, miniature chess sets, blackjacks, brass knuckles, tranquilizers, foot powder, earplugs... carotene pills for improving their night vision... just to name a few.

STEVE: Keep in mind that many infantry grunts could be out in the bush for anywhere from three to six weeks at a time. Any "luxuries" they wanted to carry would be added to the weight of their rucksacks which could top 80 pounds, depending on their mission. What was also surprising were some of the things they elected NOT to carry, in an attempt to reduce the weight of their load.

FRED: For example, a new replacement who'd just arrived in country would often be told by a combat veteran to discard all his underwear and keep just one extra pair of socks. (This was illustrated in a scene from "Platoon" where PFC Taylor, played by Charlie Sheen, is told to "get rid of this... get rid of this... you won't need this.") Each day the rookie (also known as a "cherry" or FNG, which stood for "fuggin' new guy") would wear one pair of socks and no underwear. The extra pair of socks would be hung on the outside of his pack to dry out so they could be worn the next day.

STEVE: Dry socks were extremely important for preventing a debilitating condition known as "trench foot" (technical name: immersion foot) caused by prolonged exposure to wet conditions. The skin on the foot would gradually begin to shrivel and peel off. Of course this was often a ticket to the hospital and some bedrest, so some troops might have gone out of their way to try to keep their feet wet. Which is why platoon medics in the field were often ordered to inspect each soldier's feet in the morning before breakfast— and often carried several extra pairs of dry socks for the troops.

FRED: And then there were the Death Cards— known by some as Calling Cards or Payback Cards. Most people remember the scene in "Apocalypse Now" where Colonel Kilgore, played by Robert Duvall, walks around a battlefield tossing Aces of Spades on the bodies of dead enemy soldiers. An onlooker (Charlie Sheen's father, Martin) asks the officer next to him "Hey Captain, what's that?" The answer: "That's a Death Card— to let Charlie know who did this."

STEVE: Many moviegoers assumed that routine was merely the creation of a Hollywood scriptwriter. (After all, how many decks of cards would it take to assemble an entire deck of just Aces of Spades? Answer: 52 decks!) But the practice actually did exist in Nam. In '65 or early '66, someone began circulating the idea that the Ace of Spades was greatly feared by the highly superstitious Viet Cong.

FRED: Charlie allegedly viewed it as a warning of impending death, extreme misfortune or the very real prospect of burning in hell for all of eternity. In other words, it supposedly scared the crap out of him.

The story was given coverage in Stars and Stripes, the weekly newspaper of the Armed Forces. This led some soldiers to start leaving the cards on the bodies of dead VC or leaving them as "calling cards" at the entrances to villages they had cleared of VC.

STEVE: Soon, just about every deck of cards found in their base camps had only 51 cards, with one of the Jokers being designated to fill in for the missing Ace of Spades. That's because the Aces were being left behind at battle sites to tell the enemy that "Our unit is operating in this area... and we came here to kick your ass!"

FRED: Soldiers were quoted as saying "We went into a VC stronghold and kicked butt, whereupon they all fled. We left Death Cards on the bodies and when we went back two weeks later, the place was still deserted. Charlie wanted nothing to do with us— or with the Ace of Spades!" Of course this was somewhat contrary to the stated objective of finding and killing the enemy. But what the hell— while some infantry grunts relished contact with Charlie, if only to relieve the boredom of trudging through the jungle day after day, the majority usually just wanted to serve out their 12 months and go home.

STEVE: The Death Card idea caught on quickly and in February, two officers in the 25th Infantry Division wrote a letter to the United States Playing Card Company requesting a bulk shipment of "Ace-of-Spades-only" Bicycle brand cards to be used in "psychological warfare" against the enemy. To their surprise, the company not only sent them a shipment of 1,000 aces but did so at no charge.

FRED: Soon some units of the 25th Infantry, the First Air Cavalry, the 4th Infantry and the 173rd Airborne were doing the same thing with custom-designed cards that had the Ace of Spades on one side and the unit's emblem (or some symbol of death such as a skull & crossbones) on the other.

STEVE: Often the custom designs included the name of the unit and a slogan such as "Dealers of Death," "Death from Above," "You can run, but you'll just die tired," or "If we can't win your hearts and minds, we'll burn your fuggin' hooches." Never mind that Charlie couldn't read English... the messages probably would have been in Vietnamese if they were really intended for his benefit. The fact that they were in English was a good indication that the cards were really for the morale and amusement of the GI's who carried them.

FRED: Occasionally we'd find a handful of the cards in the pocket of a patient after his clothing had been removed. The first time, I said to Carl Denton "Look at these! Why would someone carry a handful of Aces of Spades out into the jungle?" "Well, maybe he's an amateur magician and he likes to do card tricks for his buddies." I thought for a moment and said "Or maybe he's a professional card shark who likes to keep a few aces up his sleeve when he's playing poker!"

STEVE: Of course when more Aces were found in another patient's pockets several days later, we realized there had to be some other explanation. Then when others started showing up bearing a skull and crossbones and slogans like "Death from Above," we began to figure out what the Death Cards were all about. Soon the story was picked up by United Press and published in various stateside newspapers, whereupon orders began flooding in for more cards.

FRED: In '67 a team of social psychologists began looking into whether the Death Cards really did strike profound fear in the hearts of the VC or North Vietnamese soldiers. The researchers were unable to find any evidence to support that hypothesis and concluded that the Vietnamese had no cultural basis to fear the Ace of Spades as a symbol of death.

STEVE: But despite little evidence that the cards had any appreciable effect on the morale of the VC, there was absolutely no doubt about the tremendous boost in morale they provided.... to the American troops! The researchers concluded that an Ace of Spades was more likely to be viewed by the enemy not as an omen of death but as a phallic symbol and a strong suggestion that the Americans were inclined to want to have sexual relations with the corpses of the VC.

FRED: Well shoot, THAT shoulda scared the hell out of 'em!

&&&&&&&&&&&&&&&&&&

FACT OR FICTION? The story goes that after a B-52 strike on Hanoi, Ho Chi Minh's three paid impostors or "body doubles" were summoned to party headquarters and given the good news: "Uncle Ho has survived the bombing!" They all started cheering "Uncle Ho!" "Uncle Ho!" "Uncle Ho!" Whereupon a high ranking NVA General interrupted them to add that "Unfortunately, we also have some bad news. He lost his left arm in the attack!"

CHAPTER 30

HOLD ON A MINUTE, THIS PATIENT IS COVERED WITH FUR

Queen Tonic, we have three WIA's and a possible case of rabies onboard

FRED: When I was working nights in the ER (6 pm to 6 am) I'd be getting ready to hit the sack at just about the same time Steve was getting up to go to work in Headquarters from 8 to 5. So even though we bunked right next to each other, we barely had a chance to even say hello, let alone discuss what was going on in our respective little worlds. It was odd because we had spent the previous ten months together, literally seven days a week, and now whenever one of us would see the other, he was usually asleep. Such were the realities of war!

STEVE: Working nights in the Emergency Room was normally pretty easy duty for Fred since there wasn't much battle action after sundown. When patients did arrive, they'd usually come in one or two at a time, whereas during a daylight battle or ambush, the 24th Evac could at times receive as many as a dozen in the space of a half hour.

FRED: But even when it was slow, we had to carefully monitor the radio since the Dustoffs (medical evacuation helicopters) would call ahead to let us know the number and types of casualties they were bringing in. This allowed us some precious time— like 10 to 20 minutes— to make sure we had the right equipment and personnel ready as soon as the chopper touched down on our helipad.

STEVE: It also gave our people a chance to wave off the "bird" and send it to a nearby hospital if for some reason we didn't have sufficient capacity or the proper equipment or specialists to handle the types of casualties onboard.

FRED: One of my duties was to assist in unloading the wounded from the bird and bringing them into the ER to be set on litter stands. I would then perform other tasks like cutting off their clothing with a large scissors, inspecting them for multiple wounds to make sure we didn't overlook anything, and making sure we obtained their correct name, rank and serial number in case they lost consciousness. I would also collect their personal possessions to be logged in and stored in a secure area until such time as the patient was ready to leave the 24th. To prevent overdosing, we would write an "M" on their forehead to indicate they had been given morphine for pain, or a "T" if they received a tetanus booster. An IV would be started to replace lost fluids, along with a blood transfusion if needed.

STEVE: What would you say was the worst aspect of working in the Emergency Room as far as you were concerned?

FRED: For me that would have had to be whenever we had to put a deceased patient into a rubber body bag for transfer to the Morgue. Fortunately I only had to do it a couple times.

STEVE: Then when things got really busy in the ER, a doctor might have to ask one of the nurses to perform certain tasks he would normally do himself. And a nurse might then have to ask a corpsman to take on some assignments she would normally do herself, like debriding a wound by cutting away the dead tissue around it.

FRED: In a mass casualty situation, whether it involved battlefield casualties or victims of a train wreck, medical personnel often had to decide which patients to treat first, which ones could wait and which ones were not likely to survive whether they received treatment or not. This practice was known as "triage," which gets its name not from the three categories of patients but from the French verb "trier," meaning "to sort or separate out."

STEVE: And in fact some triage systems separate patients into four or five groups instead of three. The military system of triage was developed in the 1930's for the purpose of saving the maximum number of lives, sometimes at the expense of those few that were likely to be lost no matter what steps might be taken to try to save them.

FRED: In Vietnam there were two types of criteria for triage, one involving who the individual was and the other involving the type or severity of his injuries. American soldiers and civilians were treated first, followed by South Vietnamese soldiers and civilians, followed by enemy soldiers. We had two wards of VC prisoners guarded around the clock by American MP's. Naturally we assumed the guards were there to protect hospital staff from the VC. Some MP's, however, have said it was more common for them to have to protect those VC from American GI patients who wished to exact revenge on enemy soldiers for killing their friends.

STEVE: Personally I felt a lot of empathy for the VC patients since I viewed them as being mostly conscripts who had been compelled to serve in the military just like we had. And unlike a lot of American combat troops, I felt no hatred toward the enemy— especially since I worked with Vietnamese civilians every day. The ones I knew were all very decent (but primitive) people, as near as I could tell.

FRED: Agreed, I did not feel any hostility whatsoever toward the Vietnamese people we knew— although some guys did.

STEVE: Anyway, the US field medics used a form of triage when assessing battlefield casualties to determine who should be evacuated first. But triage "officially" began when the patient arrived at a hospital or aid station. A physician would normally be responsible for making triage decisions, but if things got hectic he might have to delegate that function to a nurse. And when things would get really hectic, it might have to be delegated to a corpsman.

FRED: The basic criteria were: Class I, patients who were likely to survive only if given immediate attention; Class II, patients who were likely to survive even if their treatment had to be delayed for some period of time; and Class III, patients who were not likely to survive with or without treatment and were essentially waiting to die. Over time, the hospital medics would gradually learn to recognize certain symptoms that provided strong evidence as to the category in which each patient was likely to be assigned. Had I spent more time in the ER as opposed to the Admissions Office, I'm sure I would have refined those skills as time progressed.

STEVE: But you did get an opportunity to test your surgical skills.

FRED: Yes. One evening we had nearly a dozen patients occupying the litter stands when a few more were brought in and set down over in a corner of the ER. These were South Vietnamese (ARVN) soldiers, as I recall, with gunshot wounds. One doctor took a brief look at them and said "This one needs a trache, right now!"

STEVE: What he meant was if someone didn't immediately make an incision in the patient's throat that would allow him to breathe through his neck, he could die of suffocation because his airway was blocked. The physician looked around and saw no doctor or nurse available, so he hollers "Does any corpsman wanna do a trache?"

FRED: Now back in Medic School, there were several procedures that weren't part of the official curriculum but the instructors briefly explained them to us anyway. Their theory was that we might have to perform them at some point, even if the Army didn't think we were supposed to. (The brass probably thought it would be too easy for a corpsman to make a mistake and kill somebody.)

STEVE: One of these "unofficial lectures" was about delivering a baby; another described how to perform a tracheotomy. They tried to teach us so much stuff in Medic School that I knew I wouldn't be able to retain it all. So I had a system for memorizing the key points, just like when I learned the General Orders back in Basic. In the case of a tracheotomy, I determined there were two important points I had to remember: Be sure to start the incision below the Adam's Apple, and be sure to make a vertical cut as opposed to a horizontal one— otherwise you might slice the jugular vein or carotid artery, resulting in the patient's quick demise. I figured I could pretty much handle the other aspects by operating on instinct alone.

FRED: In my case I didn't have any specific points I had memorized, so I just told the captain "I'll do it sir, but I've never done one before." He handed me a scalpel, showed me where to cut and how to stick my finger in the hole before inserting the breathing tube. With that I was off and running. I wouldn't say I was nervous about it, although if he had said "Here, take this scalpel and cut a hole in Steve Donovan's throat," I might have had some trepidation about that. But since the patient was a stranger to me, as well as a Vietnamese who was about to die if I didn't deliver, I had no second thoughts. It went pretty smoothly and in a matter of minutes, he was able to breathe as well as could be expected under the circumstances.

STEVE: I did learn later that at Fort Sam, new Army doctors and nurses (most of whom had never performed a tracheotomy) were taught to practice doing them on live goats. Apparently goats were selected because of their long necks— allowing for repeated incisions— that were very similar to those of humans.

FRED: But of course we didn't have the benefit of practicing on goats or any other living creatures. For us it was like everything else— just another case of "Look at this. Remember it!!! Next subject!" (A line that came directly from an old Bill Cosby comedy routine about when he was being trained as a Navy corpsman.) Then again, maybe they didn't teach us medics how to do tracheotomies because they just didn't have enough goats to go around.

STEVE: Naturally the first tracheotomy would be the toughest. In Medic School, I remember when I was about to give my first "practice injection" to a fellow trainee and I observed that my hand was trembling. (Probably too much coffee that morning!) Not wanting the "patient" to see it, I went ahead and quickly plunged the needle into his arm. I can only imagine what I would have done when I was about to cut into someone's throat for the first time.

FRED: At least if he were Vietnamese, he wouldn't have been able to curse at you in English! Actually I've been told that at some point after we got our Medic School diplomas, traches were added to the curriculum. Not sure about delivering babies, though.

STEVE: I do recall committing to memory the four basic life saving steps when treating a battlefield casualty: "Stop the bleeding. Clear the airway. Protect the wound. Treat for shock." The instructor said "If you don't remember anything else from your medic training, remember these four steps!!" Unfortunately I suspect there were some trainees who couldn't even remember the four basic steps. Overall, the guys in Medic School were definitely a more educated and teachable group than, say, the men in your average platoon of ground pounders. But the Army tried to give you so much information during the 10-week course that I doubt if anyone could remember it all.

FRED: And there were some guys who seemed incapable of retaining anything. We had a few of 'em at the 24th. Those were the ones who— once they got to Vietnam as an infantry or hospital medic— were put on permanent guard duty, shit burning detail or garbage detail. If nobody trusted them as medics, they weren't going to be assigned to caring for patients or treating battle casualties.

STEVE: By the way, the Field Medic's Manual dated 1984 had 20 pages on how to deliver a baby and what to do if something should go wrong. I don't think we spent 10 minutes on it in training class in '66.

FRED: Regarding the four life saving steps, I believe the Army later changed them to "stop the bleeding, clear the airway, treat for shock, prepare for evacuation." But we were inducted into the "transitional Army" that was in the process of changing its medical procedures. In the old Army, casualties traveled by ambulance from the field medic... to an aid station... to a clearing station... to a field hospital... and then to an evacuation hospital or surgical hospital, depending on what the patient needed. But in Nam, casualties were being evacuated by helicopter directly from the battlefield to the evac hospital or surgical hospital. This saved a lot of time and, of course, a lot of lives.

STEVE: The principle of the "Golden Hour" referred to the idea that if a casualty could be transported to the Operating Room in less than 60 minutes, he stood an excellent chance of surviving. The objective in Vietnam was to reduce that period to under 30 minutes, which was usually achieved. As a result, the survival rate for casualties who were still alive when they reached an evac hospital was around 97 percent. (Although I found out later that a patient had to survive for 24 hours before he was counted as being "alive on arrival.")

FRED: Usually at 2 or 3 in the morning in the ER, there was absolutely nothing going on. But we still had to constantly monitor the radio in case an air ambulance might call in to report its estimated arrival time, plus brief descriptions of the wounds suffered by the casualties onboard. So I would often be sitting in a chair right next to the radio, with the speaker less than 8 inches from my ear. Sleeping was permitted in that situation because: a) you weren't on guard duty, where sleeping could be a court martial offense, and b) the radio was so loud that it would wake you instantly if a call came in.

STEVE: Did anyone give you amphetamines to help you stay awake? Despite assertions that the Army commonly used benzedrine or dexedrine pills to keep the troops awake at night, I don't believe I ever saw or was offered any myself. Apparently you could get them from the hospital pharmacy if you needed them. Some claim that during the war, "bennies" were "handed out like candy" to the infantrymen who had to remain alert for guard duty or night ambush missions.

FRED: There were benzedrine tablets available to those of us on the night shift, although I'm not sure where they came from. I would take them occasionally, but if it was a slow night, I preferred to just sleep right next to the radio. This one night there were no radio transmissions coming in to wake me up. I slept there so long with my left arm pressed against the sharp edge of the radio that my arm went numb. Apparently I severely pinched a nerve because my arm was partially numb for three or four days before it cleared up. I was reluctant to report it due to the stigma that would be attached to my explanation that I was "asleep on duty" when it happened.

STEVE: So you were on duty— and wide awake—in the ER the night the rabid dog came in.

FRED: Yeah, it was actually early in the evening when there was still plenty of daylight. The 24th Evac had its own dedicated radio frequency (62.05 kHz) and our call sign was "Queen Tonic." I heard the radio crackle a few times, then some static, and then:

"Queen Tonic... Queen Tonic... this is Dustoff three-six-bravo-niner, inbound from Tay Ninh. Do you read, over."

Sergeant Renfro grabbed the mike as he sat down in his chair.

"Go ahead bravo-niner, this is Queen Tonic. What's your status? Over."
"Queen Tonic, ETA is 22 minutes. We have three litters, four WIA's total. One serious head wound... one bullet wound shoulder... one shrapnel wounds in lower extremities... and one dog bite. We're also bringing the dog for observation, over."
"Roger bravo-niner, we copy one serious head wound... one bullet

wound shoulder... one shrapnel in lower extremities... one dog bite...
and one naaaasty dawg. What's the disposition of this dawg? Over."
"Wait one."
"OK Queen Tonic, dog appears to be calm and relaxed, no outward
signs of agitation. We'll give you a shout when we're three minutes
from touchdown. Three-six-bravo-niner, over and out."

STEVE: And what were you guys supposed to do with a rabid dog?

FRED: Well, Captain Stiller told me to go next door and alert Headquarters about the dog. I go tell the Officer of the Day, Lieutenant Gorman, whose response is: "Where in the hell are we gonna put a rabid dog? Do we have a cage or anything like that?" A stunned silence pervades the room for a moment, then the always resourceful Company Clerk, SP4 Maxwell, says "I'll get a rope and some welder's gloves from the Motor Pool and meet the chopper. If it's calm and relaxed, I should be able to handle it. No problem, sir."

STEVE: In the Motor Pool, PFC Lovejoy was the only one on duty when SP4 Maxwell burst into the tent. Pulling a little rank and seemingly in a mild state of panic, Max panted "Quick, we've got an emergency! I need a 10-foot piece of rope and a pair of welder's gloves! Plus I gotta borrow that catcher's mask that Wendell's got in his hooch. Go grab it and meet me at the helipad in ten minutes!"

FRED: Being the Company Clerk, Max commanded more respect than most other guys of his rank— he was, after all, the Company Commander's right-hand man. Digging out some rope and gloves, Lovejoy asks "What in the hell is going on? Are we under attack?" Max replies "Not exactly... but there's definitely a rabid dog coming in on a chopper, and I get to be the designated dog handler!!!" Lovejoy says "Whooeee, whatever you do— keep him away from me, man!"

STEVE: At certain times, word could travel plenty fast at the 24th Evac. By the time Maxwell had managed to acquire his rope, gloves, and the catcher's mask that Wendell had been sent as a gag gift, a small crowd had gathered around the helipad. They were waiting to see how the medics (and especially SP4 Maxwell) were going to handle this vicious animal that was about to descend out of the skies in a green flying machine with a big red cross painted on its nose.

FRED: As soon as the bird touched down, we ran out to meet it carrying fresh litters. Once the wounded patients were offloaded, those clean, folded-up litters would be given to the chopper crew to replace the ones that were carrying the wounded.

STEVE: Later, when the chopper made its next extraction from a battle site, the clean litters would be given to the ground troops to replace the ones carrying their comrades. Litters were constantly being moved from place to place in this fashion, kind of like a five dollar bill at a shopping mall.

FRED: As the chopper medic was releasing the security locks on the patients' litters, I could see the crew chief sitting back in the corner, watching us intently. Normally he'd be assisting with the offload, so I assumed he must have had control of the dog and probably had it tied up so it posed no threat to those onboard.

STEVE: Maxwell stood off to the side, putting on his heavy gloves. As soon as the last patient was offloaded, he donned his catcher's mask, stepped up to the doorway of the chopper with his lasso and hollered "Ready for the dog!" At which point the crew chief stood up, turned toward Max and thrust out both his hands. Nestled comfortably between them was a ball of snow-white fuzz— the cutest little four-pound puppy that you're ever likely to see.

FRED: It looked like it could be a Maltese or Bichon Frise, which would have made sense since the Bichons were popularized in France in the 16th century and probably brought to French Indochina some time afterward.

STEVE: What's more, it was obviously thrilled with all the attention it was getting— and determined to lick the face of anyone who came within its reach. We never stopped to think about the fact that the rabies virus could be transmitted through the dog's saliva to humans— although it would probably have had to break the skin first. Or that rabies was a disease of the central nervous system that infected the brain and was usually fatal if not treated promptly.

FRED: I believe the virus could also enter the human body through the eyes, nose or mouth. So dog saliva should definitely have been avoided— but then, what did we know? I don't remember them covering rabies in much detail in Medic School.

STEVE: At that point Max dropped his gloves and mask and took the pup in his arms. It immediately started licking his face— and for Max, it appeared to be a case of love at first sight. As soon as all personnel cleared the pad, the chopper lifted off and was gone.

FRED: And thus began the saga of Maxwell's dog, "Pie."

&&&&&&&&&&&&&&&&&&&&

FACT OR FICTION? *The story goes that some time after MSGT Hanley retired, he was preparing to enter the Pearly Gates when he was stopped at the entrance by St. Peter. "This is a routine check on your eligibility. Have you done any good in your life?" asked the saint. "Oh absolutely," replied Hanley. "For example, I was out looking for meteorites in the desert when I saw a young lady surrounded by a bunch of mean-looking thugs from a motorcycle gang. They appeared to be working her over pretty good, so I jumped into the middle of the fray. I socked one of 'em in the jaw— he went down— then I elbowed one in the stomach and he went down. I kicked another one in the groin, and he went down too. Then I yelled "You're messin' with the US Army now, boys! If you mother truckers don't get on your little bikeys and get the hell outa here now, I'm gonna kick the snot out of every one of ya!" St. Peter was quite impressed. "That's very interesting, sergeant. When did this happen?" he asked. "About ten minutes ago," Hanley replied.*

**SEVEN MORE CHAPTERS TO GO...
DON'T FORGET TO SUBMIT
YOUR OWN BOOK REVIEW AT:
www.longbinhdaze.com**

CHAPTER 31

GOOD NEWS, MEN...
EVERYONE GETS A PIECE OF "PIE"

*They said he must be vicious, but the story
sounded rather suspicious.... Meanwhile,
the natives thought he'd be delicious*

FRED: As SP4 Maxwell took the fuzzball off the chopper and turned toward the crowd of onlookers, people began shrieking with laughter when they got a good look at the "vicious dog" that everyone had been so worried about. How could anyone possibly think this darling little puppy posed a threat to them? That thing could never hurt a flea! One guy yells "Hey Max, be careful with that dog! It might be gettin' ready to tear yer arm off!"

STEVE: Of course we all felt a great sense of relief, but we didn't realize at the time that rabies was indeed a very serious problem in many parts of Vietnam. Turns out there were rabid monkeys, dogs, rats, bats, etc., all over the place. Had we known, we undoubtedly would have taken it more seriously when we were told we had a rabies scare right there on our own turf.

FRED: Any time a soldier was suspected of being bitten by an infected animal, that animal would have to be captured or killed so it could be observed (if alive) or have its brain tested for the rabies virus (if it was already dead.) A dog would have to be quarantined and held under observation for 14 days to see if rabies symptoms might develop. If the animal could not be found, the bite victim would have to undergo a series of painful shots to avoid becoming a fatality.

STEVE: Since we had no facilities for quarantining a canine, Max volunteered to take custody. "Maxwell's dog" immediately took up residence in our hooch as a mascot. Oddly, Max named it "Pie" and fashioned a leash for it. But the pup never seemed to wander more than 10 or 15 feet away from our tent, even without a leash.

FRED: Naturally someone had to ask "Hey Max, why'd you name that dog Pie?" He said he thought it would be funny when someone called the dog by saying "Here, Pie! Here, Pie!" (It sounded a lot like the term "hair pie" which, at the time, was a bit of crude college-boy humor referring to the genitals of a female human.)

STEVE: I wasn't quite satisfied with that explanation, but I was not about to call him a liar since we all loved the guy. (After the war he became a high school math teacher, and his students all loved him too!) It wasn't until years later that I learned about two famous movie horses named "Pie" and wondered if one of 'em could have been the actual source for the name. (Then again, if Max was destined to become a math teacher, maybe what he really meant was "Pi.")

FRED: One horse named Pie was ridden by Elizabeth Taylor in the 1944 film "National Velvet" in which Velvet Brown, played by Taylor, named her horse Pie because it was short for Pirate— an epithet bestowed on the horse by its original owner.

STEVE: But the other horse named Pie belonged to actor Jimmy Stewart. It appeared with him in no fewer than 17 western movies and Jimmy insisted "Pie was the smartest horse I ever knew, and one of the best co-stars I ever had." He considered Pie to be a good luck charm as well as an old friend.

FRED: I can see where Max might not want to admit he named his dog after Taylor's horse in a sappy children's movie. But I wouldn't see any problem with naming it after Stewart's faithful sorrel from 17 Hollywood westerns.

STEVE: Or maybe he just wanted to engage in a little crude college-boy humor! After all, we could get away with lots of stuff in a combat zone that we'd never dream of trying back home in "polite society."

FRED: You mean like... farting at the dinner table? Soon, Max was feeding "Pie" scraps from the Mess Hall as well as food contributions he was getting from various other guys. We all loved that little dog, and he was without a doubt a great addition to our "family." Each night, about a half hour before lights out, someone would set a bowl of beer on the floor over in the corner. Pie would scramble over there and lap up the entire bowl— he loved the stuff— after which he would quickly pass out and keep snoring away 'til reveille the next morning.

STEVE: Now Pie was supposed to be held under observation for two weeks. If he turned out to have rabies, the soldier he'd bitten would have to undergo a lengthy series of painful shots in the abdomen. But if Pie passed with flying colors, the soldier was in the clear and everyone could rest easy. We were convinced that Pie didn't have rabies and so we assumed the pooch would just continue on being Max's best friend and our beloved hooch mascot.

FRED: When the two weeks were up, we notified the infantry unit that their soldier was out of danger. (Maybe all that beer Pie lapped up killed the rabies infection!) Next day the phone rings in Headquarters and Max answers. It's the soldier who'd been bitten, asking "When do I get my dog back?" Max says "Oh, uhh... let me check on that and I'll get back to you tomorrow."

STEVE: Sonofabitch! It never occurred to us that the guy would want his dog back after it bit him and scared the hell out of everybody. None of us wanted to give up our adorable mascot... and Max sure as hell wasn't planning to let anyone take Pie away from him!

FRED: We sat around that evening thinking up various ways to help him get out of his predicament. Several suggestions were offered. Tell them the dog ran away, tell them the dog got killed, tell them the dog got stolen or eaten by a local. Finally Max said he'd sleep on it.

STEVE: The next morning, the phone rings in HQ and it's the bite victim again. Max answers and says "Oh yeah, I checked on that and found out that the dog bit someone else yesterday— we've gotta hold him for observation for two more weeks!" After that we all hoped we wouldn't hear from the bite victim again, and we never did. He probably figured out what answer he'd get if he tried calling back.

FRED: The Vietnamese had two primary uses for dogs: As money-makers that could be sold to GI's for a tidy profit... or as a food source to be eaten. I guess they did keep some as pets, but they'd have to constantly watch 'em so they wouldn't get eaten by the neighbors. In fact I think I read that "nice" dogs would sometimes be kept as pets while the "ornery" ones would end up on the dinner table.

STEVE: But within a few days after our arrival in Nam, some of our guys quickly discovered they could buy a puppy or young dog on the streets of Bien Hoa for around ten bucks. As a result, we had a number of dogs wandering around our compound in the daytime, causing more than one senior officer to bellow "It looks like Tam Hiep in this goddam place!" (Villages like Tam Hiep often had packs of wild dogs— or unrestrained pets— roaming the streets.)

FRED: A month after Pie's arrival, the Brigade Commander did a drive-through inspection of the 24th Evac and blew a gasket when he saw the mutts roaming around loose. At first he demanded that we get rid of every single one, but someone managed to convince him to set a limit of two dogs to be kept as mascots for the entire hospital.

STEVE: It also infuriated him to see a soldier walking through the compound with an Afro hairstyle bulging out from under his Army-issue green baseball cap. "See that that man gets a haircut immediately!" he bellowed. "There's no way that's even close to a regulation haircut! What kind of operation are you guys running here?"

FRED: The problem for us was that nobody knew of anyone with an Afro— surely we would have noticed. We finally decided it was probably a friend or relative of one of our troops. Sometimes they'd catch a ride to the 24th on their day off and stop in to see their pals. But no service branch allowed Afro hairstyles as far as we knew. Nevertheless, once it was announced that everyone was required to have a regulation haircut, we considered the matter closed.

STEVE: Meanwhile, the men of the 24th had approximately eight dogs altogether. Of course nobody wanted to give up their own mutt, so it was decided that the only fair way to handle the problem was to hold an election. Ballots were created listing the names of the eight canines, with a copy being given to each enlisted man with instructions to choose any two of the pooches.

FRED: Pie was at a distinct disadvantage because he hardly ever left our hooch, so lots of guys had no idea who he was. The most popular canine was Ringo, a mutt that looked like a moth-eaten border collie. After that it was anybody's race for second place. But then Pie did have an ace up his sleeve, so to speak. That's because the job of conducting the election had been delegated to the Company Clerk... who just so happened to be SP4 Maxwell!

STEVE: Not wanting to arouse any suspicions, Max "counted" the ballots and declared Ringo the winner with a tie for second place between Pie and Tinker Bell, a spayed female with the head of a Pomeranian attached to the body of a Pit Bull. There would have to be a run-off! This prompted numerous GI's to ask "Who the hell is Pie, and what the hell kind of name is that for a dog?" Which gave Max an opportunity to show them the little white fuzzball in Tent 13 without having to mention that he was the primary owner.

FRED: Pie certainly could have won it on cuteness, but that wasn't necessarily among the most important criteria for the voters. Then again, Max WAS counting the votes... and wouldn't ya know, in the run-off election it was Pie by a wet nose! Was the fix in all along? Nobody knew that other than Max, but it was a pretty safe bet.

STEVE: And thus Maxwell got to keep his Maltese while we got to keep our beer-guzzling hooch mascot. Of course when the Battalion Commander issued his decree that all but two dogs would be banished, he neglected to add that "No new dogs are to be brought into the compound following the reduction to a maximum of two."

FRED: So within a few weeks, new mutts began appearing here and there in the hospital compound. Except that this time the troops were smart enough to not let their pooches roam loose around the company area where they would be spotted.

STEVE: Sounds like we beat the fuggin' system once again!

FRED: Roger that! But then lo and behold, the dude with the Afro reappears. Someone spotted him walking on the company street at dusk, reported it to Headquarters— and Colonel Dickerson blew his cork. But this time there was no way that whoever it was would be leaving the compound after dark. All we had to do was find him!

STEVE: The CO tells the clerks in HQ to fan out, find that man and bring him to the Orderly Room. We search the area, walking through the hooches asking if anyone had seen PFC Reynolds when we knew darn well that Reynolds was actually on guard duty. We checked the latrines, showers, beer tent, etc. We even asked the Sergeant of the Guard if any of his sentries had an Afro. And we came up empty.

FRED: Everyone was completely baffled until a few days later when, after evening chow, we saw "Afro man" strolling along from about 40 yards away. Judging from his considerable size and build, he looked a lot like PFC Buggs— except for the "big hair." He was heading into Tent 17, so I promptly went around to cover the east entrance while Steve entered the hooch from the west.

STEVE: I walked in and immediately saw Buggs sitting on his foot-locker holding an Afro wig in his hands. I said "Hey Buggsy, how's it goin'? That your wig?" (Everyone called him Buggsy.) He says "Yeah, my girlfriend sent it to me as a joke." I said "You know the brass have got their skivvies all twisted up because there's somebody walkin' around the compound with a non-regulation Afro?" He says "Yeah I know it, but I got a regulation haircut. Regulations don't say nothin' about wearin' a wig when I'm off duty."

FRED: Hmmm... a dicey situation brewing!

STEVE: I said "Well, you're probably right— but I've got orders to find the man with the Afro and report him to the CO. I'll make you a deal: If you'll promise me that this wig will never again be seen outside the confines of this tent, I'll forget that I ever saw it. Deal?" He thought for a moment and then replied "OK man, fair enough." And I felt a distinct sense of glee knowing that old man Dickerson would never have the satisfaction of hearing the true explanation!

FRED: Actually Buggs might have had a pretty good case if he had decided to challenge the assertion that he couldn't wear a wig when he was off duty. However, my guess would be that the rule was if you wanna wear a wig, ya gotta be in civilian clothes. Otherwise you'd be out of uniform if you were wearing fatigues— just like you'd be if you were wearing a Packers hat with your olive drabs.

STEVE: Sounds reasonable. Meanwhile, Maxwell was scheduled to DEROS (return home) soon, since he only had about seven months left in the service when we arrived in Nam. He was determined to take his little dog with him, despite all the required red tape... the observation periods and vaccinations needed for the animal... and the attempts by the Army to discourage or prevent him from succeeding. Most guys would have said "Hey, I can always get another dog," but Max wouldn't hear of it. He was truly obsessed.

FRED: After being repeatedly told he could not or should not take the dog home with him, Max persevered and at one point was told to fill out the paperwork, surrender the dog, pay for the dog's transportation and go home, whereupon Pie would be shipped to him after he arrived. But Max knew there'd be a good chance he would never see his dog again if he followed that procedure, and in fact for some Vietnam veterans that's exactly what happened.

STEVE: When it came time for Max to depart, he was still battling the powers that be over the fate of Pie. We think he did manage to get the dog back to the states, but we had no way of confirming it. Such is the nature of war!

FRED: Besides, even if he should manage to get the dog home, how was he going to explain its name to his family and friends?

STEVE: I dunno, but you can bet he didn't tell them he chose that name because he would get a charge out of hearing people say "Here, Pie! Here, Pie!"

FRED: If it had been me, I think I probably would have stuck with the Jimmy Stewart horse story. And I also might have fed that dog a handful of breath mints just in case they gave him a breathalyzer test when he went through customs.

&&&&&&&&&&&&&&&&&&&&

FACT OR FICTION? *The story goes that the Commander of the 44th Medical Brigade was conducting an inspection at the 24th Evac. With all personnel standing in formation, he approaches a young officer and asks "What's your job here at the 24th, Lieutenant?" "Sir, I am the Supply Officer and the Advisor to the Commanding Officer on Sexual Relations." Puzzled, the General says "Advisor on Sexual Relations? How in the hell did you ever get a job like that?" "Well sir, shortly after I joined the 24th I offered a suggestion in a staff meeting, whereupon the CO turned to me and said "When I need your fuggin' advice Penske, I'll ask for it!"*

CHAPTER 32

WE GET SHOT BY MIKE WALLACE AND LIVE TO TELL ABOUT IT
Sorry boys, the atmospheric conditions aren't
cooperating today... try again tomorrow

FRED: Among the media types that began showing up at the 24th Evac in early '67 were a number of TV correspondents who were covering the war. Most of 'em were unknown to me, but I knew Steve was an aspiring journalist as well as a news junkie— he always seemed to have his head buried in a Time magazine or some such publication. Thus when Mike Wallace of CBS News suddenly appeared one day, I knew I had to find Steve and let him know.

STEVE: It's true, I got more excited by the arrival of a Garrick Utley or a Mike Wallace than by someone like Henry Fonda or Martha Raye. Early in the war, most of the mainstream news media seemed to be solidly behind the war effort. The one exception might have been CBS News, which was already beginning to draw the ire of the US military— as well as the Johnson Administration— for what they considered "biased reporting."

FRED: A month or so prior to our induction in Milwaukee, CBS correspondent Morley Safer (who would later replace Harry Reasoner as co-host of 60 Minutes with Mike Wallace) broadcast a report titled "The Burning of Cam Ne" which immediately produced a storm of controversy. The footage purportedly showed a Vietnamese village being burned to the ground by US Marines while a woman pleaded for mercy. Apparently the village had been labeled a VC hideout with an elaborate tunnel system and was thus marked for destruction.

STEVE: This was considered one of the first TV news reports from Vietnam that cast the American military in a negative light. (It may have marked the beginning of the era of alleged "media bias"— an accusation which still flourishes to this day.)

FRED: As a result, the Marine Corps brass got hopping mad, and so did President Lyndon Johnson.

STEVE: The report also riled up TV viewers on both sides of the fence. For the anti-war types, it aroused increased anger against the war. For supporters of America's intervention in Vietnam, it aroused anger against the news media— and CBS in particular.

FRED: The Marines claimed the few huts that were burned were mostly the result of collateral damage from artillery strikes. Safer said that story was hogwash.

STEVE: As the network was being flooded with complaints from viewers, President Johnson called Frank Stanton, the president of CBS News, and said "Frank, how could your boys be so unpatriotic as this? They've just shat on the American flag!" LBJ also ordered an investigation of correspondent Safer on the grounds that he might be a communist sympathizer. After all, he wasn't an American citizen— he was just one of those shifty Canadians!

FRED: Well at least he was a "North" American. But in all honesty, I thought "shat" was just a made-up word, since the past tense of "shit" is normally "shit." But I looked it up and found that "Shat was originally a humorous and slightly sanitized version of the vulgar word shit, but it has gradually become a standardized form." So maybe Lyndon was just a few years ahead of his time.

STEVE: Meanwhile, the Marines were on the warpath against Safer. Morley claimed that a drunken Marine officer stood outside his room firing a pistol in the air and yelling "CBS— the Communist Broadcasting System!" If there hadn't been other newsmen there, Safer said, he thought he might have been killed that night.

FRED: That seems highly unlikely— after all, if you're gonna waste somebody, ya don't fire off a bunch of rounds in the air first! You approach real quiet-like. Didn't they teach us that in Basic?

STEVE: I think I might have been on KP that day. But there were also accusations that Safer had provoked the situation by handing a Zippo lighter to the marine who started the fire shown in the video clip. Safer vigorously denied it. Having heard about possible death threats against him, he started carrying a pistol for a time— not for fear of the VC, but fear of the US Marines!

FRED: Well then, he should have gotten his tail down to Long Binh where it was just us civilized Army types. His only danger from us would have been that we might have encouraged him to drink himself to death! On second thought... we hadn't arrived there yet.

STEVE: I think the first TV newsman to visit us at the 24th Evac was David Snell of ABC News in mid-April. What made his story unusual was the fact that he came to us on a litter and was offloaded from a Huey helicopter near the Emergency Room entrance. He'd been wounded while covering the 9th Infantry in the Mekong Delta, some 30 or 40 miles south of Long Binh.

FRED: Following a battle, Snell was walking across a field with two other newsmen when the soldier in front of him stepped on a mine. The explosion injured several people and seriously wounded Snell in the hand and leg. He would later describe it as a "million dollar wound"— the kind that gets one sent all the way back to the states for treatment and recovery.

STEVE: I saw him being carried on a stretcher with a cameraman filming the scene. Someone said the wounded man was David Snell of ABC News. I tried to commit the name to memory, since it was an event that would probably be shown on TV back home. As he went past me, he appeared to be speaking into a mike but I wasn't close enough to hear what he said.

FRED: And since there was no way we'd be able to see whatever was broadcast in the states on ABC News, you thought that was probably the end of the story as far as you were concerned?

STEVE: Yes, but some years later— maybe 10 or so— the network broadcast a retrospective about the Vietnam War and as I watched, there was David Snell being carried on a stretcher and talking into his mike. He said a few sentences and then closed with "This is David Snell, ABC News, flat on my back in Vietnam."

FRED: So after 10 years you finally found out what he had said?

STEVE: Well at least I thought I did. It appeared to me that he was at the 24th Evac, like I said. But I contacted him a few years ago and he said that he made the "flat on my back" statement while he was still laying in the field in the Delta. However, he also said he remembered nothing about the helicopter flight from there to the 24th Evac. My guess is the medic immediately gave him a good dose of morphine so he was "feeling no pain," as they say.

FRED: If he was full of morphine and he didn't remember the chopper flight at all, maybe he made the "flat on my back" remark twice— once in the field and once upon arriving at the hospital— but had no memory of doing it the second time.

STEVE: That would explain how we both could have been right. Either that or one of us was mistaken. He also said he had carried two canteens of water that day but drank it all by 9 am, so after that he had to drink water that "undoubtedly did not pass the rules of normal drinkability." I asked him if he had been aware of the existence of water purification tablets but he said he had not.

FRED: Some GI's in the boonies carried as many as four to six canteens, plus the purification tablets in case they ran out of potable water. If Snell had only two canteens and no awareness of the tablets, it sounds like he hadn't been given a very thorough indoctrination before heading into the swamps of the Delta.

STEVE: No, and he's lucky he didn't suffer any apparent repercussions from drinking swamp water all day. He said it had been 120 degrees in the Delta. When he went into the OR at the 24th Evac, they asked how much water he had drunk that day and he replied "gallons!" He said they gave him anesthesia to put him under and after 20 minutes he thought "I'm still wide awake, I'd better ask for some more of that stuff." He opened his eyes and discovered he was all bandaged up and had been on the operating table for five hours.

FRED: After multiple surgeries back in the states, he eventually made a full recovery except for the loss of part of a finger and the fact that he can only type with six fingers now.

STEVE: He also said that when he first went to Vietnam in '66, he believed we were winning the war. But by the time he came home he was pretty sure that was not the case. He then returned to Nam for ABC in '67 and that's when he was wounded.

FRED: Now Mike Wallace, unlike some other CBS newsmen, was considered a conservative and a "hawk" regarding Vietnam. (He had once been a game show host, among other things, before joining CBS News.) So in April of '67, when he was assigned to a two-month stint in Nam, he was greeted warmly at the airport in Saigon by none other than Commanding General Westmoreland himself.

STEVE: "Westy" personally escorted Wallace on a day-long tour of American bases and installations in the Saigon area. Ironically, some 15 years later the General would file a $120 million libel suit against Wallace (as well as CBS) on the grounds that they had falsely accused him of altering intelligence documents to make the progress of the war sound better than it really was.

FRED: The suit was dropped two years later after Westy's team of lawyers determined they'd be unable to prove their case. And as it turned out, Wallace hadn't even produced the broadcast segment in question— he was merely asked to narrate it, which he did.

STEVE: But going back to April 23rd, 1967— just nine days after Snell arrived at the 24th Evac— Mike Wallace of CBS showed up to interview one of our patients, LTC Robert Schweitzer of the First Infantry. Five days earlier, he'd been awarded eleven medals, including the prestigious Distinguished Service Cross and Legion of Merit, while lying in his hospital bed. When Fred came to tell me Wallace had just arrived, naturally I had to get over there and see right quick!

FRED: Now on that particular day, there were a couple of important details about this interview that we were not privy to. The first was that around the time Wallace arrived in Nam, the American Federation of TV & Radio Artists (AFTRA) had just gone on strike back in the states. This meant that CBS had no newswriters and no on-air talent for their evening broadcasts. The CBS Evening News with Walter Cronkite had suddenly become The CBS Evening News with Arnold Zenker, a management employee.

STEVE: But since AFTRA had no jurisdiction over foreign correspondents, Mike was free to "take over" the broadcasts with his filmed reports from the war zone. During this period he led the evening news no fewer than 31 times, with his reports sometimes consuming half the entire program. The AFTRA strike helped to make "Mike Wallace" a household name that just about everyone knows to this day.

FRED: Because of this unique situation, and because the American public had a big thirst for war news, Wallace was constantly being pushed by CBS to come up with more footage, such as the Schweitzer interview, that could be used to fill the evening broadcasts.

STEVE: The other major detail about the event was that we knew nothing about Colonel Schweitzer except that he must have said or done something weighty enough to cause Wallace to want to interview him. What we didn't realize was that he was actually a very colorful character who was already becoming famous. He would eventually achieve the rank of three-star general and serve as a member of President Reagan's National Security Council. When he died of cancer at 72 he was buried in Arlington National Cemetery.

FRED: But as we stood watching Wallace interviewing Schweitzer, we were totally unaware that we were witnessing two future American superstars in the making! Schweitzer had been wounded eight times in two different encounters with the enemy and was presently recovering from extensive shrapnel wounds incurred when VC guerrillas threw two grenades into his bunker. He hurled the first one back and was trying to find the second one when it went off.

STEVE: For the interview, Schweitzer was in a wheelchair and Wallace had selected a location outdoors between two quonset huts. The grassy area between the two wards served as a backdrop, and beyond that was open space. Since this was before the era of videotape, the CBS crew was filming with a cameraman and a sound man. A crowd of gawkers had gathered behind Mike and his film crew so that no one but Wallace and Schweitzer were visible in the shot.

FRED: After five or ten minutes it was obvious that we weren't going to be able to get close enough to hear what they were saying. So we started looking for any other opportunities to take advantage of the situation, short of "news junkie Steve" asking Wallace for an autograph. The thing that came to mind was to try to get ourselves on national TV somehow. I leaned over to Steve and said "If we circle around the two wards in opposite directions, we can walk back and forth between them and be in the background of the camera shot. Then we'll be on the CBS Evening News back in good old CONUS!"

STEVE: A brilliant idea! We took off in opposite directions and positioned ourselves out of sight at the far ends of the two buildings, roughly 20-30 yards away from the film crew. Far enough away so as not to interfere, but close enough to perhaps be recognizable on TV. I began by strolling across the open patch of ground from left to right. When I got about halfway, I suddenly turned my head to the right as if I had just noticed something going on. I kept on walking but continued to stare at the film crew as I disappeared out of sight.

FRED: Then I did likewise, crossing from right to left and turning my head in the middle. We were trying to modify our appearance each time, so on the next trip we removed our hats (which meant we were technically out of uniform. But hey, it was a combat zone, so everybody bent the rules— no big deal!)

STEVE: For the next trip we removed our shirts and took turns walking across in just T-shirts. After several passes through the background of Mike Wallace's "shot," we put everything back on and the two of us walked together for one last pass. When we got to the middle we stopped, turned toward the camera and just stared.

FRED: Either the cameraman or sound man must have noticed us by that point, because one of 'em yells "Hey, what are you guys doin'?" We point at ourselves as if to say "Who... us?" and he says "You're in the camera shot!" So we made an apologetic gesture and strolled out of the frame. As we did so, I said in a hushed voice "Hey man, we just got shot by Mike Wallace. We'll be able to tell our grandchildren!"

STEVE: I was pretty sure at least one of us was going to be on the CBS Evening News with Arnold whats-his-name. (And we didn't even know Wallace was getting 50 or 60 minutes— no pun intended— of airtime per week!) But how would we alert the folks back home to watch for us? We figured Wallace's film had to be flown to Tokyo for developing, then on to New York for airing. So we probably had at least 24-48 hours to get the word out before it would be broadcast.

FRED: Zenker! It was Arnold Zenker. (Incidentally, when Cronkite came back on the air after marching on the picket line for a while, he opened the broadcast with "Good evening, this is Walter Cronkite sitting in for Arnold Zenker.") So, how to alert the folks at home? Well, with today's satellite technology plus cell and internet service, getting a message to the homefront would be no problem. But in 1967 there were no cellphones, no satellite communications, no internet.

STEVE: A telegram might have worked, but we knew of no way to send one from a combat zone in a third-world country unless we drove all the way to Saigon, a 28-mile round trip. An airmail letter usually took a minimum of three to five days to be delivered in the states, so that left just one option— a MARS call!

FRED: You mean bounce a signal off Mars? That would sound preposterous, even if we'd had all of today's technological advances.

STEVE: Not Mars the planet! MARS stood for the Military Affiliated Radio System. It was originally formed as the Army Amateur Radio System, organized by the U.S. Army Signal Corps in 1925 to provide an alternate means of communication in the event of an emergency such as a hurricane or earthquake.

FRED: MARS allowed a soldier to call home for free by going to a MARS station operated by the nearest Army Signal Battalion. He'd have to stand in line for a couple hours to place a 5-minute call that went across the Pacific by shortwave radio to a MARS station near his home. These were manned by volunteer ham radio operators or military personnel, depending on their location. The MARS station would connect the caller to a standard telephone so the call could be completed. During the call, both parties would have to remember to say "over" each time they were done speaking so the shortwave operator would know to flip the switch allowing the other party to talk.

STEVE: So you took up the challenge and volunteered to make a MARS call all the way back to Oshkosh, Wisconsin so you could beat Mike Wallace to the punch!

FRED: I had been meaning to try it for awhile and now I had an excuse— I had to deliver our message in less than 48 hours! I got a ride over to the MARS station at Long Binh and got in line. I would tell the folks to watch the CBS Evening News each night and look for me in the background when Mike Wallace was on camera. Then I'd give them your family's phone number and ask 'em to pass the word.

STEVE: But you never got to deliver your message.

FRED: Unfortunately, no. The line was moving very, very slowly— either each guy was yakking for a good deal more than 5 minutes, or else there must have been a glitch somewhere in the system. Finally this sergeant comes out and says "Sorry boys, the atmospheric conditions aren't cooperating today. You'll have to try again tomorrow."

STEVE: And once you told me that, I began to wonder just whose fault it was that we never got to tell our friends and families to watch for us on national TV.

FRED: Let me guess... Mike Wallace? No.... the sound man who yelled at us? No.... the sergeant at the MARS station? No.... Certainly it couldn't have been me? No.... I'm drawing a blank here.

STEVE: Sunspots! As it turns out, the shortwave signals are greatly affected by a lack of sunspots on the surface of the sun— the more sunspots, the better the transmission. And on that particular day, a lack of sunspots would prevent our folks from being alerted to watch for us on TV! Then again, we had no way of knowing whether we ever made it on the air or not.

FRED: Maybe, maybe not. A year or so later I was a civilian at a party back home when one of my old classmates comes up to me and says "Hey Fred, I think I might have seen you on TV last year from Vietnam." I asked if Mike Wallace was in the foreground and the guy who looked like me was in the background. He said "I dunno, that coulda been it. I just remember seeing a guy that looked like you."

STEVE: And so ends another brief brush with greatness! Well, at least no one can ever say we didn't get shot by Mike Wallace and his CBS crew... and live to tell about it.

FRED: Damned sunspots!

&&&&&&&&&&&&&&&&&&&&

FACT OR FICTION? The story goes that as they were leaving a party and climbing atop a horse-drawn wagon, Lieutenant Danforth picked up one of the reins, turned to her husband and asked "Why on earth has Captain Bernard held such a grudge against his sister Olive for all these years?" The answer: "Because Olive— the other rein, dear— used to laugh and call him names."

CHAPTER 33

STUMPY'S LAST HURRAH

What, you say we're out of ammo? Okay then, gimme some of those grenades

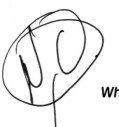

FRED: Kenny Stumpf, a fellow draftee who was inducted with us in Milwaukee back in '65, ultimately wound up in the Infantry while we wound up in the Medics. It could just as easily have been the other way around, with us being the "ground pounders" and Kenny being the "pecker checker." Such was the luck of the draw, as they say.

STEVE: We don't know how "Stumpy" would have fared as a medic, but it's highly unlikely we could ever have matched his accomplishments as an infantry grunt. Primarily because on April 25, 1967— just two days after we got shot by Mike Wallace at the 24th Evac— SP4 Stumpf did some extraordinary things that would earn him a Congressional Medal of Honor (CMH) for extreme bravery in the face of hostile enemy fire.

FRED: Most infantrymen sent to Nam were issued M-16 rifles capable of automatic or semi-automatic fire. When it came to a choice of weapons, however, some were more partial to the M-60 light machine gun... some to the M-79 grenade launcher... and some to less conventional instruments of death like the tommy gun or even the flaming arrow (used on some river patrol boats.) In Kenny's case, he had a preference for the standard M-26 fragmentation grenade.

STEVE: Like many other grunts during the first several years of the war, he found his standard M-16 rifle would often jam on him, making it somewhat unreliable (and dangerous) in combat. Thus when he went out on patrols or scouting missions he'd often have an empty sandbag slung over his shoulder— into which he had stuffed about two dozen grenades so as to make sure he had some way to defend himself and his comrades if his weapon crapped out on him.

FRED: Most GI's carried two or three grenades out in the bush, but Stumpy probably would have carried even more than 24 if they weren't so damned heavy— about a pound apiece. He was willing to lug around that extra 24 pounds, day in and day out, because he felt it gave him an edge over the average rifleman— especially one who was carrying a somewhat unreliable weapon to begin with.

STEVE: It was Kenny Stumpf's ability and willingness to drag or carry his wounded comrades out of harm's way— as well as the presence of that somewhat unorthodox bag of grenades he liked to carry— that played major roles in his earning himself a CMH.

FRED: Also we should mention before we go any further that despite the title of this chapter, Stumpy was still very much alive at the time of this writing in 2016.

STEVE: Indeed he was. As for the jamming M-16's, the problem was apparently a design flaw that allowed the weapon to start inserting the next round into the chamber before the previous cartridge had been fully ejected. Wouldn't ya know, the contract for producing those rifles had been awarded to the lowest bidder!

FRED: Yup, a classic case of the right way, the wrong way and the Army way— typical! Like a lot of other soldiers, Kenny's makeshift solution was to load only 18 rounds into each 20-round magazine. This decreased the pressure on the spring and seemed to reduce the frequency of the jamming. Later models of the M-16 were improved to the point that they performed much more reliably.

STEVE: Kenny arrived in Nam in September of 1966, just a few months after we did. Assigned to the 25th Infantry Division in the Central Highlands, he'd only been in country for a few weeks when he contracted malaria from a mosquito bite. He insists that he was taking his malaria pills just like he was supposed to, but it took a certain amount of time before they began to take effect— and he probably had not reached that point yet. That would explain why they had us start taking those pills as soon as we boarded the General William Weigel. By the time we arrived in Nam, we'd already been on the stuff for three weeks.

FRED: Ken described malaria as an unbelievable experience and said he'd never been so sick in all his life. His body temperature had climbed so high that the medics had to pack him in ice with a rubber sheet around his body. For about 10 days he says he was so sick he felt like he just wanted to die. He was also delirious for much of the time. At one point, cowboy movie legends Roy Rogers and Dale Evans came onto his hospital ward to visit the patients. There they were in their full western costumes— complete with six-guns— when the "Singing Cowboy" started to approach Stumpy's bed.

STEVE: Stumpy said he was asleep when he felt a tap on his shoulder and looked up to see this fellow in a cowboy outfit saying "Oh hello there, I'm Roy Rogers!" followed by a woman saying "And I'm Dale!" They were true icons to him, since he'd grown up worshipping heroes like Roy, Dale and Gene Autry. But the combination of his serious lack of sleep plus his delirious frame of mind caused him to react in a most uncharacteristic way.

FRED: Kenny says he was told later that he looked at Roy and Dale and said "I don't give a (blank) if you're the President of the United States, get the (blank) out of here! I want to go to sleep!" Then he rolled over and went back to sleep. He said that for a time he couldn't even identify people he knew, let alone movie stars whom he had idolized as a youth.

STEVE: That disease was definitely messing with his head! Afterward, once he had regained his faculties, he felt quite embarrassed about the whole episode— but by then it was too late for him to offer any apologies to Roy Rogers or his wife. He says once he started receiving daily doses of quinine, he began to feel better and was finally able to eat and to think coherently.

FRED: The malaria kept him out of action for a month or more, which explains why some GI's deliberately skipped taking the pills in an attempt to get about six weeks of convalescent time deducted from their 12-month tours. But Ken would be the first to tell you that having malaria was no picnic— not to mention the fact that it could be fatal if not swiftly and properly treated.

STEVE: When he finally saw his first combat action in November, his weapon jammed and he was so scared he wanted to turn around and run like hell. But after several weeks he got used to the fear, eventually reaching a point where he felt none at all. That might explain why so many GI's were able to function admirably even while being subjected to the most harsh and dangerous conditions.

FRED: In the Central Highlands he experienced the feeling of hiking through triple canopy jungle. It would be pitch dark at 9 o'clock in the morning due to the three layers of vegetation overhead that blocked virtually all sunlight. Often the undergrowth was so thick that when they made contact with the enemy, they couldn't see who they were shooting at— they'd have to just fire short bursts in the general direction of where the hostile fire was coming from. In fact at the end of their one-year tours, some infantrymen would say they never saw any live enemy soldiers for an entire year— only dead ones, along with blood trails indicating where the wounded had fled or had been dragged away by their comrades.

STEVE: To avoid booby traps and ambushes they stayed off the trails, choosing instead to hack their way through the thick vines and branches with machetes. This was generally the responsibility of the point man— a dangerous job which Stumpy often chose to take upon himself, even though he was Squad Leader and not required to do so.

FRED: Sometimes they'd get orders sent down "from above" that seemed strange, if not downright foolish. Kenny said they received one directive stating that when a man was walking point, he should not shoot at anyone until the enemy fired first. (Sort of like the old Hopalong Cassidy rule.) Kenny said his attitude toward that was "Screw you, Colonel! You come out here and walk point for awhile! Then see what you think!"

STEVE: Anyway, while Ken was hacking away at the vegetation— or watching for mines, trip wires, booby traps and enemy tracks when they were walking on a trail— the second man following some 20 meters behind (known as the "slack man") was responsible for protecting him by keeping an eye out for Charlie. If the point man should suddenly draw fire or begin shooting, the slack man had to be ready to charge forward and provide covering fire to keep the enemy's heads down so the point man could make it back to his squad. The slack position was important enough that one combat veteran was prompted to say "a point man is only as good as his slack man."

FRED: In dense jungle where there were no trails, the point and slack men were sometimes known as "the machete man and the compass man," due to the second man being responsible for watching his compass to make sure the squad continued heading in the right direction. Since wielding the machete was a very arduous task, other men in the squad would often take turns at it.

STEVE: When an infantry platoon would stop every hour or so for a water break, or to set up a Night Defensive Position (NDP), they'd often do a "Cloverleaf Recon" to scout the immediate area and see if there were any enemy troops following them— or located nearby. Four groups of two or three men would head out, one each to the north, east, south and west, for maybe 100 meters or more (depending on the terrain) and then circle clockwise until they came back on roughly the same path that the adjacent group had taken when they left. The circles made by the four teams would resemble the pattern of a four-leaf clover, resulting in the entire area being scouted around the platoon's location.

FRED: Which brings up the question— how in the hell did they navigate in dense jungle when they couldn't see where they were going? Since we never had any Advanced Infantry Training, we were never taught that stuff. But the answer turns out to be fairly simple in concept. Once they'd reviewed the maps and knew what compass bearing they were supposed to follow, all they had to do was count their paces to figure out how far they had gone. This would give 'em enough information to be able to plot their position. It wasn't very glamorous, but it usually worked.

STEVE: Normally one guy would be designated as the official pace counter, with a second man also counting to serve as a backup and to verify the official count. Of course accurate navigation also required someone who was good with a compass as well as being skilled at plotting positions and courses. (That's what lieutenants were for!) But the ones who weren't so hot at it would periodically get lost, whereupon the platoon might have to be rescued. Ditto for those who suddenly found themselves in a firefight where chaos ensued for some period of time— under such conditions, it wasn't too difficult to lose track of your pace count.

FRED: In Kenny's case, his company commander came to him and said "Stumpy, Second Platoon is lost out there somewhere and it'll be dark soon. Can you find 'em?" He thought he knew roughly where they were, so he went out searching as twilight approached. After a little while he heard movement in the dense jungle and froze in place, fearing that they might be an NVA patrol. As he fervently watched, he thought he spotted the reflections off a couple of Army steel pots.

STEVE: From watching old war movies, we all knew the thing to do then was ask for a password— or ask a question like "Who won the '64 World Series?" If you didn't get the right answer, you'd start blasting away! But Stumpy wasn't aware of any password, and in the tension of the moment he couldn't think of anything else to ask. So he said "Are you American?" Fortunately they were, and Stumpy got credit for finding the lost platoon.

FRED: Speaking of getting lost, it was fairly common knowledge that many troops had little or no desire to make contact with the enemy— especially if their tours in Nam were nearly finished, and especially toward the end of the war when everyone figured they'd soon be going home. Some soldiers did admit (after the war) that they'd sometimes get sent out with a scout team to recon an area and after they went a short distance, the group would just sit down and cool their heels for awhile. Then they'd head back to their command post and report no enemy activity seen.

STEVE: That also explains why some GI's said they would turn a "search and destroy" mission into a "search and avoid" mission by deliberately heading in the wrong direction when they were sent out to scout an area where enemy troops had been seen.

FRED: Of course if they happened to be in the wrong area when somebody called for an airstrike or an artillery barrage, they could wind up getting bombed or shelled by their own forces.

STEVE: That instinct for self-preservation also led to scenarios like this one: A couple GI's are hunkered down in a night ambush position when one spots several enemy soldiers walking past. He whispers "There's a couple VC, should we open up on 'em?" His partner thinks for a few seconds and then says "Nah, let 'em go— we'll get the next batch!" Whereupon both soldiers would promptly feel a pronounced sense of relief.

FRED: Gee, I wonder how often that happened? Now with regard to keeping themselves supplied with the essentials, each soldier had to carry enough water to last a few days. If they ran out they'd have to find more in a stream, riverbed or bomb crater and then purify it by dropping a couple halazone tablets into each canteen of water. It certainly didn't help the taste any, but at least those pills made the liquid safe to drink.

STEVE: One night Stumpy had done just that after filling his canteen with river water. He was out in a Listening Post (LP) maybe 100 or 200 meters from the NDP when he suddenly started vomiting for no apparent reason. The resulting disturbance was making it highly likely that their position would be compromised, so he called in on the radio for someone to relieve him until they could figure out what was wrong with him. He went back to camp and the next day they happened to discover two VC corpses floating in the river, just upstream from where he had filled his canteen the day before!

FRED: The moral being... maybe what you didn't know could indeed hurt you after all! About every third or fourth day, a resupply helicopter would bring out more water, ammo and C-rations. The troops always hoped it would arrive late in the day, otherwise they'd have to lug all that food and water around all day long before getting a chance to consume any of it. If it arrived toward evening, they'd get to eat one dinner and one breakfast before they'd have to pack up all the remaining rations and move out in the morning.

STEVE: Stumpy said one day a helicopter came in to pick up a wounded soldier and the door gunner jumped out to help load the casualty. The bird started taking heavy fire and its windshield got blown out, whereupon the pilot decided to take off immediately without waiting for the patient. The evacuation had to be aborted—but the gunner got left behind in the process. As he sat down on the ground feeling somewhat lost and alone, Stumpy looked at him and said "You're in the infantry now, fella."

FRED: Great. Just about the last thing a helicopter crewman ever wanted to hear! But the chopper crews were very committed to not leaving any of their own behind, so you can bet they got their gunner out of there as quickly as possible.

STEVE: Besides having to deal with Charlie and elements like rain, extreme heat and stifling humidity, infantry grunts were constantly at risk of being assaulted by various types of wild critters like snakes, leeches, scorpions, fire ants, rats and even an occasional tiger, elephant or wild boar. Some claimed most of the snakes were poisonous— and the few that weren't could crush you to death!

FRED: While that was no doubt an exaggeration, snakes would often be encountered in the morning when a GI woke up and discovered he'd acquired a silent visitor during the night. They might be found curled up inside his helmet or laying right next to him under his poncho liner, enjoying the warmth of his body heat. One soldier found one curled up inside his empty boot. From then on, he said he always slept with his boots on.

STEVE: Seems like he could have just stuck something inside the boots to prevent anything from crawling or slithering in there during the night. But anyway… Stumpy said when he woke up one morning, he started putting on his gear and couldn't figure out why his canteen wouldn't slide into its case. After several attempts he stuck his mitt in there, only to discover a hairy tarantula bigger than the palm of his hand! GI's in the field quickly learned to check all of the likely hiding places in their gear before they packed up and moved out.

FRED: He probably should have hung on to it anyway… after all, deep fried tarantulas were reputed to be very tasty!

STEVE: Too creepy for most folks, I'm thinkin'. Some of the creatures encountered in the boonies were truly exotic, too. One GI said he was out on an ambush mission one night where they had set up Claymore mines around their perimeter. (These were anti-personnel devices that were stuck into the ground with two spikes and could be aimed in a specific direction.) They also put out three concentric rings of trip wires to prevent any VC from walking or stumbling into their position by surprise. Then in the wee hours, he saw several figures moving silently toward him in the darkness. They had to be enemy, but how in the hell had they avoided all of those Claymores and trip wires that were virtually invisible at night?

FRED: At that point someone triggered an illumination flare. It shot up in the air, revealing the intruders to be a family of giant orangutans who'd been up above, in the trees, prior to nightfall. They had decided to come down to forage for food— and when the flare went off, they went berserk! It seems they were throwing rocks at the Americans to indicate their displeasure with the situation.

STEVE: Regarding the Claymore mines, Charlie had a nasty habit of sneaking up on them in the dark, pulling them out of the ground and turning them around so they faced the American troops. The GI's had three possible ways to thwart this maneuver. The first was to have someone periodically "low crawl" out to each one of the Claymores and check to make sure it was facing in the right direction.

FRED: The second, though rather ingenious, was effective only if Charlie wasn't expecting it. The strategy involved pulling the pin on a live grenade and setting it directly under the mine so that if a VC pulled the Claymore out of the ground, the grenade would go off and possibly detonate the mine as well. Good-bye Charlie, as they say.

STEVE: The third tactic— considered truly bizarre— involved deliberately placing the mines so they were facing in the wrong direction, then letting the enemy sneak up and turn them around.

FRED: Of course if Mister Charlie had been taught to feel the two sides and find the one with the raised lettering that said THIS SIDE TOWARD ENEMY, even in the pitch dark he'd be able to tell which side was the lethal one and position the mine accordingly. Any way you look at it, it could be a crapshoot for the American grunts.

STEVE: Yeah, what they really could have used was a scout dog to patrol their perimeter and tip them off when the enemy was within sniffing distance. I'm a dog lover who's been known to get overly emotional when hearing stories about a dog's unwavering loyalty to its master (or handler, in this case.)

FRED: When the infantry was in hot pursuit of some VC, they'd call on the radio to see if a tracker dog was available. In less than 30 minutes, a chopper could arrive and drop off a dog and handler.

STEVE: Ken Stumpf said his platoon was out in the field working with a tracker dog when they got in a firefight and the dog handler was badly wounded. The handler was evacuated by helicopter but the German Shepherd stayed behind.

FRED: Some time after 2 am that night, the dog suddenly began howling in the pitch dark. (The dogs were trained to never do this, since it could give away the platoon's position to the enemy.) One of the troopers wanted to immediately shoot the dog to silence him, but Stumpy said "Nooo! You can't shoot that dog! You can't shoot the dog! For one thing, if you do— Charlie will know we're right here!"

STEVE: One guy was a soft-spoken Native American who calmly said "The dog handler died." Stumpy said "What? The handler died? How would you know that?" His friend replied "It's well known in Indian lore that when the master dies, the dog knows it." When the sun came up the next morning, they received word that the dog handler had indeed died in the middle of the night.

FRED: Coincidence, perhaps? It's more likely that the dog may have been in mourning simply because he missed his master. You'd have to count me as one of those who'd be highly skeptical that the Shepherd actually knew his handler had died.

STEVE: I'd probably have to agree... good story, though! Ken's tale jibes with what an ex-dog handler once told me: When a handler died out in the field, the survivors might have to shoot the dog if no one else was able to control him. If they were able to get control and bring the dog back, he'd be sent to the Dog Training School in Nam to get retrained with a new handler. No DEROS for Rover!

FRED: Also it seems that if the Viet Cong knew the Americans were tracking them with a dog, they'd try to shoot the dog or handler at the first opportunity so they could escape. Over 3,000 "War Dogs" were used by the Army in Vietnam and were trained as Scout Dogs, Tracker Dogs, Sentry Dogs, Search Dogs or Water Patrol Dogs that could sniff out enemy swimmers.

STEVE: But GI's had to keep in mind that each type of dog had specialized skills. In one instance a tracker dog stepped on a land mine because he was trained to find the VC, not to detect booby traps or trip wires. About 300 were killed in action but others died of heatstroke, food contamination, disease, etc. The majority never made it back to CONUS, since most that survived were turned over to the South Vietnamese Army or euthanized when the Americans left.

FRED: Then on April 25th, Squad Leader Kenny Stumpf was involved in an operation near Duc Pho in the Central Highlands. His 10-man squad was down to only seven when they were ambushed by an NVA bunker complex that was well dug in and fortified.

STEVE: The enemy was pouring out machine gun fire and cutting down any Americans who tried to approach their kill zone. Three of his squad members lay wounded in an area that was in the line of fire, while Stumpy himself was pinned down in a trench.

FRED: Every time he tried to climb out, one bunker would open up on him and force him back down. He had started out with 42 magazines of ammo for his M-16 and about 25 grenades. After more than an hour, he was down to two magazines and just a few grenades left. At one point an enemy grenade landed right between Kenny's legs and another GI shouted a warning. He kicked it away and later said "I kicked that sucker as far as I could kick it— and it never went off!"

STEVE: He added that "I was unbelievably scared because I couldn't see where the enemy was. But I also knew I was the Squad Leader and it would be up to me to make some decisions. I was determined not to run from the fight. I heard the three wounded men yelling for help, so I decided I'd have to go after them, just as they would have done if it were me laying out there."

FRED: Finally Kenny got up and ran through a hail of gunfire to reach the wounded men. One by one, he dragged or carried them to safety as he continued to brave hostile fire. One of them had a broken back and Kenny had to crawl out of there on his stomach with the wounded man riding his back and clinging to his neck.

STEVE: Wow. In Basic I had enough trouble just attempting to do the low crawl on my own— it looked pretty easy but as it turned out, it involved using various muscles that the average out-of-shape weakling like me didn't normally use at all. I could not imagine trying to do it with a 180-pound soldier on top of me!

FRED: By that point, the members of Stumpy's squad had all been killed or wounded. Two of the enemy bunkers had been taken out by an air strike, but the third was proving to be impenetrable. He decided he'd have to charge the bunker before nightfall, otherwise the NVA could escape under cover of darkness. Since everyone was just about out of ammo, Ken ran out on the battlefield and policed up something like 8 or 10 weapons and ammunition from dead enemy soldiers— AK-47's, Uzi-type machine guns and so forth. He then got some of his platoon mates to give him a few more grenades and off he went to take out that remaining bunker.

STEVE: Kenny tossed the first grenade into the bunker and it was promptly thrown right back out. He had to curl up in a fetal position to avoid getting seriously injured by shrapnel from his own grenade. Then he took his two remaining grenades, pulled the pins, held them for a few seconds as a delay, and let 'em fly. Both were on the mark and the bunker was immediately silenced.

FRED: All in a day's work for one SP4 Ken Stumpf— a Wisconsin boy to boot! In the aftermath, he received a "battlefield promotion" to sergeant. Having arrived in Nam as a Private (E-3), he went home one year later as a Staff Sergeant (E-6)— a very rare occurrence indeed. He later insisted he wasn't a hero because "if the roles had been reversed, those guys would have done the same thing for me— and one of them would be getting the medal instead of me."

STEVE: Which serves to illustrate the principle that the main reason soldiers are willing to fight and take enormous risks in battle is to protect their buddies and not just themselves. Several weeks after the Duc Pho action, Stumpy was standing in the chow line back at base camp when he noticed others staring at him. He overheard someone say he was being recommended for a "CMH." At the time he was only familiar with the term in one particular context and, like many of us, was not aware that it stood for "Congressional Medal of Honor."

FRED: It seems that back in Advanced Infantry Training (AIT), one of his Drill Instructors had told a joke involving a CMH. (Just about every sergeant in a training unit had a repertoire of standard jokes he would tell over and over to each new class of recruits.)

STEVE: Yeah, I remember one we heard in Medic School when they were teaching us how to administer an enema. A young medic is told by the attending physician that a certain patient would require a hot chocolate enema to alleviate some sort of condition. The medic prepares the beverage, starts the procedure and immediately the patient begins yelling "Ooooh! Ooooh! Ooooh!" The medic says "What's the matter, too hot?" "No, too sweet!!!" I still repeat that punchline to my wife occasionally and she always chuckles! It wouldn't exactly qualify as a great joke— but then again, if we remembered it for 50 years then it must have been somewhat noteworthy, right?

FRED: One would think so. Anyway, the joke he heard in AIT went like this: While Stumpf was training on the grenade range, his sergeant said "If any one of you troops decides to fall on a live grenade to save your buddies, you will earn yourself a CMH... which stands for Casket with Metal Handle."

STEVE: Of course most new recruits wouldn't have any reason to know what the initials C-M-H stood for, so the joke would be completely lost on them. But most lifers would know what it meant— and thus appreciate the inherent humor in the alternate definition.

FRED: So as Ken continued moving through the chow line, he was baffled as to why anyone would recommend him for a casket with a metal handle. (Only later would he learn what CMH really meant.) Some four months after that, he was reassigned to base camp duty, presumably because the Army didn't want to risk having a living Medal of Honor candidate get killed before he could receive his award.

STEVE: But on September 12, 1967— just eleven days shy of two years after the three of us were inducted in Milwaukee, together with Woody Woodson— he received his honorable discharge and was sent home to Menasha, Wisconsin. Still no word about his CMH.

FRED: Then nearly a year later, he was working for a printing company in Menasha when he received an invitation to go to Washington DC to receive his CMH. Arriving at the White House, he and four other medal recipients— even those who, like Ken, were no longer in the service— were wearing their official dress uniforms. They were told that since the ceremony would be held indoors, they should not bring their military hats.

STEVE: Official protocol said that when in uniform, all military personnel had to wear their hats outdoors— but when they were indoors, they had to be "uncovered" unless they were under arms (i.e., armed with a firearm.) Any person not following this protocol would officially be "out of uniform."

FRED: When they entered the Oval Office, the group was told the ceremony would be held outdoors on the South Lawn of the White House. Stumpy said "Here was General Westmoreland, Chairman of the Joint Chiefs, plus all these other big hitters with multiple stars all over their shoulders. Someone asked if we had brought our hats and we said no, we were told not to."

STEVE: Stumpy added "Then I saw the funniest thing in the world.

Westmoreland tells all these two-star and three-star generals to go out there in the crowd and bring back a bunch of hats for these men! (Go get 'em, Bubba!) We were all enlisted, so the generals were out there telling other EM's to 'Give me your hat! Give me your hat!' They come back in and each general has brought four, five hats for us to try on so we can find the right size hat for each man."

FRED: In a scene reminiscent of the one in "Forrest Gump," during the presentation ceremony President Johnson asked Stumpy "Where are you from, son?" Ken said he was so stunned at that point that he didn't have a clue. He finally answered "Menasha, Wisconsin." Then LBJ said something like "Well, you did a fine job" and Stumpy replied "I'm more scared standing here right now than I was that day back in Vietnam, sir!"

STEVE: Stumpy was presented with the Medal of Honor by President Lyndon Johnson at the White House on Sept. 19, 1968— almost three years to the day after our induction.

FRED: This very special form of recognition qualified as being the grand finale for his tour in Vietnam— or "Stumpy's Last Hurrah," as we've chosen to call it. Except that it turned out not to be the end of the story, because he'd gotten so much attention from his CMH that soon he felt the urge to go back to Nam.

STEVE: Before long he had reenlisted and volunteered to return to the war zone. He wound up doing three tours in Vietnam and remaining in the Army for a total of 29 years.

FRED: When he went back to Vietnam, Kenny found things to be quite different in '69-71 as compared to '66-67. For one thing, that was the first time he'd seen marijuana or other drugs being used by soldiers. Not out in the field, but back at the base camps. "I never smoked marijuana before, during or after Vietnam," he said.

STEVE: Kenny explained that "When I came home after my first tour, I ran into one of my high school teachers who asked me about drug use in Nam. I honestly had no idea what he was talking about and told him I had never seen any of it over there. My second tour was when I saw guys smoking that stuff and doing other drugs."

FRED: Stumpy said it appeared to him that the officers and the senior NCO's didn't want to hear about their own troops doing any drugs because if it was revealed that they knew about it and did nothing to stop it, it could reflect badly on them and possibly prevent them from getting a promotion.

STEVE: An interesting theory, although it could also have been the case that they knew the Army had tried everything it could think of to curtail the behavior. But since drugs were so cheap, plentiful and easily obtainable, it was basically a lost cause.

FRED: Kenneth E. Stumpf retired in 1996 as a Sergeant Major— the highest enlisted rank attainable in the US Army. But little did he know that the day he received his CMH was not the last time he would ever meet a President... or see the White House either!

&&&&&&&&&&&&&&&&&&&

FACT OR FICTION? *The story goes that late one night at the 24th, PFC Kleeman was checking out a heavily sedated patient for possible shrapnel wounds when he turned him over and noticed a cork sticking out of his butt. Fearing the worst, he decided to slowly and carefully remove it, not knowing what to expect. As soon as it came out, Kleeman began hearing a male baritone voice singing "Strangers in the ni-i-i-ight, exchanging glances..." He quickly stuck it back in, whereupon the singing stopped. He called the nurse over and said "You'd better see this, lieutenant!" She removed the cork and the same exact thing happened. Since she'd never seen anything this unusual before, she said "You'd better have the CQ Runner get over to Dr. Lenehan's hooch and tell him he needs to see this!" About 15 minutes later, the doc shows up and removes the cork, whereupon he hears "Strangers in the ni-i-i-ight, exchanging glances..." Captain Lenehan sticks the cork back in, turns to the nurse and says "Do you mean to tell me you woke me up in the middle of the night and made me get dressed and come over here just to listen to some asshole singing Strangers in the Night???"*

CHAPTER 34

SAY HELLO TO YOUR NEW INTERPRETER... "LOUIE"

What, this one actually speaks English? But what happened to the ankle strap high heels?

STEVE: After several weeks of flirting with Linh and having her translate my lousy French into Vietnamese and back again on a more or less daily basis, I was somewhat surprised to hear Captain Bloom announce that my new interpreter would be arriving shortly. I knew I was going to miss seeing Linh every day— she was the only attractive female around who didn't wear either jungle fatigues or peasant pajamas— plus she wore some great perfume— but I was fully aware that she'd been only a stop-gap measure.

FRED: What you really needed was someone fluent in Vietnamese and English, not Vietnamese and French. So then the next day your new translator shows up... and he's a high school kid?

STEVE: Yeah, he was around 17 and had two years of high school English. I'm not positive about this, but I think Vietnamese kids graduated from public school at 16 instead of 18.

FRED: Of course in Vietnam, everyone's birthday was on the same day— the holiday of Tet, which was like Christmas, New Year's and your birthday all rolled into one. A newborn infant turned one on the first morning of his first Tet holiday, no matter whether he or she was (in reality) eleven days old or eleven months old.

STEVE: So if you were born the day before the first day of Tet and I was born two days later on the day after the first day of Tet, then for the rest of our lives you'd always be a year older than me, despite your actually being only two days older.

FRED: Correct. Tet, the Vietnamese New Year, occurred according to the phases of the moon and could be anywhere from January 21st to February 19th. So was this 17-year-old kid a legitimate interpreter who spoke fluent English?

STEVE: Not quite. His English was good enough to get by, but his vocabulary was quite limited. Apparently the CO elected to "steal" this kid from the Mess Hall, where he'd been serving as a translator for the kitchen workers.

FRED: So the kid had been right there in the compound already. And he had a rather unusual name?

STEVE: His birth name was Pham Duc Thinh. But Gomez, the Mess Officer, had nicknamed him "Louie." That's what everybody in the Mess Hall called him, so I continued the practice when he started working for me. Soon everyone in the compound knew him as Louie. I think I was probably about the only one who knew his real name.

FRED: So if Louie had a very limited vocabulary, you promptly set about trying to improve it?

STEVE: I did, although he was extremely soft-spoken and I guess he had a bit of a speech impediment too. There were certain English words he simply could not pronounce, no matter how many times I would repeat them and drill him on them. It was as if his mouth could not be contorted in the proper way to form certain English words.

FRED: So apparently he thought he was saying it correctly, except that in reality he wasn't. Maybe he had a tin ear. How did he take to you trying to teach him new words?

STEVE: Rather well. We quickly developed a father-son type of relationship despite the fact that I was only about four years older. I sort of took him under my wing and said "Wherever I go, you go." So he followed me around all day, just as I had instructed him to do. The only exception was for lunch breaks and latrine breaks.

FRED: That explains why some guys would come up to you and say

LONG DAZE AT LONG BINH

"What's the deal, Donovan? That kid follows you around all day like a puppy dog!" So what else did Louie do besides translate?

STEVE: Actually I would have to keep telling him it was OK to walk beside me. For the Vietnamese, walking a few paces behind was supposed to be a sign of respect or deference. When there was no translating to be done, he would help out in HQ with the civilian personnel records (which were all in Vietnamese, so they were useless to me) or perform other simple tasks. He was the official "gofer" for Headquarters, always being sent to get sodas from the vending machine or retrieve someone who was needed in the Orderly Room. I seem to recall him doing some very rudimentary typing too— while I was a two-fingered typist, he was strictly a one-finger man.

FRED: That might have been fun to watch. If you called him Louie, what did he call you?

STEVE: I suggested that he call me Steve but he expressed a preference for "Boss," so that's what he always called me. Frequently someone from the Mess Hall or Emergency Room would pop into HQ and say "We need to borrow Louie!" I'd say "Louie, they need you in the ER" and he'd say "Okay Boss!" and off he would go.

FRED: And every day he wore a long-sleeved white shirt?

STEVE: And grey or black trousers. I never saw him wear a short-sleeved shirt, even when it was 110 degrees outside. But every day he wore the traditional rubber "flip-flops" (shower shoes) with no socks, just like every other Vietnamese person who worked on post.

FRED: So it was like you half expected to see him put on a coat and tie and walk outside still wearing flip-flops on his bare feet.

STEVE: Right. Highly incongruous to us, but probably a normal occurrence to the average native. I suspect that he didn't even own a pair of shoes or perceive any need for them whatsoever.

FRED: It's possible that the white shirt and dark pants were part of his old high school uniform which the students wore in cities like Bien Hoa and Saigon. Did you ever think about the fact that he might have been a VC sympathizer or enemy spy?

STEVE: I knew it was a remote possibility, but I never actually entertained the thought. I assumed that most "city folk" (like those from Bien Hoa) were in full support of the Americans and the South Vietnamese government. The peasants and farmers out in the countryside, on the other hand, were much more susceptible to coercion, intimidation and threats by the VC.

FRED: Or to the argument that "The South Vietnamese government officials are just puppets of the Americans who've invaded our country— just like the French, the Japanese and the Chinese before them! So we need you to join with us and help drive them out."

STEVE: But there were lots of Americans who simply didn't trust any Vietnamese at all, regardless of where they were from or which side they claimed to support. Sometimes Louie and I would be talking to some GI's and one of 'em would get in his face and say "Hey Louie— you VC???" Usually they were just teasing, but he always took it very seriously— and always had the same answer.

FRED: Not too surprising— he probably realized that if he gave the wrong reply, somebody might feel justified in gunning him down on the spot! What was his standard answer?

STEVE: He'd get real animated and say "Me no VC! Me hate VC! VC kill my sista! Me want to kill one thouz VC!!!" At that point they'd usually shut up. Then I'd tell Louie they were just joking, although I was never sure of it myself. Some would continue to accuse him after he gave his answer, even though most of 'em were just having a little fun. It probably never occurred to them that Louie had been asked that question about a thousand times already.

FRED: Of course that standard answer he gave would have been the logical thing to say regardless of whether he was VC or not. But I'm sure it usually provided a quick and easy end to any discussion about whose side he was on. So how did he think he would ever be able to kill "one thouz" VC?

STEVE: He insisted his goal was to join the South Vietnamese Air Force so he could fly over the enemy and bomb the crap out of 'em. Revenge his sister's death.

FRED: That might have sounded a bit odd coming from a guy who wore flip-flops every day. How did Louie commute between Long Binh and Bien Hoa? Did he ride one of those little 50cc scooters like practically every other young, civilized Vietnamese male?

STEVE: That would have been a logical assumption, but actually he rode in the trucks with the mama-sans. Every morning at the crack of dawn we sent a couple deuce and a halfs to a pickup point in Bien Hoa to get the mess hall workers. Then they'd make a second run to get the hooch maids and a third trip for the sandbaggers. Over the course of an hour and a half, they'd transport all 80 of our civilian workers to the 24th Evac. In the evenings the process was reversed.

FRED: And so when you'd roll out of the sack at 7 or 7:30 in the morning, those mama-sans would already be in the Mess Hall stirring the oatmeal. But who in Bien Hoa decided which workers would get on the trucks? Was it sort of like "Manpower, Inc." where you had so many slots to fill and some agent at the pickup point put a sufficient number of workers on the trucks?

STEVE: It was something like that, but I must confess that I never took the trouble to find out exactly how it worked. I was curious, but I figured "If it's something I don't know anything about, then there's no way I can be held accountable for it." Obviously someone in Bien Hoa was making those decisions on a daily basis, but I had no idea who or how. Were they Americans? Vietnamese? I didn't know, and since it didn't seem to affect my job, I didn't care.

FRED: Of course if they should have to substitute for some of the sandbaggers, that would be no problem. But the mess hall workers and hooch maids were semi-skilled, trusted employees. If a substitution had to be made, the sub would have to be someone already qualified to fill in at that spot.

STEVE: Those trusted and semi-skilled workers had to have security clearances and pass health exams too, which the sandbaggers did not. So one of my first duties was to take a truckload of a dozen or so mama-sans to Saigon once a week to get security clearances and health checkups. Up to then, none of 'em had photo ID cards— a shortcoming which we were about to fix. And they were looking forward to the idea with considerable glee.

FRED: Who went on the trips to Saigon, and how did the workers get security clearances once you got there?

STEVE: Louie and I sat up front with the driver— with me and the driver being armed— while the mama-sans rode in back. It was probably 20-25 minutes to Saigon on the main highway, then another 20 minutes of weaving through the traffic jams once we got to the city. Driving in Saigon was insane on the side streets downtown. As you crawled along at maybe 10 mph, your vehicle would be completely surrounded by cars, trucks, buses, scooters, bicycles and pedestrians. They'd all be close enough that you could just about reach out the window and touch 'em. In fact on one trip an American bus, going in the opposite direction, passed so close that when we heard a loud "crack"— like a gunshot— we realized the huge driver's side mirror on our truck had suddenly vanished. There was no way you could stop in that massive sea of humanity like you would in the USA, plus the bus would have been long gone anyway.

FRED: You'd think there would be serious accidents there every day under those conditions.

STEVE: Well not as many as one might expect, I guess, but on one trip we passed by a civilian lying on the pavement— there was nothing that separated the sidewalk from the street, it was like the pavement and sidewalks expanded and contracted as necessary, depending on whether there were vehicles passing through— and this guy had obviously been run over by a large truck or bus because his head was squashed to about half its normal width.

FRED: Now in any American city, traffic would have ground to a halt immediately and people would have rushed to the aid of the victim. But in Saigon...?

STEVE: People on foot or on bicycles just kept moving right past the guy as if he weren't even there. They were practically tripping over him but they just ignored this body lying on the pavement. He was obviously dead. I was absolutely dumbfounded. It sort of gives you a different perspective on how little value those natives placed on human life. In the USA we'd normally show more respect for a dead squirrel than they were showing for one of their fellow citizens.

FRED: So what happened when you got to your destination?

STEVE: Each of the women would be carrying a few documents that they had to present at this South Vietnamese government office when we arrived. These were all in Vietnamese but I presume they included a birth certificate, a health certificate of some sort and perhaps some documentation of the individual's residence. Louie told them where to go and what to do, since the language barrier prevented me from saying or doing much of anything.

FRED: So you were pretty much just a chaperone. But the mama-sans came to realize that you were the boss-man since you would tell Louie and the driver what to do?

STEVE: They did. And when we were done and heading back to Long Binh, they each had a brand new photo ID card laminated in plastic which they wore on their tunics with considerable pride. I believe this caused them to develop a certain degree of respect and reverence for me. At least that was the impression I got.

FRED: That plus the fact that whenever the Vietnamese workers had to be assembled and addressed as a group, it was always you and Louie running the show. And you paid them too?

STEVE: I was part of the pay process, yes. I think they lined up to get paid twice a month in the Mess Hall. Seated at a table would be Louie, me and Lieutenant Jarvis. Louie had single-finger-typed a pay envelope for each worker with their name on it. Since he knew them all by name, he'd recognize them as they stood in line and hand me the envelope for the correct employee. I'd count the dough, stuff it in the envelope and hand it to the Lieutenant.

FRED: Then he'd count it out to the employee and have them sign a sheet. Were they able to sign their own names?

STEVE: Most of the younger ones could, but a lot of the older ones had to make an X or similar mark next to their name. The ones who couldn't write their names seemed somewhat embarrassed about it, but I couldn't really tell for sure— it might have been just me who was embarrassed.

FRED: That's Donovan for ya, way too much empathy! How much money did the workers make?

STEVE: I don't remember exactly but I'm pretty sure it was less than 10 bucks a week— still good money to them— so the entire bi-weekly payroll was probably something like 1400 dollars in Vietnamese currency. I believe 100 dong, also known by the French Indochina name of piastres, were roughly equivalent to one US dollar. The Lieutenant kept the cash locked up in his hooch, I think.

FRED: So there must have been periods, albeit brief ones perhaps, when you had nothing to do as Civilian Personnel Specialist?

STEVE: Yeah, I spent most of my time putting out fires, large and small. Which meant Louie and I had to be on call whenever an American and a civilian were having a disagreement about how the civilian was supposed to be performing his or her duties. For example, one day Sergeant Malmquist comes into the Orderly Room with his hooch maid, Hanh. He says someone has stolen a small gold-plated statue of Buddha that he had on his bookshelf— a decorative paperweight which someone had given him as a gift.

FRED: And he was accusing Hanh of taking it, since she was the only civilian who was authorized to be in his hooch. So you had to interrogate her using Louie as your translator?

STEVE: Right, although I didn't think any hooch maid would be dumb enough to steal something from her own hooch. We asked her if she knew what had happened to the Buddha and she said no, but she thought maybe another mama-san, Phuong, might have taken it because she had seen Phuong admiring the statue. Malmquist was convinced Hanh was the thief, so we arranged to have her searched and of course nothing was found.

FRED: Then you'd have to talk to Phuong? Meanwhile, the mama-sans knew one of 'em was likely to be fired if any strong evidence of guilt could be produced. A small fire to you, but a big one to them.

STEVE: Like Hanh, Phuong also said she knew nothing about it, so we couldn't take any further action until some sort of evidence was established. Then some 48 hours later, Malmquist goes into his hooch in the afternoon and there's the Buddha sitting in its normal spot. Whoever took it had brought it back!

FRED: Or else someone decided it would be prudent to buy another one in Bien Hoa as a replacement, rather than lose their job.

STEVE: A distinct possibility... or maybe steal another one in Bien Hoa. Regarding the many difficulties posed by the language barrier, I'm reminded of the story about the dental officer who would go out to some of the nearby villages once or twice a week to provide free dental care to the natives. Nearly all of it consisted of pulling teeth— sometimes as many as 400 in a single day.

FRED: Accompanied by a couple of medics acting as assistants, the doc would set up an assembly line where the medics would administer a shot of anesthetic to the jaw of each civilian who complained of a toothache. Then patients would wait for a half hour or so until it was their turn to have the dentist perform the necessary extractions.

STEVE: The crew was baffled by the fact that when it came time to get their teeth pulled, half the patients had left already. Then the medics realized they were leaving because the anesthetic had temporarily "cured" their toothaches and they assumed that they no longer needed the services of a dentist!

FRED: Since translators didn't exactly grow on trees, the dental officer was unable to obtain one to go out with his team. He and his crew finally had to learn some Vietnamese phrases so they could tell patients they would have to remain until their "treatment" was completed. So what did you and Louie used to talk about?

STEVE: Since the two of us spent so much time together, he would occasionally tell me about what life was like for a civilian living in Bien Hoa, and of course I would reciprocate by talking about life in the USA. One day he spotted the TV in our hooch and announced that every Saturday night, a TV station in Saigon or Bien Hoa broadcast programs featuring nude women dancing or performing various sexy routines. He said he'd turn on his TV in Bien Hoa after midnight and watch these programs every weekend.

FRED: Vietnamese porno! Except that back then, there was no such thing as a "porno flick"— they were called "stag films," intended solely for male audiences and shown at bachelor parties in the USA.

STEVE: The only TV programming available on the little 12-inch black & white portable in our hooch was Armed Forces TV, broadcast daily from Saigon from like 6 pm to 10 pm. There would be a nightly news broadcast (at one point featuring John Steinbeck IV as newscaster— son of the famous author) and reruns of old programs like Combat, Dragnet and Bonanza. Plus various sporting events like the World Series and selected NFL games.

FRED: The Air Force helped extend the range of the Armed Forces broadcasts by having a C-123 cargo plane circle continuously over Saigon, relaying the TV signal to outlying areas. I don't recall any

Vietnamese broadcasts at all, although there might have been some. For the most part we seldom watched TV anyway. But Louie seemed to be dead serious when he told you about the "Saturday night nudies." We were all highly skeptical, so you finally volunteered to stay up late on a Saturday night and see what developed.

STEVE: Yeah, it wasn't so much that I wanted to see a cheesy stag flick— it was the fact that Louie seemed so sincere and insistent that his story was absolutely true. I was hoping for his sake that he was right— otherwise he'd be lying, or trying to pull a prank on us.

FRED: So sometime after midnight, you began searching the dial (with the sound off, thank goodness) and manipulating the rabbit ears in a desperate attempt to bring in a signal— any signal at all.

STEVE: And for over an hour I got zilch. Eventually I gave up. Had Louie been lying all along, or trying to trick us? I decided that rather than confront him and call him a liar— or let him know that his prank had worked, if that's what it was— I would just never bring it up. So I never did, and neither did he. Weird, indeed.

FRED: But Louie always gave the impression that he was such a straight shooter. Maybe it was a short-range or closed-circuit broadcast that he'd been watching. Or maybe he'd been dreaming. In any event, how did you then become a Headquarters Clerk?

STEVE: Another part of my job was having to mediate disputes between two Vietnamese, since I was their authority figure of record. But some days there weren't any fires to be put out, and I might be all caught up with my recordkeeping. Since I didn't want to be just sitting around goofing off when my services were not required, I continued helping the HQ clerks whenever I could, unil I gradually became an HQ clerk myself.

FRED: And before long Captain Bloom would have you typing and editing his correspondence as well?

STEVE: Yeah, he used to write everything on yellow legal pads and one day he asked me to type a letter for him. I believe it concerned a position he intended to apply for when he returned to civilian life. I noticed that it could stand a little rewriting, so I asked if he'd like me to edit it for him. He said "Sure"— he trusted me by then— and soon he had me writing a lot of his correspondence, both military and business. At that point I had become like an executive secretary.

FRED: And then how did you become the Captain's jeep driver, in addition to being Civilian Personnel Specialist?

STEVE: I'd heard something about this jeep being involved in a motor vehicle accident but I didn't have any details. Anyway, one day he says "Donovan, I need someone to be my personal jeep driver so I'm appointing you to the job." I was both flattered and somewhat thrilled, since I loved to drive. But I had to say "Sir, I'm afraid I don't have a military driver's license." He picks up the phone, calls the Motor Pool and says "This is Captain Bloom. I'm sending SP4 Donovan over there. Fix him up with a driver's license." The next thing you know I'm taking a written test after studying the military driver's manual for all of 10-15 minutes.

FRED: But there had to be more to it than just a written test.

STEVE: I had to demonstrate my ability to drive a jeep, a three-quarter ton pickup and one of those monster "6x6" two and a half ton trucks— the "deuce and a half." The first two I just drove around Long Binh for maybe 10 minutes. But climbing into the cab of that deuce and looking out through the windshield, it felt like you were looking out the second story window of a house with a big front porch blocking your view of whatever was in front of the vehicle. Plus the steering wheel was about two feet in diameter.

FRED: So despite your having been a "wheel man" for a pizzeria when you were in college, you felt intimidated by this huge truck. Why did you have to drive the big monster?

STEVE: Well I told the guy I was never gonna be driving one of those things but he said "OK, but you have to qualify on all three to get a license, so just drive around in circles a few times here inside the Motor Pool." Sitting up in that cab, I felt like a spectator rather than someone who was actually piloting the vehicle. I let the clutch out and cranked that monster wheel all the way to the left— I'm not sure if there was any power steering, either— and we started rolling in the tightest circle possible. I hit second gear and hoped like hell that nobody would suddenly cross my path.

FRED: Did anyone tempt fate in such a manner?

STEVE: Fortunately no, and after three or four loop-de-loops around the circuit the guy says "Okay Donovan, you're good." I had my military license less than an hour after Captain Bloom had made his phone call. Never even made it to third gear!

FRED: A streamlined procedure to be sure— you'd managed to completely bypass the Army's truck driver school and obtain a license saying you were qualified to drive a six-by-six! I wonder how many other guys got their licenses by driving around in circles a few times?

STEVE: Actually I've read that it was not uncommon. Guys would get to Nam and be put in a unit where they needed to be able to drive a jeep or truck, so they'd get their license the same way I did. After all, it was wartime, ya know?

FRED: Where cutting corners and flaunting Army regulations were par for the course. Sounds like you beat the fuggin' system once more!

STEVE: True, but here's a better story than mine... Gary Burkett over at the 572nd Transportation Co. in Long Binh said he started out as a supply clerk in the Motor Pool. The 572nd (known as the "Gypsy Bandits") had to get him a license to drive a tractor trailer since everyone in the company needed to be qualified. They said "Drive this big rig to Bien Hoa, then turn around and come back. If you make it back without killing anyone, you'll have your license."

FRED: So he made it back without even causing any injuries! And just like that he was a trucker.

STEVE: But that wasn't the best part. The clerk issuing the license asked if there was any other type of vehicle he wanted on there and Gary said "Add a 3/4 ton pickup in case I might need it." The clerk said "OK, anything else?" and Gary jokingly said "Well, how about an M-109 Self-Propelled Howitzer?" Basically a big tank with a 155 mm medium-range artillery piece mounted on a turret. As a prank, the clerk added it to the license and forged the approving officer's initials, whereupon they both got a big chuckle out of it.

FRED: So now he was a tank driver too!

STEVE: Yes, but only as a joke. The closest he had ever come to an M-109 was to pose for a photo while sitting in one. Then a month or so later, they announce that the 572nd had to deliver a shipment of M-48 tanks from Saigon to various locations around the country. "Luckily," says the CO, "we have got six people in our unit with tank licenses." Gary felt half excitement, half panic. Next thing he knows, he's sitting at the controls of a tank he's never seen before.

FRED: This sounds like something out of a Jerry Lewis movie. At that point it would be time to admit he wasn't qualified, right?

STEVE: Nah, they probably wouldn't have believed him anyway. It was right there on his license, fer cryin' out loud, initialed by an officer! To his amazement, the tank was quite easy to drive— power steering and brakes, automatic transmission, etc. From that point on they delivered tanks, firetrucks, ambulances, self-propelled artillery— you name it— for the rest of his tour. They'd get a tank, deliver it by convoy, go to town and hang out for a while, then get another tank and repeat the process all over again. He loved his job.

FRED: And here all you did was drive a lousy jeep!

&&&&&&&&&&&&&&&&&&&

FACT OR FICTION? *The story goes that an infantry squad was patrolling on the outskirts of Bien Hoa, looking for VC commandos who might be trying to sabotage the airbase. Accompanying them was a "Chieu Hoi" enemy defector acting as a guide and translator. As they were passing a scrapyard full of old truck parts, they found a large hole in the ground filled with water. Puzzled as to whether it was a well or just a bomb crater, one GI says "Let's drop this old truck transmission in there and see how deep it is!" No sooner had they done so than they saw a goat come tearing out of the underbrush, leap headfirst into the water and disappear. As they stood waiting for the animal to surface, a peasant appeared and started babbling in Vietnamese. The Chieu Hoi says "Him want to know if we see his lost goat." The squad leader says "Tell him we just saw a goat come flying out of those bushes and jump into this hole!" The translator relays that to the peasant and then says "Him say that not possible, goat was chained to a big heavy transmission!"*

SEE MORE THAN 30 PHOTOS AT:
www.longbinhdaze.com

CHAPTER 35

PLEASE, LADIES... NO SQUATTING OVER THE TOILET SEATS

That's right... we're here to tell you you've been doing it wrong all your life

FRED: For our first few months in Long Binh, the hospital had no female personnel so we had no need for female latrines. We did, however, have 40 or 50 female Vietnamese hooch maids and sandbag fillers who would need bathroom facilities of some sort. Or at least the Americans thought they did, even if the mama-sans couldn't care less.

STEVE: All their lives, the Vietnamese peasants had been used to going outside and squatting to urinate or defecate. When you drove through a village like Tam Hiep, a few miles to the west of us, you could see them doing it outside their own dwellings.

FRED: But for sanitation purposes, the women in our compound were instructed to use the enlisted men's latrine and were forbidden to use the plain old ground like they were used to. This might sound a bit startling, but in fact it didn't seem to bother them at all.

STEVE: I was seated on the bench in our ten-holer latrine when a young woman entered at the far end, stepped up on the footrail, lifted the hinged lid over one of the holes, dropped her trousers and sat down. (Mind you, there were no privacy partitions of any kind in this place— it was just one long, narrow room.) I was very embarrassed for her having to be subjected to such a humiliation, so I deliberately didn't look at her. I'm not sure if she used any toilet paper or not, though I suspected that she had not. But I did notice that she didn't seem to be fazed in the least by the whole thing.

FRED: So now we had a unisex bathroom, just like some of the cities in Japan and Korea! Many of our guys were downright shocked or outraged when the same thing happened to them. But they were the only people who seemed to be embarrassed by it, so we were told to "just deal with it."

STEVE: I did most of my pooping in the evenings when the mama-sans had already gone home. I never liked pooping in a group anyway— too undignified for my taste. You'd have to either stare at the floor or else watch other guys doing their business. It was yet another sign that I was never cut out for the Army.

FRED: After some weeks, they finally built a women's latrine to accommodate the mama-sans and the influx of female nurses who'd soon be arriving at the 24th. The civilians were then told they were to use only the women's latrine and not the men's. They now had their own private shitter, which appeared to solve the problem— until the American females started showing up.

STEVE: That wasn't too long after I'd been assigned to the position of Civilian Personnel Specialist and shortly after Louie had been assigned as my interpreter. Suddenly anyone who had a problem with one of the civilians was coming to me for assistance and expecting a resolution to the conflict. As did the Chief Nurse, Major Moubry, who seemed to be quite upset.

FRED: She had a latrine problem?

STEVE: Sure did. In no uncertain terms she declared "Those Vietnamese are squatting over the holes in the nurses latrine instead of sitting down like they're supposed to. Some of them are missing the holes and making a mess all over the place. It's highly unsanitary and it's disgusting! Plus some of 'em don't use toilet paper either!"

FRED: I'm surprised she didn't say "God only knows what sorts of diseases or parasites or worms they're carrying in their feces, and it's not all going in those big drums underneath, that's for sure!"

STEVE: Well she did sort of imply that, even if she didn't say it. I assumed they were doing this out of ignorance because they didn't understand the proper way to use a western toilet. Later I found out that many Asians believed sitting on a toilet seat— where countless others had previously parked their bare buns— was far more unsanitary than the squatting method they preferred. If your butt didn't contact the seat, you couldn't possibly pick up any germs from it!

FRED: I suppose they could be right if we're talking about a bunch of strangers carrying all sorts of bacteria and parasites and leaving traces on the seat... E-coli, hepatitis, salmonella, tetanus. I never thought of it that way, other than when I'd occasionally see public toilets with paper covers that you lay over the seat for protection.

STEVE: Even those Vietnamese who had indoor toilets used the squatting method. The typical Vietnamese toilet (also known as a "French toilet," which probably explains how those fixtures made their way to Vietnam many decades earlier) looks kind of like a floor-level mop sink with a hole in the center of the floor, maybe 5 inches wide, and "foot pads" on either side. You stand with your feet on the pads and then squat over the hole to defecate. Obviously a novice might have a bit of trouble learning how to aim properly.

FRED: Then what did they do when they were done?

STEVE: Well some apparently did have toilet paper there, but the traditional method was to clean the butt with water. Next to the toilet there would be either a little hose attached to a faucet or a water bucket with a ladle in it. Using the hose or ladle, you'd dribble the water down your buttcrack with your right hand— now here's where it gets pretty gross— while wiping the surface with your left. I'm assuming you'd then wash or rinse your hands when you were done. But various sources say "In many Middle Eastern and Asian countries, this explains why people never eat or shake hands with their left hand— it's the one they wipe with."

FRED: Well gee, I sure wish someone had told us that when we got there. It doesn't do us any good to find out now!

STEVE: Yeah, I was quite surprised to read that, but at least it explains how they got by without toilet paper. Now the "fancy" toilet hose, not usually found in Asia, often has a small spray nozzle with a trigger on the end. In Europe it may be colloquially called a "bum gun" or— in the USA— a "butt blaster." Then of course there's the bastardized version— the "bum blaster."

FRED: Like that thing you nearly hosed the First Sergeant with in the Mess Hall back in Texas! What was it he said to you?

STEVE: "Donovan, you are one lucky bastard."

FRED: Meaning that you missed him by a couple inches!

STEVE: That I did. Beat the fuggin' system once again. But since we're talking about bum guns, I once heard an American nurse say that when she went to Japan on R&R "the bathrooms were really interesting— while using the toilet, they had this little hose right there so you could take a shower at the same time!"

FRED: Meanwhile you've got "Nurse Ratched" expecting you to wave your magic wand and somehow make all of those mama-sans stop crapping on the seats. How were ya gonna do that?

STEVE: Well first, my only avenue of communication with them was through Louie, which meant I first had to make sure Louie understood the problem. Not an easy task when the kid's only had a few years of high school English and the words "toilet seat," "squat" and "sit" have not yet made their way into his vocabulary.

FRED: So you drew him a picture of a toilet seat?

STEVE: I considered it, but decided it would be quicker to take him over to the men's latrine and show him what I meant by sit, squat, and seat. "Some mama-sans do this... this is squat— Numbah Ten! Some mama-sans do this... this is sit— Numbah One!" All the while he seemed somewhat dumbfounded, except when he would occasionally start giggling. So I had to keep asking him if he understood what I was trying to tell him.

FRED: And did you think he really understood?

STEVE: He indicated that he did, although it probably would have helped me immensely if he had said "You know Boss, these women have been squatting to poop ever since they were small children. And not only that, but they think the Americans are fools for sitting on toilet seats where hundreds of other nasty old bare asses have already sat before they did!"

FRED: But he didn't say that. Instead he said what?

STEVE: He didn't say zip. We set up an "assembly" for the next day at 2 pm for the 70 or so female civilians working in the compound. We used that little stage that was there for addressing the troops, and I think we had a little PA squawkbox since Louie's voice didn't carry very well. As Louie and I left the Orderly Room to go give our lecture, I said "Grab that folding chair and bring it along." He said

"Whaffo?" and I told him we might need it. I always began by asking if anyone spoke English or French— no dice. So I told Louie to say "Some mama-sans sit on the seats and some stand up and squat over them. Sitting is Numbah One, squatting is Numbah Ten!"

FRED: And was he able to get your message across?

STEVE: Well, Louie says a couple of sentences into the mike but there's no reaction at all from the crowd. I say "Tell them no can do, no squatting over the toilet seat! They must sit from now on!" Again there's no reaction as they stare intently at us. At which point I'm thinking "what the hell do I do now?"

FRED: Let me guess… time for the chair?

STEVE: You got it. I tell Louie to first sit in the chair and then to tell them in Vietnamese that this is how they're supposed to sit on the toilet. No reaction. I add "Numbah One!!" for emphasis. Then I tell him to stand up on the chair, squat over it like he's going to poop, and say this is the wrong way to use the toilet. As he does, I point to him and add "Numbah Ten!!"

FRED: Any reaction this time?

STEVE: They start laughing and cupping their hands over their mouths like they're embarrassed. An apparent breakthrough! I give them a minute to calm down, then I ask Louie if they understood the message. He says "Ya Boss, they understand." I had Louie tell them they had to use the toilet paper too. More howling, laughing and embarrassment. "Louie, understood?" "Ya Boss, they understand."

FRED: But at the time you didn't know anything about why they squatted, or why they thought we Americans were dumb for sitting, or why they didn't use toilet paper. You just thought you had succeeded in delivering your message, accomplishing your mission— and educating them on the ways of the world!

STEVE: Indeed. And afterward I didn't get any more complaints from Nurse Ratched, so I guess we must have succeeded. But I really had no idea whether they understood the message or not, since I had no way of knowing what Louie was actually telling them.

FRED: He might have been saying "This crazy American here thinks you should sit on the toilet— right amongst all those cooties on there— instead of squatting like you've been doing all your lives.

Better humor him or we'll all be in trouble!"

STEVE: Well, whatever he actually said to them, it seems to have worked— so I wasn't going to pursue the matter any further.

FRED: And then soon after that, the mama-sans in the Mess Hall began talking to you in the chow line?

STEVE: In the mornings I usually skipped breakfast in favor of an extra half hour of sleep. Like just about everyone else in HQ, I'd have a cup of java and a glazed donut when I got to the office, plus a vitamin pill from a bottle in my desk. But every day for lunch and dinner, I'd go through the cafeteria-style chow line where there were probably a dozen server stations. Each was manned by one of the KP mama-sans who normally did not speak to the GI's in line (since none of 'em spoke English anyway.)

FRED: The one exception was when they saw YOU coming through the line. They spoke to you because they knew you were their honcho. You had taken them by the truckload to Saigon to get their security clearances; you had conducted the sessions whenever they had to be addressed as a group; and you sat at the table in the Mess Hall where they lined up to collect their pay.

STEVE: Plus any time there was a grievance or dispute that had to be resolved between an American and one of the civilians, those problems were always brought to me because I was the only person in the compound who had an interpreter with me at all times. Thus in the chow line they would each give me the same greeting in a soft and reverent tone, always accompanied by a pleasant smile.

FRED: What did they say to you?

STEVE: They had apparently given me a title or nickname of sorts. I'm not sure how they spelled it— I'd guess it was probably "co-cau." In any event, they pronounced it KOE-KAW and as I went past their stations, each one would say "Hello, co-cau" in a warm, friendly manner as if it were a term of deep respect and admiration.

FRED: Since they were always nice to you and you were always nice to them, you figured there couldn't possibly be any reason why they would say it with any intent other than that.

STEVE: Right. And so to reciprocate I would softly reply to each one "Hello, mama-san" as I went through the line.

FRED: So twice a day you'd go through the line and whoever was right behind you would hear "Hello, co-cau." "Hello, mama-san." "Hello, co-cau." "Hello, mama-san." "Hello, co-cau." "Hello, mama-san." About 12 times in a row?

STEVE: Exactly. And being sort of a modest fellow, I was slightly embarrassed by all the attention they were showing me. But they did seem to enjoy it and I was flattered to a degree, so this went on for several weeks— even though I was getting a little tired of it. Then again, I did have a bit of an ulterior motive for letting it continue.

FRED: And what motive would that be?

STEVE: Well, out of the 70 or so Vietnamese women who worked in our compound, there were only two who actually turned my head. One was the PX girl, Linh, in her lovely ao-dai dresses and heels. The other was a tiny little thing who worked in the mess hall and looked about 18, although she could have been in her 20's. I always tried to steal a glance at her whenever I had the chance.

FRED: What was it about her that appealed to you?

STEVE: She had a really striking face— kind of like Liz Taylor, only with Vietnamese features— and she might have been part French. I used to dream and/or fantasize about her, although I would never even think of jeopardizing my job by actually trying to act on those impulses. Nevertheless, about the only way I could impress her was to have her think I was highly regarded by all the kitchen help.

FRED: It was often difficult to tell the ages of Vietnamese women. Some in their early 20's might appear to be in their mid-teens, while the ones over 35 tended to look 10-15 years older than their true age. So what was this little gal's name?

STEVE: Her name was Rum (pronounced ROOM) and her full name was something like Nguyen Thi Rum. (The Vietnamese put the sur-name, or family name, first and the "first" name last.) She probably didn't weigh more than 80 pounds, and like all the mama-sans she always wore long-sleeved smocks and black pajama bottoms. Her face was virtually the only visible feature on which she could be judged by us leering goons. Every day when I went into the Mess Hall I'd first look to see if she was working the serving line or not. Half of the time she wasn't— and of course I'd be disappointed— so I'm guessing that when she did, she was filling in for one of the regulars.

FRED: But then after several weeks you began to get tired of the co-cau business. So what did you do?

STEVE: Well, I did enjoy hearing Rum say "Hello, co-cau" to me as I went by, but it occurred to me that I had absolutely no idea what "co-cau" meant. I assumed it was probably a title like dai-uy (DYE-WEE) which meant "Captain" in Vietnamese. Maybe co-cau meant something like "boss man" or "fearless leader" or "super stud."

FRED: So you decided to ask Louie, your interpreter. He knew the answer, but since his English vocabulary was quite limited, he had no idea how to translate it from Vietnamese.

STEVE: Right. Louie would say "Me no can say, don't know word in Ingrish." Now at this point I need to explain that at the time, I was 6 foot 1 and about 145 pounds with really long, skinny arms and legs plus a long, skinny neck. Not an ounce of fat— or muscle either— on my frame at all. I was literally a ghastly bag of bones and was always surprised that no one ever tried to nickname me "Spider."

FRED: So if you had to venture a guess, you would have said co-cau probably meant Spider?

STEVE: Yeah, plus I always thought Spider would be kind of a cool nickname anyway. But I had to get it out of Louie somehow, so I got a pad of paper and told him to draw me a picture. It took him several tries to come up with anything that was recognizable, but eventually he did. I studied it and then decided he was trying to draw me a picture of an ostrich with its head buried in the sand!

FRED: But you couldn't ask him if he meant "ostrich" because that word was totally unfamiliar to him.

STEVE: Correct. So instead I drew another picture of an ostrich standing up with its head in the air. I said "Is this it?" and he said "Ya, thass it!" We both laughed out loud. "This is co-cau?" "Ya, thass it! For sure!" And we both laughed again.

FRED: The mama-sans had been saying "Hello, ostrich!" to you twice a day, seven days a week, for three weeks! Were you pissed by this monumental display of disrespect?

STEVE: Nah, some guys might have been, but I thought it was hilarious. I could appreciate a good prank even if it was at my own expense. But now I had to figure out how I would get the last laugh on them! That was one thing I learned living in a college dorm— somebody pranks you, you prank 'em right back— only better!

FRED: So you thought it over for a day or two and eventually came up with a plan?

STEVE: Well I knew it would have to happen in the chow line since that's the only time the crew was all together in one place. I knew that "khong biet" meant "I don't understand," but I had to ask Louie how to say "I understand." He said "toi biet" (pronounced TOO-E BE-ICK.) I rehearsed it until I had it down cold. I had to make it sound like I could speak proper Vietnamese so that when I said "I understand," they'd believe that I really did know what co-cau meant.

FRED: And then you launched your attack!

STEVE: I had to wait until I saw that Rum was working the serving line, since I didn't want her to miss my performance. I pushed my tray along the track with the usual "Hello, co-cau." "Hello, mama-san." "Hello, co-cau." "Hello, mama-san"— until I got down to the very end of the line, where I stopped dead in my tracks.

FRED: What happened then?

STEVE: Any time the line stopped moving, one by one each mama-san would lean forward and turn her head to the left to see what the hold-up was. I waited until I had all 12 of 'em staring at me, and I was staring back. Then I took my index finger and started poking myself in the chest as I said in a loud voice "HEY MAMA-SAN!" (poke, poke, poke)... "TOO-E BE-ICK!!" With that they started shrieking, howling and slapping their hands over their mouths to try to conceal their embarrassment. I had scored my coup, so I gave them a chuckle and a smile, then turned and walked away with my tray. And no one else in the entire Mess Hall had the slightest idea what had just happened. But I knew... and those 12 mama-sans knew that I knew!

FRED: So did that finally mark the end of having them calling you an ostrich every day?

STEVE: Yeah, except every once in a while one would quietly say "Hello, co-cau," and then give me a big grin as if to say we could both appreciate a good joke. Besides, shortly after that episode they came up with a new taunt for me. One day I made the mistake of innocently asking Louie if he knew anything about Rum— how old she was, what her background was, etc. He didn't know much about her but he said "You rike-a Rum?" I said "No, no, no, I was just curious— she looks so young compared to many of the others."

FRED: And then Louie promptly went and spilled the beans to the Mess Hall workers?

STEVE: I think he must have. Apparently he was too young or too "culturally naive" to understand the single guy's code of silence which says that when they're discussing a specific female, that conversation is to remain private. So a couple days later I'm going through the chow line and one of the mama-sans says "Hey, co-cau!" She points at Rum and says "Rum!!" I start laughing, she starts laughing and Rum starts looking extremely embarrassed, like she'd like to crawl under the serving counter. At which point I decide I should go looking for Louie so I can strangle the little bastard.

FRED: Well, look at it on the positive side— at least she didn't give you the finger!

&&&&&&&&&&&&&&&&&&&&

FACT OR FICTION? *The story goes that a LRRP (Long Range Reconnaissance Patrol) Team leader was approached by a village elder who had a dog for sale that could not only talk, but translate from Vietnamese into English. The lieutenant had to see this for himself, so he met with the dog alone in one of the huts. The dog said his name was Chipper and he used to work as a spy for the Green Berets, going into villages and eavesdropping to see if there were any Viet Cong hiding there. In addition, he rattled off a string of over a dozen major operations in which he played a key role in flushing out the enemy, earning him many decorations. Eventually he took some shrapnel in his leg and had to retire, but he said he was now fully recovered. The lieutenant gave him several Vietnamese phrases and Chipper translated them all into flawless English. Amazed, the officer asked the elder how much he wanted for the dog. "Twelb dollah!" came the reply. Shocked, the Team leader said "Why only twelve dollars? This dog ought to be worth a fortune with skills like that!" The elder explained that "Dog be big phony. Him no do half that crap like he tole you!"*

CHAPTER 36

THANKS FOR THE MAMMARIES

Proving that a slight mispronunciation can get
you in a considerable amount of hot water

FRED: So now you're driving Captain Bloom to Saigon once or twice a week. Did you ever have to make the trip by yourself?

STEVE: I believe I did several times, accompanied by an armed guard of course. In one case our new Chief Nurse was going to be arriving at Tan Son Nhut Airbase in Saigon. She asked that someone be there to pick her up, but no big shots were available on such short notice. So Captain Bloom sent me in the jeep with PFC Rossini as shotgun. Her flight arrived early, so when we got to the pickup point we were told we'd find her at the Tan Son Nhut Officers Club. We arrived there, padlocked the jeep and went inside with our M-14 rifles slung with the barrels down.

FRED: You were allowed into the Officers Club?

STEVE: No, we went into this lobby with signs that said OFFICERS ONLY BEYOND THIS POINT and NO WEAPONS BEYOND THIS POINT. We sent word in to tell her we'd arrived. She brought out a couple of Cokes with ice and told us to relax in the lobby while she visited with some old friends.

FRED: But the only place to sit down in that lobby was at two little podium-type things on either side with seats similar to barstools.

STEVE: Yeah, it was probably two in the afternoon and soon some Air Force officers walked in. Seeing two armed guards seated at these little desks, they started whipping out their wallets and showing me their ID's. I was startled of course, but rather than try to explain why we were there, I just said "Thank you, sir" to each one of 'em as they passed by.

FRED: What was Rossini doing?

STEVE: He was drinking this in with great fascination. So after they went inside, I said "Just play along!" Soon more were coming in and now we were checking more ID's. Eventually one officer said "Oh shoot, I don't have my wallet with me! No ID!" By this time Rossini had decided to play it to the hilt and said "Sorry sir, I can't let you in without it!" The lieutenant was starting to beg when I intervened and said "It's OK this one time, Rossini. Let him in."

FRED: Didn't anyone wonder why the two of you were armed and drinking Cokes, or why you were wearing Army fatigues and checking ID's on an Air Force Base?

STEVE: Well nobody had up to that point— maybe they thought the security threat level had been raised. But I was starting to get a little nervous, so I sent Rossini outside to watch the jeep and soon the Major came out. I think she talked non-stop all the way back.

FRED: Did driving the CO's jeep make you feel important?

STEVE: Well I would have to say privileged, for sure. What really made me feel like somebody important was when I would occasionally have to strap on a .45 pistol, depending on where we were going and what we were gonna be doing.

FRED: Normally they were only worn by officers or people with important duties like military couriers or military police.

STEVE: Correct. I distinctly remember going into the 24th Mess Hall wearing that piece on my hip and figuring strangers would think "Who's that guy wearing the .45?" while my buddies would see me and wonder "Where in the hell did Donovan get a .45?"

FRED: Did you ever fire one of those things?

STEVE: Nope, practiced for all of five minutes (without a clip) the first time Captain Bloom told me I needed to wear one. Then I loaded it and strapped it on. But he said "If you ever need to use that thing, you might as well just throw it at your target because you'll stand a better chance of hitting something!" The weapon was notoriously inaccurate due to its short barrel and huge kick.

FRED: But why would you need to wear a .45?

STEVE: Mainly for the monthly payday ritual. The Captain and I would have to drive over to the heavily guarded Paymaster's office to pick up the payroll, which at the time was around 60 grand in military currency. There the two of us would take the money inside one of these big wire cages and sit at a table surrounded by armed MP's. I'd count each stack of bills and hand them to Bloom so he could count 'em again. We'd both keep score as we did this and hopefully everything would come out right when we finished.

FRED: What if it came out wrong?

STEVE: At that point we'd have to count it all over again. I think it only happened once. When the count was right, Bloom would have to sign for it and we'd head back to the hospital. I remember one time we were driving along and he said "Do you realize that if anything should happen to this money I just signed for, I'll probably be working for the next 30 years to pay back Uncle Sam?" We both had a good laugh and I especially appreciated his candor, since it was the sort of thing you'd say to a personal friend.

FRED: So then once you got back to the 24th Evac, what did you do with all that cash?

STEVE: We'd set up a table in the Mess Hall and the troops would line up at their allotted times like "A thru F, 1300 hours; G thru L, 1400 hours" and so on. As each soldier approached I'd look him up on my sheet, count out his money and hand it to the Captain. He'd count it again to the recipient and then have him sign for it— like we did with the civilians.

FRED: Meanwhile there you were, guarding that money with a weapon you were told to throw at anyone who tried to steal the dough!

STEVE: True, but unless the guy was a masked bandit, where was he gonna go with all that loot? Besides, don't forget that in Basic Training I got a nearly perfect score on the grenade throw— it was the only thing that saved my skinny butt from flunking the Physical Combat Proficiency Test!

FRED: So now when you weren't tooling around in the CO's jeep you had Louie following you around the compound to serve as your interpreter. Which meant you no longer needed the services of Linh, the PX girl, any more. Did you explain that to her?

STEVE: Yes, and I stopped going into the PX since I no longer had any excuse for chatting with her. It had been fun while it lasted, as they say. A week later, Louie comes into the Orderly Room with a message from Linh: She wanted to invite me to dinner at her home in Bien Hoa— with her and her parents— on a Saturday evening.

FRED: Sounds like wedding bells, for sure!

STEVE: At that point all sorts of thoughts started racing through my brain. What if she was actually looking for a husband to take her across the "Big Pond" to the Land of Plenty? Or what if she was in love with me? What if her parents were looking to marry her off and get their own ticket out of that nasty hellhole in the process? Or what if she was really an enemy agent working for the VC? Or... what if she just wanted a good old roll in the hay?

FRED: Sounds like an awful lot of "what ifs" there.

STEVE: But there's more! What if I should accept her invitation, thereby giving her the impression that I was romantically interested in her? Would I just be leading her on, only to break her heart in the end? Or what if her parents were just desperate to find an American whom they could converse with, since they spoke French but no English? I knew my facility for conversational French left a hell of a lot to be desired.

FRED: Well, maybe she just wanted to show her gratitude for your friendship and the fact that you weren't a rude, slobbering Neanderthal like a lot of the GI's she must have encountered. But despite all the time you'd spent talking to her, you had no idea what her actual feelings or intentions were?

STEVE: No. There was no way to tell what was really going on in her head since the language barrier prevented us from having anything approaching a deep conversation. She spoke fluent French, but mine was woefully weak.

FRED: In the USA, when a girl brought a guy home to meet her parents it usually meant it was a pretty serious deal. But there's no telling what it might have meant in the Vietnamese culture.

STEVE: Exactly. I asked some of the other guys— including you, as I recall— what they would do in my situation and most of 'em said "Go for it!" I was sure I wasn't interested in a serious romance with a Vietnamese girl who didn't speak English. But ultimately I decided that in the interests of being polite as well as satisfying my curiosity, I would accept Linh's offer.

FRED: Way to go! Did you think at all about taking one of us 24th Evac guys with you?

STEVE: I would have felt more comfortable having a buddy with me, but she never mentioned it so I didn't think I should either. She wrote her address on a piece of paper so I could show it to the Lambretta driver when I got to Bien Hoa.

FRED: Did you bring the family a gift?

STEVE: I brought a bottle of French wine, partly as a gesture and partly because I'd heard the rice wine consumed by the natives was pretty awful stuff. The driver took me past a lot of crudely built shacks before stopping at a larger home that had probably been a French villa at one time but was now divided into a multiple-family dwelling. I think the area we were in was actually supposed to be off limits to Americans, but I wasn't sure— and in any event, I wasn't about to try to find out.

FRED: How were you planning to get back to Long Binh?

STEVE: There was a bus or convoy that left Bien Hoa Airbase for Long Binh a half hour before dusk. I figured I'd leave Linh's home around 8 pm, flag down a Lambretta and have him take me to the pickup point, keeping in mind the warning we'd heard when we first arrived in Long Binh: "Never go to Bien Hoa after dark."

FRED: By this time had you learned enough Vietnamese to be able to converse with the civilians?

STEVE: Not really. Most of their words consisted of no more than four letters, sometimes five. One might wonder how you could construct an entire vocabulary out of mostly three and four-letter words, but the spelling of those words could be very deceptive.

FRED: The natives had a half a dozen accent marks that could change the way words were pronounced, such as having the voice go up or down at the end of a word. A single word might have five different meanings, depending on the pronunciation. For those who knew nothing about the language, it would be easy to mispronounce words and create a lot of confusion among the civilians.

STEVE: Right. Take the three-letter word "pho." If you pronounced it "FUH" (like the English word "foot" without the t) it meant a soup made with rice noodles that was very popular in Vietnam for breakfast, lunch or dinner. But most Americans would look at "pho" and pronounce it "FOE" which apparently meant "lady of the evening."

FRED: So a little caution was in order when having dinner with a Vietnamese family! And having read the pamphlet about Vietnamese Culture and Customs, you knew you were supposed to remove your shoes when entering the home? And that if they put their palms together and bowed their heads slightly, you were supposed to do the same instead of trying to shake hands?

STEVE: And never, ever pat them on the back! I went in, removed my shoes and Linh introduced me to her parents who appeared to be in their late 40's. There were two pre-teens who I think were Linh's brother and sister, plus some old geezer in his 60's. I'm not sure if he was her grandfather or uncle, but everyone showed great reverence for him, as was the custom in their culture.

FRED: Nobody spoke English, so you had to rely on your French?

STEVE: Yeah, the parents and the kids spoke French but Gramps only spoke Vietnamese and seemed grumpy. (Perhaps he didn't like having an American there.) I brought my trusty notepad, plus a pocket-sized and rather dog-eared French/English dictionary.

FRED: What did you talk about?

STEVE: Just as I had suspected, we spent most of our time trying to figure out what was being said back and forth, with me writing or drawing on the pad and consulting my dictionary about every two minutes. Each time something was successfully communicated, they'd have to translate it into Vietnamese for Gramps. There was a lot of giggling with an occasional laugh here and there, so everyone seemed to be having a good time... except for "Grumpy the Dog."

FRED: Who was that?

STEVE: They introduced Gramps to me as "Chien." In Vietnamese it means "warrior"— pronounced with a hard "ch" as in "chicken." But if you pronounce it with a soft "ch" as in "champagne," it's the French word for dog. So I had to caution myself not to be calling Linh's grandfather a pooch. As soon as my brain visualized "chien" it would want to pronounce it with that soft "ch" just the way my Belgian French teacher taught me in high school.

FRED: Another verbal land mine to be avoided at all costs! So then everyone sat down and ate Hen's Foot Soup?

STEVE: We sat on floor mats around a large table that was about a foot high. The menu consisted mainly of vegetables, fish and rice plus a bowl of pho— the soup— and thin slices of marinated beef as an appetizer.

FRED: Were you able to tell if it was actually beef, or was it water buffalo? I'm not sure they had any cows in Nam.

STEVE: I wondered about that and would have asked Linh, but I couldn't figure out how to do it without possibly sounding rude, so I didn't. The main course turned out to be sauteed eel, which is very popular among the natives. They also had spring rolls dipped in the infamous nuoc mam fish sauce which smelled awful but tasted pretty good. Linh showed me how to pinch my nose shut as I ate it so as to avoid the smell.

FRED: And then what about the hen's feet?

STEVE: They set a bowl of soup in front of me with a hideous giant claw floating on top. I thought it was either a grotesque mistake or perhaps a prank someone was playing on the new guy.

FRED: Maybe old Grumpy didn't like having to watch some punk American G.I. leering at his granddaughter!

STEVE: But Linh had a claw in her bowl, too. I asked "qu'est-ce que c'est?" ("what is that?") and she said it was "FUH" (pho) with a "pied du poulet" (a foot of a chicken) on top. I asked her to write the name of the soup on my pad, then watched as she wrote P-H-O. Unfortunately my photographic memory immediately processed and stored this information as "FOE" instead of "FUH."

FRED: What was the point of putting a chicken foot in your soup?

STEVE: In many parts of the world, hen's feet are reputed to be the tastiest part of the chicken. Linh showed me how to strip the meat off the claw without swallowing the fragile bones. I quit about halfway through, so she happily finished my claw for me. The fact that I had never seen or eaten a chicken's foot prompted considerable discussion around the table, mostly in Vietnamese.

FRED: So did you think it was tastier than plain old chicken?

STEVE: I couldn't really say. But my wife, having grown up on a farm in Wisconsin, says her parents loved eating chicken's feet. She, on the other hand, refused to try them because they were so creepy.

FRED: And then you saw your first Vietnamese toilet?

STEVE: Yeah, I asked Linh to direct me to the toilette (that's French.) The next thing I know I'm looking at this "mop sink" on the floor. It had a round hole in the middle and what looked like foot rests on each side, plus a small hose attached to a receptacle on the wall. I stared at it and finally decided that one was apparently supposed to squat over the hole, take a dump and then wash everything down the hole with the hose after you were done.

FRED: And you thanked your lucky stars that you only had to pee! Then how were you planning to get back to Long Binh?

STEVE: I had to leave by 8 pm to beat the curfew. I planned to walk out on the street and flag down a Lambretta to take me to the bus pickup point. But the streets were deserted. No Lambrettas.

FRED: So you started walking... but you immediately got lost because you had no idea which way to turn, or how to get to the pickup point. On top of that you were in an off-limits area and the MP's would soon be doing a drive-through, looking for violators to toss into the pokey. At which point you'd be AWOL. You were in the proverbial pickle, so to speak!

STEVE: Indeed I was. Plus I remembered the old warning that "the Americans own Bien Hoa in the daytime, but Charlie owns it at night!" At which point I was sincerely hoping that was simply another wild rumor, like so many others we had heard. Finally I spotted a Lambretta and flagged him down. It was nearly dark out, so I figured I'd probably missed the bus already. I told him I wanted to go to Long Binh and he said "No go Long Binh! Too late!"

FRED: It was about a 10 or 12-mile round trip to Long Binh and back— and the normal fare was like a buck and a quarter, if that. He probably didn't want to drive Route 15 all alone in the pitch dark. So you had to do some persuading, right?

STEVE: Yeah, but with the natives— money talks! Being in no position to argue, I whipped out a 10-dollar bill in military currency (which technically we weren't allowed to give to civilians, but which was highly coveted by them.) He said "OK, Long Binh! We dee-dee now!" Meaning "OK soldier boy, let's get the heck out of here!"

FRED: And so you were off on another wild ride?

STEVE: Well, those Lambrettas probably had a top end of maybe 35 carrying a single passenger as opposed to four GI's, but as soon as we hit the edge of town he cranked that baby up to full throttle— never let off it 'til we got to the main gate at Long Binh. I'm sure he realized he was in some danger from both the Americans as well as the VC, if either side should spot him on that road at night.

FRED: By the way, didn't you make a big "faux pas" when you were getting ready to leave Linh's house in Bien Hoa?

STEVE: Yeah, I got up and everyone began smiling and bowing as we said our "au revoirs." I thanked them for the dinner and since everyone had made such a big deal about the hen's foot soup, I added "merci pour le FOE extraordinaire," meaning thanks for the excellent noodle soup. Unfortunately this caused quite a commotion because what I had actually said— as I was gazing fondly at Linh, decked out in her beautiful ao-dai dress which was slit up the sides all the way to her waist, revealing her floor-length silk pants underneath— was "thank you for the excellent high-class prostitute!"

FRED: Ooops!

STEVE: Well, "Gramps" might not have known much French, but he surely understood what he thought he had just heard! Suddenly he gets very agitated and starts jabbering away in Vietnamese as he's gesturing wildly with his hands.

FRED: And there was no way you could apologize to him, since you didn't speak Vietnamese and he didn't speak English or French.

STEVE: Right. Linh immediately turns to me and says "FUH, pas FOE! FUH, pas FOE!" which meant "it's FUH, not FOE, you idiot!" She then starts trying to explain to the family members what I really meant. Eventually things start to calm down and everyone begins to laugh. It was only later that I found out what FOE actually meant.

FRED: Well, look at it this way... surely it could have been even worse. At least you didn't tell Chien— AKA Gramps— "Nice to have made your acquaintance, you Dog!"

STEVE: I don't think I did. But anyway, a couple days later I found myself staring at a naked French woman!

FRED: Where? In your dreams?

STEVE: No, in real life. While the big USO shows were headlined by superstars like Bob Hope and Nancy Sinatra, there was a completely separate "circuit" for little shows that traveled around the country under contract to the US military. Their main function was to bring a modicum of entertainment— cheesy though it might have been— to the troops at small bases out in the boonies. This was supposed to boost morale as well as dissuade the average infantry grunt from wanting to spend his free time consorting with prostitutes.

FRED: You mean entertainment like acrobats from New Zealand or rock bands from the Phillippines. They'd also hit the hospitals along the way, and they'd show up unannounced.

STEVE: True, they'd just come rolling into our compound in their beat-up van once the guards waved them in. So one afternoon someone comes into the Orderly Room and says "Hey, there's a USO show setting up over in the Mess Hall, and we need an audience!"

FRED: The performers didn't really care how big the audience was— they just had a contract that said they were supposed to put on so many performances at so many locations. I don't think the 24th even had very many patients yet. So the CO sent you over there as a spectator and told you to round up some more along the way. Did you find anyone?

STEVE: I managed to collar a couple guys, but few were eager to attend a show when they didn't even know who or what it was. So we had maybe half a dozen troops and a few patients sitting at tables in the Mess Hall watching this group set up their stuff.

FRED: And the performers were French?

STEVE: Well they were speaking French— they could have been from Belgium or Switzerland or whatever, but none spoke English. There were two men plus a blonde woman who appeared to be on the high side of 40— and at least 20 pounds overweight. One of the guys— her husband, perhaps— was like the manager or emcee, while the other was in charge of the record player and sound system.

FRED: So the blonde woman was the only performer?

STEVE: Yeah, the DJ started playing records and the woman began singing in French. With each subsequent number, she'd remove an article of clothing. At first I thought she was just hot due to the lack of air conditioning. But soon I realized she was performing a strip-tease— and apparently doing so in the twilight of her career.

FRED: So half a dozen GI's sat dumbfounded as they watched her perform at 3 in the afternoon. At what point did she stop?

STEVE: I think she'd gotten down to a thong and pasties, where-upon the music stopped and we applauded— all eight of us— mostly out of politeness. She put her clothes back on as the men packed up their gear, then hopped in the van and left.

FRED: And since none of 'em spoke English, no words were ever exchanged between the trio and the audience?

STEVE: No, and it's probably just as well that we didn't have many patients there— a bunch of combat veteran hecklers might not have been as polite as we were.

FRED: Did you ever in your wildest imagination think you'd be sent off to war and then have your commanding officer in a combat zone order you to sit and watch some blonde taking her clothes off?

STEVE: Can't say as I did, but it reminded me of a peculiar situation in which I had found myself back in civilian life.

FRED: Your boss ordered you to watch women disrobe?

STEVE: Yup. In college I had a summer job working for a printing company in Manhattan, just a block or so from the United Nations. I worked from noon 'til 8 pm as a combination messenger, gofer and typesetter's assistant. The shift changed at 4 pm, when the big pressroom went dark. The night shift consisted of just one typesetter—"Gino"—plus me there to do whatever he instructed me to do, such as operating the proof press or going out to get him some lunch.

FRED: So there weren't any women there.

STEVE: Not in our building. Our plant occupied the entire 5th floor and after 5 pm, the back side of the shop was completely dark. Right across the alley was a high-rise hotel . Since our building was dark, a lot of the hotel guests didn't bother to close their drapes. Whenever things were slow in the type shop, Gino would instruct me to "patrol" the dark side of our building by strolling back and forth to see if anything interesting was going on across the way.

FRED: Meaning you got paid to watch women disrobe! If you saw anything happening you were supposed to go get Gino, right?

STEVE: Exactly. Naturally I had to wait a bit to see if the situation really merited my interrupting Gino's work. So I'd be sitting there in the dark, watching something develop, and of course if it looked really good I wasn't about to jump up and run to find Gino.

FRED: And what would happen then?

STEVE: Well he wore these work shoes with thick rubber soles, so of course I couldn't hear him approaching. I'd be sitting there in the dark, watching the windows, when all of a sudden I'd feel a hand on my shoulder. Gino would say "Anything goin' on over there?"

FRED: Aha, caught in the act!

STEVE: Invariably I would say "Uh, this just started right here, I was just about to come and get ya!" Sometimes it was like watching a live sex show— the best views were of the 4th floor participants, one level below ours. I have no idea if those people were married couples or hookers with johns or what. But whoever they were, they weren't about to wait 'til bedtime to start gettin' it on!

FRED: Maybe they were honeymooners. But you went home at 8 pm, so you probably missed most of the action, don't ya think?

STEVE: I suppose I did. Gino was there alone after that, since he didn't get off until midnight.

FRED: Or sometimes a bit sooner, perhaps?

&&&&&&&&&&&&&&&&&&&

FACT OR FICTION? *The story goes that a small touring USO Show arrived unexpectedly and set up in the 24th Evac Mess Hall. The first act was a ventriloquist dressed in a cowboy outfit with a dummy wearing a nicely tailored set of jungle fatigues. The show begins and soon the dummy is telling a series of dumb blonde jokes. After the fourth or fifth one, a young blonde nurse suddenly stands up in the audience and shouts "Hold on there! We've heard about enough of your stupid blonde jokes. What makes you think you can stereotype blonde women that way? It's people like you who make others think all blondes are dumb!" The somewhat embarrassed ventriloquist starts to apologize, whereupon the nurse yells "You stay out of this! I'm talking to that little twerp sitting on your knee!"*

SEE MORE THAN 30 PHOTOS AT:
www.longbinhdaze.com

CHAPTER 37

WOODY AND STUMPY
TAKE THE WHITE HOUSE
Our fellow inductees are reunited...
at 1600 Pennsylvania Avenue

STEVE: It was only a few weeks after my dinner in Bien Hoa with Linh and her family that she suddenly wasn't working at the PX any more. I surmised that she'd probably been transferred to a different PX, or maybe quit her job for some reason.

FRED: You didn't think her departure had anything to do with the fact that you failed to commence a romantic relationship with her? Or that maybe the Army had discovered she was an enemy spy?

STEVE: Well I had no idea, but I decided not to try to draw any conclusions. Maybe she already knew she'd be leaving when she invited me to meet her family. Then again, maybe she'd met her maker while on a night raid with her VC commando squad. At any rate, you and I were getting too "short" to be concerned about such things.

FRED: A GI was "short" when he had less than 30 days remaining before his DEROS (Date Eligible to Return from Overseas.) Inside his wall locker he'd put up a "Short Timer's Calendar" divided into 30 numbered squares. Each day he'd fill in a new square with a colored marker. When they were all filled in, it meant he would be climbing aboard a "Freedom Bird" (jet airliner) the next morning to fly home to CONUS. Maybe Linh was too heartbroken to want to stick around and wave goodbye as you disappeared forever.

STEVE: Seems unlikely, although Louie did have a reaction that was somewhat in that vein. The issue of "how short are you?" is where the expression "23 days and a wake-up" came from, as well as the lament that "Aw Sarge, I'm too damned short for this!" The latter meant to imply that an assigned task was too menial, nasty or dangerous for someone who was just days away from being set free for good.

FRED: In infantry units, troops were often pulled out of the field when they had only a week or two to go before the end of their tour. This was done partly to avoid the panic that would often set in among superstitious GI's who felt that the closer they got to those final few days, the more likely they were to get wounded or killed. It was also considered to be bad for troop morale if a soldier should buy the farm just a couple days before his DEROS.

STEVE: In the case of our fellow inductee Ken "Stumpy" Stumpf, his unit pulled him out of action once they learned he was going to receive the Medal of Honor. They wanted to be sure he'd still be alive for the ceremony at the White House. But Stumpy fooled 'em. At the urging of a friend, he volunteered to go out on a "four day ambush" anyway, since he had never been on one before.

FRED: And of course he would eventually volunteer for two additional tours in Nam as well. Some would say that might qualify him as either an adrenaline junkie or a glutton for punishment. Or both.

STEVE: Meanwhile, most of the guys in the 24th Evac had come over together on the Weigel in June of '66. Which meant nearly all would be going home in June '67. And many would spend their final 30 days religiously working on their suntans whenever possible so as to look like combat veterans when they got home.

FRED: Or at least to avoid having people say "You just spent a year in Vietnam? Where the hell is your tan?" But there were a handful of guys like us who had to extend our tours by about 10 days so that when we arrived in CONUS, we'd be under the 90-day cutoff. If you arrived in the continental USA with 89 or fewer days left in the service, you automatically got an "early out" since the Army figured you'd be of little use to them anyway— just hanging around, eatin' their chow and takin' up space while continuing to draw a paycheck.

STEVE: And doggedly defying the orders of your superiors! I was glad those guys were leaving together because I hated saying goodbye to friends when I knew I'd probably never see 'em again. Although I'd learned to lighten it up a bit by saying "Well, so long Frankie... have a nice life!" When everyone left together, you could just sort of wave goodbye to the whole group at once. Less emotional that way.

FRED: And the guys in our hooch were from states ranging all the way from California to New Jersey, so it was unlikely we'd ever run across 'em again. I thought about trying to collect everyone's home address, but someone volunteered to gather all that info and make copies for everyone so I thought "Great, that's all taken care of!" Unfortunately whoever it was apparently dropped the ball, since we never received any such document after we got home.

STEVE: Which meant that when we decided to try to have a reunion with those guys some 35 years later, we had to try to track down each one. We found most of 'em, but it would have been impossible without the internet since in a lot of cases we couldn't remember what city or state they were from. Ultimately we managed to have a reunion with about a half dozen of our pals in 2002.

FRED: Meanwhile as our DEROS approached in Long Binh, we were convinced we had "beaten the fuggin' system" enough times to be able to go home with a clear sense of having accomplished our goals. But we were rank amateurs at it when compared to SP4 Bengston, who took over as Company Clerk after Maxwell went home. One of the more devious individuals we'd ever met, he was always looking for ways to subvert the system, either for his own benefit or to try to make himself more popular among his peers.

STEVE: And popularity was indeed a problem for him. Whereas his predecessor was loved by all, Bengston always seemed to rub people the wrong way, even though he did try to be friendly much of the time. I worked with him for 4-5 months and I'd swear he didn't have a single friend that I knew of. I was probably the closest thing to it, now that I think about it, since we were both originally from the east coast and I sort of understood his brand of aloofness.

FRED: Bengston also bunked in our hooch. About every two weeks he'd get a really gushy, somewhat lurid love letter from his "squeeze" back in the states who, judging by the snapshot in his wallet, was quite a looker. He reveled in reading passages aloud to his buddies or passing the letters around for us to read. We marveled at how he could have so charmed that lovely damsel as to cause her to be thoroughly enthralled with him. Charm did not seem to be his strong suit.

STEVE: For some reason I began to get suspicious about the origins of those juicy typewritten missives. I noticed they looked like they could have been composed on the same brand of typewriter we used in HQ. Also the lower case "w" had a slight break in it that made it quite distinctive. One day Bengston was about to head over to the shower, wrapped in a towel, when I said "Hey, lemme read that latest letter you got." He handed it to me and headed out the door of our tent.

FRED: And you immediately scurried over to the office with it?

STEVE: Purely on a hunch, yes. I opened his desk drawer, found a document he'd typed and compared it to the love letter. Not only was the same broken "w" there, but there were several other idiosyncrasies that matched on both documents. Sonofabitch, Bengston!

FRED: So he'd been writing and addressing those mushy letters himself? Sending them home in a larger envelope to a confederate who would turn around and mail them back to him?

STEVE: Apparently so. It was pretty hilarious but also kind of pathetic, so I decided not to confront him with it. That is until one day when he did something that pissed me off and I blurted "How come this letter looks like it was typed on your own typewriter???" He snatched it out of my hand, locked it in his footlocker and stomped out of the tent without saying a word.

FRED: Did any more love letters to Bengston arrive after that?

STEVE: Well let's just say that if they did, he wasn't showing 'em to anybody. In 2002 I did attempt to locate him to invite him to our reunion, but nobody could remember his first name— a good sign that he probably didn't have any close friends at the 24th Evac. Everyone just called him Bengston.

FRED: But there were also times when Bengston's devious methods were put to good use for the benefit of many of us. Like when he cooked up fake travel orders for just about anyone who wanted them.

STEVE: True. Those of us who were due to be discharged as soon as we set foot on California soil were supposed to be given travel orders allowing us to fly "Military Standby" (half price) for up to 72 hours after our discharge. We were also given enough airfare in a travel voucher to get us to our homes, wherever they might be. But you and I, for example, wanted our travel orders to cover a 14-day period so we could visit friends and relatives in California before flying back to Wisconsin.

FRED: Our CO was due to leave several weeks ahead of us but his replacement hadn't arrived yet. Since his only remaining duty was to sign travel orders for each soldier as they departed, he took a whole stack of blank order forms, signed them and handed them to Bengston to fill them out on his typewriter as they were needed. Then the Captain caught a ride on the next Freedom Bird and was a civilian in less than a week.

STEVE: So now Bengston had this stack of signed orders on which he could type any damned thing he wanted. He immediately started asking guys what they wanted on their "custom" travel orders, so we asked for 14 days and I think he gave us 21.

FRED: I was always saving documents for posterity, like our travel orders from Milwaukee to Missouri and from Long Binh back to Wisconsin after our separation from the service. I've checked and sure enough, Bengston's broken "w" is right there on that document. And it was valid for 21 days after its issuance.

STEVE: When a GI flew Standby, he had to be in uniform and have a valid Military ID, plus a set of of travel orders authorizing him to be in that airport on that particular date. It was routine for the MP's— while looking for AWOL's, deserters or impostors— to stop soldiers in an airport and ask to see their ID cards and travel orders.

FRED: But we surrendered our ID's when we were discharged.

STEVE: So there we were, having already been civilians for two weeks (which technically made us impostors, since we were still in uniform) flying on fake travel orders that authorized us to fly Military Standby for half price. All thanks to our buddy SP4 Bengston.

FRED: And having no ID's made us a bit nervous when we'd see MP's patrolling in an airport. We tried to maintain proper military bearing so as not to arouse their suspicions, making sure to salute all officers— Air Force, Marines, Salvation Army, whatever.

STEVE: But of course if we had confronted some Marine Captain and the bastard chewed us out for not saluting, we probably could have just said "Screw you, jarhead! The Uniform Code of Military Justice doesn't apply to civilians, which is what we are, so you can just take a hike! You can't touch us, pal!'"

FRED: Sure enough... and we wind up in the brig! But Bengston's crowning achievement had to be when he promoted himself to sergeant just two days before he left for the states. Unlike most of us who were draftees, he'd enlisted for three years— which meant he'd have another year to serve when he returned to CONUS. So naturally he thought "Well, why not go back as a Sergeant instead of a Specialist Fourth Class? I've got the blank documents and copies of the CO's signature that I need to forge my promotion orders, and by the time I put those stripes on my sleeve (after a 30-day leave) I'll be surrounded by complete strangers at Fort Lewis. They won't be any the wiser!" So that's exactly what he did.

STEVE: But he just couldn't resist telling someone... so he told me. Then on the day before we were supposed to catch our Freedom Bird back to the states, we were getting ready to leave for the Departure Center that afternoon. We had to circle through the compound to bid adieu to the few remaining friends who hadn't gone home yet. I noticed that Louie wasn't anywhere to be found, so I started asking everyone "Where the hell is Louie?"

FRED: Finally someone said he was hiding in the back of the Supply office because he didn't want to have to say goodbye to you.

STEVE: Yeah, I went in and found him sitting there alone. I said "Louie, what are you doin' in here?" "I dunno." I said "Don't you wanna say goodbye before I leave?" He stared at the floor without saying a word, so I asked "What's the matter?" He softly answered "I think maybe I never know anybody like you again."

FRED: Undoubtedly referring to the fact that you had taken him under your wing and bonded with him, whereas most everyone else treated him like he was just some dumb gook.

STEVE: Apparently so. I said "Well you might be right, but you'll probably meet someone else even better than me."

FRED: Did you believe that when you said it?

STEVE: Naaah! But I shook his hand and told him I never could have done my job without him and I'd be grateful to him for the rest of my life. Those things I sincerely did believe. Six months later I tried writing him a letter, care of the 24th Evac. But I never heard back, so I figured the CIA probably intercepted it and was busily trying to decode it to figure out what secret spy messages I was sending to some heretofore unknown enemy agent.

FRED: By then he'd probably been drafted into the South Vietnamese Army... or shanghaied by the Viet Cong. Of course if he was still alive when the Communists eventually took over, he probably would have been executed for collaborating with the Americans.

STEVE: And on that pleasant note... we shift to the next morning when we were bussed to Bien Hoa Airbase to catch our flight. We stood waiting in line in our Class B khaki uniforms as a planeload of troops disembarked from the chartered Continental Airlines jet that would soon be taking us home.

FRED: Then as that "new meat" slowly walked past us on the tarmac, you were treated to a "last laugh" moment, brief though it was.

STEVE: Yeah, I spotted my old Drill Sergeant from Basic Training and hollered "Hey Sergeant Blackburn, remember me?" He said "Why sure I do, Long Dick! How ya doin'?" I said "I'm doin' great—goin' home today!" Of course he was facing another 364 days in Nam, while I was about to be set free!

FRED: Was he still wearing his Smokey Bear hat?

STEVE: It seems like he might have been, I'm not sure. But if he was, that would explain how I was able to spot him so easily. In Basic he was the one with the gruff baritone voice that made him sound like a real hard-ass. (Reminiscent of Karl, the character played by Billy Bob Thornton in the movie "Sling Blade.") He's also the one who asked why a big long-legged sumbitch like me couldn't run any faster. But I could tell he was really a softie at heart. Plus I'm pretty sure no one else has ever called me Long Dick, either before or since.

FRED: Not that they wouldn't have had any reason to! So then when our plane took off and we saw the shoreline of Nam disappearing below us, we all let out a big cheer. Since planes didn't want to stay on the ground any longer than necessary in Bien Hoa, we were scheduled for a refueling stop in either Guam or Okinawa. As we approached the airfield, they announced "Absolutely NO picture taking allowed!" Sounded rather odd until, from the air, we saw row after row of B-52 bombers parked on the ground. So naturally I grabbed my Nikon and started snapping away.

STEVE: I suppose you just had to "beat the fuggin' system" one more time, didn't ya?

FRED: Well hell, what were they gonna do— send me to Vietnam? We took off once more in daylight, but since we were flying east at 600 mph, soon it was pitch dark.

STEVE: I was too excited to sleep, so I watched the two inflight movies thinking I'd catch some Z's as soon as the second one ended. But by then the sun was already coming up ahead of us, and once more I couldn't sleep! (After all, how often does one get to witness dawn at 30,000 feet?)

FRED: As each hour of flight time went by, we'd pass through another time zone. So a 10-hour eastbound flight might eat up 20 hours of "wristwatch time." Once we could see the coast of California it was nearing twilight again. Everyone was happy as hell except for the two flight attendants who were sitting stone-faced in their little rear-facing jumpseats.

STEVE: I figured they probably did this three or four times a week, so it was nothing special to them. We circled the airfield three, four, maybe five times. I think it was Travis Air Force Base, about 30 miles north of the Oakland Army Terminal, which is where we would eventually be processed out. Seemed a little odd, but no big deal— hell, we were practically home!

FRED: Finally they gave us clearance to land and as we started our approach, we could see fire engines and emergency vehicles racing along the frontage road right next to our runway.

STEVE: I slapped Fred on the shoulder and jokingly said "Look, they're all coming out to greet us!" Little did we know that was exactly what they were doing. It seems we had blown one or more tires on our previous takeoff and the pilot had no way of knowing how many tires were left. So he had to circle to dump fuel, then wait for the emergency vehicles to get in position, ready for the worst.

FRED: And from that day on, our friends and families would have spoken with great reverence about the day we flew home from the war and almost made it back to California! When we finally landed they had us exit the plane right there on the runway as soon as it could roll to a stop. That's when they told us what the flight attendants had already known when they looked so somber during the approach— we had been attempting a landing on some unknown number of flat tires. They had just decided not to tell us, figuring "these guys are so elated, why ruin their day at this point?"

STEVE: By the time we were bussed to the Oakland Army Terminal it was approaching midnight. We had to stand in line for more outprocessing despite not having eaten for something like eight or ten hours, and I for one had not slept for about 24. But they put us on another bus and some NCO climbed aboard to make an announcement: "Gentlemen, welcome back to CONUS. President Johnson has decreed that every soldier returning from Vietnam shall immediately be served a first-class steak dinner with all the trimmings! We're on our way to the Mess Hall now."

FRED: Which would have been great, except that by then it was like 2:30 am. That steak, onion rings and apple pie was probably the best meal we ever had in the service, but most of us just wanted some sack time at that point. (Thanks anyhow, Lyndon!)

STEVE: The next day we finally were separated from the Army and immediately called our 24th Evac buddy Dave McMillan, who lived just a few miles from Oakland. He picked us up (as he had promised) and took us to his parents' home in Berkeley.

FRED: We already knew Dave's dad was a physics professor at UC Berkeley... plus a key member of the Manhattan Project team that built the first A-Bomb... and a Nobel Prize winning physicist. Seems he had merely helped invent radar and sonar as well as create the elements neptunium and plutonium. That evening we had a great dinner with Dave, his brother and his parents at their home.

STEVE: The whole time I couldn't stop thinking "How many guys get to come home from Nam and 24 hours later be having dinner with a Nobel Prize winner?" Soon afterward we visited my two sisters who lived in San Jose and North Hollywood, respectively. Then it was back to Wisconsin (flying Military Standby on fake orders, of course) to finish working on our college degrees before launching our careers in Marketing (Fred) and Journalism (me.)

FRED: Now as for our fellow inductees "Woody" Woodson and "Stumpy" Stumpf. The Army trained Woody as an aircraft mechanic and sent him off to Germany, where he eventually became an Air Traffic Controller, which he really enjoyed. After his separation from the service he became a staff photographer for the Washington Post, later authoring a book about "roadside diners across the USA."

STEVE: Eventually Woody wound up back in France (where he had grown up) and was working as a French-to-English translator prior to his retirement. Stumpy, meanwhile, served his three tours in Nam and then, after 29 years in the Army, retired as a Sergeant Major. He had already received the Congressional Medal of Honor (CMH) following his first tour in Nam.

FRED: Woody had been Stumpy's squad leader in Basic Training, which is how they became friends, after which they never saw each other again until sometime after they were discharged. When Stumpy was invited to the White House in '68 to receive his CMH, Woody was assigned to cover that same event as on-scene photographer for the Washington Post.

STEVE: Stumpy proceeds to march into the White House Reception Hall with the other CMH honorees to meet the President and who should he see standing there holding a camera but his old squad leader— Woody Woodson! After the ceremony the two had a chance to visit. They subsequently ran into each other again at a similar event in Los Angeles.

FRED: Then in 1984, Stumpy was honored at a "Welcome Home" parade in New York where he had a chance to meet and talk to none other than Donald Trump, in the flesh. By then Mister Trump had become old enough to run for President. Despite his denials that he would ever consider doing so, he might have thought it prudent to start getting cozy with the veterans and the veterans groups. Especially since "bone spurs" on his heel had kept him out of Nam.

STEVE: It's too bad that Trump's grandfather had changed the family name from Drumpf to Trump when he came to the USA as an immigrant from Germany.

FRED: Why? What difference would that have made?

STEVE: Well if he hadn't changed it, they could have introduced the two of them to each other by saying "Kenny Stumpf, I'd like you to meet Donny Drumpf!" Some 25 years later, Stumpy would be invited to another ceremony honoring the living CMH recipients at the White House, where he would meet President Obama.

FRED: Hold on a minute, there's a phone call for you... it's Brigadier General Bengston, our old buddy— right up there with Trump as a veritable master of self-promotion! He wants to know if we're planning to have a 50th reunion for the 24th Evac.

STEVE: Tell him we'd be happy to, if we weren't stuck in the brig at San Francisco International Airport— no thanks to him! By the way, here's a little footnote to our story. While having a CAT scan to search for kidney stones, I was recently surprised to find out I was born with only one kidney. According to the Army's Standards of Medical Fitness, "Absence of one kidney... is a cause for rejection for appointment, enlistment or induction into the US Army."

FRED: So in other words, while I was getting on the train to go to Leonard Wood, you should have been riding a bus back to Madison! At least having only one kidney sounds more legit than having bone spurs on your foot. Tough luck, I guess. It might have kept you out of the draft. But if you think it'll keep you off my list of potential kidney donors— should I ever need one— you are wrong, my friend!

STEVE: But I'm the one who's more likely to need a donor. I'll be pounding on YOUR door yelling "You gotta be kidneying me!"

&&&&&&&&&&&&&&&&&&&&

FACT OR FICTION? The story goes that SP5 Linderman wrote his wife and asked for a harmonica, explaining that learning to play it would help occupy his free time and keep his mind off all the readily available women in Bien Hoa. She sent the best one she could find, along with some instruction books. When his tour finally ended and he arrived home, he said "Why don't we go out and have a fancy dinner and some wine— then we'll come back and make love all night long!" Whereupon his wife said "Not so fast, Buster... Let's hear you play that harmonica first."

SEE MORE THAN 30 PHOTOS AND SUBMIT YOUR OWN BOOK REVIEW AT:
www.longbinhdaze.com

GLOSSARY

Air ambulance: A medical evacuation helicopter, AKA "Dustoff."

Air Cav: Air Cavalry— troops who ride into battle on helicopters.

AIT: Advanced Individual Training in a specific Military Occupation such as Radio Repairman, Tank Driver or Medical Corpsman.

AK-47: Russian or Chinese assault rifle carried by VC and NVA troops.

AOD or OD: Administrative Officer of the Day.

Ao-dai: Ankle-length tight-fitting formal dress of brightly colored silk worn by Vietnamese women. Slit up the sides to the waist revealing black or white silk slacks underneath.

Article 15: A disciplinary measure by which a commanding officer can administer punishment (such as docking of pay) to a soldier guilty of a petty crime or violation of regulations.

ARVN: Army of the Republic of Vietnam (the South Vietnamese army.)

AWOL: Absent without leave.

Ba Moui Ba: The brand name of a Vietnamese beer ("33 Beer") that was rumored to be brewed with formaldehyde as a preservative.

Base camp: "Home base" for an infantry company; a resupply base offering hot food and showers. Standard location for unit headquarters.

Bird: Army slang for any helicopter.

Boo-coo: A Vietnamese bastardization of the French word "beaucoup" which means much, many or "a whole lot."

Boom-boom: Vietnamese slang for having sex, presumably for money.

Boonies or bush: Infantry slang meaning a rural area out in the field.

BP: Blood pressure.

C-123: Twin-engine cargo plane used to haul troops or supplies.

C-4: A plastic explosive compound carried by GI's for blowing up stuff. Also used in tiny amounts for quickly heating coffee or C-rations.

Charlie: Nickname for a Viet Cong (VC) soldier, derived from the words "Victor Charlie" in the Military Phonetic Alphabet.

Chieu Hoi: A program by which enemy soldiers were offered a financial reward for laying down their weapons or defecting.

Chinook: The CH-47 twin-rotor cargo helicopter used for the transporting of supplies, troops and hospital patients.

Choi oi!: A Vietnamese exclamation of surprise similar to "Holy cow!"

Chopper: Slang for helicopter, often frowned upon by Army crewmen who preferred to refer to their aircraft as "birds."

CID: Criminal Investigation Division charged with investigating criminal activity such as homicides and drug use among American troops.

Claymore: A portable anti-personnel mine carried by infantry soldiers and packed with C-4 explosive. It could be set out at night to fire hundreds of little steel balls in a 60-degree fan-shaped spray when triggered by a trip wire or handheld detonator.

CMH: Congressional Medal of Honor.

CO: Commanding Officer; often referred to as "the Six" in radio code. Could also mean a "Conscientious Objector" who was drafted with the understanding that he would not be required to carry a weapon.

COL: Colonel.

Concertina wire: Barbed wire or "razor wire" that comes in long coils which can be expanded or contracted like a musical squeeze box.

CONEX: A heavy corrugated steel shipping container used for transporting cargo overseas. Often retained for use as storage containers, sleeping quarters or bomb shelters.

CONUS: The continental United States.

Corpsman: Medical Corpsman; another name for a medic. An Army infantry company usually had one Medical Corpsman assigned to each platoon, plus a senior Medical Corpsman assigned to the command post.

Court martial: A court of military officers that tries soldiers who are accused of serious offenses against military law.

Crew chief: The helicopter crew member responsible for the mechanical condition of the aircraft at all times. In flight, he functions as one of the two door gunners.

CP: Command Post.

CQ: Charge of Quarters. An officer or NCO assigned to remain in Headquarters overnight and assist the AOD (Officer of the Day) by taking phone calls, relaying messages and alerting the appropriate personnel of any impending dangers or problems.

CQ Runner: An enlisted man assigned to assist the CQ at night by delivering messages, retrieving equipment or summoning specific personnel to Headquarters.

C-rations: Boxed individual meals containing canned meat, vegetables, fruits, dessert, crackers, etc., plus essentials like toilet paper, gum, one P-38 can opener, matches, sugar, instant coffee and four cigarettes.

Dai uy: Vietnamese word for Captain, pronounced "dye-wee."

Dee-dee: Short for "didi mau," Vietnamese for "run away quickly" or "get out of here fast!" as in "we just saw three VC dee-dee down the hill!"

DEROS: Date Eligible to Return from Overseas. The day everyone awaited because it meant they'd be climbing aboard a Freedom Bird.

Deuce and a half: The two and a half ton, six-wheeled truck used to carry troops or supplies. Marines called them "six-bys" since all six wheels were drive wheels (6 by 6.)

Dink: A somewhat derogatory slang term for a Vietnamese person.

Dinky Dow: American bastardization of the Vietnamese phrase "dien cai dau" meaning crazy, as in "Mama-san, you dinky dow!"

DMZ: The Demilitarized Zone. A three-mile wide strip of "No Man's Land" separating North and South Vietnam.

Dong: A Vietnamese unit of money, AKA "piaster."

Door gunner: One of the two enlisted men who operate M-60 machine guns in the open side doors of a Huey helicopter in flight. The second gunner is usually the crew chief or a medic.

Dung lai: Vietnamese for "Halt!"

Dustoff: Nickname for an unarmed medical evacuation helicopter.

EM: Enlisted man: Any male member of the Army who's not a commissioned officer or warrant officer.

ETA: Estimated Time of Arrival.

Field-stripping: Tearing down a cigarette butt to reduce it to a few shreds of tobacco plus a tiny ball of white paper. The filter went into the soldier's pocket so that no trace was left out in the field.

Firebase: A temporary artillery encampment used for fire support of forward ground operations.

First Sergeant: The highest ranking enlisted man in a unit, usually a Master Sergeant (E-8) or Sergeant First Class (E-7.) Often nicknamed the "First Shirt" or "Top Sergeant" or just "Top" as in "Hey, Top!"

Flak jacket: A heavy vest filled with layers of fiberglass to protect soldiers from shrapnel and (to a limited degree) small arms fire.

Fragging: The attempted assassination of an officer or NCO with a fragmentation grenade that would leave no ballistic evidence.

Freedom Bird: The commercial jetliner that would land at Bien Hoa or Tan Son Nhut airbase to pick up troops who were ready to go home at the end of their one-year tour.

Gook: A somewhat derogatory slang term for a Vietnamese person.

Green Berets: U.S. Special Forces troops.

Grunt: An Army infantryman.

GSW: Gunshot wound.

Gunship: A Huey helicopter that's heavily armed with rocket pods, mini-guns, machine guns and/or grenade launchers.

Hooch: Any overnight living quarters which could be a tent, a hut, a building or a couple of ponchos fastened together to provide shelter.

Hot LZ: A helicopter landing zone that was believed to be under fire from the enemy.

HQ: Headquarters.

Huey: The Bell UH-1 single-rotor helicopter with many uses including ferrying troops to an LZ, resupplying them, evacuating casualties and providing close air support for infantry units on the ground.

In-country: Anywhere within the boundaries of Vietnam.

Jungle boot: A combination leather and canvas boot that was lighter and quicker to dry out than a traditional leather combat boot.

Jungle penetrator: A device used by a medevac helicopter crew to "hoist" a casualty from a combat zone via a winch and cable when the jungle canopy was too thick to allow the Huey to land.

KIA: Killed in Action.

Kill zone: The area around an explosive device in which a majority of all personnel will be killed when it detonates. Also can mean the area in front of an ambush setup or perimeter defense bunker in which a majority of all personnel will be killed when firing commences.

Kit Carson Scout: An enemy defector who would travel with an American infantry company as a guide and interpreter. Some defected for ideological reasons, others did it to become well-paid mercenaries.

KP: Kitchen police. Typically a soldier would get "stuck on KP" a couple times a month, having to spend all day in the Mess Hall washing dishes, peeling potatoes and assisting with food preparation.

Lambretta: Three-wheeled taxi built on a scooter platform; normally hauled four GI's at a time— or up to 12 Vietnamese.

Laterite: A reddish soil that got its color from heavy amounts of iron oxide. It could harden like cement when dry but turn to thick, gooey mud when it rained, especially during the annual monsoon season.

LBJ: A nickname for the Long Binh Jail, which in turn was a nickname for the Long Binh Stockade where American soldiers were incarcerated for various criminal acts or violations of military regulations.

Lifer: Any soldier or officer who was, or appeared to be, intending to make a career of the military. Often used in a derogatory sense, especially by draftees.

Litter: A stretcher used to carry the wounded from a battlefield.

Log flight: A helicopter mission in which a logistical resupply chopper flew out to the area where ground troops were situated to deliver food, water, ammo, mail and fresh clothing.

LP: Listening post. A concealed two-man guard post set up 30 or 40 yards outside the perimeter of an NDP (Night Defensive Position) to serve as an early warning system if enemy troops should approach.

LRRP Rations: Freeze-dried dehydrated meals designed to be carried by Long Range Reconnaissance teams who could be way out in the boonies (alone) for weeks at a time.

LRRP Team: A five to seven man team of daredevils who conducted "Long Range Reconnaissance Patrols" by sneaking far out into the jungle to observe and listen to enemy activity without initiating contact.

LT: Lieutenant.

LTC: Lieutenant Colonel.

LZ: Helicopter landing zone, often a makeshift clearing.

M-14: The standard infantry rifle (with a heavy wooden stock) issued to combat troops prior to 1966. Held a 20-round magazine.

M-16: The standard rifle issued to combat troops starting in about 1966. Its plastic stock made it much lighter than the M-14.

M-60: Standard light machine gun used by helicopter door gunners, also carried by the lone machine gunner in a light weapons platoon.

M-79: A hand-held grenade launcher for hurling 40mm grenades at enemy positions.

Malaria pills: Pills taken to prevent the serious tropical disease malaria. One type was taken weekly while the other was taken daily.

Mama-san: Term used by American soldiers that could refer to any Vietnamese female, but usually those over the age of 20 or 30.

MARS: Military Affiliate Radio System. A network of shortwave radio operators (both military and civilian) who would enable troops in Vietnam to talk to loved ones back home, if only for a few minutes.

MASH: Mobile Army Surgical Hospital

Medevac: A medical evacuation helicopter, often called a "Dustoff."

MFW: Multiple fragment wounds from a grenade, mine, bomb, mortar shell or artillery round.

MIA: Missing in action.

Military Intelligence: The process of acquiring vital information about the enemy, terrain and weather, then evaluating and disseminating it to those making decisions regarding combat operations.

Million-dollar wound: A combat wound that was serious enough to warrant the soldier's return to CONUS.

Mini-gun: An aircraft-mounted machine gun with six rotating barrels capable of firing up to 6,000 rounds per minute.

MOS: Military Occupational Specialty— the job you were trained for by the Army. Not necessarily the one you would wind up performing.

MP: Military police.

MPC: Military Payment Certificates paid to soldiers in a combat zone. Denominations ranged from 5 cents to 20 dollars (by 1968.)

MSGT: Master Sergeant (E-8.)

Napalm: Jellied petroleum used as an anti-personnel weapon. Burned so fiercely that enemy soldiers often suffocated from lack of oxygen.

NCO: Any Non-Commissioned Officer (Sergeant.)

NCOIC: Non-Commissioned Officer in charge.

NDP: Night Defensive Position where an infantry platoon or company would bed down for the night after first setting up defensive measures.

Number One: Vietnamese "pidgin-English" slang ("numbah wan") meaning very good or the best.

Number Ten: Vietnamese "pidgin-English" slang meaning very bad, really lousy or the worst.

NVA: The North Vietnamese Army— the enemy, along with the VC.

OD: Officer of the Day, assigned to remain in or near Headquarters overnight to be the officer in charge while everyone slept.

OP: Observation post. Similar to a Listening Post but operated during daylight when enemy infiltrators could be seen as well as heard.

OR: Operating Room.

P-38: A tiny folding metal can opener, could be carried in a pocket.

Papa-san: Term used by American soldiers that could refer to any Vietnamese male, but usually those over the age of 30.

Parachute flare: An illumination flare dropped from an aircraft or fired into the air by hand or by artillery.

PCPT: Physical Combat Proficiency Test given at the end of Basic Training to demonstrate a soldier's degree of physical fitness.

PFC: Private First Class (E-3.)

PIO: Public information officer; a "public relations man" or news media liaison for the US Army.

Point man: The first man in a column hiking through the bush. In jungle settings, the point man's primary responsibility was to watch for trip wires, ambushes and booby traps.

POW: Prisoner of war.

Pugil stick: A padded pole used for simulating bayonet combat.

Punji stakes: Sharpened bamboo sticks used in a primitive form of pit trap. Often smeared with excrement to cause infection.

Purple Heart: A U.S. military decoration awarded to any member of the Armed Forces wounded by enemy action.

PVT: Private (E-1 or E-2.)

PX: Post Exchange, a military store selling goods at discounted prices and ranging in size from a convenience store to a department store.

Quick Kill: Also known as "Instinct Shooting" or "Point and Shoot." A method of rapidly aiming and firing at an enemy soldier who suddenly appeared in thick jungle, perhaps only 20 yards away.

Red Alert: A warning of a possible imminent attack by the enemy.

Regiment: A military unit comprised of two or more battalions.

Repo depot: A replacement detachment where new replacements were processed in before being assigned to a specific unit.

Rock 'n' roll: Firing a weapon on full automatic in short bursts.

ROK: Republic of Korea. ROK soldiers were considered extremely tough.

ROTC: Reserve Officer Training Corps.

R & R: A "Rest and Recreation" period of either three days (in-country) or seven days (outside of Vietnam, such as in Bangkok or Tokyo.)

RTO: Radio telephone operator. Carried the PRC-25 radio and remained with the commanding officer. If the officer became incapacitated, the RTO might have to call in airstrikes, artillery fire or medevac choppers.
Rucksack: The back pack carried by US soldiers in the field.

Same-same: Vietnamese pidgin English phrase meaning "the same as" or "the same thing."
Sappers: Enemy commandos who would sneak through base perimeter defenses to commit sabotage, usually by planting explosive charges.
SFC: Sergeant First Class (E-7.)
SGT: Sergeant (E-5.)
Short timer: A soldier whose 12-month tour in Nam was near completion, i.e., he had less than 30 days (or some other number) to go.
Shrapnel: Pieces of sharp metal sent flying by an explosion.
Sin loi: (Actually spelled xin loi) Vietnamese phrase meaning "too bad!" or "sorry about that!" or "tough luck, buddy!"
Slack man: The man following behind the point man in an infantry platoon. His job was to protect the point man by watching for enemy activity while the point man was watching for trip wires, mines or booby traps. The slack was also expected to cover the point man with suppressive fire if anyone started shooting at them.
Slick: A Huey helicopter with no external armament, used for transporting troops or cargo and for making regularly scheduled resupply flights to bring food, water, ammo and clothing to troops in the field.
SMAJ: Sergeant Major (E-9.)
SMBL: Semimobile. Prior to Vietnam, the 24th Evac was designated as SMBL because it could be moved to a new location in roughly 48 hours.
Soc mau: Vietnamese term meaning hit or punch, as in "I soc-mau you!" Usually said in jest.
Spider hole: A camouflaged enemy foxhole.
SP4: Specialist Fourth Class (E-4.)
SP5: Specialist Fifth Class (E-5.)
SSGT: Staff Sergeant (E-6.)
Starlight scope: A night scope that intensified images at night by using reflected light from the moon, stars or any other source of light.
STD: A sexually transmitted disease; venereal disease (VD.)
Steel pot: The steel helmet worn by US soldiers. It fit over a fiberglass "helmet liner" which could be worn separately without the pot.
STRAC: Slang describing a soldier who did everything by the book and placed a higher importance on military appearance, grooming, regulations and conduct than on common sense and group camaraderie.

Tee-tee: Vietnamese slang meaning very little, tiny or a very small amount. The opposite of boo-coo.

Tet: The Buddhist lunar New Year.

Three-quarter: An Army three-quarter ton 4x4 pickup truck.

Throwing smoke: Releasing a colored smoke grenade to alert approaching aircraft as to a unit's position on the ground. The smoke came in different colors so the pilot could say "I've got blue smoke" and the ground troops could then verify via radio that he was in the right place. If the pilot saw the wrong color of smoke, he knew that either he was in the wrong place or the enemy was trying to bait him into an ambush.

TPR: A patient's temperature, pulse and respiration as recorded by medical personnel.

Tracer round: A bullet which, when fired, glows in the dark (from the burning of a colored chemical) to show where the rounds are hitting.

Tracheotomy: Making an emergency incision in a patient's throat to facilitate breathing when his windpipe is blocked.

Trench foot: Slang for immersion foot, caused by prolonged submersion of feet in water. The skin may start to shrivel, crack and bleed.

Triage: A procedure for deciding what order in which to treat casualties in a "mass casualty" situation.

Trip flare: A ground flare or parachute flare triggered by a trip wire to reveal the presence of an advancing enemy at night.

USO: United Service Organization. Provided recreation centers and entertainment including "USO Shows" featuring celebrities.

UW: University of Wisconsin.

VC: Nickname for the Viet Cong soldiers.

VD: Venereal disease (a sexually transmitted disease or STD.)

Viet Cong: Communist rebels who were attempting to overthrow the South Vietnamese government.

White mice: American nickname for the South Vietnamese police found in cities like Saigon or Bien Hoa. They wore white gloves and helmets and, like all Vietnamese males, were very diminutive in size.

WIA: Wounded in Action.

XO: Executive Officer, the second in command to the Commanding Officer (CO.) The XO is prepared to take command if anything should happen to the CO.

SEE MORE THAN 30 PHOTOS AND
SUBMIT YOUR OWN BOOK REVIEW AT:
www.longbinhdaze.com